GENERAL
STERLING
PRICE

and the

CIVIL WAR IN THE WEST

General Sterling Price

GENERAL STERLING PRICE

and the
CIVIL WAR IN THE WEST

Albert Castel

LOUISIANA STATE UNIVERSITY PRESS
BATON ROUGE AND LONDON

Library of Congress Catalog Card Number: 68-21804
ISBN 0-8071-1854-0 (paper)

The paper in this book meets the guidelines for permanence and durability of the Committee
on Production Guidelines for Book Longevity of the Council on Library Resources.♾

Louisiana Paperback Edition, 1993
02   01   00   99   98   97   96   95   94   5   4   3   2

2001.43

To Ann, Charles, and Rudolph

INTRODUCTION

A general must be successful in order to be great, but he need not be great in order to be important. General Sterling Price, Confederate States Army, falls into this last category. Measured by the standard criteria of military leadership, he was at best a respectable mediocrity. Yet his actions decisively influenced the course of the Civil War as a whole, and he was the central figure in the Civil War west of the Mississippi. This, then, is the excuse for this book.

There will be no attempt in it to magnify the accomplishments and significance of its hero beyond their just proportions. It is written out of the conviction that an account of Price's role in the Civil War will prove interesting in itself, and at the same time contribute to the knowledge and understanding of an important but neglected phase of that conflict.

An additional word: Although Price was without doubt a colorful, vital, and unique personality, unfortunately he must in these pages remain a somewhat shadowy figure. The reason for this is that the prime requisite for bringing back to literary life a historical character— his personal papers—no longer exists in the case of Price. Although his family retained these valuable documents following his death in 1867, they were totally destroyed by fire about 1885. All that is available today is his official correspondence and military reports, which he left in the custody of his adjutant general Colonel Thomas L. Snead, who later turned them over to the War Department for publication in the *Official Records of the Union and Confederate Armies*. These provide most of the essential facts about Price the general, but offer only brief glimpses of Price the man.

Apart from the *Official Records*, the main sources on Price's Civil War exploits are the recollections of his contemporaries, both friends and enemies. In the first category, most important by far, are Colonel Thomas L. Snead's *The Fight for Missouri*, published in 1886, and his articles on the war in the West in *Battles and Leaders of the Civil War*. These writings contain much valuable information, but since Snead sought to glorify Price and since he also had strong animosities against

Jefferson Davis and certain other Confederate leaders, their use requires much care.

Outstanding in the second category is "Gen. Sterling Price and the Confederacy," an unpublished manuscript written shortly after the war by Thomas C. Reynolds, Confederate governor of Missouri from 1862 to 1865 and a close associate of Price. It provides a great deal of significant information about Price, especially as regards personal and political matters, that is available nowhere else. However, Reynolds became a bitter foe of the General and in this manuscript endeavored to expose him as an opportunist, incompetent, and a traitor to the Confederate cause. Consequently this source also must be used with great caution. To do otherwise would be the same as depending for the private life of Alexander Hamilton on an account written by Aaron Burr, if such existed!

Besides "Gen. Sterling Price and the Confederacy," Reynolds left behind a large collection of his personal and official papers. These are to be found in the collections of the Library of Congress and the Missouri Historical Society, and they are of great value both as supplement to and check on "Gen. Sterling Price and the Confederacy." Because of his importance and because of the need to rely heavily on his papers as a source, Reynolds looms large in this book, which to a degree at least can be considered a study of him as well as of Price.

A surprisingly large amount of other manuscript material pertaining to Price and the Civil War in the West was also uncovered during the course of my researches, all of which, along with newspapers, published memoirs, and other sources, is listed where such things are customarily listed.

Few secondary works of scholarly worth have been written about the Civil War in the West. Of them I found most helpful the following (full citations will be found in the bibliography): Major Arthur Roy Kirkpatrick's series of articles on early events in Missouri in the *Missouri Historical Review*; Joseph H. Parks's definitive biography of Edmund Kirby Smith; and Norman Potter Morrow's excellent but, unfortunately, unpublished M.A. thesis, "Price's Missouri Expedition, 1864."

To my knowledge only two biographies of Price have been written. One is Lucy Simmons' "The Life of Sterling Price" (M.A. thesis, University of Chicago, 1922), the other is Ralph R. Rea's *Sterling Price: The Lee of the West* (Little Rock, 1959). These works contain some useful information, especially that of Rea, whose grand-father served under Price. However, both are based on very sketchy research and contain many errors.

The present work is not intended to be a full biography of Price and so makes no attempt to relate either his long prewar or his short post-war careers in detail or depth. For the former there is, with the exception of his participation in the Mexican War, no satisfactory study (here is a good subject for a dissertation). As regards the latter, the best account is to be found in George D. Harmon's "Confederate Migration to Mexico," *Hispanic American Historical Review*, XVII (1937), 458–87.

In conclusion, I would like to thank for their friendly and efficient assistance the staffs of the National Archives, the Library of Congress, the Missouri Historical Society (St. Louis), the Missouri State Historical Society (Columbia), the University of Missouri Library, the Kansas State Historical Society, the University of Michigan Library, the University of Chicago Library, the Western Michigan University Library, and the University of Texas Library. In particular I wish to record my gratitude to Mrs. Frances H. Stadler of the Missouri Historical Society—a most charming and gracious lady. I also desire to thank the Faculty Research Committee of Western Michigan University, headed by my colleague Dr. Alan Brown, for providing funds for travel, research, and the preparation of maps; Dr. Willis Dunbar, former chairman of the Western Michigan University history department, for arranging my teaching schedule so as to facilitate my work; Dr. Rainer Erhart of the Western Michigan University geography department for his skilled work in preparing the maps that appear in this book; and Miss Jan Frizzel, sometime secretary in the Western Michigan University history department, for typing the manuscript. I wish, too, to thank Mr. Francis M. Wilson of Kansas City, Missouri, for permission to quote from the Wilson Family Papers, University of Missouri. And, last but not least, I extend my thanks to the staff of the Louisiana State University Press, and in particular Mrs. Ruth B. Hubert, for their friendly and efficient assistance in preparing my manuscript for publication.

I will pass up the customary expression of sentiment, gratitude, etc., to my wife, not because it is undeserved, but rather because we agree that it is unnecessary.

I have written two previous books dealing with aspects of the Civil War in the West. With the present work I terminate my active scholarly interest in this area. Much more could be done, much more should be done, but others will have to do it.

KALAMAZOO, MICHIGAN   ALBERT CASTEL
DECEMBER, 1967

CONTENTS

ILLUSTRATIONS

xiii

MAPS

GENERAL STERLING PRICE

and the
CIVIL WAR IN THE WEST

1

MISSOURI

Sterling Price's soldiers referred to him with affection as "Old Pap." It is easy to see why from his Civil War photographs. They reveal a portly, handsome, dignified man with white hair and sideburns. The expression on his face is firm and commanding, yet benign, almost gentle. He is obviously a man capable of inspiring confidence and even devotion in other men. One senses, too, that he was accustomed to the exercise of authority and that over the years he had enjoyed much in the way of success and good fortune.

The story of Price's antebellum career confirms this impression. He began life in Prince Edward County, Virginia, on September 11, 1809. His father, a moderately wealthy planter, was of Welsh ancestry and belonged to an old Virginia family. Upon completing his primary education Price attended Hampden-Sidney College for one year, then studied law under the famed Virginia jurist Creed Taylor. But instead of entering the legal profession in the Old Dominion, he migrated with his parents to the new state of Missouri where he engaged in various commercial enterprises. In 1833 he married Martha Head, who also was of Virginia birth, and settled on a farm near Keytesville in Chariton County, just north of the Missouri River. The union proved not only happy but fruitful, eventually producing five sons and one daughter, not counting several children who died at birth or in infancy. In naming his offspring, Price displayed a certain originality: Amanda, Celsus, Heber, Athol, and Quintus—the last so named because he was the fifth child to live. Price's devotion to his family was, by all accounts, extremely, even unusually, strong.

By 1840 he was a prosperous tobacco planter and owned several dozen slaves. In that year his neighbors on their own initiative elected him to the state legislature. Two years later he became speaker of the Missouri house of representatives, and then in 1844 secured a seat in the House of Representatives in Washington.[1] This spectacular political rise derived in part from his membership in the dominant Democratic

[1] Thomas L. Snead, *The Fight for Missouri* (New York, 1886), 81–82; "Unveiling of General Sterling Price Monument, Keytesville, Missouri, June 17,

3

party, but was primarily a consequence of the splendid personal impression he made on others. A Missouri newspaper described him at the time of his election to Congress as being "in the prime of his young manhood, possessing a tall, straight, majestic figure of perfect proportions. His face fair and full, with regular, dignified features, [has] every appearance of manliness and gentility."[2]

Price served but briefly in Washington. Much to his disgust he did not obtain renomination, and in August, 1846, following the outbreak of the Mexican War, he resigned from Congress to become colonel of a regiment of Missouri volunteers. President Polk gave him the command at the request of Senator Thomas Hart Benton, leader of the Democratic party in Missouri. His only previous military experience consisted of an occasional militia muster and participation in the campaign that drove the Mormons from western Missouri.[3] However, there were many other colonels, and even generals, in the Mexican War whose qualifications for command were in no way greater who gained their commissions in the same fashion. This was the American and democratic way of fighting wars.

Price quickly recruited his regiment, which had been designated for service under Brigadier General Stephen Watts Kearny in New Mexico. Kearny had requested that it be infantry, but Price ignored him and made it into a cavalry outfit. Although this action aroused criticism from his political foes, it won him the favor of his soldiers, who did not fancy walking all the way to Santa Fe. When, in accordance with good militia tradition, an election for officers was held in the regiment, they unanimously "confirmed" Price as colonel.[4]

Late in the summer of 1846 the regiment moved from Fort Leavenworth across the plains and mountains to Santa Fe. The movement took place without mishap, but during it Price suffered an attack of cholera, a disease which was to plague him the rest of his life and

---

1915," (pamphlet, n.p., n.d., in Price Family Papers, Missouri Historical Society, St. Louis); Lucy Simmons, "The Life of Sterling Price" (M.A. thesis, University of Chicago, 1922), 2–33.

[2] *Missouri Statesman* (Columbia, Mo.), January 30, 1844.

[3] Thomas C. Reynolds, "Gen. Sterling Price and the Confederacy" (Typescript in Missouri Historical Society, St. Louis), 1; Justin H. Smith, *The War with Mexico* (New York, 1919), I, 290.

[4] *Missouri Historical Review*, XXV (1946), 579.

ultimately cause his death. He arrived in Santa Fe on September 28 and shortly afterwards assumed command of the American occupation of New Mexico.[5] In this capacity he displayed a laxness in enforcing discipline, a tendency to quarrel with other officials, and a penchant for acting in a highly independent, almost insubordinate, fashion— characteristics that were to manifest themselves in a subsequent war.[6]

At first it appeared that he would have no opportunity for active service. But suddenly, in January, the Pueblo Indians rose in bloody revolt against American rule, killing the territorial governor, Charles Bent. Although caught off guard, Price displayed decisiveness and vigor in quelling the insurrection, winning a number of pitched battles at little cost to his own forces while at the same time inflicting heavy losses on the poorly armed Indians. Later on, when faced with another uprising, he led his army in a swift campaign into Mexico itself, where he gained new victories and captured the city of Chihuahua.[7] He returned to Missouri at the end of the war with the brevet rank of brigadier general and a greatly enhanced reputation. Henceforth he considered himself first and foremost a military man.

During the next several years he devoted himself to his tobacco plantation, which was located near Keytesville on the banks of the Missouri River and named Val Verde after the beautiful valley of the same name which he had seen in New Mexico. He constantly added to his holdings and became in time one of the largest landowners in Missouri. However, like so many other Southern planters he was in effect "land poor," and he supported his lavish scale of living only through, an equally lavish indebtedness.[8]

Beginning in 1849 a split developed in the Missouri Democratic party over the slavery issue. For several years Price avoided com-

[5] John T. Hughes, "Journal of John T. Hughes," in William E. Connelley (ed.), *Doniphan's Expedition and the Conquest of New Mexico and California* (Topeka, 1907), 74, 256–61.

[6] Reynolds, "Price and the Confederacy," 1–2. One incident of note in New Mexico was the arrest by Price of Frank P. Blair, Jr., of the politically powerful Blair family. Blair resented the arrest and some supposed that the resultant enmity between Blair and Price influenced Price's subsequent political course. However, Price himself indicated that he attached little importance to the incident and that he had no special feelings about Blair. See *ibid.*, 2–3.

[7] Smith, *The War with Mexico*, II, 166, 217, 419, 453, 510–24; "John T. Hughes Journal," 298, 517.

[8] Simmons, "Life of Sterling Price," 39–41.

mitting himself to either side, but ultimately, like most Missourians of his class, he joined the proslavery, anti-Benton faction—thus causing Benton to denounce him as a traitor and ingrate. In 1853 the anti-Bentonians gained control of the party and nominated him for governor. Price won the election by a substantial majority, for his war record plus his personal charm and impressive physical presence had made him, in the words of one supporter, "unquestionably the most popular man in Missouri." Among his fellow politicians he had a reputation for sagacity, secrecy, and an ability to detect the winning trend and act accordingly. However, his friends admitted he was "somewhat slow of thought and speech" and a mediocre orator, and his enemies accused him of vanity and double-dealing.[9]

Price occupied the governorship during one of the most crucial periods in Missouri's history. The Kansas-Nebraska Act of 1854 opened the way for a violent and momentous struggle between North and South for control of the Kansas Territory. In this contest Missouri, by reason of geographic proximity and political and economic interest, represented the South. Price, as might be expected, sympathized with the effort of his constituents to make Kansas a slave state. Thus in 1855 he endorsed a resolution drawn up by a convention at Liberty which declared that if Congress refused to admit Kansas as a slave state this would mean the "destruction of the Union."[10] And although he refrained from using his official powers to aid the Missouri "Border Ruffians" in their campaign to conquer Kansas for slavery, he did nothing as governor to restrain them or prevent their invasions of Kansas.

Taken as a whole, his administration was competent if not distinguished, and he gained much praise for not taking advantage of a legislative act increasing the governor's salary, even though it would have been legal for him to have done so.[11] On leaving office in 1857 he

[9] Snead, *The Fight for Missouri*, 182–84; Reynolds, "Price and the Confederacy," 4–11; A. P. Richardson to James O. Broadhead, May 20, 1861, in James O. Broadhead Papers, Missouri Historical Society, St. Louis; Eugene M. Violette, *History of Missouri* (Boston, 1918), 277–84; C. R. Barnes (ed.), *Switzler's Illustrated History of Missouri from 1541 to 1877* (St. Louis, 1877), 264–82; Thomas C. Reynolds, "Memoranda relative to appointment of Confederate Senators from Missouri," in Thomas C. Reynolds Papers, Library of Congress.

[10] Allan Nevins, *Ordeal of the Union* (New York, 1947), II, 393.

[11] Barnes, *Switzler's History of Missouri*, 282–84; "Unveiling of Price Monument" in Price Family Papers.

sought a United States senatorship, but the Democratic caucus passed
him over. He then retired to Val Verde, where for the next few years
he managed his plantation and engaged in railroad promotion.[12] In
the spring of 1860 he participated in the Democratic state convention
as a delegate from Chariton County and for awhile received consideration as a possible compromise candidate for governor. During the convention his friends learned that he was in financial difficulty and hence
arranged for his appointment as state bank commissioner. This was
the best-paying office in Missouri and it "came just in time to save him
from serious business and pecuniary embarrassment."[13]

During the 1860 presidential campaign, Price backed Stephen A.
Douglas, the Northern Democratic advocate of sectional compromise.
For although proslavery, Price was not a secessionist. Rather he was a
Southern moderate who opposed secession except as a last resort on
the part of the South to protect itself against Northern oppression. He
hoped that the Union could be preserved and feared that disunion
would lead to a disastrous war. Most Missourians shared these feelings
and so voted either for Douglas or the Constitutional Union nominee
John Bell of Tennessee. They considered Lincoln, the "Black Republican" candidate, as much an enemy of the Union as John Breckinridge,
the Southern secessionist nominee, and the Railsplitter received only
a few thousand votes in the entire state.

But Lincoln, not Douglas or Bell, was elected. The resultant secession crisis found Missouri badly divided, for, politically as well as
geographically, it was neither North nor South but rather both. At one
extreme stood the unconditional Unionists. A small but powerful minority, they insisted on full support of the federal government and declared that secession was treason. Their stronghold was St. Louis, with
its large antislavery German element, and their principal leaders were
Frank P. Blair, Jr., of the influential Blair family, and Captain Nathaniel Lyon, abolitionist and commander of the United States Army
garrison in St. Louis. Blair organized the Germans into home guard
regiments and equipped them with muskets furnished by Lyon.

At the other extreme, and also a definite minority, were the secessionists. They hailed mainly from the hemp and tobacco counties along

[12] "Unveiling of Price Monument" in Price Family Papers; Reynolds, "Price
and the Confederacy," 5–9.
[13] Reynolds, "Price and the Confederacy," 9–11.

the Missouri River, a region which contained the bulk of the state's
slave population.[14] Probably their most important leader was Lieutenant-Governor Thomas C. Reynolds. Because this man will play a
vital role in the story of Sterling Price and the Civil War in the West,
it is appropriate at this point to introduce him in some detail. A South
Carolinian by birth, and thirty-nine years of age, he was "of medium
height and compact mould, with regular features, that were at once
refined and strong—a rather handsome man. His jet-black hair and
beard were always closely cut, and his dark eyes always shaded by
gold-rimmed glasses, which served a two-fold purpose."[15] He graduated
from the University of Virginia in 1838, obtained a doctor of laws
degree (*summa cum laude*) from Heidelberg in 1842, and was admitted to the Virginia bar in 1844. After a period in the diplomatic
service, during which he was United States *chargé* in Madrid, he moved
in 1850 to St. Louis where he practiced law, became United States district attorney, and rose rapidly in Democratic politics. His wife was
French; and in addition to her language he spoke fluent German and
Spanish and was proficient in Latin and Greek. A contemporary who
knew and liked him well described him quite accurately as a man of
"indomitable will," with a brilliant mind that "bored into the heart of
every question with the pitiless auger of common sense."[16] However, he
was proud and sensitive, inclined to be contemptuous of those who did
not measure up to his own high standard of competency, and despite
(or perhaps because of) his intellectual background and appearance
was extremely pugnacious. He fought several duels, including a famous
one in which he wounded B. Gratz Brown, a prominent St. Louis
politician who in later years was the vice-presidential candidate of the
Liberal Republican and Democratic parties. Moreover, his "busy intellect delighted to devise schemes, which it pleased his tireless energy
to carry out; and the more difficult and the more intricate the pathway
to success, the more did it fascinate his diplomatic brain, and the more
command his unwearied efforts to thread its mazes and overcome all

[14] John N. Edwards, *Shelby and His Men, or, The War in the West* (Cincinnati, 1867), 14.

[15] Snead, *The Fight for Missouri*, 30–31.

[16] Memorandum by Thomas C. Reynolds, in Thomas C. Reynolds Papers,
Missouri Historical Society, St. Louis; St. Louis *Republican*, March 31, 1887
(clipping in Thomas L. Snead Papers, Missouri Historical Society, St. Louis).
The quote is from Edwards, *Shelby and His Men*, 195.

its difficulties."[17] In other words, he had a strong streak of the busy-body in him.

As soon as Reynolds' native state seceded he began campaigning to have his adopted one follow suit. On January 4 at Jefferson City, he called a conference of other Missouri secessionists to formulate strategy. Several days later he presided over a mass meeting in St. Louis which resulted in the organization of "Minute Men" to counteract Blair's home guards. And on January 17 he delivered a widely published address before the Missouri senate denouncing the North for revolutionary usurpation and urging that the South, instead of forming a new nation, reconstitute the United States. Following this, and largely through his efforts, the legislature passed an act providing for the election of a state convention "to consider the relations of Missouri to the United States." He and the other secessionists confidently expected this convention to take Missouri out of the Union when it met.[18]

The governor of Missouri at this time of crisis was Claiborne Fox Jackson, fifty-five and head of the proslavery "Central Clique" of the state Democratic party. In his opinion, the election of Lincoln made necessary and inevitable the secession of all the slaveholding states, and hence he fully sympathized with Reynolds' activities. However, he refrained from openly advocating secession because he knew that most Missourians were not prepared as yet for such a drastic step. For the same reason he restricted himself in public utterances to castigating the North and declaring that Missouri would side with her sister states of the South if the federal government attempted to "coerce" them.[19]

Jackson's evaluation of public opinion was correct and his caution justified. The vast majority of Missourians early in 1861 stood between the unconditional Unionists and the secessionists. Instead, they were conditional Unionists, which meant that they were opposed to secession but that they also believed that the federal government had no right to use force to keep states in the Union. This attitude reflected the conflicting loyalties and interests of Missouri, with its blood ties to the South and its economic links to the North, and also the fact that

[17] Snead, *The Fight for Missouri*, 30–31.
[18] *Ibid.*, 31–33; James O. Broadhead, "St. Louis During the War" (MS in James O. Broadhead Papers), 21.
[19] Snead, *The Fight for Missouri*, 17–26; William H. Lyon, "Claiborne Fox Jackson and the Secession Crisis in Missouri," *Missouri Historical Review*, LVIII (1964), 422–33.

most of its citizens were either Douglas Democrats or Old Line Whigs who held the Northern Republicans and the Southern Democrats equally responsible for disrupting the Union. Furthermore, many conditional Unionists were slaveholders, who for that very reason opposed secession. As one of their spokesmen put it, "So long as we remain loyal, the General Government is bound . . . not only to respect, but to maintain and defend our slave property." Secession, on the other hand, would "bring the Canada line down to our borders" and leave Missouri exposed to the Kansas "murderers and bandits."[20]

But more than anything else, most Missourians in the first weeks of 1861 hoped that somehow their state could avoid choosing between North and South and, if civil war occurred, remain neutral, thus sparing themselves and others the necessity of fighting against either side.[21] Yet, unfortunately for this totally unrealistic desire, both the unconditional Unionists and the secessionists demanded with ever-growing impatience that Missouri take a stand, one way or the other. And all the while, too, the march of events made this decision increasingly difficult to postpone.

On February 18 the election of the state convention took place. Its outcome was a severe blow to the hopes of the secessionists. Of 140,000 ballots cast, 110,000 went to antisecessionist candidates, and not a single avowed disunionist was elected.[22] Among the delegates chosen was Price, who campaigned actively as a conditional Unionist.[23] The secessionists were angered by his stand, for they had assumed that he was a "Southern rights" man. Indeed, according to Reynolds, because of Price's position as bank commissioner the "money power" was exercised against the secessionists, and this along with his reputation for always picking the winners was the main reason for the Unionist victory.[24] However, in view of the vote tally, this undoubtedly assigns too great an effect to too minor a cause.

[20] St. Louis *Missouri Republican*, quoted in Kansas City *Daily Journal of Commerce*, May 25, 1861.

[21] Snead, *The Fight for Missouri*, 54, 66–74, 80–88; John S. McElroy, *The Struggle for Missouri* (Washington, 1909), 24–49; Edward Conrad Smith, *The Borderland in the Civil War* (New York, 1927), 126–32, 149–55.

[22] Arthur Roy Kirkpatrick, "Missouri on the Eve of the Civil War," *Missouri Historical Review*, LV (1961), 104; Snead, *The Fight for Missouri*, 66–67.

[23] Thomas Shackleford, "A Chapter of the Unwritten History of Missouri" (MS in Price Family Papers), 1–2.

[24] Reynolds, "Price and the Confederacy," 12–13.

The convention first met on February 28 in Jefferson City, but immediately moved to more comfortable quarters in St. Louis. By almost unanimous vote it named Price president, a tribute to his prestige and proof that the conditional Unionists were in control. On March 9 it adopted, by an 89 to 1 margin, a resolution declaring that "there is no adequate cause for the withdrawal of Missouri from the Union," but also stating that the federal government should not "employ force against the seceding states."[25] Passage of this resolution ended any danger of Missouri's seceding in the near future, a fact realized by Governor Jackson, who in a private letter bitterly denounced "the miserable, base, and cowardly conduct of Gov. Price's submission convention."[26]

A short time later the convention provided further evidence of its antisecessionist sentiments by overwhelmingly rejecting a resolution which proposed that if the other border states left the Union, Missouri would follow their example. However, among the twenty-three delegates who supported the resolution was Price—a clear sign that his Unionism was very conditional indeed.[27] To a friend, Price explained his vote in pessimistic terms which foreshadowed his subsequent course: "It is now inevitable that the general government will attempt the coercion of the southern states. War will ensue. I am a military man, a southern man, and if we have to fight, will do so on the part of the South."[28]

Price proved to be a good prophet. On April 12 the Confederates bombarded Fort Sumter and three days later Lincoln issued a call for volunteers to suppress the rebellion. What Missourians had dreaded, happened—civil war. Their initial reaction was sympathy for the South, and in the subsequent opinion of James O. Broadhead, an unconditional Unionist leader in St. Louis, it was "an undoubted historical fact . . . that [for the moment] a large majority of the people of Missouri were in favor of secession and uniting the fortunes of Missouri with the states already seceded."[29] But, as Thomas Snead, the prosecessionist historian of the "fight for Missouri" has recorded, "The

[25] Snead, *The Fight for Missouri*, 78–81.
[26] Claiborne F. Jackson to J. W. Tucker, April 28, 1861, in James O. Broadhead Papers.
[27] Snead, *The Fight for Missouri*, 81.
[28] Shackleford, "Unwritten History of Missouri," 3.
[29] Broadhead, "St. Louis During the War" (MS in Broadhead Papers), 7.

enthusiasm of the Southern Rights people . . . quickly subsided in view of the unanimity with which the North was responding to the President's call for troops, and in contemplation of the dangers which they would have to encounter who should dare to take up arms against the Federal Government."[30] Before long, most Missourians reverted to their original and basic hope that through neutrality they could escape the horrors of civil war.

But this was not to be. On the one side Jackson arrogantly rejected the President's request for troops from Missouri as "inhuman and diabolical," called the legislature into special session and urged it to prepare for war in alliance with the Confederacy, mobilized the militia, and made secret arrangements to obtain arms from the government of Jefferson Davis. Secession, he believed, was just a matter of time and manner: "Who does not know," he wrote a friend, "that every sympathy of my heart is with the South?"[31]

On the other side Blair and Lyon regarded Jackson's rejection of Lincoln's troop request as treason. At once they began bolstering the Unionist forces in St. Louis, at the same time calling for reinforcements from Illinois. Missouri, they were resolved, would support the federal government in the war. If drastic action was needed to achieve this end, they were prepared to resort to it.

Early in May seven hundred militia assembled on the outskirts of St. Louis at Camp Jackson under the command of Brigadier General Daniel M. Frost, a Northern-born West Pointer of Southern sympathies. Jackson and Frost planned to use this force to capture the United States arsenal at St. Louis, and for that purpose had induced Jefferson Davis to send two cannons from Baton Rouge in crates labeled "Marble." However, Blair and Lyon frustrated the scheme by transferring the arms from the arsenal to Illinois. Nevertheless, despite the fact that they had ten thousand soldiers of their own, and despite many (now sincere) assurances that the militia had no hostile intentions, they saw in the encampment a dangerous threat to the Unionist position in St. Louis. Its streets bore such names as "Beauregard" and "Jefferson Davis," Confederate flags were openly displayed, and the militiamen boasted of what they would do to the "Dutch" when they got the chance. Therefore on May 10 (the day the state troops were

[30] Snead, *The Fight for Missouri*, 158.
[31] Jackson to Tucker, April 28, 1861, in James O. Broadhead Papers.

scheduled to go home) Lyon surrounded the camp with four regiments of federalized home guards and a battalion of regulars, then demanded that Frost and his men surrender. They did so, with only a verbal protest against the illegality of such high-handed proceedings.

So far things had gone smoothly for Lyon—if one excepts his having been kicked in the stomach by a horse! But as the Unionists escorted the prisoners into the city a large mob of Southern sympathizers collected along the sidewalks shouting "Damn the Dutch!" and "Hurray for Jeff Davis!" Clods and stones soon followed the yells. Then someone shot and mortally wounded a German home guard officer. As he fell, another officer ordered his men to open fire. Fusillades of musket balls swept the streets. The mob scattered in panic-stricken flight. But left behind, sprawled bleeding in the streets and on the walks, were twenty-eight dead civilians, including two women and a small child.[32]

News of the "Camp Jackson Massacre" aroused fierce excitement throughout Missouri and produced a strong reaction in favor of the pro-Confederate party. Thousands of indignant Missourians called for secession and still more thousands felt their loyalty to the federal government badly strained. Everywhere "military meetings" took place and newspapers featured notices of special sales of powder, lead, caps, rifles, and shotguns. In fact, some of the towns near St. Louis sent armed bands marching towards the city for the purpose of rescuing its citizens from the "blood thirsty Dutch," who "drunk with beer and reeking of sauerkraut," were reportedly engaging in a wholesale slaughter of the population! All in all, Lyon and Blair, far from aiding the Union cause with their militant conduct, had created a situation which might easily engulf that cause in disaster.[33]

Camp Jackson marked not only a turning point in the history of Missouri but also in the career of Price. He was (as were two other Civil War generals of note, U. S. Grant and W. T. Sherman) an eye-

[32] Arthur Roy Kirkpatrick, "Missouri in the Early Months of the Civil War," *Missouri Historical Review*, LV (1961), 235–39; William E. Parrish, *Turbulent Partnership: Missouri and the Union, 1861–1865* (Columbia, Mo., 1963), 15–24; Snead, *The Fight for Missouri*, 158–72.

[33] Snead, *The Fight for Missouri*, 174–76; James W. Covington, "The Camp Jackson Affair," *Missouri Historical Review*, LV (1961), 209–10; Liberty (Mo.) *Tribune*, May 17, 24, 1861; Kansas City *Weekly Journal of Commerce*, June 5, 1861; Barnes, *Switzler's History of Missouri*, 356–57; Smith, *The Borderland in the Civil War*, 240–41.

witness of the affair. The seizure of the camp he considered as a flagrant violation of Missouri's sovereign rights, the massacre as the natural consequence of Lincoln's coercion policy. Accordingly he now abandoned his quasi-Unionism in favor of secession. At the same time he decided that it was his duty to help Missouri resist Northern subjugation. On the evening of May 10 he denounced the Camp Jackson "outrage" before a large crowd in front of his hotel, then in the morning took a train to Jefferson City to offer his services to Governor Jackson.[34]

Even as Price traveled to the capital, the legislature, infuriated by what had happened in St. Louis and expecting Lyon's troops to attack at any moment, rushed through a "Military Bill." This authorized the recruitment of a state guard, divided Missouri into eight military districts, and empowered the governor to appoint a major general to command the state's forces. In addition it appropriated all of the money in the state treasury, $82,000,000, for the purchase of war materials, and gave the governor almost dictatorial powers to put down rebellion and repel invasion.

Price reached Jefferson City on May 12, and that afternoon met Jackson and Reynolds in the governor's office. He informed them that he now supported "southern rights," and was at Jackson's disposal to aid in defending the state. As soon as he left, Reynolds urged Jackson to appoint him commander of the state guard. But Jackson planned to offer that post to Alexander Doniphan, and he distrusted Price as head of the "submission convention." Reynolds then pointed out the advantage of having Price publicly and irrevocably side with the pro-Confederate party, and reminded Jackson of Price's prestige as president of the convention and of his Mexican War reputation. Jackson bowed to these arguments and authorized Reynolds to draw up a commission appointing Price commander of the state forces. Later that afternoon Reynolds presented the commission to Price. Much to his surprise Price, who previously had said he would accept it, remained motionless and silent, and seemed to be in "a deep study." Reynolds

[34] Snead, *The Fight for Missouri*, 183; Thomas L. Snead, "The First Year of the War in Missouri," in Robert U. Johnson and Clarence O. Buel (eds.), *Battles and Leaders of the Civil War* (New York, 1887), I, 266 (hereinafter cited as *Battles and Leaders*); St. Louis *Missouri Republican*, May 11 and 12, 1861.

thereupon asked Price as a personal and political friend to take the commission. General Robert Wilson, an influential state senator who was also present, likewise called on Price to accept. After a pause of a few minutes Price replied, in a tone as if he had come to a sudden decision, "Well, gentlemen, I accept it, and rely on your support in the performance of my duties to the best of my ability." He then went to the adjutant general's office and began his new task.[35]

Price had good reason to hesitate before accepting the commission which Jackson had reluctantly granted him. He must have known that the moment he took it he became in effect a rebel against the United States government. And although he could not have known this at the time, by taking it he linked his fortunes irretrievably to the cause of the Southern Confederacy.

During the days that followed, Price labored to establish some semblance of order among the hundreds of ill-armed volunteers who poured into Jefferson City to defend it against the expected attack of Lyon. In this work he was greatly aided by Captain Henry Little, a highly competent ex-regular army officer from Maryland who had offered his services to the Missouri government. Curiously enough, for awhile Price, although commander of the state guard, did not possess any formal military rank. Under the military bill the commander was to be a major general, but Jackson withheld the necessary commission. Only when Price threatened to resign did he confer it. Since it gave Price enormous powers, civil as well as military, the governor's attitude is understandable. Furthermore, several secessionist leaders had protested to Jackson against Price's being commander of the state troops.[36] But on the whole, as Reynolds had anticipated, Price's appointment was very popular in the state and undoubtedly strengthened the pro-Confederate party.[37]

On May 13 Price, Jackson, and Reynolds conferred on future strategy. Reynolds proposed that the governor exploit the universal indignation over Camp Jackson by calling on the citizenry to form military organizations. Then, if Lyon marched on Jefferson City, Jack-

---

[35] Reynolds, "Price and the Confederacy," 13–16.

[36] Ibid., 15–18; R. S. Bevier, *History of the First and Second Missouri Confederate Brigades, 1861–1865* (St. Louis, 1879), 325, 333.

[37] Snead, *The Fight for Missouri*, 184–85; St. Louis *Missouri Republican*, May 16, 1861; Liberty (Mo.) *Tribune*, May 24, 1861.

son would order a mass uprising against him. The Union army would be destroyed, the Southern rights party would gain control of the state, and the way would be open for secession.

Initially Jackson and Price agreed to this plan.[38] Then, for a number of reasons, they changed their minds. First, Lyon was superseded by Major General William S. Harney as commander of the United States Army in Missouri. Harney upheld the action against Camp Jackson and denounced the military bill as an "indirect" ordinance of secession. But he was known to be more conservative than Lyon, independent of Blair, and anxious to avoid bloodshed. When approached by a group of influential Missourians, he indicated that he would be willing to enter into negotiations with Jackson and Price, and word of this was passed on to Jackson. Second, Reynolds' plan, if put into effect, almost surely would precipitate full-fledged war, and this would be disastrous at the present juncture for the secessionist cause. The one thousand or so poorly armed, unorganized, and untrained militiamen at Jefferson City were no match for the powerful Union force at St. Louis, and it required little reflection to realize that Reynolds' idea of a mass uprising was impractical. Third, the legislature had no power to pass a secession ordinance. Only the convention could legally do this, but it was adjourned and its members scattered over the state. Yet until Missouri formally seceded, it remained part of the Union and subject to federal laws and authority. Fourth, secession presented an extremely difficult problem for Missouri. It was surrounded on three sides by Northern states, its principal city was held by the Unionists, it had no direct rail connections with the South, the Mississippi was closed, and the only slave state from which help could come directly, Arkansas, was very weak and itself had not yet seceded. Thus from a purely strategic standpoint, breaking away from the Union would be inexpedient until effective Confederate military assistance was forthcoming. And finally, popular indignation over Camp Jackson subsided rapidly, and the desire for peace and neutrality once again became the dominant feeling in Missouri.

What was needed, decided Jackson and Price, was time—time in which to organize and strengthen the state guard, time to make arrangements for Confederate military intervention, time to reassemble

[38] Reynolds, "Price and the Confederacy," 16–18.

the convention. Therefore, in order to gain this time, they decided to enter into negotiations with Harney. They would do so in the name of maintaining Missouri's sovereignty and preserving peace, so that when war did come (as inevitably it must) the blame would fall on the Unionists. Moreover, to accomplish this end, they were prepared to make almost any concessions, promise nearly anything, that would appease and lull the Federal authorities and prevent a premature showdown. Or, in other words, while talking peace they would prepare for war and under the cloak of neutrality attempt to lead Missouri into the Confederacy. Obviously it was a strategy in which reasons of expediency prevailed over considerations of morality. Whether it would be sanctioned by success remained to be seen.[39]

Jackson and Price did not consult Lieutenant-Governor Reynolds about their decision to negotiate with Harney, presumably because they knew he would be strongly opposed and might try to interfere. However, Price did tell him that contact had been made with Harney and that he personally did not object to some sort of pacific arrangement, as it would give him time to increase and organize the state forces. This news, plus Jackson's failure to move immediately for secession, alarmed the Lieutenant-Governor. Jackson, he feared, intended to follow the example of his native state of Kentucky and adopt a neutrality

[39] This interpretation of Jackson's and Price's motives in negotiating with the Federal authorities is derived largely from Snead, *The Fight for Missouri*, 185–87 (Snead at this time was an aide and advisor to Jackson); Reynolds, "Price and the Confederacy," 17–23; and other relevant primary sources. It follows essentially the view presented by Kirkpatrick in "Missouri in the Early Months of the Civil War," 239–40. A different view is presented by William H. Lyon in "Claiborne Fox Jackson and the Secession Crisis in Missouri." Lyon contends that Jackson and Price genuinely sought neutrality, and that the issue in Missouri after Camp Jackson was no longer Unionism versus secession, but state sovereignty versus federal domination. Some of the points he makes in support of this thesis are good, if not fully convincing, and he is correct in emphasizing the vacillations and frustrations of Jackson, an aspect of the story which could not be covered adequately in this work. However, in my opinion the weight of the evidence, as well as inherent logic, seems to support the belief that Jackson and Price were sincere in seeking neutrality only in the short run, that their long-run objective was secession. It must have been apparent to men of their experience and sagacity that Missouri could not permanently occupy a peaceful half-way house between North and South, and their whole previous record, especially that of Jackson's, indicates a belief in the inevitability of secession for Missouri which certainly Camp Jackson did not destroy. Furthermore, as will be seen, Jackson and Price, while negotiating with Harney, sought through agents and letters Confederate military intervention.

policy. Hence he decided to go south at once and seek Confederate military intervention. To this end he obtained written authorization from Price, whom he informed of his intention, to ask the Confederate government to protect the convention (of which Price was still president) so that it could pass an ordinance of secession. In the interest of absolute secrecy both Price and Reynolds agreed to keep Jackson in the dark as to Reynolds' mission. Before leaving Jefferson City, Reynolds told the Governor that he was going to Richmond and offered his services. Jackson replied that he had already sent an agent to the Confederate government, but did not name him or divulge his instructions. Neither did he say anything about negotiating with Harney. As Arthur Roy Kirkpatrick has stated in his excellent study of Missouri during the early months of the Civil War: "It is indeed a strange and, for them, unfortunate thing that these men who were so passionately devoted to the same cause felt it necessary to keep so many of their actions secret from each other, while their only hope for success lay in complete understanding and in concerted planning and action."[40]

On May 20, at Harney's invitation, Price traveled to St. Louis. By coincidence Reynolds set out the same day for the south. Price's train left first, and as he boarded he told Reynolds that he had consented to confer with Harney in order to gain time in which to prepare the state guard. His parting words were, "Get Jefferson Davis to send in Confederate troops as soon as possible."[41]

The next day, in St. Louis, Price and Harney signed an agreement, the key provision of which stated:

General Price, having by commission full authority over the militia of the State of Missouri, undertakes, with the sanction of the governor of the state, already declared, to direct the whole power of the State officers to maintain order within the State among the people thereof, and General Harney declares that, this object being thus assured, he can have no occasion, as he has no wish, to make military movements, which might otherwise create excitements and jealousies which he most urgently desires to avoid.[42]

---

[40] Reynolds, "Price and the Confederacy," 18–21; Kirkpatrick, "Missouri in the Early Months of the Civil War," 259.

[41] Reynolds, "Price and the Confederacy," 21.

[42] *The War of the Rebellion: A Compilation of the Official Records of the Union and Confederate Armies* (Washington, 1880–1901), Ser. I, Vol. III, 375–76 (hereinafter cited as *Official Records*). Unless otherwise indicated, all citations are to Series I.

In addition, before Price left St. Louis, Harney warned him through a mutual friend that the state guard might come under Lincoln's proclamation ordering the dispersal of all armed bodies hostile to United States authority, and that consequently he hoped that Price would suspend the organization of the militia until its legal status was determined. Price answered that he had to obey the laws of his state and hence could not halt the mobilization of the militia. Nevertheless, on returning to Jefferson City he instructed all of his troops except a company from St. Louis to go back to their homes, where they would be organized by district commanders.[43] This order (which was fully consistent with Price's ulterior purposes) aroused so much anger among the guardsmen, who had come to the capital anxious to fight, that according to an eyewitness Jackson and Price for awhile actually feared for their lives![44]

Jackson's and Price's motives in making an agreement with Harney have already been described. As for Harney, he was aware of the great excitement aroused by the Camp Jackson affair, and realized that further military action would plunge Missouri into civil war. In his estimation, Missouri could be kept in the Union by a firm but conciliatory policy in which force would be used only when strictly necessary. The agreement with Price, he believed, would reassure and calm the people, weaken the secessionists, and set the stage for a gradual, peaceful establishment of Union control. Thus, like Jackson and Price, but for a diametrically different reason, he sought to gain time.[45]

Most Missourians, if their newspapers are indicative, welcomed the agreement as restoring peace and security to the state. Not so Reynolds. He learned of it in Arkansas and was astonished and chagrined. In his opinion it represented an adoption of the neutrality policy he feared and hence checkmated the object of his journey. Moreover, it caused him to experience his first doubts about Price's integrity and loyalty to the Southern cause. He could not reconcile its terms with Price's previous statements or the authorization to ask for Confederate military intervention, and he suspected that Price had reverted to Unionism.[46]

[43] Snead, *The Fight for Missouri*, 187–88.
[44] Richardson to Broadhead, May 24, 1861, in James O. Broadhead Papers.
[45] Parrish, *Turbulent Partnership*, 25–26; William S. Harney to Simon Cameran, May 31, 1861, in *Official Records*, III, 381–83.
[46] Reynolds, in "Price and the Confederacy," 22, blamed the "fatal" Price-

So strong was Reynolds' anger that he even seriously considered issuing a proclamation assuming the governorship on the grounds that Jackson was a prisoner in the capital and unable to exercise his constitutional functions! But before resorting to this drastic measure, he decided to proceed to Memphis and ascertain whether Price's agreement with Harney signified a sincere commitment to neutrality, or was merely a trick (though a "reprehensible" one) to secure time, or else was a scheme by Harney and Price to disarm the secessionists. In Memphis several pro-Southern refugees from St. Louis told him that they regarded the treaty as a return by Price to Unionism and a betrayal of the cause, but that they were confident that the federal authorities would soon break it—a view which St. Louis newspaper reports seemed to confirm. Therefore, on June 3 Reynolds, in his official capacity as lieutenant governor, wrote Jefferson Davis asking that he be given a Confederate army with which to occupy Missouri and enable it to secede in accordance with the will (so he claimed) of the overwhelming majority of its people. He accompanied this letter with Price's authorization and a personal evaluation of the state of affairs in Missouri.[47]

Reynolds was not the only person to deplore the Harney-Price accord. His opposite numbers on the Unionist side, Blair and Lyon, likewise looked askance at it. With good cause they suspected that the agreement was simply a device on the part of Jackson and Price to gain time. More important, it stood in the way of their prime objective, namely absolute support by Missouri, under their leadership, of the federal government and the war. Consequently, Blair urged Lincoln to

---

Harney treaty completely on Price, who (he declared) became frightened of the Federal forces and who came under the influence of the "timid counsel of his convention colleagues at St. Louis." He also claimed that friends of Jackson subsequently told him that the governor approved the agreement only because of Price's opinion that the state forces were too weak to justify any rejection of Harney's demands. Here, as in many other instances, Reynolds' hatred of Price is all too obvious. The entire history of the negotiations between the state and federal authorities in Missouri clearly demonstrates that Price did not act independently of Jackson and that Jackson fully concurred in Price's acts. Furthermore it appears rather unlikely that Jackson, who according to Reynolds manifested such extreme reluctance to appoint Price commander of the state guard and to commission him a major general, would suddenly give Price free rein in dealing with the Federals, or that he would rely unduly upon his advice. Finally, there is much evidence indicating that Jackson, not Price, was the one most anxious to avoid a premature clash with the United States forces.

[47] *Ibid.*, 23–27.

remove Harney from command on the grounds that he was playing into the hands of the secessionists. Lincoln was reluctant to take this step but finally wrote an order dismissing Harney and replacing him with Lyon, who was promoted to brigadier general. He sent the order to Blair with an authorization to deliver it to Harney only if such action became "indispensable."[48]

During the rest of May and early June the secessionists organized military companies, held drills, and purchased and manufactured arms. They also persecuted Unionists, causing hundreds of them to flee their homes in central and western Missouri. Reports of these activities, sometimes exaggerated or false, intensified the fears and suspicions of Blair, Lyon, and other Unionist leaders, and strengthened their conviction that "treason" must be crushed in Missouri before it was too late.[49]

Harney, on the other hand, saw in the situation an opportunity to put pressure on the state authorities and extract concessions. On May 28 and 29 he telegraphed Price concerning rumors that Confederate troops from Arkansas (which had now seceded) intended to enter Missouri, then called Price to account for the outrages being committed against Unionists. He concluded by offering federal assistance in protecting against Confederate invasion and by declaring that unless Price guaranteed the safety of Union adherents, it would be necessary to organize home guard units for their protection.

Price answered that he knew nothing about an incursion from Arkansas, but that if Confederate forces entered Missouri he would cause them to return "instanter." As for outrages against Unionists, they were the acts of irresponsible parties and not sanctioned by the state government. In closing he cautioned Harney against organizing home guards, as this would provoke civil war.[50]

Price's declaration that he would oppose a Confederate invasion

[48] Kansas City (Mo.) *Weekly Journal of Commerce*, May 23, 1861; *Official Records*, III, 9, 375–79; James O. Broadhead to Montgomery Blair, May 22, 1861, in James O. Broadhead Papers; John G. Nicolay and John Hay, *Abraham Lincoln: A History* (New York, 1890), IV, 217.

[49] Richardson to Broadhead, May 24, 1861, and Richard C. Vaughn to James O. Broadhead, May 30, 1861, in James O. Broadhead Papers; F. P. Wright to J. F. Snyder, May 23, 1861, in John F. Snyder Collection, Missouri Historical Society, St. Louis; Liberty (Mo.) *Tribune*, June 14, 1861; Parrish, *Turbulent Partnership*, 30.

[50] *Official Records*, III, 377–81; Smith, *The Borderland in the Civil War*, 249–50.

illustrates his and Jackson's appeasement policy and also the dissemblance that it engendered. At the same time, an agent of Jackson's, Aaron H. Conrow, was in Arkansas to obtain military aid from that state, and another one, E. C. Cabell, was in Richmond on a similar mission to the Confederate government. Price would have done better simply to have denied any knowledge of Confederate military movements and let it go at that.[51]

Harney was satisfied with Price's response and believed that his gradualist strategy was succeeding. But the following day Blair delivered Lincoln's dismissal order and Lyon resumed command. The little red-bearded general quickly began preparing to march his troops into the interior. There was to be no more shilly-shallying with Jackson and Price. They must choose either submission or resistance to the federal government.

Most historians, of whom Edward Conrad Smith and Allan Nevins are conspicuous examples, have accepted Harney's assessment of the situation in Missouri in the late spring of 1861, and hence have been highly critical of Blair and Lyon, even going so far as to blame them for all the subsequent woes of the state.[52] However, besides making the dubious assumption that Jackson and Price were sincere in their neutrality professions, they overlook (as did Harney) the simple fact that it was not enough merely to keep Missouri in the Union, that instead, given its wealth, population, and geographic position, it was absolutely necessary that Missouri participate actively on the side of the North in the war—something it most obviously would never have done so long as Jackson and the pro-Southern legislature remained in power at Jefferson City. Nor is there much point to the corollary argument that Union control could have been established gradually: Blair and Lyon, unlike twentieth-century historians, did not know in the spring of 1861 that the Civil War was scheduled to run four years; most likely they thought, as did most other Americans at the time, that it would be won or lost before the summer was over.

[51] Reynolds, "Price and the Confederacy," 23–27; Thomas C. Reynolds to Jefferson Davis, January 20, 1880, in Thomas C. Reynolds Papers, Missouri Historical Society. It is possible, of course, that Price was unaware of the Conrow and Cabell missions, but this is unlikely. But if so, then the mutual mistrust and cross-purposes of Jackson, Price, and Reynolds assume comic-opera qualities.
[52] Smith, *The Borderland in the Civil War*, 260–62; Allan Nevins, *The War for the Union* (New York, 1959), I, 128–29.

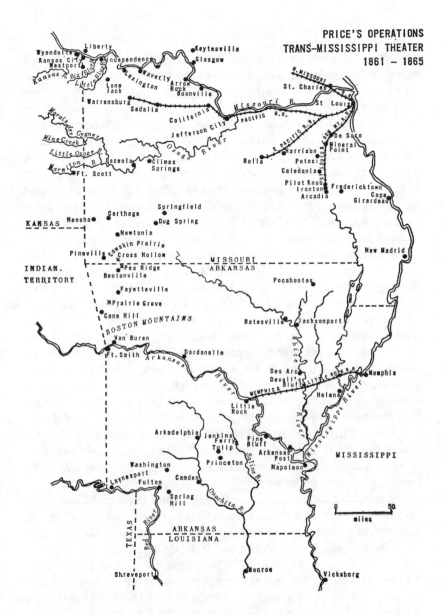

When Price learned that Harney no longer commanded, he took the official position that Lyon was bound to respect the agreement of his predecessor, and even published a communication to his district commanders stating that there was no truth to the rumors that the Federals would soon invade the state. However, he went on to assert that the replacement of Harney by Lyon had created much concern among the people, and that it was Lyon's obvious intent to arm Unionist home guards, thereby violating the agreement. In addition, he sent secret instructions to the military districts advising them to get ready for active service. Each regiment was to unfurl a flag "made of blue merino with the arms of the State emblazoned in gold on each side."[53]

In a last-minute effort to advert armed conflict, a group of prominent St. Louis citizens persuaded Jackson and Price to ask Blair and Lyon for an interview. The Unionist leaders consented on condition that Jackson and Price meet them in St. Louis. This being agreed to, Lyon promised safe conduct from and back to Jefferson City.

The conference, which was to decide peace or war in Missouri, took place in a room at the Planter's House hotel on June 11. Present with Jackson and Price was Thomas L. Snead, a young newspaperman serving as the governor's aide. Lyon and Blair demanded that the state government cooperate in suppressing the Southern rebellion, and that it permit federal military occupation and the organization of home guards. Price and Jackson, for their part, insisted that the national government disband the existing home guards and promise not to station troops in any part of the state not already occupied; in return they promised to preserve order in the state and to keep Confederate forces out of it. The two positions were irreconcilable, both sides distrusted the other, and in the opinion of Snead neither really expected or even wanted an agreement. After four hours of futile wrangling Lyon abruptly ended the meeting:

"Rather," he shouted, "than concede to the State of Missouri for one single instant the right to dictate to my government in any matter however important, I would see you, and you, and you, and you, and every man, woman, and child in the State, dead and buried!"

He paused, then rasped out: "This means war. In an hour one of my officers will call for you and conduct you out of my lines." Then, spinning around on his heel, he strode out of the room, his sabre clanking.[54]

[53] Snead, *The Fight for Missouri*, 196–97.
[54] *Ibid.*, 197–200.

2
WILSON'S CREEK

Leaving the Planter's House, Price, Jackson, and Snead impressed a train and on cleared tracks sped back to Jefferson City, stopping only to cut the telegraph wires connecting the capital and St. Louis. As soon as they arrived, Jackson issued a proclamation, drafted by Snead and dated June 12, describing the conference with Blair and Lyon and calling for fifty thousand volunteers to come to the defense of the state. Simultaneously Price ordered the district commanders to muster all available men, had the railroad bridges over the Osage and Gasconade rivers burned, and directed Brigadier General John B. Clark of the North Missouri District to march his men to Boonville. Price despaired of defending Jefferson City, with its predominantly pro-Union German population, and had already transported the state armory farther up the river to Boonville. This town was located in the most pro-Southern section of the state, and he hoped to hold it at least long enough to permit the concentration of the State Guard there. He then planned to defend western Missouri until reinforced by Confederate troops from Arkansas. After that, he would take back the entire state.

On June 13 word came that Lyon was embarking his troops at St. Louis with the obvious intent of steaming up the Missouri to Jefferson City. Price immediately ordered a small force under Brigadier General Monroe M. Parsons to move down the Pacific Railroad line to a point south of Boonville and there await further orders. Then, along with Jackson, various state officials, many legislators, and a few troops, he boarded a steamboat and went to Boonville.

He found General Clark already there, with several hundred soldiers. During the next two days more men came in, arriving in squads or alone, and bringing with them their shotguns and fowling pieces. Most of them belonged to a regiment headed by twenty-eight-year-old Colonel John Sappington Marmaduke, West Pointer and nephew of Governor Jackson. Although eager to fight, they were completely without discipline or training.

Price next received the alarming intelligence that a large body of federal cavalry and Kansas jayhawkers was threatening Lexington to the west. This town he considered to be one of the most strategic spots on the river, and a door through which recruits from northern Missouri could enter his army. Hence he hurried to Lexington in person, leaving Clark in command at Boonville with instructions to defend it as long as possible and then join Parsons to the south. He was at this time suffering from a flare-up of his Mexican War ailment and was not physically capable of taking the field in active operations. For this reason, and, more significantly, because Lyon had moved too quickly and forcibly to permit execution of his original plan, he now was merely trying to gain time in which to collect additional troops before abandoning the Missouri River line and retreating to the southwest corner of the state. There, close to Confederate support from Arkansas, he hoped to be able to organize his embryonic army in security, then launch a counteroffensive.[1]

Lyon conducted his campaign with the vigor and boldness that made him the outstanding Union military leader of the early months of the war. In a matter of hours after the Planter's House conference he began moving against Price. He occupied Jefferson City on June 15 and two days later landed two thousand men near Boonville. Governor Jackson, assuming personal command of the state troops there, ordered Marmaduke to engage Lyon. Marmaduke reluctantly obeyed, with the inevitable result that his four or five hundred men were quickly routed. Jackson then fled southward with the remnants of Marmaduke's regiment, Clark's and Parsons' commands, and the pro-Confederate legislators.

Price was delayed by his illness and did not reach Lexington until the day after the engagement at Boonville. On hand were several thousand men under Brigadier Generals James S. Rains and William Y. Slack. He had just begun to organize these forces when the news of the Boonville fiasco arrived. Realizing that Lexington was no longer tenable, he instructed Rains to take command of all the troops there and retreat to the southern border by way of Lamar. Afterward, accompanied only by his staff and a small escort, he set out for Arkansas and Confederate help. Lyon, after securing the Missouri River, sent columns fanning southward in pursuit of the state forces.[2]

---

[1] *Official Records*, LIII, 696–98; Snead, *The Fight for Missouri*, 200–201.
[2] *Official Records*, III, 12–14; Snead, *The Fight for Missouri*, 210–14.

Jackson and Rains met at Lamar, from where, after a brief rest, they continued to retreat. On July 5, near Carthage, a Union detachment under Colonel Franz Sigel, a bespectacled veteran of the German Revolutionary War of 1848, tried to intercept them, but in a lively artillery skirmish they drove him back—a minor victory which greatly bolstered morale. The following day all immediate danger of pursuit ceased as Price, accompanied by twelve hundred Missourians and a Confederate army from Arkansas under Brigadier General Ben McCulloch, joined them. Price resumed command of the state guard and established a camp at Cowskin Prairie south of Carthage. McCulloch, who had not been authorized by the Confederate government to enter Missouri, and who had done so only at Price's urging to rescue Jackson, withdrew to Maysville, Arkansas, within easy supporting distance. Lyon, distracted by problems elsewhere and lacking transport, halted his advance at Springfield. Except for mounting guerrilla warfare along the Kansas border and in northern and southeastern Missouri, the rest of July did not witness any noteworthy military action as both sides paused to regroup and reorganize.[3]

Quite clearly the first round of the war in Missouri had gone to the Federals. They now controlled the wealthy northern and central areas, all the principal towns including the capital, and the Missouri River and the railroads. The pro-Confederates, on the other hand, had been deprived of their main source of recruits and were reduced to a few thousand ill-armed and penniless fugitives (the state treasury was scattered about in various local banks and so in Union possession), now forced into the poor and thinly populated Ozark country. Furthermore, Jackson's proclamation, instead of producing a mass uprising against "Federal invasion," had caused such influential conservative newspapers as the St. Louis *Republican* to denounce him for plunging the state into war. But most important of all, and basic to the entire subsequent course of the war in Missouri and the West, most Missourians, when at last compelled to make a choice, either rallied to the Union or else were cowed into quiescence by the speed, vigor, and success of Lyon's operations. Only a minority were prepared to give active support to the state government and the Confederacy, and but a small portion of this minority was in a position to do so.

[3] *Official Records*, III, 15–37, 606–607, 743–44; Snead, *The Fight for Missouri*, 234–38.

Price's force at Cowskin Prairie numbered a mere seven or eight thousand men. Almost without exception they lacked uniforms, tents, and the other ordinary military accoutrements. Moreover, they were unorganized, undisciplined, and untrained. In fact, several thousand of them were even unarmed! The rest considered themselves lucky to possess the shotguns and squirrel rifles they had brought from their homes. There were only seven small caliber, smoothbore field pieces.

Price set to work to convert this mob into an army as quickly as possible. He was aided by the fact that he had good human raw materials with which to work. All of his troops had taken up arms (at least figuratively) out of the strong and sincere conviction that the sovereignty of their state had been wantonly violated and that their own rights and liberties were in danger. According to one of their number, "among them all there was not a man who had come forth to fight for slavery." By and large they were young, hardy men of middle-class farming families, intelligent, and in many instances well educated. Given proper training, adequate weapons, and good leadership, they would be excellent soldiers.

Nor were all of them inexperienced in warfare. Some of the older men had served in Mexico under Doniphan and Price, others had ridden with the Border Ruffians in Kansas, and a number had fought the Indians on the great plains. Such veterans as these, plus the sprinkling of former regular army officers, such as Little, provided the cadres needed to drill and instruct the others. Indeed, the strength of the state guard lay in the rank and file, whereas its greatest weakness was the fact that few of its numerous colonels and generals possessed military training (Marmaduke soon left in quest of a Confederate commission) or had any previous experience in commanding large forces in combat (except Price himself). And so great was the lack of qualified personnel for the staff positions that Price was obliged to appoint Snead chief of ordnance, although Snead, a journalist by profession, admittedly "did not know the difference between a howitzer and a siege gun." And scarcely had he discovered the difference than Price named him to the even more important post of adjutant-general (in place of Little, who went on leave to Richmond), despite the fact that he had "never heard of a morning report." [4] Yet, like so many other military

[4] Snead, *The Fight for Missouri*, 239, 241–43.

amateurs during the Civil War, Snead rapidly learned his new duties and became quite competent in their performance. In fact, along with Little he became Price's principal military advisor and was to serve as his adjutant general almost to the end of the war.

Weapons and staff officers were not the only items in short supply in the state guard: "There were no quarter-master's supplies [recalled Snead], nor subsistence; and neither the quartermaster-general nor the chief commissary had a dollar of funds. The men were not fighting for pay, they wanted none, nor did they get any; but they and their thousands of horses and mules had to be fed. For the animals there was nothing but the grass of the prairies, and for themselves nothing but a scant supply of lean beef and coarse corn-bread."[5]

Two military necessities the Missourians did have in abundance—powder and lead, the latter coming from the nearby Granby mines. This made it possible to manufacture cartridges and also to supply, through a little improvisation, ammunition for the artillery. As described by a lieutenant in one of the batteries:

A turning lathe in Carthage supplied sabots; the owner of a tin-shop contributed straps and canisters; iron rods which a blacksmith gave and cut into small pieces made good slugs for the canisters; and a bolt of flannel, with needles and thread, freely donated by a dry-goods man, provided us with material for our cartridge bags. A bayonet made a good candlestick; and at night . . . the men went to work making cartridges; strapping shot to the sabots, and filling the bags from a barrel of powder placed some distance from the candle. . . . My first cartridge resembled a turnip rather than the trim cylinders from the Federal arsenals, and would not enter a gun on any terms. But we soon learned the trick, and at the close range at which our next battle was fought our home-made ammunition proved as effective as the best.[6]

Also, as indicated above by Snead, there were a great many horses and mules. Like Price's earlier followers in the Mexican War, the members of the state guard did not care to march on foot. As a consequence, about three-fourths of them were mounted, and according to General McCulloch there were enough surplus steeds to provide for an army of fifty thousand. This disproportionate number of horse-

[5] Snead, "The First Year of the War in Missouri," 269–70.
[6] Quoted in Snead, *The Fight for Missouri*, 242.

men made it far more difficult to control and provision the army, and their lack of training and equipment for cavalry action seriously impaired their military effectiveness.[7]

While Price thus endeavored to create an army, an equally urgent effort was taking place to obtain Confederate assistance. As noted earlier, Jackson had sent a commissioner, E. C. Cabell, to Richmond for this purpose. Following the outbreak of hostilities in Missouri, Cabell asked President Davis to dispatch an army to the state. To his dismay Davis refused on the grounds that he could not deal with Governor Jackson until Missouri formally seceded! At once Cabell telegraphed Reynolds, who was still in Memphis, to hasten to Richmond. Reynolds arrived on June 19, and the next day he and Cabell had an interview with Davis.

The two Missourians presented various reasons why the Confederacy should waste no time in sending troops to Missouri. At first Davis answered with legal-constitutional objections. Then, as described by Reynolds, Davis, "with the air of a man conscious of the weakness of these arguments, and suddenly resolving to give his ruling reasons at whatever risk of offending, drew himself up in his chair, and compressing his lips," said:

I find, gentlemen, by your Governor's proclamation of June 12, which I have in my hand, that in the conference between General Price and himself and General Lyon at St. Louis, he offered to use his state troops to drive out of Missouri, any Confederate troops entering it. . . . Now at the very moment he made this offer, you, Mr. Cabell, were here with a commission from him to me, and presenting his request for those Confederate troops to be sent into Missouri, so that had I asserted to the request, those troops, even though with your Lieutenant Governor at the head of them, might have had to fight against, instead of with, General Price's army. Now I think General Lyon acted very unwisely in not accepting Governor Jackson's proposals, and Mr. Lincoln may send him orders to accept them. Governor Jackson in his proclamation makes a merit of having proposed them; now if I agree to send Confederate troops into Missouri at your request, can you give me *any* guarantee that Mr. Lincoln may not propose and Governor Jackson assent to the agreement rejected by General Lyon, and compel those troops to retire before their joint forces? [8]

---

[7] Ephraim M. Anderson, *Memoirs: Historical and Personal, Including Campaigns of the First Missouri Confederate Brigade* (St. Louis, 1868), 49.

[8] Reynolds, "Price and the Confederacy," 27–29; *Official Records*, III, 603–

Davis' tone and manner manifested great disgust at what he obviously considered double-dealing and an insult to his dignity by Jackson
and Price. Cabell and Reynolds could only reply that whatever their
earlier "vacillation," the governor and his general had "taken the final
leap into the secession camp and could be trusted accordingly." But
Davis' mind was made up, and the interview soon ended. Two days
later Cabell and Reynolds received a formal written answer to their
solicitations, rejecting Confederate military intervention in Missouri
for the technical reasons previously assigned.[9]

In brief Jackson and Price, while failing in their attempt to out-
maneuver the Unionists, had unwittingly succeeded in offending the
President of the Confederacy and arousing his suspicions as to their
loyalty and integrity. As a consequence, a great obstacle was placed in
the way of their efforts to liberate Missouri from Federal control,
irreparable damage was done to their personal standing with the Confederate government, and, to quote one historian, "Missouri's position
and influence in the Confederacy and her ability to contribute in any
important way to the common cause were jeopardized from the beginning."[10] Obviously, from this standpoint, they made a great mistake
in not following the course of action originally proposed by Reynolds.
Had they done so, the outcome in so far as events in Missouri were
concerned could not have been worse, and it assuredly would have
been better as regards relations with Richmond.

However, Davis' refusal to deal with Jackson did not mean that he
meant to ignore the plight of the state forces. Missouri's importance
was too great for that; perhaps also Cabell's and Reynolds' arguments
made some impression. On June 26 the Confederate War Department
authorized McCulloch to render whatever assistance he thought proper
to the Missourians as long as it was consistent with his main mission,
the protection of Arkansas and the Indian Territory from Federal
invasion. On July 4 Confederate Secretary of War L. P. Walker repeated these instructions, but at the same time he cautioned McCulloch
that "the position of Missouri as a Southern State still in the Union
requires, as you will readily perceive, much prudence and circumspec-

606; *ibid.*, LIII, 707; Reynolds to Davis, January 20, 1880, and November 13,
1880 in Thomas C. Reynolds Papers, Missouri Historical Society; Kirkpatrick,
"Missouri in the Early Months of the War," 261–62.
    [9] Reynolds, "Price and the Confederacy," 28–29.
    [10] Kirkpatrick, "Missouri in the Early Months of the War," 266.

tion, and it should only be when necessity and propriety unite that active and direct assistance should be afforded by crossing the boundary and entering the State."[11]

Besides Cabell and Reynolds, two other Missourians sought help from the Confederacy during July—Jackson and former United States Senator David R. Atchison. They left Cowskin Prairie on the twelfth and journeyed to Memphis where they urged Major General Leonidas Polk, at the time commanding Confederate troops along the Mississippi, to aid Price in recovering Missouri. Polk, although sympathetic, held back because his forces were extremely weak and because Richmond had instructed him, like McCulloch, to be very cautious in regard to Missouri affairs. Eventually, however, he ordered Major General

---

[11] *Official Records*, III, 599, 603. Twenty years after the war Daniel M. Frost (commander of Camp Jackson and subsequently a Confederate general) stated in a paper read to the Southern Historical Society of St. Louis that in September, 1861, he was told by General Albert Sidney Johnston, then commander of all Confederate forces in the West, that the Richmond government did not want to become so involved with Missouri as to make it a *sine qua non* that it insist upon an impossible boundary line when the time came to make a peace treaty with Washington ["That State Secret," St. Louis *Missouri Republican*, February 19, 1886]. When Jefferson Davis learned of this assertion he strongly denied that any such consideration influenced Confederate policy regarding Missouri, and Frost hastily disavowed it, claiming that he had been misquoted [Jefferson Davis to R. I. Holcombe, St. Louis *Missouri Republican*, March 20, 1886; D. M. Frost to Jefferson Davis, March 22, 1886, and Davis to Frost, May 30, 1886, in Dunbar Rowland (ed.), *Jefferson Davis, Constitutionalist: His Letters, Papers, and Speeches* (Jackson, Miss., 1923), IX, 409–410, 453–55]. In addition Colonel John F. Snyder, a Missouri secessionist, in a memorandum prepared for Snead in the 1880's, and to be found in the Thomas L. Snead Papers, Missouri Historical Society, St. Louis, stated that he went to Richmond in June or July, 1861, and found that the feeling there was that the spirit of Missouri had been crushed, that the state guard was of no military use, and that Cabell was unable to communicate with the Confederate authorities. Also, that "it was whispered that a subtle and damaging influence had been brought to bear on the President by Lt. Governor Reynolds . . ."; that Reynolds had prejudiced Davis against Jackson; that "it was said" that Reynolds was seeking a general's commission and the command of the Missouri troops; and finally, that he, Snyder, supplied the Richmond government with its first accurate information about affairs in Missouri, which caused it to "order" McCulloch into the state. No doubt there is a substratum of truth in Snyder's words, and it is also easy to see how a rumor that Reynolds was prejudicing Davis against Jackson and seeking a general's command could come into being. But Snyder's story is contradicted by several established facts, and it was related in private to a man—Snead—who was known to be an admirer of Price and a past enemy of Davis and Reynolds.

Gideon Pillow with six thousand men to invade southeastern Missouri and join with the state troops in that region under Brigadier General M. Jeff Thompson in an attack on St. Louis. Pillow did as instructed, but he got only as far as New Madrid before becoming bogged down. Nevertheless this thrust later proved to be of great indirect help to Price, for it caused Major General John C. Frémont, overall Union commander in the West, to withhold troops from Lyon out of fear for the safety of strategically vital Cairo, Illinois.[12] Had Lyon obtained these reinforcements, chances are that subsequent military events in Missouri would have taken a radically different course.

By the last week of July, Price considered his army ready to take the field. True it was still, in the words of one of its members, "a great awkward squad,"[13] but at least it was capable of marching and fighting. Not only that, Price was anxious to assume the offensive against Lyon. The state convention, with a new president, had reconvened at Jefferson City and was about to depose Jackson and install a Union administration; Price hoped to prevent, or in any event challenge, this action. Second, he had learned that Lyon's army was decreasing in strength because the enlistments of its troops (three month's volunteers) were expiring; by attacking it now while it was weak, he perhaps could forestall its ever getting stronger. And finally, his own forces were threatened with disintegration unless they moved away from Cowskin Prairie. They had nearly exhausted the available supplies of food and forage and would either have to advance, retreat, or disband. Therefore when McCulloch, who had been proposing a joint movement against Lyon for several weeks, came to him and again urged such an operation, he quickly agreed.[14]

On July 25 Price's army left Cowskin Prairie and made a three-day

[12] *Official Records*, III, 612–13; Arthur Roy Kirkpatrick, "The Admission of Missouri to the Confederacy," *Missouri Historical Review*, LV (1961), 369. In addition to seeking aid from McCulloch and Polk, Price also requested Brigadier General William J. Hardee, commanding Confederate forces in northeast Arkansas, to invade Missouri. But Hardee informed Price that his army was not yet capable of active operations. See William J. Hardee to Sterling Price, July 27, 1861, in *Official Records*, III, 616. Early in August, however, Hardee did move a short distance into Missouri, threatening Ironton.

[13] Joseph A. Mudd, "What I saw at Wilson's Creek," *Missouri Historical Review*, VII (1913), 92.

[14] Snead, *The Fight for Missouri*, 243; *Official Records*, III, 607–609, 611, 622–23, 744.

march eastward across the Ozarks to Cassville. Here it was augmented by seven hundred state troops under Brigadier General J. H. McBride. Natives of the Ozark hill country, McBride's men were a martinet's nightmare. They knew almost nothing of drill and discipline, and the backwoods lawyers who served as their officers did not even attempt to remedy these deficiencies. The only drum and fife in the outfit sounded all the calls, and the sergeants assembled their units by bawling out, "Oh, yes! Oh, yes! all you who belong to Captain Brown's company fall in here." Officers and men messed together, and there was no such thing as saluting. Nor did anyone take offense when a private sauntered casually into General McBride's headquarters tent, lounged about listening to all that was said, and then addressed the general as "Jedge" while advising him on how to run matters! However, in compensation for their military crudeness, McBride's hillbillies were crack shots with their deer rifles, and they were to show themselves good fighters when the time came.[15]

McCulloch joined Price at Cassville on July 29. He brought with him an army of 5,700, consisting of a brigade of Confederate troops from Louisiana and Texas, and a "division" of Arkansas militia commanded by Brigadier General N. Bart Pearce. Famed as leader of the Texas Rangers during the Mexican War, McCulloch was fifty years old, tall, spare, and slightly stooped. His long black hair fell back over his ears, he had a short but full beard, and his deepset grey eyes were shaded by heavy brows "which gave an expression of almost suspicious scrutiny to his countenance." In manner he was cool, serious, and taciturn. He wore no uniform, and instead of a sabre carried a hunting rifle. The Missourians, impressed by his reputation and liking his looks, cheered him whenever he rode by. In him they saw the man who would make it possible for them to redeem their state.[16]

McCulloch—and this must be emphasized—likewise was eager to drive the Federals out of Missouri. But, as we have seen, his instructions from Richmond restricted his freedom of action on this score. Moreover, he had serious doubts about the military efficiency of the state guard and its commander. "I find," he wrote the War Department on July 18, "that [Price's] force of 8,000 or 9,000 men [sic] is

[15] Snead, "The First Year of the War in Missouri," 270–71; Mudd, "What I Saw," 95.
[16] Bevier, *First and Second Missouri Confederate Brigades*, 317.

badly organized, badly armed, and now almost entirely out of ammunition. This force was made by the concentration of different commands under their own generals. The consequence is that there is no concert of action among them, and will not be until a competent military man is put in command of the entire force."[17] Consequently he was more than a little wary of becoming too deeply involved in Missouri or with the Missourians.

Nor did close association improve McCulloch's opinion of the state guard and Price, whom in private he characterized as "nothing but an old militia general." Before leaving Cowskin Prairie, Price had promised McCulloch that his unarmed men—about two thousand— would remain behind. But on arriving at Cassville, McCulloch found these men very much in evidence. He immediately remonstrated with Price, who then issued an order (composed by McCulloch) stipulating that all unarmed soldiers were to keep at least one day's march to the rear of the army. However, without notifying McCulloch, Price rescinded the order—probably because of the loud protests of those affected. Thus, when the combined armies set out from Cassville on August 1, McCulloch was startled to see the unarmed men accompanying General Clark's command. Thinking that Clark was responsible, he urged him not to set such a bad example of insubordination. But Clark paid him no heed, and to the Texan's disgust the unarmed troops continued to tag along—an unruly, plundering, and encumbering mob.[18]

On the morning of August 2, as the Southern column approached Crane Creek, Federal artillery began shelling the woods on either side of the road. Thinking this might presage a full-scale enemy attack, McCulloch promptly ordered his troops into a line of defense and sent forward pickets. William Watson, a sergeant in the Third Louisiana, later recalled that as he was posting his men, McCulloch came riding up accompanied by "a stout farmer-looking old gentleman dressed in a suit of white linen clothes, not over clean, who I took to be one of the farmers of the neighbourhood the general was often talking with about the roads, passes, and country in general." Watson continued:

[17] *Official Records*, III, 611.
[18] *Ibid.*, 103–104, 745; *ibid.*, LIII, 717–18.

The general asked me what I was doing and having told him, he gave me some directions about placing the pickets, telling me to keep them a little further back from the road and more out of sight, and, although the enemy passed on the road, to be certain not to fire unless they tried to enter the pass. The old gentleman then said something to the general which I did not hear, but the general turned to me and said, "Remember that there is a body of our own troops to come in first; take care that you don't fire upon them."

"How are we to distinguish our own men from the enemy?" said I. "The enemy's troops we saw yesterday were so covered over with dust and dirt that we could not tell them from our own men."

"That is a compliment to your own men," said the old man, laughing. "But there should be something to distinguish them,—a piece of white cloth tied around every man's left arm would do very well."

"Yes," said the general, "that will do very well, and it should be done; they can tear up a tent or something."

I did not like the idea of tearing up our only tent, and I asked the old gentleman whom I took to be a farmer, whether he thought we could not get an old white shirt or two.

"I can't give you any," said he, "unless I give you the one I have on, and it is not very white."

"Tut," said the general to me, "that is General Price you are talking to." I laughed and apologized. He laughed and said it was all right.[19]

No Federal attack developed, but later in the day General Rains's Missouri "huckleberry cavalry," serving as the advance guard, was routed by a Union detachment less than half its size at Dug Springs. As subsequently described by McCulloch in a report to the Secretary of War: "It was at this point I first saw the total inefficiency of the Missouri mounted men under Brigadier-General Rains. A thousand, more or less, of them, composed the advance guard, and whilst reconnoitering the enemy's position, some eight miles distance from our camp, were put to flight by a single cannon-shot, running in the greatest confusion, without the loss of a single man except one, who died of overheat or sunstroke . . . ."[20] The conduct of Rains's command,

[19] William Watson, *Life in the Confederate Army* (New York, 1888), 195–96.
[20] *Official Records*, III, 745. McCulloch's account is based on the report of Captain James McIntosh, who witnessed the affair. Rains reported that he encountered 5,000 Federals and Price accepted his version. However the federal reports make it clear that the McCulloch-McIntosh version is substantially correct. See *ibid*., 47–52, 99, and Watson, *Life in the Confederate Army*, 197–98.

later wrote Snead, caused McCulloch "to lose all confidence in the Missouri troops . . . ."[21]

So far the state guard, although in effect in Confederate service, had remained an independent force, merely cooperating with Mc-Culloch's army and not subject to his orders. Two days after the Dug Springs fiasco this awkward and potentially disastrous situation came to an end as Price relinquished command of the guard to McCulloch. Just how and why he did so, however, is a matter of dispute. If we are to credit Snead, McCulloch in order to obtain command of the entire army "refused to advance any further, alleging as an excuse that the Confederate Government had declined to give him leave to move into Missouri except for the defense of the Indian Territory; and that to advance another foot into the state might endanger the safety of that Territory and subject himself to the censure of his Government." Price, sensing McCulloch's desire, and willing to subordinate his own pride to the common cause, thereupon rode over to McCulloch's tent and declared in a "loud, imperious tone":

I am an older [two years older!] man than you, General McCulloch, and I am not only your senior in rank now, but I was a brigadier-general in the Mexican War, with an independent command when you were only a captain; I have fought and won more battles than you have ever witnessed; my force is twice as great as yours; and some of my officers rank, and have seen more service than you, and we are also upon the soil of our own State; but General McCulloch, if you will consent to help us to whip Lyon and to repossess Missouri, I will put myself and all my forces under your command, and we will obey you as faithfully as the humblest of your own men. We can whip Lyon, and we will whip him and drive the enemy out of Missouri, and all the honor and all the glory shall be yours. All that we want is to regain our homes and to establish the independence of Missouri and the South. If you refuse to accept this offer, I will move with the Missourians alone, against Lyon. For it is better that they and I should all perish than Missouri be abandoned without a struggle. You must either fight beside us, or look on at a safe distance, and see us fight all alone the army which you dare not attack even with our aid. I must have your answer before dark, for I intend to attack Lyon tomorrow.[22]

[21] Snead, *The Fight for Missouri*, 254.

[22] *Ibid.*, 255–57. Snead gave a somewhat different account of the matter in a newspaper interview in 1877, reprinted in Barnes, *Switzler's History of Mis-*

McCulloch, however, later contended that while he did hesitate to advance farther, it was solely because he lacked adequate information about Lyon and because food supplies were running low. Furthermore, with reference to his seeking command of the combined forces,

. . . the generals of the Missouri forces, by common consent on their part and unasked on mine, tendered me the command of their troops, which I at first declined, saying to them that it was done to throw the responsibility of ordering a retreat upon me if one had to be ordered for the want of supplies, which seemed likely to be the case, their breadstuffs giving out about this time; and, in truth, we would have been in a starving condition had it not been for the young corn . . . .

McCulloch then added: "At this juncture Major Dorn, of Missouri, arrived, bringing a letter from General Polk, saying General Pillow was advancing into Missouri from New Madrid with 12,000 [sic] men. After further reflection on our condition I consented to take the command and to march upon the enemy."[23]

Snead published his account in 1886; McCulloch wrote his in December, 1861. Snead was not above playing fast and loose with the facts, especially where the reputation of his hero Price was concerned; there is no known reason to doubt McCulloch's essential truthfulness. Therefore, in all likelihood McCulloch's version is the more accurate, as it is the more probable and circumstantial. This is not to say that Price did not go to McCulloch and offer him command of the state guard; but he probably did so only under pressure from his own generals and from General Pearce. By the same token, McCulloch, without actually seeking the command, most likely forced the Missourians to offer it to him by speaking of retreat and manifesting his

----

souri, 377, from which is taken the "loud imperious tone." Quite obviously the long speech of Price's quoted by Snead is not verbatim. In evaluating all controversial matters in Snead's *The Fight for Missouri* it should be kept in mind that its primary purpose was to glorify Price and to show that Jefferson Davis was responsible for the Confederate failure in Missouri. Robert Bevier, who was a state guard colonel at the time, gave a different account of the affair than Snead, but agreed that McCulloch in effect forced the Missourians to give him overall command. See Bevier, *First and Second Missouri Confederate Brigades*, 41.

[23] *Official Records*, III, 745.

lack of confidence in the guard. In other words, neither Snead nor McCulloch was completely candid in relating this affair.

Price announced the change in command to his troops on the evening of August 4, at the same time carefully reserving the right to resume control whenever he deemed it necessary.[24] At midnight the army began marching, hoping to surprise Lyon, who, according to a report from Rains's cavalry, had advanced west of Springfield to a spot known as McCulla's store. But neither the surprise nor Lyon's army materialized, and the Confederates pushed on through the day in suffocating heat and over dusty roads to Moody's Spring where, nearly exhausted, they halted for the night. On August 6 they moved forward two more miles along the Telegraph Road to Wilson's Creek, ten miles southwest of Springfield, and encamped in a straggling line some three miles long amidst cornfields which provided food for both men and animals. During the next two days they rested while McCulloch vainly endeavored to obtain accurate intelligence concerning Lyon's movements and the defenses at Springfield. He blamed Rains's cavalry for this failure and again sneered openly at the state guard.[25]

All the while Price became increasingly concerned over the delay in attacking Lyon. But whenever he urged McCulloch to strike, the Texan replied that he would not budge until he had reliable information about the enemy. In addition, McCulloch once more talked of retreat—however (he later explained), merely to stimulate the Missouri cavalry into greater scouting efforts. Finally, on August 9, Price's patience gave out. Riding to McCulloch's tent, he found him marking diagrams on the ground with a stick. "General McCulloch," he demanded loudly, "are you going to attack Lyon or not?" McCulloch gave a noncommittal reply. "Then," shouted Price, "I want my own Missouri troops, and I will lead them against Lyon myself if they are

---

[24] Snead, *The Fight for Missouri*, 257–58. In his report on the campaign Price stated, "Reasons which will hereafter be assigned induced me on Sunday, the 4th instant, to put the Missouri forces under the direction, for the time being, of General McCulloch." *Official Records*, III, 99. However, if Price ever assigned the reasons, the record has been lost. But it is obvious from his tone that he resented McCulloch's taking over "direction" of the state guard.

[25] Snead, *The Fight for Missouri*, 258–61; *Official Records*, III, 745. Snead states that McCulloch personally reconnoitered towards Springfield, then blamed the Missourians "for his own want of success." But that a commanding general would feel obliged to act as a scout is the significant fact.

all killed in the action, and you, General McCulloch, may go where in the devil you please!" Faced with this ultimatum, and realizing that the only alternative to an advance was a disastrous retreat, McCulloch therewith issued orders to march on Springfield at nine o'clock that night.[26]

However, just as the march was about to get under way, a slight rain began falling, with portents of heavier showers to follow. Strange as it may seem, this produced a near crisis. Most of the troops, for want of regular containers, carried their cartridges in cotton sacks or in their pockets. If their ammunition became rainsoaked, the result would be disaster, for each man had only twenty-five rounds on the average, and no more was to be had closer than Arkansas or Louisiana. Therefore McCulloch, after conferring with Price, countermanded the movement and directed the army to hold itself in readiness to march on instant notice. During the rest of the night the Confederates remained under arms, and since it did not rain after all, some of the Missourians passed the time fiddling and dancing about the campfires.[27]

Meanwhile the Union army was on the march. Lyon, although outnumbered more than two to one, had decided to seize the initiative and strike the rebels before they attacked him. Several factors prompted him to make this desperate gamble, rather than adopt the more prudent course of retreating, as advised by Frémont. First, the enlistments of several of his regiments were about to expire and if his army was to fight at all it would have to be at once. Second, except for McCulloch's Louisiana and Texas troops, estimated at four thousand, he considered the Confederates too poorly armed and badly trained to be of much military consequence. And last, he was by nature aggressive and could not tolerate the idea of retreat as long as there was a chance of defeating the enemy.

Originally he envisioned a spoiling operation, in which he would strike the head of the Confederate column with the full strength of his army, inflict as much damage as possible, and then fall back to Springfield. But at the last moment he was induced by his second in command, Colonel Franz Sigel, to employ a more ambitious plan. Under it Sigel,

---

[26] Snead, *The Fight for Missouri*, 261–63; Barnes, *Switzler's History of Missouri*, 378; *Official Records*, III, 745–46.

[27] *Official Records*, III, 99–100; Bevier, *First and Second Missouri Confederate Brigades*, 43.

with one thousand troops, swung around the Confederates and advanced from the south. At the same time Lyon, with the rest of his army, four thousand men, moved in from the north. Just as dawn broke on August 10, first Sigel's, then Lyon's column, smashed into the Wilson's Creek camp.[28]

The Confederates were taken almost completely by surprise—the result, McCulloch later charged, of the failure of Rains's cavalry to perform the picket duties assigned it, but which the Missourians attributed to McCulloch's not putting the pickets out again after pulling them in prior to the rain-aborted march on Springfield.[29] In any case, a goodly number of the Southern soldiers were shot or captured while drawing water from the creek or gathering corn in the fields. As for McCulloch and Price, they had just sat down with Captain James McIntosh and Snead to a breakfast of corn bread, lean beef, and coffee in Price's tent, which was located not far from where the Fayetteville Road crossed Wilson's Creek. Then, breathless with excitement, Colonel John F. Snyder of Rains's command came running up and cried out: "Thirty thousand Yankees are attacking Rains' line!"

"Oh, pshaw," scoffed McCulloch, understandably skeptical, "that's another of Rains' scares; I'll see about it when I finish breakfast," and they all continued eating. But a few minutes later a second officer dashed up and declared that Rains was falling back before overwhelming numbers.[30] This time McCulloch, Price, and their aides decided to take a look. To the northwest they saw, in Snead's words, "a great crowd of men on horseback, some armed, and others unarmed, mixed in with wagons and teams and led horses, all in dreadful confusion . . . and rushing down toward us—a panic-stricken drove." At the same instant Union batteries opened up from both north and south. McCulloch and McIntosh immediately left to take personal command of the Louisiana, Arkansas, and Texas troops. Price, bareheaded, in his shirtsleeves, and still buttoning his suspenders, ran out of the tent calling for his horse. Swinging his 250 pounds into the saddle he galloped off, followed by Snead, to rally his men.[31]

[28] *Official Records*, III, 94, 96.
[29] Snead, *The Fight for Missouri*, 268, 271, 298; Edwards, *Shelby and His Men*, 37; *Official Records*, III, 746.
[30] Barnes, *Switzler's History of Missouri*, 378.
[31] Snead, *The Fight for Missouri*, 271–72.

Despite the fact that they had achieved a surprise, the impact of the Federals' onslaught was not as great as it might have been. Indeed, following the battle, McCulloch declared that he did not consider anything lost by the manner of the enemy attack, "as we never were in a better condition to make a battle, every man being ready with gun in hand to receive the enemy [an exaggeration, but generally true], when at other times thousands of our men would be miles from camp hunting something to eat for themselves and horses."[32]

Lyon's main blow fell on the Missourians, striking first Rains's hapless cavalry and a large number of camp followers (the "panic-stricken drove" described by Snead). However, a portion of Rains's command held together, and while retreating managed to check the Union advance. Price, taking direct command, ordered his brigades to hasten to the front. As each unit came up he hurled it into the fray. Soon he had about three thousand men and four cannons in line. He, of course, had far more troops than this available, but many of the mounted men—the bulk of his army—could not be brought into action. Consequently the brunt of the battle was borne by the infantry, especially McBride's Ozarkers, Although they could not stand in a straight line, and were "barefooted, hungry, and ragged," they "seemed devoid of fear and eager for the hottest place in the conflict."

The fighting centered on Oak Hill, a knoll which both sides renamed "Bloody Hill." The ground was covered with trees and underbrush so dense that the opposing forces were able to move within a few score yards of each other and still be invisible. Only the thick clouds of powder smoke marked the positions and provided targets. Such close-range fighting worked to the advantage of the Missourians, since in open country their shotguns and smoothbores would have been no match for the rifles of the enemy.

The battle developed into a stubbornly contested fire fight, with neither side gaining nor losing ground. Meanwhile, the other half of the Confederate army came close to disaster. Sigel's attack was initially much more successful than Lyon's, and he advanced for a considerable distance, driving hundreds of terrified Southerners ahead of him. But many of his men—short-term volunteers without sufficient training or officers—thought that the victory had been won and so dropped out

[32] *Official Records*, III, 746.

of ranks to plunder. At this point McCulloch brought up a battalion of Missouri cavalry and part of the Third Louisiana regiment under Colonel Louis Hébert. The Louisianians wore grey uniforms and Sigel's men mistook them for an Iowa regiment that was similarly attired (blue had not yet become the standard Federal uniform, nor grey the Confederate). Hébert's troops rocked them with a devastating volley delivered at close range, then utterly routed them with enfilading artillery fire. Many of the survivors surrendered and the remainder scattered in confusion over the field. Sigel himself fled all the way back to Springfield, accompanied only by a private. He made no attempt whatsoever to rally his men, and he did not report his defeat to Lyon, who was left to carry on the battle alone.

After disposing of Sigel, McCulloch went to the aid of Price. Gradually the Confederates built up a strong superiority in numbers along Oak Hill. Twice they charged forward, and twice the tough Kansans, Iowans, and regulars of Lyon beat them back. In like manner the equally stubborn Missourians, Arkansans, Louisianians, and Texans under McCulloch and Price repulsed the Federals' assaults. Sometimes the opposing lines moved to within fifty yards of one another, fired, then staggered back to reload, reform, and advance again. The deafening roar of rifles and cannons gave way occasionally to an inexplicable lull, only to thunder forth once more with new fury. By mid-morning the slopes of Bloody Hill were littered with dead and wounded, some places in heaps and rows.[33]

Price displayed the bravery that always distinguished him on the battlefield and which did so much to gain him the respect and devotion of his men. He rode up and down the battle line, encouraging the Missourians and bringing up fresh troops to bolster weak points. Whenever the firing subsided, he rode far out in front and attempted to see through the thick, low-lying smoke for signs of enemy movements. Once Lyon recognized him and started forward to engage him in

[33] The above account of the Battle of Wilson's Creek is based on *ibid.*, 60–61, 66–67, 87–88, 94–97, 100, 104–105; William M. Wherry, "Wilson's Creek and the Death of Lyon," in *Battles and Leaders*, I, 289–97; N. B. Pearce, "Arkansas Troops in the Battle of Wilson's Creek," in *Battles and Leaders*, I, 298–303; Franz Sigel, "The Flanking Column at Wilson's Creek," in *Battles and Leaders*, I, 304–306; Snead, *The Fight for Missouri*, 263–94; Mudd, "What I saw at Wilson's Creek," 95; Edwards, *Shelby and His Men*, 34–35; Anderson, *Memoirs: Historical and Personal*, 49.

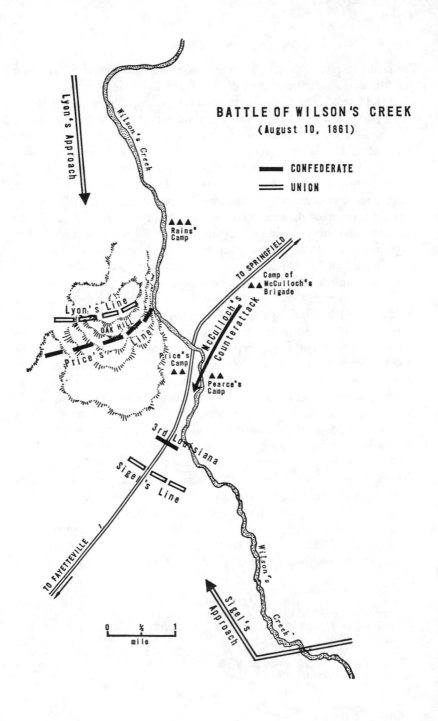

BATTLE OF WILSON'S CREEK
(August 10, 1861)

CONFEDERATE
UNION

Lyon's Approach

Wilson's Creek

Rains' Camp

TO SPRINGFIELD

Camp of McCulloch's Brigade

Lyon's Line

OAK HILL

Price's Line

McCulloch's Counterattack

Price's Camp

Pearce's Camp

3rd Louisiana

Sigel's Line

TO FAYETTEVILLE

0   ½   1
mile

Sigel's Approach

Wilson's Creek

personal combat but was dissuaded by an aide.[34] Long afterwards, one of his soldiers recalled his "superb figure, large, and faultless in every detail," and how he and his fellows were inspired by the presence of "this grand man, a few feet away, watchful of every movement on the field, silent, calm, and dignified, with countenance expressive of serene confidence in his Missourians."[35]

Price's reckless self-exposure caused his men to cry out again and again, "Don't lead us, General; don't come with us; take care of yourself for the sake of us all; we will go without you." But he paid them no heed, and continued to ride wherever the fighting was hottest. Several times his clothing was ripped by bullets, and one ball wounded him painfully in the side. But with the exception of an officer who was nearby at the time, no one in the army realized it until after the battle. To this officer, probably Snead, he said when hit, "That isn't fair; if I were as slim as Lyon that fellow would have missed me entirely."[36]

Slowly but inevitably the superior numbers of the Confederates began to tell, as the Union soldiers approached the limits of their endurance. Lyon, leading a desperate charge, fell mortally wounded. His successor, Major Samuel D. Sturgis, consulted the other Federal officers as to what should be done. All, except one, agreed that they were in the gravest peril and must retreat. Sturgis thereupon issued orders to break off the battle. The Northern troops withdrew from the field—not in a rout, but nevertheless so hastily that they left behind Lyon's body. Soon the firing died away.

It was then early afternoon. Price, Snead claimed later, called for an immediate pursuit, only to have McCulloch refuse to order it, thereby throwing away an opportunity to destroy the defeated enemy. For, according to Snead, the Confederates had available 2,700 cavalry and 2,000 infantry who had seen little or no action and had fired scarcely a shot.[37] But, as might be expected, McCulloch told a different story. According to him, when the Federals retreated he issued orders "for the wounded to be removed from the battlefield, the dead to be buried, and the army to be ready to march after the enemy that night."

[34] Snead, *The Fight for Missouri,* 285–86.
[35] Mudd, "What I Saw at Wilson's Creek," 95.
[36] Snead, *The Fight for Missouri,* 286.
[37] *Ibid.,* 293–94.

However, several of his officers then informed him that many of the
men had expended all their ammunition. So, following a conference
with Price, "it was thought best to 'let well enough alone.' "[38] General
Pearce supported McCulloch's version, adding that the Confederates
were simply too exhausted and disorganized by the battle for effective
pursuit in any case.[39]

Wilson's Creek, in the words of an Arkansas soldier, was "a might
mean-fowt fight."[40] In fact it was the fiercest and bloodiest engagement
of the entire war up to that time. Raw Northern and Southern farm
boys had slugged it out almost literally toe to toe, hour after hour, and
in the process inflicted casualties on each other which veterans were
not supposed to withstand. Over a fourth of the army which Lyon
and Sigel led into action was killed, wounded, or missing. Confederate
losses were almost equally heavy, the number of killed and wounded
probably being greater than that of the Union.[41] Price's Missourians in
particular had suffered (732 casualties out of the total Confederate loss
of 1,230), and with ample cause they felt that had redeemed the disgrace of Dug Springs on the slopes of Bloody Hill.

Lyon deserved credit for daring and determination but not for
judgment. He divided his army in the face of a much superior foe in
order to attempt with inexperienced officers and troops one of the most
difficult maneuvers in warfare—a coordinated attack from two widely
separated directions. He would have done much better to have carried
out his original plan of falling on the Confederates with his full force,
cutting them up, then retiring to Springfield. As for McCulloch and
Price, they displayed courage, steadiness, and resourcefulness in a time
of crisis, but they had been outgeneraled by Lyon and owed their
success mainly to luck and superior numbers. All in all it was a soldier's fight, and the side with the most soldiers won it.

The consequences of the battle were thus: Lyon, the most able and
dynamic Federal leader in the West, had been killed. His army, although escaping destruction, ceased for the moment to be a factor in
the war. Union prestige suffered a damaging blow, and Southern

[38] Victor M. Rose, *The Life and Services of Gen. Ben McCulloch* (Philadelphia, 1888), 184.
[39] Pearce, "Arkansas Troops in the Battle of Wilson's Creek," 303.
[40] *Ibid.*, 296n.
[41] *Ibid.*, 306; Snead, *The Fight for Missouri*, 290–92, 310, 312–15.

morale, already soaring as a result of Bull Run, rose even higher. And, of greatest importance, all of western Missouri now lay open to the victory-flushed troops of McCulloch and Price, and the tide of the war in the West had been reversed.

3

LEXINGTON

The battered remnants of Lyon's army retreated to Rolla, where it had a direct rail link with St. Louis. On August 12, two days after the battle, the Confederates occupied Springfield. Price at once urged McCulloch to participate in an advance to the Missouri River. McCulloch, however, refused. He informed Price that his troops lacked ammunition; they were needed to protect Arkansas and the Indian Territory; and Pearce's division was about to return home, thereby leaving him with only 2,500 men. In addition, he argued that a movement to the Missouri could not succeed without the support of Hardee's and Pillow's armies, both of which (he had just learned) had fallen back towards the Arkansas line.[1]

McCulloch's reasons for opposing an advance to the Missouri were sincere and, except for the one concerning the protection of Arkansas and the Indian Territory, valid. But he had at least two others which he did not mention. The first was that, despite the bravery they showed in the fighting on Bloody Hill, he still had no confidence in Price's troops, whose lack of discipline he feared would demoralize his own forces. The second was that he, along with many of the other non-Missourians, was disgusted with what he considered to be the selfish and unfriendly conduct of the state guard. At the beginning of the campaign Pearce loaned the Missourians 615 muskets—only 10 were returned. In marching up from Cassville, Parsons' division "borrowed" ninety-five tents left there, along with spare clothing, by the Louisiana regiment. During the battle Price's unarmed men picked up and kept the small arms of all the dead and wounded, including those of McCulloch's forces. And finally, Price's report on Wilson's Creek, published August 12, was so worded that it appeared that his troops had captured Sigel's five cannons, whereas in fact they had been taken by the Louisianians. Little wonder, then, that McCulloch remarked in

[1] *Official Records*, III, 747.

48

a letter to Hardee that "we had as well be in Boston as far as the friendly feelings" of the Missourians were concerned.[2]

McCulloch's response angered and disappointed Price, but it did not deter him. He was convinced that Missouri's hour of deliverance was at hand and that not to take action now would only give the Federals a chance to recover from their defeat and more time to consolidate their hold on the state. He believed, too, that with his advance the great mass of Missourians would rise up against the Northern invaders, negating thereby the strictly military risks involved in the venture. Hence, on August 14 he resumed independent command of the state guard, which began preparing for the march to the Missouri.[3]

Shortly after he occupied Springfield, Price sent Rains's cavalry to "clear out" some Kansas jayhawkers under Jim Lane, United States Senator and part-time general, who were "marauding and murdering" in the Missouri counties east of Fort Scott, Kansas. Rains proceeded to Stockton, then reported back (erroneously, as usual) that the Kansans were too numerous for him to attack alone. Price, having completed his preparations, accordingly decided to seize and destroy Fort Scott before heading to the Missouri. On August 25 he moved westward out of Springfield, and a few days later McCulloch withdrew to Arkansas.

On the evening of September 2 Price's advance guard encountered about five hundred jayhawkers at Drywood Creek along the Kansas-Missouri border. For almost an hour the two forces skirmished amidst prairie grass higher than a man's head, with neither side inflicting any particular damage on the other. The badly outnumbered Kansans then

[2] *Ibid.*, 104, 672, 747. In a letter to the Secretary of War, December 22, 1861, McCulloch stated that if Price had asked him for advice, which he did not, he would have recommended that the Missouri army fortify Springfield, that Jackson and the legislature establish their capital there and carry out the secession of the state, and that proper preparations be made for a campaign to recover the rest of Missouri in conjunction with other Confederate armies, *ibid.*, 747. The passage in Price's report on Wilson's Creek to which McCulloch —quite rightly—objected, read: "The forces under my command have possession of three 12-pounder howitzers, two brass 6-pounders, and a great quantity of small-arms and ammunition taken from the enemy. . . ." *ibid.*, 100.

[3] *Official Records*, LIII, 435, 727–28; Snead, "The First Year of the War in Missouri," 273.

fled, followed by the Missourians who discontinued their pursuit only with the coming of darkness.[4] In his report, written two days afterwards, Price referred to the engagement as a "trifle" and stated that he did not take Fort Scott only because he had learned that it had been abandoned (which was true). He concluded by declaring that he did not want to invade Kansas "unless her citizens shall provoke me to do so by committing renewed outrages," in which case he would "lay waste the farms and utterly destroy the cities and villages of that State."[5]

Content with thus "chastising" the jayhawkers, Price resumed his northward march. The weather was warm and fair, he encountered no opposition, and hundreds of recruits flocked to his banner. On the morning of September 13 Rains's cavalry approached the outskirts of Lexington, then fell back under the fire of Union pickets. Price brought up infantry and artillery, and after a brief action the Federal garrison retreated to its fortifications.[6]

Set on a bluff north of Lexington and overlooking the Missouri River was the white-pillared, three-storied, brick building of the Masonic College. Around it the Union troops had a rampart of sod and earth twelve feet high and twelve feet thick. Beyond this was an irregular line of earthworks and rifle pits, protected by traverses, ditches, sharpened stakes, and trip wires. Behind these formidable defenses stood 3,500 men supported by seven cannons. In command was Colonel James A. Mulligan of the "Irish Brigade," a young Chicago politician turned soldier. Although he had two steamboats available and could have escaped easily, Mulligan decided to make a stand. He believed that his orders required him to protect the large quantities of confiscated property which he had buried in the basement of the college— property that included the Great Seal of Missouri and $900,000 taken from the Lexington bank. Moreover, he was confident that a relief column would soon come to his rescue.[7]

---

[4] *Official Records*, LIII, 435–36; Elwood (Kansas) *Free Press*, September 24, 1861; Albert Castel, *A Frontier State at War: Kansas, 1861–1865* (Ithaca, 1958), 50–53.

[5] *Official Records*, LIII, 435–36.

[6] *Ibid.*, III, 185–86.

[7] James A. Mulligan, "The Siege of Lexington, Mo.," in *Battles and Leaders*, I, 307–309; Susan A. Arnold McCausland, "The Battle of Lexington as Seen by a Woman," *Missouri Historical Review*, VI (1912), 129–30; Barnes, *Switzler's History of Missouri*, 395; *The Battle of Lexington fought in and around the*

Price had to wait for his ammunition wagons to come up before attacking the fort. Meanwhile, his army continued to swell in numbers as more volunteers arrived each day. Among the reinforcements were nearly two thousand troops from northeast Missouri under Brigadier General Thomas A. Harris—a division which earlier had numbered in its ranks a Missouri river pilot named Sam Clemens who had quit after deciding that he was not cut out to be a soldier.

On September 18, the ammunition having arrived, Price invested the fort. Mulligan himself later described the Confederate advance: "They came as one dark moving mass, their guns beaming in the sun, their banners waving, and their drums beating—everywhere, as far as we could see, were men, men, men, approaching grandly."[8]

The garrison poured a heavy artillery fire on the Missourians, causing most of their officers to dismount. Price, however, galloped to the front, his clothes covered with dust, his face glowing with the excitement of battle. "Perfectly self-possessed," later wrote one of his men, admiringly, "he seemed not to heed the storm of grape and canister, and taking position in the rear of Parsons' battery directed the handling of the guns. Many officers urged him to retire or dismount, but he refused. A grape shot struck his field glass, breaking it in pieces, but without the slightest apparent emotion, he continued giving his orders. After twenty minutes he retired, leaving a lasting impression upon his men, who have ever loved him as their chief, and admired him as their 'beau ideal' of honor and chivalry."[9]

Price's divisions completely encircled the fort—Slack's on the west, Parsons' on the south, Rains's on the east, and McBride's and Harris' on the north by the river. They then began an all-out and incessant attack. The garrison quickly pulled back to the inner works, abandoning the outpost which protected the fort's water supply. The fiercest fighting occurred around the Anderson house, a large brick structure which stood (and still stands) on a hill only 125 yards from the Union ramparts on the west. The Federals were using it as a hospital, and when the Missourians captured it, Mulligan's Irishmen became incensed at what they considered to be a barbaric violation of the laws

city of Lexington, Missouri on September 18th, 19th, 20th, 1861 (Lexington, Mo., 1903), 5–10.

[8] Mulligan, "The Siege of Lexington," 309.

[9] Anderson, *Memoirs: Historical and Personal,* 65.

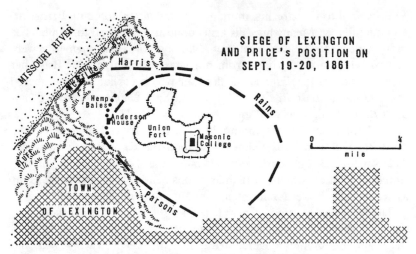

SIEGE OF LEXINGTON
AND PRICE's POSITION ON
SEPT. 19-20, 1861

of warfare. Sallying forth, they retook it, killing without quarter every Confederate they found with arms in hand. But the Missourians quickly drove them out again, then held it for the rest of the siege. Because of its location it had great military value, and so should never have been used as a hospital.[10]

Darkness ended the day's fighting. Late that night Price's provost marshal brought to his headquarters, located on the second floor of a waterfront store, one Francis B. Wilkie, war correspondent of the New York *Times*. Wilkie had gotten drunk, and in that condition he had decided to visit Price's army. Price, whom Wilkie described as a "stout, courtly man," did not know what to make of the rowdy, unkempt-looking Wilkie, or his claim that he was a Northern reporter. Adjusting his spectacles, Price examined papers found on Wilkie—among them a pass signed by Frémont. Then, deciding not to question Wilkie while he was still in a drunken conditon, Price ordered him locked up for the night.

In the morning a sobered Wilkie was brought before Price, who listened thoughtfully as he explained that he had come to do a sympathetic story on the Missouri army. Price remained skeptical, however, until Wilkie mentioned that he had been with Lyon's army at Wilson's Creek and had written an objective account of the battle

[10] *Official Records*, III, 186–87, 190; *Battles and Leaders*, I, 311n; *The Battle of Lexington . . .* , 32–57; McCausland, "The Battle of Lexington," 131.

that appeared in the St. Louis *Republican*. Price obtained a copy of that particular issue of the *Republican* and read the account through slowly. He then took a pen and sheet of paper and wrote:

The bearer, Francis B. Wilkie, newspaper correspondent, is hereby authorized to observe operations of this Army at Lexington, Mo. Treat him courteously, but keep an eye on him. He is a Yankee.

Sterling Price
General Commanding

Wilkie remained with the state guard four days, then escaped and made his way to St. Louis, where he filed the first detailed report on the Lexington battle to appear in the Northern papers.[11]

On the second day of the siege Price's men kept up a steady musket and artillery fire on the fort. This did little damage, but the Federals began to suffer from thirst, their dry, cracked lips bleeding as they bit open their cartridges. Several cannonballs of the "hot shot" variety tore through the walls of the college, but soldiers tossed them out with shovels before they started a fire. In turn, stray projectiles from the fort smashed into buildings in Lexington, including one that buried itself in a corner of the courthouse, where its mark can be seen to this day. But because Price had ordered the town evacuated, there were no civilian casualties. Some of the local inhabitants joined in the fighting, among them a sixty-year-old farmer who appeared every morning with a basket of food in one hand and a trusty flintlock in the other. Taking position behind a large tree, he banged away at the· Yankees all day, then at dusk returned home.[12]

Members of Price's staff urged him to order an assault on Mulligan's works, arguing that, unless the garrison was captured soon, a Federal relief column would rescue it. But Price refused to follow this advice. "It is unnecessary to kill off the boys here," he said. "Patience will give us what we want."[13]

Mulligan and his men were sustained by the hope and expectation of a relief column. In fact, such a column, under General Sturgis, set out for Lexington from Mexico, Missouri. But Price learned of its

[11] Emmett Crozier, *Yankee Reporters, 1861–1865* (New York, 1956), 160–65.

[12] *Official Records*, III, 187; Mulligan, "The Siege of Lexington," 311; McCausland, "The Battle of Lexington," 131.

[13] Bevier, *First and Second Missouri Confederate Brigades*, 617.

approach and sent three thousand men under Parsons across the river to intercept it. A Negro warned Sturgis of Parsons' movement and caused him to turn off in the direction of Kansas City. Thus the garrison was left to its fate.[14]

On the evening of the nineteenth some of Harris' men began using hemp bales, which they found in a warehouse on the riverbank, as mobile breastworks. Others followed their example, and General Harris, liking the idea, requested additional bales from Price and he promptly obtained 132 of them. Several days earlier Captain Thomas Hinkle had suggested this use of hemp bales to Snead, who told Price, who in turn had his chief of artillery, Colonel John Reid, park several wagonloads of them in front of his headquarters.

Harris first had the bales soaked in the river so as to prevent them from catching fire when hit by bullets. However, this so increased their weight that the tired and hungry Missourians were unable to haul them up to the top of the bluff. Harris thereupon instructed his men to wet the bales after putting them in position. By morning a long, snake-like line of bales faced the fort on the north and west, generally about four hundred yards distant, but in places as close as one hundred yards.

Shortly after 8 A.M. Price's soldiers began moving the bales forward. In some cases they propelled them by poles or dragged them by ropes, but usually three unarmed men pushed them along by crawling on their knees and butting them with their heads. Behind the bales advanced Harris', McBride's, and portions of other divisions, firing as they came. The Union troops opened a heavy fire in a frantic attempt to keep the hemp coil from closing, but to no avail. Bullets merely buried themselves harmlessly in the bales, and cannon balls caused them only to "rock a little and then settle back." Heated shot also failed, and fortunately for the success of the stratagem the Federals lacked shells. After several hours the Missourians were nearly close enough to the fort to take it in one quick rush.[15]

By then the garrison's ammunition was practically exhausted and it was without food or water. One of Mulligan's officers, disobeying orders, hoisted a white flag and the Union troops stopped firing. Price ordered his men to do likewise, then sent a note to Mulligan asking why the firing had ceased. The Irish colonel, unaware of his subordi-

[14] Harold F. Smith, "The 1861 Struggle for Lexington, Missouri," *Civil War History*, VII (1961), 162.

[15] This account of the origin and use of the famous hemp bale stratagem

nate's action, returned the note with the gallant but rather absurd reply written on the back, "General, I hardly know, unless you have surrendered."[16] A few minutes later Price's soldiers resumed pushing their hemp bales.

Mulligan knew that he was merely delaying the inevitable—that barring the sudden appearance of a relief column the only choice was surrender or massacre. He put the question to his senior officers; by a large majority they voted in favor of the former. Immediately he sent out a flag of truce, at the same time asking for terms. Snead, speaking for Price, demanded unconditional surrender, to be made within ten minutes, for he suspected that Mulligan might merely be trying to gain time in hopes of help arriving. Mulligan could only comply. A little after 2 P.M. the garrison marched out and laid down its arms—not, however, without much grumbling from the still defiant Irish. Mulligan and his officers came before Price and offered their swords. But Price, in a characteristic action, declined them: "You gentlemen have fought so bravely that it would be wrong to deprive you of your swords. Keep them. Orders to parole you and your men will be issued, Colonel Mulligan, without unnecessary delay."[17]

Price was not simply being gallant. Lacking proper facilities, he could not have kept such a large body of enemy troops prisoner in any case. After being lined up and forced to listen to a speech by Governor Jackson, who had accompanied the state guard to Lexington, all the Federals were released except Mulligan. He refused a parole and remained with Price until October 30 as a privileged captive, being joined by his pretty nineteen-year-old wife who had remained near Lexington during the siege. The couple rode in Price's

is based on an interpretation of the following materials: Price's report, in *Official Records*, III, 187; Harris' report, in *ibid.*, 191–92; John Reid to L. A. Maclean, July 21, 1863, in *ibid.*, XXII, Pt. 2, pp. 1146–47; Isaac Hockaday to His Mother, Lexington, Mo., September 26, 1861, *Missouri Historical Review*, LVI (1961), 56–57; T. A. Fagan, "The Battle of Lexington," St. Louis *Globe-Democrat*, September 19, 1897 (Civil War Clippings, Missouri Historical Society, St. Louis); McCausland, "The Battle of Lexington," 134; Anderson, *Memoirs: Historical and Personal*, 70; Bevier, *First and Second Missouri Confederate Brigades*, 306; Edwards, *Shelby and His Men*, 44. Other interpretations are possible. To collate and evaluate all the conflicting testimony on this affair would require a special monograph. Interestingly, Sepoy mutineers employed mobile barricades of cotton bales in attacking the British at Cawnpore in 1857.
16 Mulligan, "The Siege of Lexington," 312–13.
17 *Ibid.*

carriage and slept in a tent pitched near his.[18] The war was still young in the fall of 1861, and, even on the frontier, chivalry was not yet dead.

At Lexington, Price achieved the outstanding victory of his career. It had been made possible by his own daring and determination, by the courage and inventiveness of his soldiers, and by the ineptitude and confusion of the Federal commanders in Missouri, who were unable to concentrate a sufficient force either to prevent his advance, rescue Mulligan, or sever his communications. Besides nearly 3,500 Union troops, his army captured 7 cannons, over 3,000 desperately needed rifles, 750 horses, and a large quantity of other items, including sabers, saddles, and commissary stores. In so doing it inflicted 159 casualties and suffered less than 100.[19] It was, moreover, the most complete success so far gained by a Confederate army, one made all the more spectacular by the ingenious device of the hemp bales. Coming on the heels of Wilson's Creek, it made Price a popular hero in the South and gave him a lasting hold on the confidence and esteem of pro-Confederate Missourians. But, unfortunately, it also gave him an exaggerated opinion of his own military abilities, and led him to underestimate the hazards involved in assaulting fortified positions.

Price remained at Lexington for over a week following Mulligan's surrender. During that period he distributed the captured equipment among his troops, received large numbers of new recruits, and—in an action that was almost Quixotic in view of the state guard's slender financial resources—restored all but $37,000 of the money taken by Mulligan from the Lexington bank.[20] In addition, Jackson and he sent Snead on a special mission to obtain greater aid and cooperation from the Confederate authorities. For although Jackson had proclaimed on August 5 that Missouri was a "Sovereign, Free and Independent Republic," it had neither formally seceded nor officially joined the Confederacy. En route Snead stopped at Fort Smith, Arkansas, where he tried to persuade McCulloch to reinforce Price or at least supply him with percussion caps for the muskets captured at Lexington. But McCulloch turned down both pleas, repeating his earlier objections to the northern movement and stating that he had no musket caps to spare.

---

[18] *Ibid.*

[19] *Official Records*, III, 188; Snead, "The First Year of the War in Missouri," 273.

[20] *Official Records*, III, 188; Snead, "The First Year of the War in Missouri," 273.

In Richmond, Snead joined with E. C. Cabell in negotiating a "treaty of alliance" between Missouri and the Confederacy. He also denounced McCulloch's failure to support Price and called for the immediate appointment of Price to command of all Southern forces in Missouri and Arkansas.[21]

Frémont finally gathered his forces, 38,000 strong, and on September 26 took the field against Price. A day or two later Price learned that the Union advance had reached Sedalia. At once he began preparations for retreat, for now he was in danger of being cut off from the south. As McCulloch had anticipated, he could not maintain himself on the Missouri without the active support of Confederate forces to the east, and this was not forthcoming. Moreover he lacked the arms and equipment to supply more than a fraction of the recruits that had come flocking to his army. Consequently he had to advise many of them to return home and wait for a more favorable opportunity. Hundreds of others left on their own, declaring that they had to "arrange their business affairs, and set their houses in order." These were men who had joined in a holiday mood and had enjoyed themselves hugely in the balmy September weather peppering the Masonic College with bullets and buckshot. But the prospect of retreat, cold weather, long marches, and short rations was less appealing.

On September 29 the state guard marched southward out of Lexington. By the time it reached the Osage River nine days later it had dwindled through desertions to a mere seven thousand, nearly thirteen thousand fewer than its peak strength immediately after Mulligan's surrender. Instead of a great campaign of liberation, the march to the Missouri had merely been a raid, and the triumph at Lexington, however dramatic, had proved strategically barren. As one of Price's officers later observed, the brutal truth of the matter was that "the sentiment of Missouri was not in harmony with the secession movement," and that even those who sympathized with the Confederate cause "were more interested in the conservation of their property and scalps than in abstract principle." Price, however, refused to admit this fact, even to himself, but remained convinced that if he could only hold on long enough in central Missouri, a popular uprising against Federal rule would take place. In his mind two men were to blame for the failure

[21] *Official Records*, III, 717–18; *ibid.*, LIII, 749–52; *Battles and Leaders*, I, 313n; Reynolds, "Price and the Confederacy," 32–33.

of the campaign—McCulloch, for not supporting it, and Jefferson Davis, for his general policy regarding Missouri.[22]

Among those who left Price's army as it retreated was a tall, slender former Ohio schoolteacher and Kansas jayhawker named William Clarke Quantrill. He made his way to the Kansas City area, where he had friends who believed his story that he was from Maryland and that he had a brother who had been murdered by the jayhawkers. Before long he headed a gang of bushwhackers—one of dozens that were springing up in west Missouri as a result of jayhawker raids and Unionist persecutions of Confederate sympathizers. At first he took prisoners, at least most of the time. But when the Federal authorities outlawed his men and ordered them killed without quarter, he retaliated in kind. He also began raiding into Kansas, giving the people there, he vowed, a taste of their own medicine. By the spring of 1862 his was the most powerful and active partisan band in the region, and the name Quantrill had become synonomous with death.[23]

Frémont's pursuit was characterized by every quality except rapidity. Consequently, Price conducted his retreat at a leisurely pace, taking three days to cross the Osage. Pro-Southern farmers along the way provided his men with hot food and pitchers of cold buttermilk, and their daughters invited them to dances when they camped for the night. During the day there was more music, as the Lexington brass band, which had left with the army, played such pieces as "Dixie" and "O Listen to the Mockingbird."[24]

On October 20 the retreat ended at Neosho in the southwest corner of the state. Here, in a two-week "rump session," that portion of the legislature which still adhered to Jackson passed an ordinance of secession and elected senators and representatives to the Confederate Congress. These actions were taken in defiance of the Missouri Convention, which had recently deposed Jackson and established a provisional gov-

[22] *Official Records*, III, 720; Snead, "The First Year of the War in Missouri," 273–74; John F. Snyder, "The Capture of Lexington," *Missouri Historical Review*, VII (1912), 8–9.

[23] Albert Castel, *William Clarke Quantrill: His Life and Times* (New York, 1962), 61–63, 65–70.

[24] *Official Records*, III, 547; Snyder, "The Capture of Lexington," 7; Bevier, *First and Second Missouri Confederate Brigades*, 308–10; Edwards, *Shelby and His Men*, 51; Milo M. Quaife (ed.), *Absalom Grimes: Confederate Mail Runner* (New Haven, 1926), 25.

ernment under Hamilton R. Gamble. Legally they were invalid, for a quorum of the legislature was not present and only the convention was empowered to carry out secession. Practically, however, they had the advantage of ending the Jackson administration's anomalous position in respect to the Confederacy and the war. On November 28 the Confederate Congress declared Missouri the twelfth member of the Confederate States of America, and measures were initiated to transfer the state guard into Confederate service.[25]

Early in November, Price retreated to Pineville near the Arkansas border. Frémont, who had occupied Springfield on October 27, planned to pursue him. However, before he could do so Lincoln, on November 2, removed him from command—an act prompted by the "Pathfinder's" alleged military and administrative ineptitude. His successor was Major General David Hunter, who promptly rescinded an agreement recently made by Frémont and Price for the exchange of prisoners, the outlawing of guerrilla warfare, and the cessation of political arrests.[26]

Price's plan in retreating to Pineville was to make a stand there in conjunction with McCulloch. The extremely rugged terrain of this region, Price believed, would compensate for the Southern inferiority in numbers. Once the Union army was defeated, then the Confederate forces would sweep through Missouri again. In fact, he even wrote General Albert Sidney Johnston, new commander of all Confederate armies in the West, outlining grand strategy for capturing St. Louis![27]

But McCulloch, as usual, was not nearly so optimistic. While Price dreamed of marching into St. Louis, he was writing the War Department that he hoped "by resorting to the partisan mode of war" to make the Union forces withdraw "ere they reach Fort Smith." At the same time he advised Price to retire into the refuge of the Boston Mountains of northwestern Arkansas. However Price replied that he was confident their combined armies could meet and defeat the Federals in Missouri, and that in any case his men would refuse to leave

[25] *Official Records*, LIII, 754–55, 757–58; Kirkpatrick, "The Admission of Missouri," 379–81, 383–85.

[26] *Official Records*, III, 540–54, 559, 561–65, 722, 727–28, 731–33; John C. Frémont, "In Command in Missouri," in *Battles and Leaders*, I, 287.

[27] Sterling Price to Albert Sidney Johnston, November 7, 1861, in *Official Records*, III, 731–32.

the state without a battle. So once again McCulloch, contrary to his better judgment, agreed to join Price.[28]

But even as the Southern generals debated, the Union army, instead of advancing, began retreating. On instructions from Lincoln, Hunter on November 8 evacuated Springfield and fell back to the Sedalia–Rolla region. McCulloch and Price did not learn of the retreat until a week later—a significant commentary on their scouting and intelligence arrangements. Price at once ordered his army to Newtonia, and McCulloch made a forced cavalry march to Springfield in hopes of overtaking Hunter's rear guard. But when he arrived, the Union army was at least a hundred miles away. Considering it useless to pursue farther, he remained. As for Price, he retraced his September route northward, finally encamping on the Sac River near Osceola.[29]

This town, the seat of St. Clair County, had been destroyed during the Lexington campaign by Jim Lane's Kansans. Following the skirmish at Drywood Creek, and after Price had gone to Lexington, Lane had re-entered Missouri and proceeded to plunder, burn, and kill indiscriminately. In subsequent weeks other jayhawkers led by Charles Jennison, Dan Anthony, and Marshall Cleveland did the same—proclaiming all the while that they were avenging the Missouri Border Ruffian invasions of the 1850's, destroying slavery, and stamping out rebellion. However, far from achieving the latter, these raids merely intensified pro-Southern feeling in western Missouri. Indeed, Major General Henry W. Halleck, who replaced Hunter as overall Union commander in the West, declared: "A few more such raids will make Missouri as Confederate as Eastern Virginia."[30]

Shortly after Price reached the Sac River the terms of service of three-fourths of his men expired. Most of them were willing to re-enlist, but large numbers wanted first to return to their homes. Winter was nigh, and they were poorly clad and had received no pay since taking up arms in the summer. They insisted that they be furloughed for a few weeks in order to procure warm clothing for themselves and make some provision for their families. Price had no choice except

[28] *Official Records*, III, 733, 736, 748.
[29] *Ibid.*, 553–54, 740, 742–43, 748–49; Snead, "The First Year of the War in Missouri," 274.
[30] Castel, *A Frontier State*, 54–64.

to give them leaves of absence, and his army became so small that for the time being it was incapable of offering battle.[31]

Price tried to make up for the loss, either temporary or permanent, of many of his veterans by obtaining new recruits. On November 26 he issued a "Proclamation to the People of Central and North Missouri." Although, it declared, he had called for fifty thousand volunteers in June, less than five thousand had responded, and most of them had been "boys and small-property holders." It continued, "Are we a generation of driveling, sniveling, degraded slaves? Or are we men who dare assert and maintain the rights which cannot be surrendered . . . ? [Let us] drive the hireling bands of thieves and marauders from the State . . . . Do I hear your shouts? Is that your war-cry which echoes through the land? Are you coming? Fifty-thousand men! Missouri shall move to victory with the tread of a giant!" Monetary losses, Price added on a more mundane note, incurred from enlisting would be made good after the war by confiscated Union property.[32]

Price followed up the proclamation by sending a detachment of 1,100 men to Lexington, where in a few days it collected 2,500 recruits. North of the Missouri many more were eager to join also but could not penetrate the Federal cordons along the river.[33] However, not all pro-Southern Missourians desired to serve in Price's or any other army. Hundreds of them much preferred to fight the Yankees "on their own hook" as guerrillas under the leadership of such men as Quantrill, "Bloody Bill" Anderson, George Todd, John Thrailkill, Clif Holtzclaw, "Coon" Thornton, and Dick Yaeger. These hard-riding freebooters ravaged the Kansas-Missouri border region throughout the war and spawned such postbellum outlaws as Frank and Jesse James and Cole Younger. Occasionally they cooperated with regular Confederate forces, as when Quantrill assisted in the capture of Independence in the summer of 1862. But most of the time they operated without orders or control from the Confederate military authorities, ambushing Union patrols, attacking Federal posts, raiding Kansas border settlements, and terrorizing Missouri Unionists. The latter, who were armed and organized into militia regiments by the Federal army, retaliated by

[31] *Official Records*, VIII, 730.
[32] *Ibid.*, 695–97.
[33] *Ibid.*, 730.

persecuting all those suspected of secessionist proclivities or of aiding the guerrillas. Thus a civil war within a civil war raged in Missouri, especially in the country between Kansas City and Jefferson City.

Price believed that if he could establish himself in strength on the Missouri during the winter his "numbers would be indefinitely increased." Hence on December 6 he wrote McCulloch, who had retreated again to Arkansas, asking him to cooperate in such a movement.[34] McCulloch, however, did not receive Price's letter: he had just left for Richmond to defend his conduct of operations in the West from the criticisms of Price's friends in the capital. The answer came instead from McIntosh, now a colonel and commanding in McCulloch's absence. McIntosh declared that his troops were needed in Arkansas, and that in any case they were not adequately equipped or clothed to march "in the depth of winter over the bleak prairies of Missouri." And for good measure he added: "The facility with which the enemy could concentrate a force on the Missouri River renders such a project at this season of the year almost madness."[35]

It is easy to see why Price inspired contempt in professionals such as McIntosh. Too often his military proposals, as in this instance, were utterly impractical. However, in his defense it can be said that at least he wanted to do something, instead of constantly finding reasons for doing nothing, as did McCulloch and McIntosh. Also he realized, as these officers apparently did not, that the war in Missouri was as much political and psychological in character as it was military, and that consequently it might sometimes be necessary to take great military risks in order to arouse or at least keep alive the spirit of opposition to Union domination.

Finally, it should be kept in mind that he had not favored secession originally and had drawn the sword solely to defend his own state against what he deemed Northern invasion. And although he now supported the Confederacy, his primary interest was, and ever remained, most passionately Missouri.

[34] *Ibid.*, 702.
[35] James McIntosh to Sterling Price, December 14, 1861, *ibid.*, 712–13. It is worth noting that the Federals agreed with McIntosh's analysis. Wrote Lincoln to General David Hunter, October 24, 1861: ". . . it would be so easy to concentrate and repel any army the enemy returning on Missouri from the southwest, that it is not probable any such attempt to return will be made before or during the approaching cold weather." *Ibid.*, III, 554.

On December 23 Price wrote General Leonidas Polk expressing bitter resentment against what he considered to be the inexcusable lack of Confederate assistance. By failing to reinforce him, McIntosh had deprived him of a golden opportunity to recruit his army "to any desirable extent," destroy the Missouri railroads, and force the Union armies into the confines of St. Louis. His troops and the people of Missouri were becoming disillusioned with the Confederacy and distrustful of its competency and intentions. The two main obstacles to the successful prosecution of the war in Missouri were that the great majority of those desiring to take up arms on the part of the South were prevented from doing so by the Federal occupation of the state, and "the dissatisfaction which General McCulloch's constant refusal to cooperate with us has engendered in the minds of the people of Missouri, and which leads them to doubt whether the Confederate Government really sympathizes with them and desires to aid them."[36]

At about the same time that Price penned this letter, J. W. "Deacon" Tucker, editor of the *Missouri Army Argus*, camp newspaper of the state guard and Price's personal organ, published a long address to the people of the Confederate States, also denouncing the Richmond government and especially McCulloch for not helping Missouri. "With the exception of the battle of Springfield," he asserted, "not a sword has been drawn for the release of Missouri, save by her own sons."[37] While in Richmond, McCulloch read Tucker's diatribe, which was widely reprinted in Southern journals. Immediately and angrily he responded with a long letter to the Secretary of War[38] and a shorter one to the Richmond *Whig*.[39] In both he described his efforts to assist Price, explained why he was unable to do more, condemned the inefficiency of the Missouri forces, and derided Price's generalship. In addition, John Henry Brown, a member of McCulloch's staff, published a reply to Tucker in the Fayetteville *Arkansasian*, likewise widely copied by the Confederate press, upholding his chief and castigating Price and the Missourians.[40]

Needless to say these newspaper exchanges merely intensified the

---

[36] *Official Records*, III, 729–30.
[37] Quoted in Washington (Ark.) *Telegraph*, January 15, 1862.
[38] *Official Records*, III, 743–49.
[39] Quoted in Rose, *Life of McCulloch*, 184–86.
[40] Quoted in *ibid.*, 186–91.

ill feeling between Price and the Missourians on the one hand, and McCulloch and his troops on the other. Furthermore, Price's and Tucker's denunciations of Confederate policy, combined with Mc-Culloch's and Brown's charges, did nothing to improve the Missouri general's standing with the President, who was already prejudiced against him because of his original Unionism and his mysterious deal-ings with Harney.[41] Price and Tucker would have done much better to have remained silent, or at least been more moderate and concilia-tory in their utterances. A penchant for becoming involved in vitupera-tive personal controversy with others would again and again injure Price, and through him the cause he represented, as the war progressed.

Late in December, Price left his camp on the Sac River and fell back to Springfield in order to shorten his supply line and better pro-tect the southwestern part of the state. He did not plan, and indeed was incapable of, active operations in the field. Instead, his men erected log huts and went into winter quarters. During the weeks that followed they began to transfer into the regular Confederate service. They did so, however, reluctantly and only at the personal urging of Price, who told them that this was the best, indeed only, way to achieve the libera-tion of their state. By February, a two thousand-man infantry brigade under Henry Little (who had returned from Richmond with a brigadier general's commission) had been formed, and a second one commanded by Slack was in process of being established.[42]

In spite of this reorganization, the Missouri forces, or at least most of them, remained much as they had been at Cowskin Prairie, if a Union report is to be credited. Wrote Colonel Frederick W. Steele to Halleck on January 2, 1862: "Two of my spies just in from Springfield humbugged Price completely; went through all his camps safely; saw everything. . . . At present he has no discipline, no roll-calls, no sen-tinels, nor picket to prevent passing in and out of Springfield. Rains drunk all the time. Price also drinking too much."[43]

Although the disparaging reference to Price's personal habits can be discounted, for spies always tend to pass on the sort of gossip which they think their superiors will like to hear, there can be little doubt

[41] Reynolds, "Price and the Confederacy," 32–33.
[42] *Official Records*, VIII, 756; *ibid.*, LIII, 759–60; Anderson, *Memoirs: His-torical and Personal*, 110–12, 163.
[43] *Official Records*, VIII, 478–79.

that he was fond of the bottle. However, to his followers this was an amiable weakness which in no way lessened their affection and respect for "Old Pap." "It has been said that a genuine Missourian can smell whisky a mile and a half," wrote one of Price's officers, who added that during the fall and winter of 1861 the state guard was "besieged by retail dealers in rotgut" wherever it marched.[44]

Towards the end of January, Price's scouts reported that a well-equipped Federal army of over twelve thousand under Major General Samuel Ryan Curtis had assembled at Rolla with the obvious intent of moving on Springfield. By the second week of February this force, to which Halleck had assigned the mission of driving Price permanently from Missouri, was only a few dozen miles away. Price knew that it would be suicidal for him to make a stand with his army, which numbered barely seven thousand effectives, but nevertheless he held on until the very last moment in the vain hope that McCulloch would reinforce him. Then, on February 12, he hastily evacuated, leaving behind sizable quantities of stores and equipment for lack of transportation. Skirmishing constantly with Curtis' advance guard, he retreated into Arkansas, marching literally day and night.[45] It was necessary, recalled one of his veterans after the war, "to post guards to prevent men from dropping out of the column and falling asleep in the bushes. . . ."[46] In addition, the weather was so cold that the water in the canteens froze and beards turned white with frost. Not until the army reached Cross Hollows on February 17 did it halt its flight.

Price had been driven from Missouri, but the struggle for the state would continue in Arkansas.

[44] Bevier, *First and Second Missouri Confederate Brigades*, 312.

[45] *Ibid.*, 313–14; *Official Records*, VIII, 58–59, 554, 756–57; Franz Sigel, "The Pea Ridge Campaign," in *Battles and Leaders*, I, 316–17; Edwin C. Bearss, "From Rolla to Fayetteville with General Curtis," *Arkansas Historical Quarterly*, XIX (1960), 225–59.

[46] "John Wilson Reminiscences" (MS in Wilson Family Papers, Western Historical Collection, University of Missouri, Columbia, Missouri).

4

ELKHORN TAVERN

Contrary to the allegations of Price, Tucker, and other disappointed Missourians, the Confederate government was not blind to the importance—"the supreme importance," as Secretary of War Judah P. Benjamin put it—of Missouri.[1] If Southern armies could gain control of the state, and in particular St. Louis, they would outflank the whole Federal position in the West and could threaten the heartland of the North itself. Moreover, they would obtain access to the state's great wealth, natural resources, and manpower, at the same time denying them to the Union. In brief, Missouri might prove the difference between victory or defeat in the war as a whole. Certainly the side which held it would materially improve its chances of winning, while the side which lost it would probably find it hard to keep from losing.

Nor was it lack of desire that had prevented effective Confederate aid to Price's army during the summer and fall of 1861. Instead, it was simply that the Confederacy had practically no trained and equipped troops to spare for Missouri. All that were available, and even more, were urgently needed to guard the long, ragged front which extended from the Potomac through Virginia, Kentucky, and Tennessee to the Mississippi. But if Richmond could not send men, it could send a man —a general to take overall command of the various independent forces operating in Missouri and Arkansas and transform them into an army capable of achieving victory in the West. In December, President Davis began searching for a general to perform this task.

Governor Jackson, who likewise saw the pressing need for unified command, proposed Price. Snead, Cabell, and even Reynolds seconded him.[2] But Davis was aware of the ill feeling between Price and Mc-Culloch and knew that to place the former over the latter would merely exacerbate matters. Furthermore, despite Wilson's Creek and Lexing-

[1] Judah P. Benjamin to Braxton Bragg, December 17, 1861, in *Official Records*, VI, 788.
[2] *Ibid.*, III, 718; *ibid.*, VIII, 724–25; Reynolds, "Price and the Confederacy," 32–34.

ton, he had strong reservations about Price's military competency, reservations that stemmed not only from McCulloch's trenchant observations but from the adverse reports of others as well. And finally, it is more than likely that he was unwilling to entrust a top command to a man who had so long opposed secession, who only a few months before had at least pretended to be ready to fight Confederate forces, and whose friends were so rancorous in their criticism of his, Davis', policies.[3]

In any case, when the Missouri delegation to the Confederate Congress went to Davis and urged him to name Price commander of the Western armies, the President was "firm and even impatient in his opposition" and he declared that he was not going to appoint anyone who was a native of Missouri, Arkansas, or Texas. He added, too, that in the future the Federals could be expected to employ real generals, not "pathfinders."[4]

Davis' first choice for the Trans-Mississippi command was Colonel Henry Heth, a West Pointer and Virginian. But the Missouri delegates threatened to block his promotion to major general and Heth thereupon announced that he had no desire for the post.[5] Davis then adopted a suggestion from McCulloch (who had ruled himself out of consideration because of his poor relations with the Missourians) and appointed Braxton Bragg, but that general too declined the command.[6] Finally Davis selected Major General Earl Van Dorn, a Mississippi-born West Pointer who, in addition to being a personal friend of the Confederate President, had a high military reputation, considerable experience in the West, and a desire for an independent command.

Van Dorn proved a popular choice, even with the Missourians, now that Price obviously had no chance.[7] Forty-one, short, slim, and dapper, he was the very incarnation of the Southern Cavalier and was dedicated to the achievement of military glory. Unfortunately, however, he suffered from an excess of his virtues. He was bold to the point of

[3] *Official Records*, III, 601, 733–34; Reynolds, "Price and the Confederacy," 33–34.

[4] Reynolds, "Price and the Confederacy," 34; *Official Records*, LIII, 761–63.

[5] *Official Records*, LIII, 762; Jefferson Davis to W. P. Harris, December 13, 1861, in Rowland, *Jefferson Davis, Constitutionalist*, V, 179.

[6] *Official Records*, III, 734; *ibid.*, VI, 788–89, 797.

[7] *Official Records*, VIII, 734; Snead, "The First Year of the War in Missouri," 275; Reynolds, "Price and the Confederacy," 35–36.

rashness, liked fighting for its own sake, and had a disdain for death that was matched only by his lack of regard for the lives of others.[8] And even worse for a general, he was unlucky.

The day Van Dorn received his new assignment he wrote his wife gleefully, "I must have St. Louis—then huzza!"[9] En route west he visited Albert Sidney Johnston's headquarters at Bowling Green, Kentucky, and with him drew up plans for a flanking movement against the Missouri metropolis, to be carried out by McCulloch's and Price's armies, for the purpose of disrupting Grant's offensive in Tennessee and so relieving the pressure on Confederate forces in that area.[10] He then went on to Little Rock, where on January 29 he formally assumed command of "The Military District of the Trans-Mississippi."[11]

At once he began preparing for the campaign against St. Louis. Besides Price's army, which then was still at Springfield, and McCulloch's at Fort Smith, he had available the Confederate Indian Brigade under Brigadier General Albert S. Pike in the Indian Territory. On February 7 he wrote Price, announcing that he proposed to combine all these forces (plus additional levies to be raised by the governors of Arkansas, Louisiana, and Texas) into one army, which he optimistically estimated would be 45,000 strong, and move northward late in March. "With these," he asked rhetorically, "can we not hope to take St. Louis by rapid marches and assault?"[12] A week later, in another letter to Price, he provided further details of his plans and even spoke of invading Illinois![13] Here, most definitely, was a commander after the Missourians' own hearts—no cautious, critical, and contemptuous McCulloch, but one who thought only of attacking and conquering!

However, before Van Dorn could proceed much further with his preparations, Curtis advanced, Springfield fell, and Price retreated. News of these alarming developments reached Van Dorn on February 22 at his field headquarters at Pocahontas. Immediately he sent orders

[8] In October, 1858, Van Dorn, while a captain of U.S. cavalry, carried out a deliberate massacre of sixty Comanche Indians, among them women and children. See Anna Heloise Abel, *The Slaveholding Indians* (Cleveland, 1915–19), I, 55.

[9] E. Van Dorn Miller, *A Soldier's Honor: With Reminiscences of Major-General Earl Van Dorn* (New York, 1902), 63.

[10] William Preston Johnston, *The Life of Gen. Albert Sidney Johnston* (New York, 1880), 523.

[11] *Official Records*, VIII, 734, 745–46.

[12] *Ibid.*, 748–49.

[13] *Ibid.*, 750–52.

to McCulloch and Pike to join Price, then set out on horseback across the mountains, accompanied only by two staff officers, to take personal command. His intention, he wrote Albert Johnston before departing, was to give battle to Curtis. "I have no doubt of the result," he declared. "If I succeed I shall push on."[14]

Price continued to fall back before Curtis' army, leaving in his wake much material and many stragglers. From Cross Hollows he retreated to Bentonville and from there through Fayetteville. On February 21 he reached Cove Creek, where he linked up with McCulloch. Curtis, on orders from Halleck, halted his pursuit at Fayetteville.[15]

On the night of March 1 Van Dorn's party rode up to Price's headquarters, a little farmhouse beside a mountain road. As Price came forward to greet them, Major Dabney H. Maury, Van Dorn's chief of staff, was struck by the "grand proportions and stately air" of the "man who up to that time had been the foremost figure of the war beyond the Mississippi." He later described the Missouri general as one of the handsomest men he had ever seen.

He was over six-feet two inches in stature, of massive proportions, but easy and graceful in his carriage and his gestures; his hands and feet were remarkably small and well shaped; his hair and whiskers, which he wore in the old English fashion, were silver white; his face was ruddy and very benignant, yet firm in its expression; his profile was finely chiseled, and bespoke manhood of the highest type; his voice was clear and ringing, and his accentuation singularly distinct.[16]

Maury was equally impressed by Price's numerous staff—"as thoroughly good fellows as I ever met"—and by the "luxurious accomodations" of their camp, which was pitched in a "beautiful little meadow" near the farmhouse. Nor did he ever forget the food that was served, especially a breakfast (and the italics and exclamation mark are his) "*of kidneys stewed in sherry!*" This was, he wrote in after years, "the first and last time I enjoyed that dish."[17]

Following this rare breakfast, Van Dorn, to the martial accompani-

[14] *Ibid.*, 283; Bevier, *First and Second Missouri Confederate Brigades*, 94.

[15] *Official Records*, VIII, 283, 755, 763–64; Bevier, *First and Second Missouri Confederate Brigades*, 92–94.

[16] Dabney H. Maury, "Recollections of the Elkhorn Campaign," *Southern Historical Society Papers*, II (1876), 181–83.

[17] *Ibid.*

ment of Price's headquarter's band and a forty-gun salute, assumed command of "The Army of the West," as he dubbed the combined Missouri-Arkansas forces.[18] He announced his presence in a proclamation to the troops which no doubt was designed to be inspiringly Napoleonic: "Soldiers! Behold your leader! He comes to show you the way to glory and immortal renown. . . . Awake, young men of Arkansas, and arm! Beautiful maidens of Louisiana, smile not on the craven youth who may linger by your hearth when the rude blast of war is sounding in your ears! Texas chivalry, to arms!"[19]

Van Dorn looked upon the Union invasion of Arkansas as more of an opportunity than a danger. Curtis had moved far from his base deep into thinly populated, mountainous country, and in order to obtain food and forage had dispersed his forces widely. If the Confederates could strike him before he regrouped, he would not merely be defeated but destroyed, and the way would be open to St. Louis. And what with the recent fall of Fort Henry and Fort Donelson to Grant, it was more imperative than ever that the pressure on Johnston be relieved. Accordingly, Van Dorn's order to the Army of the West was to prepare three days' rations and make ready to march.[20]

On March 4 the Confederates set out northward on the Telegraph Road, the main highway of the region, connecting Fort Smith, Van Buren, Fayetteville, Bentonville, and Springfield. A cold wind blew wet snow into their faces, but did not dampen their morale, which ran high. On the afternoon of March 5 they reached Elm Springs, where they were joined by Pike's Indian Brigade. This gave Van Dorn approximately sixteen thousand men in all, supported by sixty cannons.[21] But it also added to his army a unit of extremely dubious military value. Most of Pike's force consisted of semicivilized Cherokees, Choctaws, Chickasaws, Seminoles, and Creeks, their faces daubed with war paint. They totally lacked discipline and training, were in large part armed only with tomahawks and warclubs, and had no conception

[18] Bevier, *First and Second Missouri Confederate Brigades*, 316; Edwards, *Shelby and His Men*, 49; Anderson, *Memoirs: Historical and Personal*, 162.

[19] Washington (Ark.) *Telegraph*, April 2, 1862.

[20] *Official Records*, VIII, 283; Wiley Britton, *The Civil War on the Border* (New York, 1899), I, 214–15; Maury, "Elkhorn Campaign," 183–85.

[21] *Official Records*, VIII, 196–97, 209–10, 283; Britton, *War on the Border*, I, 215–18; Snead, "The First Year of the War in Missouri," 276.

whatsoever of regular warfare. Furthermore, they were disgruntled because they received no pay or uniforms from the Confederacy; in fact, one Cherokee regiment was merely waiting for the first good opportunity to desert *en masse* to the Federals! Their commander, long-haired and bewhiskered Pike, looked picturesque in feathers, leather leggings, and beaded moccasins, but although a canny Arkansas politician, a leading Mason, and an accomplished poet, he was by no stretch of the imagination a soldier.[22]

Meanwhile, Curtis had retired first to Bentonville, and then, after learning of Van Dorn's advance, to the north bank of Sugar Creek, an excellent defensive position at the base of Pea Ridge (a mountain so named because of the wild peas growing on its sides), near the now extinct hamlet of Leetown. Here he began concentrating his forces behind a line of log and dirt breastworks running across the Telegraph Road, up which he expected the Confederates to deliver their attack. He chose to stand on the defensive, for his army had been reduced by the attrition of campaigning to less than 10,500 effectives. However, it possessed a powerful, well-served artillery train and the infantry were better drilled and equipped than the majority of the Southern foot soldiers. And while Curtis himself was at best a mediocre commander, deliberate and unimaginative, he had some very able subordinates—among them a stocky, Tartar-visaged, regular army captain named Phil Sheridan, whose superb work as quartermaster had made it possible for the Federals to come as far south as they had.[23]

Two Union divisions under Sigel still lingered at Bentonville when March 6 dawned. Learning of this, Van Dorn promptly pushed forward with the intention of gobbling them up. But his cold and weary soldiers "moved so very slowly" that the attempt failed. As the Confederates entered Bentonville on the south, the Federal rear guard left it on the north. Van Dorn pursued vigorously, but Sigel (who specialized in retreating) experienced little difficulty making good his escape. Dusk found the Army of the West strung out along the Telegraph Road

[22] Wiley Britton, "Union and Confederate Indians in the Civil War," in *Battles and Leaders*, I, 335–36; Fred W. Allsop, *Albert Pike, A Biography* (Little Rock, Ark., 1928), 205–208; Anderson, *Memoirs: Historical and Personal*, 159–60.

[23] *Official Records*, VIII, 196–98; Sigel, "Pea Ridge Campaign," 319.

below Sugar Creek. On the other side of that stream the Union forces waited tensely but confidently for the Confederates to attack on the morrow.[24]

Van Dorn had failed to catch Curtis' army in a dispersed condition. Moreover, his troops were tired, hungry, and cold. And, in addition, he himself was suffering from chills and fever, the consequence of falling into an icy river while on his way to join Price and McCulloch. Nevertheless he remained determined to strike the invaders a decisive blow. Indeed, the only alternative to attack was an ignominious retreat.

Late that afternoon he conferred with Price, McCulloch, and McIntosh. Price favored attacking Curtis from the southwest, driving him from his position, and finishing him off with cavalry as he retreated to Springfield. McCulloch and McIntosh, on the other hand, suggested swinging the army around Curtis' right flank by way of the Bentonville Detour, a rough dirt trail which branched off from the Telegraph Road to the west, then rejoined it northeast of Pea Ridge about two miles above the Elkhorn Tavern—a distance in all of some eight miles. In this fashion the Confederates would not only be able to surprise Curtis and attack him from the rear, but would cut his line of retreat to the north and force him to fight under circumstances in which defeat meant destruction. Van Dorn adopted this plan. It would be a maneuver worthy of Napoleon, and if successful he would have the distinction of staging the first battle of annihilation of the war.[25]

The Confederates masked their flanking march by throwing out pickets, lighting campfires, and pretending to bivouac for the night south of Sugar Creek. Then, as soon as it was dark, they reformed in line of march and moved off on the Bentonville Detour. Price's division, accompanied by Van Dorn, took the lead, followed by McCulloch and Pike in that order. One thousand of McCulloch's troops,

[24] *Official Records*, VIII, 197–99, 283; Sigel, "Pea Ridge Campaign," 319–21. Maury, "Elkhorn Campaign," 189, states that if the Confederates had marched "at the hour appointed" on the morning of March 6, they "would have cut off Sigel at Bentonville." However, Sigel strongly denies that he was ever in any danger of being cut off. The statement that the Confederates marched slowly appears in Van Dorn's report. One of Price's officers later declared, however, that the army did the last ten miles to Bentonville "at double quick." See Bevier, *First and Second Missouri Confederate Brigades*, 317.

[25] *Official Records*, VII, 283; Maury, "Elkhorn Campaign," 182–83; "John Wilson Reminiscences," 4.

plus two thousand state guards under Brigadier General Martin Green, remained behind to protect the wagon train. Consequently Van Dorn took into the forthcoming battle about fourteen thousand men.

Van Dorn calculated that Price's division would reach the Telegraph Road, only eight miles distant, by sunrise. However he had not bothered to have the Bentonville Detour reconnoitered. This proved to be a terrible blunder. Curtis, foreseeing the possibility of an enemy turning movement by this route, had ordered it obstructed with fallen trees, and as a consequence, Price's march was greatly slowed. In addition, Van Dorn had neglected to make any provision for crossing Sugar Creek, with the result that the Confederates had to pass almost single file over a hastily erected bridge of rails and poles, causing further delay. Thus it was that when morning came, Price was still several miles from the Telegraph Road, and McCulloch and Pike had not even gotten all their forces across Sugar Creek.[26]

Curtis, meanwhile, was deceived by the Confederate campfires into believing that Van Dorn would oblige him with a frontal assault. Also, despite his precaution against a flanking movement, he did not station pickets on the Bentonville Detour. As a result, not until about 8 A.M. did he discover that the Confederates had given him the slip and were attempting to turn his right flank. But Price did not reach the Telegraph Road until nearly 10 A.M., thus giving Curtis ample time in which to redeploy his forces. However, the Federals were still in an extremely perilous situation and would have to fight hard to save themselves.[27]

Van Dorn had intended to strike down the Telegraph Road with his entire army. But when McCulloch saw that it would take several more hours to get his division into position, he obtained permission from Van Dorn to attack from the west.[28] As a result the Confederates went into battle in two widely separated wings which, because of the intervening bulk of Pea Ridge, were unable to see each other or to communicate readily. The right wing, commanded by McCulloch and consisting of the Arkansas, Louisiana, and Texas troops under McIntosh and the Indians under Pike, advanced from the Bentonville

[26] *Official Records*, VIII, 198, 283, 287, 305, 316–17; Maury, "Elkhorn Campaign," 187; Anderson, *Memoirs: Historical and Personal*, 163–64.
[27] *Official Records*, VIII, 198–99, 283–84; Maury, "Elkhorn Campaign," 187–88; Bevier, *First and Second Missouri Confederate Brigades*, 98.
[28] *Official Records*, VIII, 305–306, 308; Maury, "Elkhorn Campaign," 187–89.

Detour against what was now Curtis' left. The other wing, headed by Van Dorn and Price, turned directly south on the Telegraph Road and marched two miles through a deep valley until it came in view of the Union right, stationed on a plateau north of the Elkhorn Tavern.

As the Missourians moved into position, Van Dorn told Price that McCulloch would attack on the other side of Pea Ridge. Price, surprised and disturbed, declared that this would enable the enemy to concentrate against each wing separately. Van Dorn replied that Price was right, but that it was then too late to do anything about it.[29]

Price deployed his troops, which totaled about 5,500 with eight batteries of light artillery, into line of battle. Slack's and Little's brigades moved to the right, and the remaining state guard units under Rains and Daniel M. Frost (who had been exchanged following his capture at Camp Jackson) debouched to the left. They all then advanced and occupied heights on either side of the Telegraph Road, gaining thereby commanding positions from which to attack the Union line. Price enjoyed a 2 to 1 superiority in numbers, and his soldiers drove forward courageously, slowly pushing the stubborn Northern infantry back. Little's brigade, which contained the best-trained and best-armed troops, bore the brunt of the engagement. Slack fell mortally wounded while leading his men, and Price suffered painful flesh wounds in the abdomen and right arm. In a final charge just before darkness, Little forced the Federals beyond the Elkhorn Tavern and seized two cannons. Price's men, as they hungrily gulped down captured Yankee commissary stores, were confident that they would complete their victory in the morning.[30]

[29] Account of Colonel R. H. Musser, St. Louis *Missouri Republican*, November 21, 1885 (Newspaper clipping in the Daniel Marsh Frost Papers, Missouri Historical Society, St. Louis).

[30] *Official Records*, VIII, 305–306, 308; Anderson, *Memoirs: Historical and Personal*, 163–73. According to Maury, "Elkhorn Campaign," 187–89, the Confederate left wing was driving the Federals back and seemed to have a decisive victory in their grasp, but then Price "stopped the pursuit and ordered the troops to fall back to take up a position for the night." Although Maury was in a position to know whereof he wrote, there is no confirmation of this assertion in either Confederate or Union accounts. Instead all sources agree that the Federal line, while falling back, was still unbroken and far from routed, and that Price did not suspend the battle until darkness fell. Maury wrote, at least in part, from memory, as is obvious from the many minor factual errors that appear in his account (he has, for instance, the battle taking place on March 5 and 6, and McCulloch attacking Curtis' "front," whereas McCulloch was nearly as much

Unknown to them, however, the right wing had met with disaster. At first McCulloch's attack went well, pressing the Federals back to new positions. Even Pike's Indians, in a wild rush, captured a Union battery. But after accomplishing this feat they stopped fighting and began plundering and—at least in a few instances—scalping the enemy dead. Suddenly they came under heavy artillery fire. Panic-stricken, they scurried into some woods, from which they refused to budge. At the same time the white troops began to waver before murderous Federal volleys. Recklessly exposing himself, McCulloch rallied them for another charge, only to fall dead with a bullet through his heart. McIntosh also was killed, and Colonel Hébert taken prisoner. The loss of these leaders demoralized the Confederates, and a strong Union counterattack routed them. All semblance of discipline and organization gave way as they fled back towards the Bentonville Detour. Pike, on whom the command had devolved, wandered aimlessly over the battlefield in quest of such missing items as his infantry, cavalry, and artillery. No more than two thirds of the right wing managed to reach Van Dorn and Price during the night, and they were "staggering with fatigue and half-dead with cold and hunger." Fortunately for the defeated Confederates, the immediate necessity of reinforcing his hard-pressed right made it impossible for Curtis to follow up this triumph.[31]

That night Van Dorn, who did not learn of McCulloch's defeat and death until 2 A.M., took stock of the situation and found it far from encouraging. His right wing had been routed, the men were famished and bone tired, and the artillery and cavalry horses were "beaten-out." But worst of all, owing to the "strange and criminal mistake" of an unknown ordnance officer the reserve ammunition train had gone back to Bentonville; this meant that it would be impossible to replenish the

in the rear of the original Union line as was Price). Also, while no enemy of Price, he was a close friend of Van Dorn, and in his postwar narratives of Van Dorn's military career tended to seek excuses for the Mississippi general's failures. Of course, it still remains possible that Price withdrew his troops from battle too soon. But even if he did, it probably made little difference in the ultimate outcome of the battle. Heavy reinforcements were coming up to the Union right, and there can be scarcely any doubt that the Confederate drive would have been checked, no matter how persistently pressed.

[31] *Official Records*, VIII, 199–200, 217–18, 287–90; Sigel, "Pea Ridge Campaign," 324; Britton, *War on the Border*, I, 224, 242–59; Washington (Ark.) *Telegraph*, April 2, 1862; Watson, *Life in the Confederate Army*, 304.

army's almost exhausted ammunition supply. Quite understandably, therefore, he viewed the coming day of battle with "no little apprehension." Nonetheless he resolved to "accept the gage" and hope for the best.[32]

The fighting recommenced at dawn. Curtis' entire army now confronted Price's troops and such remnants of McCulloch's division as could be brought into action. The Federals took the offensive, advancing slowly but steadily under the cover of their powerful batteries. As Van Dorn's cannons expended their limited stock of powder and projectiles, their roar died away to a stuttering whisper. The Southern infantry soon came under deadly artillery cross-fire and began losing heavily. Price, his arm in a sling and his silver hair streaming in the wind, rode up and down the battle line, urging his Missourians to stand firm. Then Van Dorn, deciding that his rapidly dwindling ammunition supply would make continuation of the battle suicidal, issued the order to retreat. Weeping, Price passed it on to his men. Most of them, not knowing of McCulloch's debacle nor realizing that they had been defeated, thought that they were merely withdrawing in order to make a flank attack on the enemy. Not until they had marched four or five miles to the east along the Huntsville Road did they discover the truth. Then, wrote a young Missouri cavalryman in his diary, "there seemed to be a gloom spread over the men in an instant." This in turn gave way to anger and to denunciations of Van Dorn that verged on the mutinous.[33]

Van Dorn and Price declared in their reports that the retreat was made voluntarily and conducted in an orderly and deliberate manner.[34] However, some of the Confederate artillery fled in panic across the Missouri line before returning, and Van Dorn himself became so rattled that he sent word to General Green to destroy the wagon train

[32] *Official Records*, VIII, 284, 317–18; Maury, "Elkhorn Campaign," 188; Bevier, *First and Second Missouri Confederate Brigades*, 103.

[33] *Official Records*, VIII, 214, 284, 290; Snead, "The First Year of the War in Missouri," 277; Britton, *War on the Border*, I, 262–72; Homer L. Calkins (ed.), "Elk Horn to Vicksburg: James H. Fauntelroy's Diary of the Year 1862," *Civil War History*, II (1956), 14; Bevier, *First and Second Missouri Confederate Brigades*, 104, 320; Anderson, *Memoirs: Historical and Personal*, 178–181; "John Wilson Reminiscences," 6.

[34] *Official Records*, VIII, 284, 306.

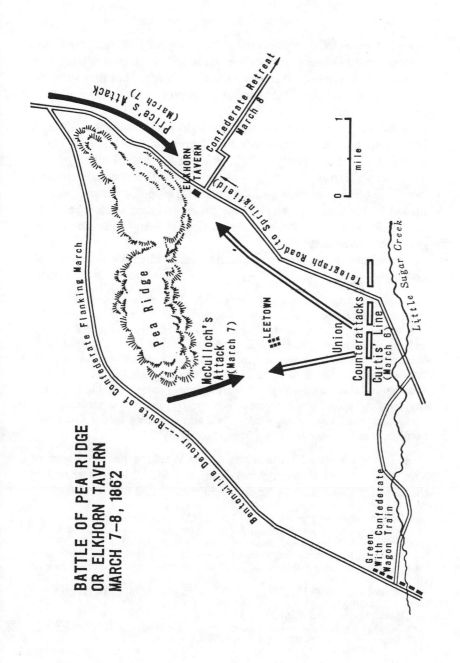

BATTLE OF PEA RIDGE
OR ELKHORN TAVERN
MARCH 7–8, 1862

Price's Attack
(March 7)

Confederate Retreat

March 8

ELKHORN
TAVERN

Telegraph Road (to Springfield)

Pea Ridge

McCulloch's
Attack
(March 7)

LEETOWN

Union
Counterattacks

Curtis' Line
(March 6)

Little Sugar Creek

Route of Confederate Flanking March

Bentonville Detour--

Green
With Confederate
Wagon Train

0   1
mile

—an order which Green disregarded.[35] Even more fortunate, the Union forces were too battered and exhausted to follow up their victory with a vigorous pursuit—or at least so Curtis believed. Had they done so, complete destruction of the Army of the West probably would have resulted.[36]

For a week the Confederates continued to retreat, passing through Huntsville, then turning towards Van Buren on the Arkansas River. Rain fell almost constantly and (later wrote a Missouri officer) "hunger added its terrors to the misery of the march. The mountain streams, swollen by incessant rains and the sudden melting of the snows, were forded by the ragged soldiers in the bitter, freezing weather, and the oozing blood from the still running wounds of many a poor hero congealed in icicles as it fell."[37]

During the retreat Price personally looked after his wounded followers, although suffering severely himself. According to one account:

. . . every few hundred yards he would overtake some wounded soldier. As soon as [the wounded soldier] would see the old general, he would cry out, "General, I am wounded." Instantly some vehicle was ordered to stop, and the poor soldier's wants cared for. Again and again it occurred, until our conveyances were covered with the wounded. Another one cried out, "General, I am wounded!" The general's head dropped upon his breast, and his eyes, bedimmed with tears, were thrown up; he looked in front, but could see no place to put his poor soldier. He discovered something on wheels, however, and commanded: "Halt! and put this wounded soldier up; I will save my wounded, if I lose the whole army!"[38]

At last, on March 16, the Army of the West reached the haven of Van Buren, "weak, broken down, and exhausted." Here it remained the rest of the month, reorganizing, reinforcing, and recuperating.[39] Its

[35] Britton, *War on the Border*, I, 274; Calkins, "Fauntelroy's Diary," 14; Walter L. Brown, "Albert Pike, 1809–1891" (Ph.D. dissertation, University of Texas, 1955), 650–54. Brown states that Van Dorn neglected to inform Pike of the retreat, with the result that Pike and the remaining Indians were left alone on the battlefield. When they discovered this alarming fact, they fled in wild panic.
[36] *Official Records*, VIII, 195, 215, 282, 284, 306; Sigel, "Pea Ridge Campaign," 329–30.
[37] Edwards, *Shelby and His Men*, 51.
[38] Bevier, *First and Second Missouri Confederate Brigades*, 107.
[39] Anderson, *Memoirs: Historical and Personal*, 178.

losses at Pea Ridge, or Elkhorn Tavern as the Southerners named
the battle, were between eight hundred and a thousand dead and
wounded, and included two to three hundred prisoners. In addition,
several regiments of Indian and Arkansas troops disbanded, and there
were uncounted hundreds of stragglers and deserters. On the Union
side, slightly in excess of a tenth of Curtis' army was killed, wounded,
or captured, and some time passed before it was able to resume active
operations.[40]

The Confederate defeat at Pea Ridge was a case of a sound stra-
tegical concept being ruined by poor tactical execution. As noted, Van
Dorn originally proposed to strike the Federal rear at daylight on
March 7. When it became apparent that because of the obstructions
on the Bentonville Detour Price's division could not reach the Telegraph Road by that time, he should have abandoned this portion of
his plan and hurled the bulk of his army on Curtis' west flank, at the
same time sending a smaller force to block the Union escape route to
the north. In this way he would have surprised Curtis and avoided the
wide gap between his two divisions. As it was, Curtis not only had
sufficient time in which to react to the Confederate maneuver, but (as
Price feared) he was able in effect to deal with McCulloch and Price
separately and in sequence.

During the actual battle, Price failed to overpower the smaller force
opposed to him, which compensated for its inferiority in numbers by
superiority in artillery firepower. He did, nevertheless, push the Union
line back and inflict heavy casualties, and the morale of his men remained high and their fighting edge sharp despite hunger and fatigue.
Had McCulloch's division done as well, the battle, even with Van
Dorn's mistakes and misfortunes, might have had a different outcome.
However McCulloch attacked in a piecemeal fashion, led his men
into action as if he were a captain rather than a general, and thus set
the stage for his disastrous death. Furthermore, except for Hébert's
Louisianians and several regiments of Texas cavalry, most of McCulloch's force consisted of raw, poorly equipped Arkansas recruits—or

[40] *Battles and Leaders*, I, 337. Watson, *Life in the Confederate Army*, 315,
317, 344, stated that the Third Louisiana alone suffered 270 casualties at Pea
Ridge, and that the Confederate high command deliberately minimized its
losses in the battle.

else Pike's hapless Indians. Once such troops as these lost their commanders, they were finished.[41]

Van Dorn's official report on the battle praised Price and his men highly: "During the whole of the engagement I was with the Missourians, under Price, and I have never seen better fighters than these Missouri troops, or more gallant leaders than General Price and his officers."[42] Significantly, however, he did not mention the discipline of the Missourians, nor the competence of their officers. On these subjects his opinion was less complimentary, as witness the letter he wrote on March 17 to the Adjutant General in Richmond: "In the recent operations against the enemy on Sugar Creek I found the want of military knowledge and discipline among the higher officers to be so great as to countervail their gallantry and the fine courage of their troops. . . . I cannot convey to you a correct idea of the crudeness of the material with which I have to deal in organizing an army out here. There is an absolute want of any degree of sound military information, and even an ignorance of the value of such information."[43]

In this same letter Van Dorn requested the promotion of a number of West Point-trained staff officers (such as Maury) to higher ranks, stating that if some of these officers had been substituted at Elkhorn for "some of the highest commanders, my orders would have been promptly and intelligently carried out and the enemy's army put to utter rout."

Undoubtedly there was much truth in what Van Dorn said. However, his strictures (which hint strongly towards Price) probably should be discounted to some degree as representing an effort to explain away a failure which in large part was the consequence of his own blunders. On subsequent occasions this Mississippi glory-hunter was to display a pronounced tendency in that direction.

The rank and file of the Army of the West, especially the Missourians, refused to admit that they had been defeated at Elkhorn. In their opinion Van Dorn had retreated from victory. In addition, they blamed him for the hardships they suffered during the campaign, especially on the long march to Van Buren. Consequently, whereas they

[41] Washington (Ark.) *Telegraph*, April 2, 1862; Anderson, *Memoirs: Historical and Personal*, 164, 174.
[42] *Official Records*, VIII, 285.
[43] *Ibid.*, 787.

had cheered him at first, they now stood in sullen silence whenever he rode by.[44] Price, on the other hand, emerged from the battle more popular with the troops than ever. Wrote a Texas soldier to his parents: "Maj. Gen. Sterling Price has immortalized himself at [the] Battle of Elk Horn for his bravery never was a man more beloved by southern soldiers than [by] his."[45]

The strategic significance of the Pea Ridge campaign was as follows. By invading Arkansas when they did the Federals disrupted Van Dorn's plan for taking St. Louis and by throwing back the Confederates at Pea Ridge, they ended any immediate threat to Union control of Missouri. However, contrary to the view of most historians, the battle in itself was not the decisive engagement of the Civil War in the West. Despite his victory Curtis was too battered to advance, and despite their defeat Van Dorn and Price did not consider the situation hopeless. As soon as he reached Van Buren the indomitable Van Dorn sent cavalry to cut Curtis' communications and began preparing for a new offensive, this time into southeastern Missouri.[46] As for Price, nothing short of death could quench his determination to redeem Missouri. Thus there can be little doubt that within a month or two the Army of the West would have marched northward again had not the Confederacy needed its services elsewhere.

Late in March, Johnston, fearful that the loss of Fort Henry and Fort Donelson would lead to the complete collapse of Confederate resistance west of the Appalachians and east of the Mississippi, began concentrating all available units at Corinth, Mississippi, for an attack on Grant at Pittsburg Landing on the Tennessee River. To this end he ordered Van Dorn on March 23 to transfer the Army of the West to the other side of the Mississippi.[47] Van Dorn responded promptly, marching to Des Arc on the White River, from which point his troops were to be ferried to Memphis. It was this movement, not the setback

[44] "John Wilson Reminiscences," 6; Anderson, *Memoirs: Historical and Personal*, 203.

[45] Thomas A. Coleman to parents, April 23, 1862, in Thomas A. Coleman Letters, Missouri State Historical Society, Columbia.

[46] *Official Records*, VIII, 282, 813–14; Maury, "Elkhorn Campaign," 190; Calkins, "Fauntelroy Diary," 14. The orthodox view concerning the importance of Pea Ridge is presented in Walter L. Brown, "Pea Ridge: Gettysburg of the West," *Arkansas Historical Quarterly*, XV (1956), 15–16.

[47] *Official Records*, X, Pt. 2, p. 354.

at Elkhorn, that brought an end for the time being to any major Confederate effort in the Trans-Mississippi and rendered Missouri completely secure from invasion. Or in other words, Grant's victories at
Henry and Donelson had as much effect on the war in the West as
Curtis' success at Pea Ridge.

Price's soldiers objected strongly to leaving Arkansas—they had
enlisted, they declared, to fight for Missouri. For awhile it even seemed
as if they might mutiny. But Van Dorn assured them that they would
be brought back as soon as the impending battle against Grant had
been fought and won; and Price, although opposed to the transfer,
used his great influence to reconcile his followers, telling them that
the road back to Missouri lay through Tennessee.[48]

By now five thousand of Price's men had been mustered into the
Confederate service, leaving only a few thousand in the old state
guard. Consequently, on April 8 Price resigned as commander of the
guard and became formally as well as actually a major general of the
C.S.A. That same day he embarked for Memphis with Little's brigade; the remainder of the Missouri troops, including most of those
still in the state guard, were to follow later. Before departing Price
vowed that soon he would return and reconquer Missouri.[49]

But the fates of war were to decree otherwise. Few of the approximately eight thousand soldiers who followed Price across the Mississippi ever saw their Missouri homes again. Instead they died fighting
on the battlefields of Tennessee, Mississippi, Alabama, Georgia, and
the Carolinas. Moreover, they did not arrive in Tennessee in time to
participate in the Battle of Shiloh, which as a matter of fact ended
the day before they boarded the boats at Des Arc! Thus the redeploy-
ment of the Army of the West did not achieve its original purpose,
although it did help the Confederate forces east of the Mississippi
make good their heavy losses at Shiloh. By the same token, however,
the removal of Van Dorn's army from Arkansas released several times
its number of Union troops in Missouri for service in the east also.[50]

As Governor Jackson and Governor Rector of Arkansas were
quick to point out in protest, the transfer of the Army of the West

[48] Snead, "The First Year of the War in Missouri," 277; Thomas L. Snead,
"The Conquest of Arkansas," in *Battles and Leaders*, III, 441–43.
[49] *Official Records*, VIII, 813–14.
[50] Snead, "The Conquest of Arkansas," 443.

to the other side of the Mississippi was tantamount to abandoning Missouri all together and leaving Arkansas practically defenseless. Furthermore, the transfer meant that the Confederacy had decided to treat the Trans-Mississippi as strictly a secondary theater to be subordinated and even sacrificed to the requirements of Virginia and Tennessee. Such a policy, given the military situation that existed in the spring of 1862, was probably the only practical one open to the Confederate high command. And since this situation never materially improved but steadily worsened, the policy remained in effect to the end.

5

IUKA

A large crowd cheered lustily and a band played "Dixie" as the Missourians disembarked at the Memphis levee on April 15. Resplendent in a new grey Confederate general's uniform, "his fine face in full view, and his white locks fluttering in the breeze," Price stood on the hurricane deck of his steamer and acknowledged the shouts of welcome. That night the town officials held a ball at the main hotel in honor of Price and his officers. When Price appeared, a fanfare of music sounded, the ladies waved their handkerchiefs, and the men hurrahed for "Ol' Pap." To the insistent demands for a speech, Price replied: "The time for speech-making has passed, and the time for action has arrived. However, I expect soon to be heard from in the thundering tones of the cannon, the roar of musketry, and the clashing of bayonets." Renewed cheering greeted this short flight of hackneyed eloquence, then the dancing began.[1]

From Memphis the Missourians traveled by train to Corinth, Mississippi, arriving on the night of April 24. Following Shiloh, Johnston's army, now commanded by Beauregard, had retreated to this strategic railroad center. Every available Confederate unit was being rushed there in a desperate effort to hold it against the huge Union army under Halleck which was ponderously advancing towards it. Should it fall, not only would the Federals clinch their control of western and central Tennessee, but also Beauregard would be forced to retreat deep into Mississippi, thus exposing the vital river city of Vicksburg to overland attack.

Confederate nurse Kate Cumming, serving in the military hospital at Corinth, noted in her diary the arrival of Price's soldiers, "as brave and daring a set of men as the world has ever seen." A few days later she met Price, who entered the hospital to receive treatment for his wounded arm. "I told him I felt we were safe in Corinth now, since

[1] Anderson, *Memoirs: Historical and Personal*, 191–92; William P. Snow, *Southern Generals, Who They Are, and What They Have Done* (New York, 1865), 453.

he and his brave followers had arrived. He gave me a very dignified bow, and, I thought, looked at me as if he *thought* that I was talking a great deal of nonsense. He was not behind his sex in complimenting the ladies for the sacrifices they are making. . . . I felt quite proud of the honor I enjoyed in shaking hands with him whose name has become a household word with all admirers of true patriotism, and whose deeds of heroism in the West have endeared him to his followers, so that they look on him more as a father than any thing else."[2]

After having his wound tended, Price visited the other patients, many of whom had fought under him, and all of whom were delighted to see him. The next day he rode back to camp, impressing Mrs. Cumming with his handsome appearance. "I think he is," she confided to her diary that night, "one of the finest looking men on horseback that I have ever seen. I have a picture of Lord Raglan in the same position, and I think that he and General Price are the image of each other." Then, on a more sober note, she added: "General Price is in bad health, but could not be induced to stay longer with us, as his abode is with his soldiers in the camp, where he shares their sorrows and joys. It is this that has so endeared him to them. Missouri may well be proud of her gallant son."[3]

Soon after arriving at Corinth, Price toured the town's elaborate system of earthworks with Beauregard. His only comment was, "Well, these things may be very fine; I never saw anything of the kind but once, and then I took them." This remark received wide circulation in the press and helped bolster Price's reputation as a rough and ready general who scorned "pick and shovel warfare."[4] Rather ironically, however, before the year was over he would be leading his men against these very same fortifications.

On April 30 Van Dorn with the Arkansas, Louisiana, and Texas troops reached Corinth. Six days later the Army of the West, reinforced to about twenty thousand, went into the front lines. During the next three weeks it engaged in almost constant skirmishing and marching as the Federal forces slowly but relentlessly pressed closer to the town.

[2] Richard B. Harwell (ed.), *Kate: The Journal of a Confederate Nurse* (Baton Rouge, 1959), 27.
[3] *Ibid.*, 28.
[4] Columbia (Mo.) *Statesman*, June 27, 1863; Reynolds, "Price and the Confederacy," 40–41.

Only one action, fought at Farmington on May 8, deserved to be called a battle. Here Price's division helped drive back with heavy losses a Union probing operation. However, despite the lack of major fighting, the men suffered severely. The countryside was low and swampy, the heat and humidity were intense, and the water, unhealthy. These conditions, added to fatigue and poor rations, resulted in a great amount of sickness, even among the Missourians who, as one of them observed, "had better constitutions than most of the Southern troops."[5]

In spite of all efforts, the Confederate high command was unable to increase Beauregard's strength to much more than fifty thousand troops, two-fifths of whom belonged to the Army of the West. Halleck, on the other hand, had over twice that number, and his super-cautious tactics afforded no opening for an effective counterthrust. Hence Beauregard decided to evacuate Corinth before being encircled and crushed. During the night of May 29 to 30 his forces carried out this extremely dangerous operation with complete success. First they sent out by railroad the surplus supplies and all the sick and wounded who could be moved safely. Then, as the empty cars returned, they cheered lustily, creating the impression that they were receiving reinforcements and concealing the fact that they were leaving. The trick worked as desired —some of the Union troops even stayed awake all night anticipating attack! By daybreak all the Confederates, except a rear guard of cavalry, had pulled out and were well to the south.[6]

Beauregard halted his retreat at Tupelo, Mississippi. Halleck, instead of pursuing, dispersed his mighty host into a number of separate armies—and thereby lost a golden opportunity to smash Confederate power in the West and end the war in 1862. By the same token the Southern army gained a desperately needed chance to recuperate and rebuild. Braxton Bragg took over the command from the ailing Beauregard and thousands of fresh troops arrived to make good the losses at Shiloh. As soon as possible Bragg planned to launch a counteroffensive into Tennessee and Kentucky.[7]

[5] Bevier, *First and Second Missouri Confederate Brigades*, 117–20; Anderson, *Memoirs: Historical and Personal*, 194–97.

[6] Thomas L. Snead, "With Price East of the Mississippi," in *Battles and Leaders*, II, 717–22; Bevier, *First and Second Missouri Confederate Brigades*, 121.

[7] John C. Ropes, *The Story of the Civil War* (New York, 1898), 95, 218, 384.

Early in June, Price secured leave of absence and, accompanied by Snead, journeyed to Richmond. His purpose was to obtain the Trans-Mississippi command, which Van Dorn now only nominally exercised. In addition, he wished to have the Missouri brigades ordered back to Arkansas. He could see no need for their continued presence in Mississippi, whereas he believed that the time was ripe for a new campaign into Missouri. Not only had the Federal forces there been greatly reduced to bolster Halleck, but large-scale uprisings were taking place in the northern part of the state because of a law requiring all able-bodied men to enroll in the Union militia. Moreover, a thrust into Missouri, even if it were not fully successful, would relieve the pressure on Mississippi by drawing off troops from Halleck's army.

Van Dorn, who had no desire to return to Arkansas, was quite willing to relinquish the Trans-Mississippi command to Price. In fact, he wrote Davis that "the love of the people of Missouri is so strong for General Price, and his prestige as a commander so great, that wisdom would seem to dictate that he be put at the head of affairs in the West." Also, Bragg recommended that Price be allowed to recross the river—but alone. The Missouri troops, he advised Davis, were needed in the forthcoming campaign.[8]

Price's trip to Richmond was a triumphal progress. All along the way crowds turned out to cheer him, and in Richmond the state legislature honored him with a formal reception followed by a public banquet. His spectacular victory at Lexington, coupled with stories of his courage in battle and his impressive appearance, had made him perhaps the most popular man in the South. Vice-President Alexander Stephens proposed making him commander of all Confederate armies, and there was even talk of his becoming the next President.[9]

On June 16 he visited the President. Davis (who at this time was ill and preoccupied with McClellan's advance on Richmond) listened in noncommittal silence while he expressed his wishes, then asked him to submit in writing his plans and proposals for the Trans-Mississippi. On June 19 he delivered a memorandum to Secretary of War George W. Randolph. In it he recommended that "the Trans-Mississippi District should be constituted into a separate department, under the

[8] *Official Records*, XIII, 831–32.
[9] Snead, "Price East of the Mississippi," 717–22; Reynolds, "Price and the Confederacy," 40.

command of an officer enjoying enough of the confidence of the Government to be left untrammeled by specific instructions to the guidance of his own judgment and the ever shifting circumstances of an active and aggressive campaign." Following this, a "movement should be made immediately in the direction of Missouri" which would compel the "withdrawal of General Halleck's army from the extreme south."[10] Price asked the President to place him in command of the proposed Trans-Mississippi Department because he felt he would be more useful there than anywhere else, and requested that he be allowed to take the Missouri division with him.

Several days later Price had a second interview with Davis, at which Snead and Randolph were present. Davis expressed regret over the transfer of the Missouri troops from the West and said that it had been done by Johnston without his prior knowledge. However, he continued, Price and his men for the time being must remain on the east side of the river, for that was where they were needed most. As for the Trans-Mississippi command, that had already been assigned to Major General John Bankhead Magruder, presently commanding a division in Lee's army.

Price became incensed. He believed that the promise of speedy return made to his troops before they left Arkansas had been broken and that Davis was selfishly denying him a chance to fight for the freedom of Missouri. "Well, Mr. President," he said, his face flushed, "well, Mr. President, if you will not let me serve *you*, I will nevertheless serve my *country*. You cannot prevent me from doing that. I will send you my resignation, and go back to Missouri and raise another army there without your assistance, and fight again under the flag of Missouri, and win new victories for the South in spite of the Government."

Davis glared back at Price and in contemptuous tones replied: "Your resignation will be promptly accepted, General; and if you do go back to Missouri and raise another army, and win victories for the South, or do it any service at all, no one will be more pleased than myself, or—more surprised."

"Then I will surprise you, sir!" shouted Price, banging his fist on the table with such violence that the inkwells jumped. And with that

[10] *Official Records*, XIII, 838; Snead, "Price East of the Mississippi," 724.

he stalked from the room, returned to his quarters at the Spottswood Hotel, and wrote and sent to Davis his resignation. As he did so, Snead angrily denounced the President to a crowd in front of the hotel, tore the Confederate insignia from his uniform, and declared that Price would go to Missouri and fight again under the "bear flag." Price also made some "turbulent remarks" to the crowd, stating that he would act and plan by himself to save Missouri, without regard for Davis.[11]

In the meantime, Davis had some second thoughts about the advisability of letting Price quit the army. For if he did so, chances were that the Missouri troops would become disaffected, the Missouri and Arkansas congressional delegations would kick up a fuss, and Price would cause trouble in the West, where Governor Rector of Arkansas and others reportedly were talking of establishing a separate confederacy. Also, he recognized that Price had some valid reasons for dissatisfaction.[12] Therefore, the next day he returned Price's resignation and at the same time notified him that Bragg would be instructed to transfer him and the Missouri brigades back to Arkansas as soon as the military situation in Mississippi and Tennessee permitted. In addition, Randolph informed him that he would be appointed second in command to Magruder in the Trans-Mississippi, and Magruder in turn promised to make an immediate and all-out effort to liberate Missouri. Placated by these concessions and assurances, but still resentful towards Davis, Price left Richmond to rejoin his division.[13]

Then and later, Price's friends charged Davis with being willfully unfair in his treatment of Price. Davis, they claimed, was jealous of the Missourian's popularity, prejudiced against him because he was not a West Pointer, and indifferent to the fate of the West.[14] In fact, one Price partisan went so far as to assert that Davis had a grudge against

[11] Snead, "Price East of the Mississippi," 724–26; Reynolds, "Price and the Confederacy," 36–38, 43–44. Snead is the main source for the altercation with Davis. Undoubtedly Davis would have given a different version, as Reynolds indicates.
[12] Reynolds, "Price and the Confederacy," 39; *Official Records*, XIII, 815–16, 828–29, 833–35.
[13] *Official Records*, XIII, 837, 841–42, 845; Snead, "Price East of the Mississippi," 726; Douglas Southall Freeman, *Lee's Lieutenants* (New York, 1942–45), I, 610.
[14] John B. Clark to Sterling Price, July 17, 1862, in *Official Records*, LIII, 816–17; John Tyler to William Lowndes Yancey, October 15, 1862, in Western Historical Collection, University of Missouri, Columbia.

Price dating back to the Mexican War, when Price allegedly turned down the Mississippian's request that they trade military assignments so that Davis would not have to serve under his ex-father-in-law, Zachary Taylor![15]

Unquestionably Davis had little liking for Price, whom he described as the "vainest man he had ever met."[16] And because of this feeling, he doubtless was not as sympathetic to Price's aspirations as he might otherwise have been. But there is no substantial reason for believing that personal animosity was Davis' sole, or even main, motive in rejecting Price's request that the Missouri troops be sent back to Arkansas, or in denying Price the command of the Trans-Mississippi. On the first count, he was merely following the advice of Bragg as to the necessities of the existing military situation—the only course he could have taken under the circumstances. On the second, his decision undoubtedly was based on the same considerations as before. He believed that only a non-Westerner could successfully fill the post, he did not consider Price sufficiently competent, and he distrusted his loyalty and intentions.

Regarding this last, a recent development had served to keep it very much present in the President's thoughts. Taking its cue from the series of Confederate defeats in early 1862, a group of disgruntled anti-administration politicians in Richmond began talking of deposing Davis and proclaiming Price as President or "generalissimo!" Prominent among this element were John B. Clark, then a Senator, and William M. Cooke, also a member of the Missouri delegation to the Confederate Congress. Price, it appears, knew nothing of the scheme

[15] J. R. Perkins, "Jefferson Davis and Gen. Sterling Price," *Confederate Veteran*, XIX (1911), 473. According to this story, which several writers have accepted as fact, Davis did not want to serve under Taylor because the two had become estranged after Davis had eloped with Taylor's daughter and married her without Taylor's consent. Davis therefore asked Price to switch assignments, Davis' Mississippi regiment to go to New Mexico, Price's Missouri regiment to northern Mexico, only to have Price refuse. However, not only is there no evidence supporting this rather improbable tale, there is considerable evidence contradicting it. For example, Taylor soon forgave Davis for eloping with his daughter, who died shortly after the marriage, and he cordially welcomed Davis to his army during the Mexican War. Perkins, who apparently was a friend or associate of Price, gives Price himself as the source for this story— but with what accuracy and authority there is no way of determining. His entire article is a vicious attack on Davis, filled with distortions, innuendoes, halftruths, and downright falsehoods.

[16] Reynolds, "Price and the Confederacy," 44.

(it never became an actual plot), but it so happened that he appeared in Richmond just as McClellan's army besieged the city, and just as the talk about overthrowing Davis reached its peak. Davis, for his part, never took the matter seriously, but naturally it did nothing to allay his suspicions of the Missouri general.[17]

The only concrete result of Price's trip to Richmond was an open quarrel with the Confederate President. Not even the promise that he would be second in command to Magruder came to anything. For when Magruder set out early in July to assume his new post, the War Department almost immediately ordered him back to Richmond and appointed in his stead Major General Theophilus H. Holmes, a North Carolinian, West Pointer, and personal friend of Davis. Magruder was recalled because of charges (subsequently proved false) of misconduct during the Battle of Malvern Hill.[18] Price's friends, however, believed that Davis had superseded Magruder with Holmes because he had promised to cooperate with Price in liberating Missouri. Wrote Clark to Price on July 17: "I have thus spoken of Magruder's recall . . . to show how determined and persistent the President is in his neglect and disregard of the interest and manifest wishes of the whole West . . . as well as his continued neglect and insult to you . . . . [Davis] is your enemy, everybody knows . . . ."[19] Thus Price had a fresh grievance against the President.

Governor Jackson, it is worth noting, played no role whatsoever in the controversy over the transfer of Price's troops. During the winter of 1862 he had established a "government-in-exile" at Little Rock which controlled a remnant of the state guard, issued bonds and currency, and performed other sovereign functions. However, not only was he physically isolated from affairs east of the Mississippi, he became seriously ill with cancer and hence was incapable of acting with his former vigor. In any case, Price was now generally regarded as the real leader and spokesman of the Southern cause in Missouri—a situation that must have been the cause of much bitterness to the governor.

Price arrived back at Tupelo on June 27. On July 2 he went to Bragg and showed him a letter from the War Department authorizing

[17] *Ibid.*, 37–38; Perkins, "Davis and Price," 473, 477.
[18] Freeman, *Lee's Lieutenants*, I, 606–608.
[19] Edwards, *Shelby and His Men*, 106–107; Clark to Price, July 17, 1862, in *Official Records*, XIII, 817.

the return of the Missouri division to the Trans-Mississippi at Bragg's discretion. Bragg replied that the Missouri troops could not be spared at this time, but that Price would be given command of the Army of the West in place of Van Dorn, who had gone to take charge of the defense of Vicksburg against a threatened attack by Farragut's fleet.[20]

The following day Price assumed his new command, to the accompaniment of loud cheering by the troops. On July fourth the men of the Missouri division went to his headquarters and called for a speech. Price came out and said that he had never made a Fourth of July speech and never would. However, he told his followers that he had obtained permission from the President to take them back to Missouri, but that he was going to stay in Mississippi awhile and see if a battle was to come off. If it did not, he would have one of his own, for he was going to Missouri anyhow. He concluded by declaring that he could "make up as big an army as this one out of the states of Missouri, Arkansas, and Texas." It was, wrote one of the Missourians in his diary, "a short speech but what he said was to the point and just what we wanted to hear."[21]

Price's assurances did much to restore the morale of his troops. Not unnaturally they believed that the Confederate authorities had dealt unfairly with them, and they resented having (as they saw it) to fight to protect other people's homes while their own were in the hands of the enemy. Also, many of them were unhappy over being dismounted and converted into infantry. Even after Price's July 4 speech desertions were frequent, the deserters usually going back to Missouri where some of them joined guerrilla bands. However, the great majority, trusting the good intentions of the government and dedicated to the cause of Southern independence, remained steadfast in their duty.[22]

After taking command of the Army of the West, Price split it into

[20] *Official Records*, XVII, Pt. 2, pp. 645–46; Snead, "Price East of the Mississippi," 725; Calkins, "Fauntelroy's Diary," 23.

[21] Calkins, "Fauntelroy's Diary," 24; *Official Records*, XVII, Pt. 2, p. 636.

[22] *Official Records*, XIII, 15, 855; *ibid.*, XVII, Pt. 2, pp. 29, 645–46, 677; Snead, "Price East of the Mississippi," 728; Calkins, "Fauntelroy's Diary," 25–26. On July 13 the Missouri state guard unit under Parsons, which had accompanied Price to Mississippi, was allowed to return to Arkansas. It had considerable trouble crossing the Mississippi River, which would seem to justify the opinion that Bragg gave at this time to the War Department that even if the Missouri division could be spared, it would probably find it extremely difficult to cross.

two divisions. The first was composed mainly of the Missouri troops and was under the command of Henry Little. Price justly regarded Little as his best lieutenant, leaned heavily on him for advice, and strongly urged his promotion to major general. The other division, made up largely of Louisiana, Arkansas, and Texas regiments, was headed by Dabney Maury, who had been elevated to brigadier general. He too was a highly capable officer with West Point training. In addition, Price established a separate cavalry brigade of about fifteen hundred troopers under the command of Brigadier General Frank C. Armstrong, a native of Louisiana. His total force came to slightly over fifteen thousand men, with some forty pieces of artillery.

And thanks to the work of Little and Maury it soon became the finest force he ever commanded. When it held a review at Tupelo late in July, General William Hardee pronounced it to be the "most efficient, best drilled and most thoroughly disciplined body of troops" in Mississippi. And Bragg turned to Little and said, "You had the reputation of having one of the finest companies in the old army. General, this is certainly as fine a division as I have ever seen."[23] The quasi-mob that had gathered at Cowskin Prairie the previous summer were now soldiers—they had always been fighters.

However, Price's notions of discipline still remained below Bragg's martinet standards. When some of Price's soldiers were arrested for stealing corn, he released them after several days. Bragg angrily denounced this leniency and said that the men should have been executed as examples. Price replied that he would never shoot any of his boys for taking a few roasting ears. Such an attitude endeared "Ol' Pap" to his troops, but not to the West Pointers.[24]

During the last week of July, Bragg began transferring the bulk of his forces to Chattanooga as the first step in his projected northern offensive. Only Van Dorn's army at Vicksburg and Price's at Tupelo remained behind. To Price he assigned command of the misnamed District of Tennessee with instructions to watch Grant in northern Mississippi and prevent him from going to the assistance of Buell's Union army in Middle Tennessee. As for Van Dorn, he was authorized

[23] Snead, "Price East of the Mississippi," 726–28; Anderson, *Memoirs: Historical and Personal*, 227; Bevier, *First and Second Missouri Confederate Brigades*, 124, 325, 333; *Official Records*, XVII, Pt. 2, pp. 683–85.
[24] Anderson, *Memoirs: Historical and Personal*, 204.

to join Price if this should prove necessary or desirable, and could do so without endangering Vicksburg.[25]

The last of Bragg's army left Tupelo on July 29. Price at once began preparations to move against Corinth, where a large Federal force under Major General William S. Rosecrans was stationed. Rosecrans constituted Grant's left wing, and thus was most likely to reinforce Buell. However, since Grant's available troops outnumbered his own two to one, Price could not hope to make a serious advance without support from Van Dorn. Therefore, on July 31 he wrote Van Dorn that he was ready to take the field and that he would place himself under Van Dorn's command if he would join him.[26] But Van Dorn was unable to comply. After beating off Farragut's attack on Vicksburg, he had sent a force under Brigadier General John C. Breckinridge to capture Baton Rouge. Breckinridge had gotten bogged down in swamps and other difficulties, and Van Dorn, far from reinforcing Price, asked him for a brigade with which to extricate Breckinridge![27]

Before leaving Tupelo, General Hardee had told Snead to use his influence to prevent Price from weakening his forces to aid Van Dorn. Bragg, he stated, would "sternly disapprove the sending of any re-enforcements whatever to Van Dorn," for the success of the invasion of Tennessee and Kentucky depended "greatly upon Price's ability to keep Grant from re-enforcing Buell," and Bragg expected Price "to keep his men well in hand, and ready to move northward at a moment's notice."[28] So, when Van Dorn's request for a brigade arrived, Snead informed Price of Hardee's warning. And as if to confirm it, a telegram came from Bragg stating that Grant was reinforcing Buell and that consequently "the road was open" into West Tennessee. Price accordingly replied to Van Dorn on August 4 that it was impossible to detach a brigade for the Baton Rouge front. Bragg, he stated, "says very pointedly that West Tennessee is now open to my army, intimating that he expects me to enter it." He concluded by again urging Van Dorn to join him at an early date in a campaign against Grant.[29]

[25] *Official Records*, XVII, Pt. 2, p. 656; Snead, "Price East of the Mississippi," 725–26.

[26] *Official Records*, XVII, Pt. 2, p. 665; Snead, "Price East of the Mississippi," 726–27.

[27] *Official Records*, XVII, Pt. 2, p. 663.

[28] Snead, "Price East of the Mississippi," 726–27.

[29] *Ibid.*; *Official Records*, XVII, Pt. 2, p. 663.

On the same day Price sent this answer to Van Dorn, he also transmitted copies of his correspondence with that general to Bragg's headquarters at Chattanooga. The result was that on August 11 Bragg telegraphed Van Dorn to add his army to Price's, to take command of the joint forces as senior in rank, and to lead them into West Tennessee as quickly as possible. On receipt of these instructions Van Dorn wrote Price that he would act on them, but that it would be two weeks before he could join him. Meanwhile, would Price lend him a brigade to assist Breckinridge? It would be back, he promised, in time for the Tennessee campaign.[30]

However, not only did Van Dorn fail to reinforce Price in two weeks, but for some unknown reason his message saying that he would do so took nearly that long to reach Tupelo! Furthermore, Price received no other word from Van Dorn, and had not Bragg written to appraise him of his instructions to Van Dorn, Price would not even have known that the Mississippian had been ordered to join him for an advance into Tennessee![31] Thus August went by with Bragg urging Price to move against Grant, Price impatiently waiting for Van Dorn, and Van Dorn lingering in Vicksburg while still vainly seeking to capture Baton Rouge.

During this time Price endeavored to further improve his army's battle readiness. He had money brought from Richmond, and for the first time in several months his troops were paid. He also collected a large number of wagons and obtained enough new rifles to re-equip his own men and to supply five thousand exchanged prisoners who had been promised him. Finally, by prevailing on the governors of Alabama and Mississippi to call out several thousand militia, he released a sizable force of regular Confederate soldiers who had been on garrison duty for service in the field.[32]

At the same time he did all he could to worry and harass the enemy. Early in August he instructed the Mississippi Partisan Rangers of Colonel William C. Falkner (great-grandfather of the novelist) to round up pro-Union men in the northern part of the state, and authorized Captain George L. Baxter to make an attempt to capture Grant—

[30] *Official Records*, XVII, Pt. 2, pp. 675–76. Van Dorn's renewed request for a brigade to reinforce Breckinridge pinpoints his fatal defect as a general—a lack of realism and practicality, combined with self-centered obstinacy.
[31] *Ibid.*, Pt. 1, pp. 120–21.
[32] *Ibid.*, Pt. 2, pp. 664, 666–68, 674–77, 682–85.

a venture which obviously did not succeed.[33] Later in the month he sent Armstrong's cavalry raiding into Tennessee with orders to slash Grant's communication lines and secure information about Union strength and movements. Augmenting his brigade with eleven hundred men at Holly Springs, Armstrong struck for Bolivar, Tennessee, where he defeated a small Federal detachment. He then cut (temporarily) the railroad between Bolivar and Jackson, Tennessee, following which he returned to Tupelo, overcoming a second enemy unit on the way.[34]

Meanwhile, Van Dorn received another communication from Bragg instructing him to join with Price in a movement against Grant's forces in West Tennessee: "If you hold them in check we are sure of success here; but should they re-enforce here so as to defy us then you may redeem West Tennessee and probably aid us by crossing to the enemy's rear."[35] Van Dorn considered this, then on August 24 wrote to Price that he would be ready to join him in twenty days with ten thousand men for an "aggressive campaign" through West Tennessee toward Paducah, Kentucky, and from "thence wherever circumstances may dictate." Price replied on the twenty-ninth with a proposal that their combined armies drive the Federals from Corinth. "I fear that my own forces are hardly sufficient to accomplish this, as the enemy are equal to them in numbers and strongly intrenched, and I am not willing to risk a doubtful engagement under present circumstances." Price also urged Van Dorn to hasten his preparations, as "success must depend in a great measure, and may depend altogether, upon the rapidity of our movements."[36]

Before Van Dorn could reply, Price on the night of September 1 received a dispatch from Bragg stating that Buell was retreating towards Nashville, that every effort must be made to prevent Rosecrans from joining him, and that if Price could not do this he was to pursue Rosecrans into Tennessee. Price realized that he could not tarry longer and informed Van Dorn the following day that he intended to march northward on the fifth, and that he hoped that Van Dorn

[33] *Ibid.*, 667–68.
[34] *Ibid.*, Pt. 1, p. 120.
[35] *Ibid.*, Pt. 2, pp. 675–76.
[36] *Ibid.*, Pt. 1, p. 121; *ibid.*, Pt. 2, p. 687. The records do not contain Van Dorn's August 24 letter, the contents of which must be deduced from Price's reply and subsequent report.

would support him. Van Dorn sent back word that he would move his troops to Holly Springs on September 12. He advised Price not to follow Rosecrans into Middle Tennessee if he could avoid it, for their combined forces could do more by pushing Grant out of West Tennessee, after which they could join Bragg if necessary.[37]

Price first advanced to Guntown, where on September 11 he learned that Rosecrans was at Iuka, a small resort town on the Memphis and Charleston Railroad twenty miles southeast of Corinth. This seemed to indicate that Rosecrans was heading for Nashville, as Bragg had feared, and Price hastened his army towards Iuka. If Rosecrans was still there he would attack him; if not, he would press on into Tennessee in pursuit. On the morning of September 14, following an all-night, forced march, Armstrong's cavalry galloped into Iuka hard on the heels of a small Federal rear guard which left behind immense quantities of military stores. Inquiry soon established that although part of Rosecrans' army (three divisions in all) had gone to Buell, Rosecrans himself had fallen back to Corinth with about ten thousand men. After some hesitation, Price decided not to enter Tennessee. "As Rosecrans had retreated westward with his forces," he subsequently explained in his report, "I did not think it was my duty to cross the Tennessee and move upon Nashville as had been ordered by General Bragg, under the belief, as I presumed, that Rosecrans had eluded me and was marching to the relief of Buell, but that I should continue to hold Rosecrans in check and prevent if possible his junction with Buell." To this end he sent a message to Van Dorn proposing that they make a joint attack on Corinth.[38]

Years later Snead deplored the fact that Price did not march on to Nashville, and implied that he was guilty of excessive deference to Van Dorn's wishes.[39] However, the records amply demonstrate that any move by Price to Nashville was contingent on Rosecrans' going to that city, and this he had not done in the sense meant or supposed by Bragg. Moreover, had Price tried to cross the Tennessee, most likely Grant and Rosecrans would have cut his line of communications, then

[37] *Official Records*, XVII, Pt. 2, pp. 690–92.
[38] *Ibid.*, Pt. 1, p. 121; *ibid.*, Pt. 2, pp. 695–96, 698–99, 702–703; Snead, "Price East of the Mississippi," 730–31. Price also promptly reported to Bragg's headquarters on Rosecrans' movements.
[39] Snead, "Price East of the Mississippi," 730–31.

pounced on him with superior forces from flank and rear. Therefore, contrary to Snead (who was trying to pin the blame on Van Dorn for the eventual failure of Bragg's Kentucky campaign), Price acted wisely in not obeying Bragg's orders, which obviously were based on an underestimation of Union strength in West Tennessee and on misleading intelligence concerning Rosecrans.[40]

However, Price remained doubtful as to what course to follow, and Bragg continued to try to direct his movements from afar. On September 14 Price received a telegram from Bragg, dated September 6, instructing him to "march rapidly for Nashville," as Buell was falling back and "Rosecrans must follow." Then on September 17 yet another telegram arrived from Bragg, this one sent September 12 while "En Route to Kentucky": "I have anxiously expected your advance, and trust it will no longer be delayed." This second message caused Price to write Van Dorn again, quoting Bragg and stating that he could not remain inactive any longer, but must either move with Van Dorn against Rosecrans or else march alone into Tennessee.[41]

Van Dorn in the meantime had moved with about nine thousand troops to Holly Springs. But before doing so he had wired Secretary of War George Randolph on September 9: "I ought to have command of the movements of Price, that there may be concert of action." Randolph referred this request to President Davis. After some hesitation, for he did not want to interfere with Bragg's plans, Davis advised Van Dorn: "The troops must co-operate, and can only do so by having one head. Your rank makes you the commander . . . ."[42] Thus, unknown to both Bragg and Price, the latter now came under Van Dorn's control. However, such an arrangement was not only logical but also was perfectly acceptable both to Price, who several times had offered to put his army under Van Dorn, and to Bragg, who had recommended that this be done as soon as Van Dorn could free

[40] Kenneth P. Williams, *Lincoln Finds a General* (New York, 1949–59), IV, 70, 482, comes to the same conclusion. True, Halleck on September 17 telegraphed Grant: "Do everything in your power to prevent Price from crossing the Tennessee River. A juncture of Price and Bragg in Tennessee or Kentucky would be most disastrous." But this merely proves that the Federals would have made an all-out effort to smash Price if he had crossed the Tennessee. In fact, the very possibility that he might led to a heavy concentration against him.

[41] *Official Records*, XVII, Pt. 1, p. 121; *ibid.*, Pt. 2, pp. 694, 705–706; Snead, "Price East of the Mississippi," 731.

[42] *Official Records*, XVII, Pt. 2, pp. 697–700.

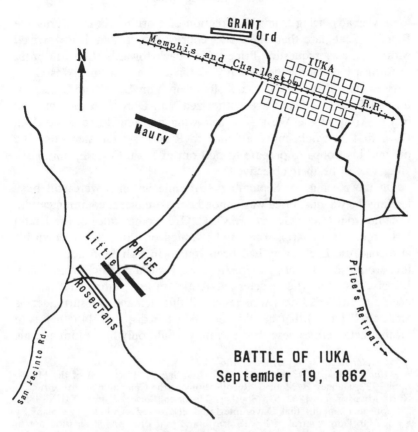

BATTLE OF IUKA
September 19, 1862

his forces from the defense of Vicksburg. It was not, as some of
Price's staff later charged, the result of a sinister plot hatched by
Davis and Van Dorn to ruin Price.[43]

Price was still lingering at Iuka on September 18 when two events
occurred which removed all uncertainty from his mind as to what to
do. First, in the evening Armstrong reported that a strong Union

[43] Snead, "Price East of the Mississippi," 730–31; Tyler to Yancey, October
15, 1862, in Western Historical Collection. Tyler was an aide-de-camp to Price.
Son of the ex-President Tyler, he was a somewhat eccentric character with a
tendency to alcoholism. He wrote a number of letters to Yancey, Confederate
Senator from Alabama and leader of the anti-Davis faction in the Confederate
Congress, denouncing the West Pointers and complaining of Davis' unfair treatment of Price. His testimony must be used with caution.

force was advancing from the direction of Corinth via the Burnsville Road.[44] Next, late that night two couriers from Van Dorn arrived with dispatches requesting Price to fall back towards Rienzi in order to form a junction of the two armies for a campaign into West Tennessee. One of the couriers, an officer on Van Dorn's staff, also informed Price that Davis had authorized Van Dorn to take command of the Army of the West. The following morning Price wrote Van Dorn that he would move at once to Rienzi. At the same time he ordered his troops to prepare to pull out of Iuka. Corinth, not Nashville, was to be their objective.[45]

On the morning of September 19, while his men were still busy loading the wagons, Price was handed a most unusual communication. It came from Major General E. O. C. Ord, commander of the Union force reported by Armstrong, and it called on Price to lay down his arms because Lee's army had been routed in Maryland and the war thus would soon be terminated. Appended was a dispatch from Cairo, Illinois, describing Lee's defeat at Antietam and stating that he had been surrounded. Price, who regarded this demand for surrender as "insolent," replied that he did not credit the dispatch, but that even "if the facts were as described . . . they would only move him and his

[44] *Official Records*, XVII, Pt. 2, 706–707.

[45] *Ibid.*, Pt. 1, p. 121; *ibid.*, Pt. 2, 707–708; Snead, "Price East of the Mississippi," 732; Dabney H. Maury, "Recollections of the Campaign against Grant in North Mississippi in 1862–63," Southern Historical Society *Papers*, XIII (1885), 288. Snead maintains that Davis interfered disastrously with Bragg's plans by giving Van Dorn control of Price's army, and that Price's final decision not to march on to Nashville was the result of Van Dorn assuming command and ordering Price to pull back to Rienzi. The official records, however, do not support this contention. Indeed, Price in his report and the correspondence between Price and Van Dorn for this period do not even mention Van Dorn's assumption of command. Even Tyler, in his October 15 letter to Yancey, gives no support to Snead's accusation, although he implies criticism of Davis for ordering Van Dorn to take command of Price's army. But in any case, by the night of September 18 it was much too late for Price to head north from Iuka, for if he had done so he would have been destroyed by superior Union forces poised to strike him. Also, Price had already committed himself to joining forces with Van Dorn and was only waiting for definite word from Van Dorn agreeing to such a juncture. Snead hated Jefferson Davis and despised Van Dorn. As a consequence, his testimony concerning Price's operations in Mississippi is badly warped where those two are concerned. Williams, *Lincoln Finds a General*, IV, 485, also discounts Snead's account. Robert G. Hartje, *Van Dorn: The Life and Times of a Confederate General* (Nashville, 1967), 208–13, takes the easy way out and ignores the whole issue of the relations between Price and Van Dorn.

soldiers to greater exertions in behalf of their country, and that neither he nor they will ever lay down their arms . . . until the independence of the Confederate States shall have been acknowledged by the United States."[46]

By early afternoon Price's troops had nearly completed their preparations to leave Iuka. Then, at 2:30 P.M., the pickets south of the town were driven back by an advancing enemy column. Grant, who had taken the field in person, had set in motion a two-pronged offensive against Price. In addition to Ord's eight thousand soldiers to the northwest of Iuka, Rosecrans with nine thousand men was closing in from the south: Price was to be caught and crushed between them. Curiously enough, this marked the third major battle in succession involving Price in which one of the commanders attempted such a combination attack. And like Lyon and Van Dorn before him, Grant too was destined to fail. Originally, Ord and Rosecrans were to attack simultaneously at a preset time. But when Rosecrans reported that he would not be in position by then, Grant instructed Ord to attack when he heard Rosecrans' guns opening up on Price. However, a strong wind, blowing from the north, carried the noise of the firing south of Iuka away from Ord, who waited expectantly but motionless throughout the day. Thus, Rosecrans alone attacked, and thus the Army of the West escaped a serious defeat, perhaps annihilation.[47]

Price had posted his forces northwest of Iuka to hold off Ord. Consequently, when he learned that the Federals were advancing from the south, he ordered Little to rush first one, then two brigades to the threatened point. These units responded quickly and engaged the

[46] *Official Records*, XVII, Pt. 1, pp. 121–22; *ibid.*, Pt. 2, pp. 229–301; Jefferson Davis, *The Rise and Fall of the Confederate Government* (New York, 1881), II, 387; Williams, *Lincoln Finds a General*, IV, 74–75.

[47] *Official Records*, XVII, Pt. 1, pp. 65–67, 122; U. S. Grant, *Personal Memoirs of U. S. Grant* (New York, 1885), I, 412–13. Considerable mystery still shrouds the Union side of the Battle of Iuka. Grant, who was with Ord's column, is the principal authority for the statement that the sound of Rosecrans' guns was not heard. Ord and others second this assertion, but as William L. Lamers points out in his revisionistic biography of Rosecrans, *The Edge of Glory* (New York, 1961), 103–30, other Union officers located at approximately the same distance and direction from Iuka as Grant and Ord heard the firing of Rosecrans' guns. He raises the question of whether Grant perhaps was drunk at the time, citing the late Professor William B. Hesseltine of the University of Wisconsin to the effect that Iuka "seems to be the only place where an issue [concerning Grant being incapable of command because of drink] could arise."

Federals about one mile from the town. Price accompanied them, and on seeing that the Union force was stronger than expected, turned to Little and told him to bring up the rest of his division. Hardly had he spoken when a bullet crashed through Little's head, killing him instantly. Horrified, Price jumped from his saddle and knelt over the body, weeping "as he would for a son." Then, pulling himself together, he remounted and took personal charge of the battle, at the same time sending word to Brigadier General Louis Hébert (who had been exchanged following his capture at Elkhorn) that he now commanded Little's division.[48]

Price's counterattack had caught the leading Federal division only partially deployed. In addition, Rosecrans was prevented by what he called the "horrid" ground from employing his full manpower or making effective use of his artillery. In fact, if Little's death had not caused a temporary pause in the Confederate assault, Rosecrans' forces might have been routed. As it was, Price's men drove the Federals back six hundred yards and captured nine cannons before darkness brought an end to the conflict, which Price subsequently described as having been "waged with a severity I have never seen surpassed." Confederate losses were slightly over five hundred as compared to about eight hundred for the enemy.[49]

Price planned to renew the battle in the morning, confident that he then would complete his victory. Therefore he ordered Maury's division to Rosecrans' front, leaving only the cavalry to check Ord. Then, after instructing Snead not to let anyone disturb him until dawn, he went to a friend's house rather then his headquarters to seek badly needed rest.

Snead helped bury Little, then went to the headquarters building. Sometime after midnight Hébert, Maury, and Colonel Wirt Adams of the cavalry came to see him. They all predicted disaster if the army did not immediately retreat from Iuka and demanded to see Price, but Snead was undecided as what to do. When a courier arrived with important dispatches from Van Dorn, he hesitated no longer and took

[48] *Official Records*, XVII, Pt. 1, p. 122; *ibid.*, Pt. 2, p. 708; Bevier, *First and Second Missouri Confederate Brigades*, 333.

[49] *Official Records*, XVII, Pt. 1, pp. 67, 122; Major General C. S. Hamilton, "The Battle of Iuka," in *Battles and Leaders*, II, 735; Snead, "Price East of the Mississippi," 732–33, 736.

the officers to Price's lodgings. It was nearly dawn, and Price thought
that they had come to summon him to battle. On learning their actual
purpose he evidenced great disappointment and tried to persuade them
that their fears were groundless and that victory was in their grasp.
Wrote Maury ten years later:

The old man was hard to move. He had taken an active personal part
in the battle that evening; his Missourians had behaved beautifully under
his own direction, the enemy had been so freely driven back, that he
could think of nothing but the complete victory he would gain over Rose-
crantz [sic] in the morning. He seemed to take no account of Grant [Ord]
at all. His only reply to our facts and our arguments, as he sat on the side
of his bed in appropriate sleeping costume, was: "We'll wade through him,
sir, in the morning; General, you ought to have seen how my boys fought
this evening; we drove them a mile, sir."[50]

But the generals persisted, and in the end Price reluctantly agreed to
retreat. However, he rejected absolutely a further proposal that the
wagon train, ladened with captured Union spoils, be burned.

By sunrise the Confederate army had left Iuka. With Armstrong's
cavalry acting as a rear guard, it marched southward by way of the
Fulton Road, which had been left open by the Federals. During the
retreat Price himself acted as "wagon boss." He "would hurry up the
teamsters," wrote one of his soldiers, "and tell them he would have
them hung if they didn't keep the wagons closed up—he kept them
scared all the time in that way and they drove in double quick."[51]

Rosecrans did not discover the Confederate retreat until shortly
after dawn. Although he promptly pursued, he failed to overtake
Price's column. As one of his generals subsequently commented, "pursuit . . . can amount to little in a country like that of northern Mississippi, heavily wooded and with narrow roads, when the enemy has time
enough to get his artillery and trains in front of his infantry."[52] When
they entered Iuka the Federals found only several hundred seriously

[50] *Official Records*, XVII, Pt. 1, p. 122; Snead, "Price East of the Mississippi,"
733; Bevier, *First and Second Missouri Confederate Brigades*, 335; Maury, "Campaign against Grant," 290. Maury's article was published originally in the *Southern Magazine* in 1872.
[51] Calkins, "Fauntelroy's Dairy," 32.
[52] Hamilton, "Battle of Iuka," 735–36.

wounded Confederates in the Methodist church, plus several dozen bodies covered by tarpaulins lying outside. Both Rosecrans and Price claimed a victory, but Grant felt that the Union forces had in effect suffered a defeat by failing to destroy the entire Confederate army.[53] Price, on the other hand, did gain a tactical success, but he had a freak of nature—the strong north wind that prevented Ord from hearing Rosecrans' cannons—to thank for escaping Grant's trap. Furthermore, his stubborn reluctance to retreat, while doing honor to his courage and fighting spirit, was not a credit to his generalship.

The Army of the West retreated until it reached Baldwyn on the Mobile & Ohio Railroad on September 23. It remained there several days, the men resting their "wearied limbs" and filling their "empty craws" with bacon and crackers. It then marched northwest to Ripley, where on September 28 it finally linked up with Van Dorn. At this point a crisis erupted in Price's official family—Snead submitted an angry letter of resignation:

I had once before . . . quit the army rather than serve under General Van Dorn and his staff. I could not endure the incompetency and rashness of the one, nor the inefficiency of the others. I could not consent to be any longer the instrument in their hands of doing gross injustice to the Missouri and other Trans-Mississippi troops in your division. I foresaw that what had happened before was going to happen again. I foresaw from the correspondence that was passing between you that General Van Dorn, as soon as he got control over you, would take away your wagons and teams and give them to his own unprovided troops, unprovided by want of his

[53] *Official Records*, XVII, Pt. 1, 68, 122. Price, in his report written six days after the battle, stated that if he had renewed the fight on the morning of September 20 he had little doubt but he would have been victorious. This is fatuous. Grant, *Memoirs*, I, 413, criticizes Rosecrans for leaving the Fulton road open and falsely accuses him of failing to pursue Price promptly and vigorously. Lamers, *Edge of Glory*, 108–109, 126, defends Rosecrans, arguing that if he tried to block the road he would have divided his forces badly and so invited disaster. Williams, *Lincoln Finds a General*, IV, 79–80, 464, who generally is very partial to Grant and critical of Rosecrans, agrees with this contention in substance, but maintains that Rosecrans should have thrown a cavalry force across the road and blocked it with fallen trees so as to delay at least any Confederate retreat. However, in answer to this it can be said that Rosecrans operated on the entirely reasonable assumption that Grant and Ord would support his attack and that Price hence would be trapped and crushed before he could retreat on the Fulton or any other road. The Union failure to destroy Price at Iuka cannot be pinned on Rosecrans alone.

own foresight and the inefficiency and carelessness of his officers. I foresaw in the same way that he would take away the arms that your foresight had provided for your exchanged prisoners. I foresaw that he would, after doing this, take away your men. As I have always said, I nevertheless resolved to remain and endure everything for the sake of aiding you and rather than resign in face of the enemy. But my anticipations are being realized so rapidly that my indignation against General Van Dorn is too intense, and my aversion to serve under him too great, to permit me to hesitate any longer. You will see from the enclosed note that General Van Dorn has invaded your district and in the most insulting terms ordered one of his sergeants to go, even to your headquarters, and take away, not ask for, the arms which are now in the hands of your troops. The same thing will be done with reference to the wagons and teams which you have been buying with the bounty money sent expressly for the Missouri Army of the West. The same thing will be done with the exchanged prisoners, and finally with your army. Forseeing all this and being unwilling to endure these wrongs and indignities, I ask to be relieved from duty with the Army of the West.[54]

There is probably no way of determining today the exact truth of Snead's charges against Van Dorn. No doubt they reflect personal dislike and a parochial view of military affairs. Yet that they had some basis in fact is demonstrated by Van Dorn's own correspondence in the official records, which shows that repeatedly during September he sought control over Price's army, endeavored to obtain the exchanged prisoners and surplus arms that had been ordered to Price, and solicited wagons from the Army of the West.[55] Also it is apparent from Price's reply to Snead's letter of resignation that Price himself shared his chief of staff's views:

Major: I desire to express . . . my deep and unfeigned regret at your determination, and desire that you do not consider it as a censure for me to say that I believe every Missourian here is impressed with feelings corresponding with yours, but the military position we at present occupy toward the enemy, with an engagement where the odds are heavy against

[54] *Official Records*, LII, Pt. 2, p. 366. Snead's letter was dated September 28, Tupelo.

[55] See *ibid.*, XVII, Pt. 1, pp. 696–716, *passim*. At the beginning of the Pea Ridge campaign some of Price's tents and surplus arms were turned over to the Arkansas troops, although this was reported to be a voluntary act on the part of the Missouri contingents [perhaps to make up for their behavior during the Wilson's Creek campaign]. See Washington (Ark.) *Telegraph*, March 19, 1862.

us immediately impending, calls imperatively for a sacrifice on my part
and that of my army of all that we feel to be due us to secure a victory
to our arms in the impending conflict.[56]

This letter, in which Price subordinates what is obviously a strong
personal resentment against Van Dorn to the good of the cause, re-
flects great credit on Price as a patriot, general, and man. In the end
Snead, persuaded by his hero's words and example, withdrew his
resignation. But although relations between Price and Van Dorn remained officially harmonious, true respect and trust did not exist.

Van Dorn optimistically named the force assembled at Ripley "The
Army of West Tennessee." Besides Maury's and Hébert's divisions
under Price, about fourteen thousand effectives, it consisted of a
division of Mississippi, Alabama, and Kentucky infantry commanded
by Major General Mansfield Lovell, and the cavalry brigades of
General Armstrong and Colonel William H. Jackson. In all it numbered about twenty-two thousand men, plus a sizable artillery train.
Most of the troops, furthermore, were veterans, well-armed and fully
trained.[57]

In a conference with Van Dorn and Lovell, Price advised against
attacking Corinth until they were reinforced by a contingent of twelve
or fifteen thousand exchanged prisoners then at Jackson, Mississippi.
The recent engagement at Iuka had demonstrated how quickly the
Federals could concentrate their forces, and he feared that the army
lacked sufficient strength to be sure of taking Corinth, or that if it did
so its losses would be so heavy as to preclude following up the success.
But Van Dorn, as eager now to strike as he previously was slow to
obey Bragg's instructions, replied that to bring up the exchange prisoners, most of whom were unarmed and unorganized, would occasion
much delay, and that in the meantime the Federals would have an
opportunity to strengthen the defenses and reinforce the garrison at
Corinth. Price made no attempt to argue the matter further, and he

[56] *Official Records*, LII, Pt. 2, pp. 366–67. In a paper written in 1886 Celsus
Price asserted that friendship and respect existed between his father and Van
Dorn, but there are many reasons to believe that he was being less than candid.
See Celsus Price, "Gens. Price and Van Dorn" [newspaper clipping in the Earl
Van Dorn Collection, Alabama State Department of Archives and History,
Montgomery, Alabama].
[57] *Official Records*, XVII, Pt. 1, pp. 374–75, 378, 385.

agreed with Van Dorn that the importance of Corinth was so great that it "warranted more than the usual hazards of battle." However, he retained obvious misgivings about the venture.

"You seem despondent, General Price," said Van Dorn.

"No!" Price answered. "You quite mistake me. I have only given you the facts within my knowledge and the counselling of my judgment. When you reach Corinth you shall find that no portion of the army shall exceed mine either in courage, in conduct, or in achievement."[58]

On the morning of September 29 the Confederate troops marched northward from Ripley. Their morale was high, they were confident of victory, and the prospect of entering Tennessee filled them with enthusiasm—especially the Missourians, who were anxious to leave Mississippi. "No army," wrote Van Dorn in his report a few weeks later, "ever marched to battle with prouder steps, more hopeful countenances, or with more courage than marched the Army of West Tennessee . . . on its way to Corinth."[59]

[58] *Ibid.*, 377–78, 441, 455; Tyler to Yancey, October 15, 1862, in Western Historical Collection. The direct quotations are from Tyler's letter. Tyler represented Price as being absolutely opposed to attacking Corinth without the exchanged prisoners and gave the impression furthermore that the idea of attacking the town originated with Van Dorn. He also stated that Price knew the exact size of the Union garrison at Corinth, that he correctly predicted the strategy the Federals subsequently used in trying to trap Van Dorn, and he claimed that the exchanged prisoners were armed and organized and ready to be brought up to Ripley by railroad. Only so much of Tyler's account has been used in the narrative as appears consistent with the known facts of Price's and Van Dorn's views regarding the attack on Corinth. The wisdom of this attack will be discussed later.

[59] Calkins, "Fauntelroy's Diary," 34; *Official Records*, XVII, Pt. 1, pp. 377–78. The Missourians found Mississippi almost alien country, and they had utter contempt for the fighting ability of the Mississippi troops, who had run at the first fire at Iuka.

6

CORINTH

Corinth was the most vital and, at the same time, most vulnerable point held by Grant's army. Nowhere else, Van Dorn believed, could the Confederates hope to achieve more at less risk. Should they capture Memphis, they could not hold it against the dreaded gunboats. If they attempted the center of the Union line at Bolivar, they would be in danger of an enveloping attack on both flanks. But Corinth was an exposed salient on Grant's extreme left. By taking it the Confederates not only would gain control of the two strategic railroads which bisected it, but would also open the way for the recovery of West Tennessee—and perhaps for a march to the Ohio River![1]

The town itself consisted of a small cluster of wooden buildings beside the junction of the railroad lines which gave the place its importance. Surrounding it was a low, flat countryside of sluggish, steep-banked streams, swampy bottoms, and dense oak forests through which twisted a few miserable dirt roads. First the Confederates, then the Federals, had fortified its approaches, so that there were now actually more defenses than the available Union forces could properly utilize. Two and a half miles to the north were the old Confederate works of Beauregard; a mile closer and on the south side was another row of trenches constructed by Halleck; and immediately about the town was a final line built under Grant and anchored by a number of detached redoubts or "batteries." Rosecrans, with an army of 23,000 battle-hardened midwestern troops, commanded the Corinth area. Although he believed that his old West Point classmate "Buck" Van Dorn would strike elsewhere, he maintained strong outposts and instructed his engineers to improve the inner fortifications, which were still in large part unfinished.[2]

Van Dorn knew Corinth and its environs well as a result of his

[1] *Official Records*, XVII, Pt. 1, pp. 376–78, 452–53, 457–58; *ibid.*, Pt. 2, pp. 703–704, 712.
[2] William S. Rosecrans, "The Battle of Corinth," in *Battles and Leaders*, II, 739–43.

service there in the spring. Also, scouts and spies had provided him with reasonably accurate information as to Rosecrans' strength and preparations. Therefore, he realized that it would be extremely difficult to carry out a successful assault. Yet, by deception, speed, and surprise, he hoped to reduce the odds sufficiently to gain victory. He first would keep the Federals guessing until the last possible moment as to where he intended to strike. Then he would march rapidly to Corinth and attack it before Rosecrans could call in his scattered outposts, thus achieving the advantage of superior numbers at the point of contact. Once Rosecrans was defeated and Corinth seized, he would bring up the exchanged prisoners, equip them with captured material, and sweep into West Tennessee, outflanking Grant and forcing him to fall back to the Ohio.[3] As in the case of Elkhorn it was a brilliant plan—at least on paper.

A three-day march northward from Ripley brought Van Dorn's army to Pocahontas, Tennessee, from which point it threatened simultaneously Bolivar and Corinth, equidistant away. This move not only kept the Federals in the dark as to Van Dorn's objective, but his own men as well. However, their uncertainty soon ended. On the night of October 1 Van Dorn swung the army eastward to Davis' Bridge on the Hatchie River, which it crossed during the early morning.[4] Not until then did the brigade and regimental commanders learn officially that he intended to take Corinth. Brigadier General Albert Rust of Lovell's division at once declared that the venture would fail. To this Lovell answered, "If we cannot succeed we had better lay down our arms and go home."[5]

The Confederates bivouacked for the night at Chewalla, ten miles from Corinth. Rosecrans, whose cavalry encountered them on the way, was aware of their presence, but believed that they were merely a small force designed to pin him down in Corinth while Van Dorn's main body cut the Mobile and Ohio Railroad north of the town. Nevertheless he sent an infantry brigade to Chewalla with orders to develop Confederate strength and intentions by offering stiff resistance to any advance. At the same time he called in all his outlying detach-

---

[3] *Official Records*, XVII, Pt. 1, pp. 376–78, 441, 452–53, 457–58.
[4] *Ibid.*, 377–78, 385.
[5] *Ibid.*, 417.

ments to the south and east and intensified work on the inner ring of fortifications.[6]

At daybreak on October 3 Van Dorn's army resumed its march towards Corinth. As at Elkhorn, it advanced on a Friday to strike the enemy from the north, but if any of the men at the time noticed the coincidence, there is no record of their commenting on it or being disturbed by it. In any case there was a much more ominous occurrence for them to ponder—three distinct earthquake tremors shook the gloomy forests around Corinth that morning. And as usual when battle was in the immediate offing, many of the soldiers threw away playing cards, entrusted personal possessions to friends to be sent home "in case," or carefully placed Bibles in the breast pocket just over the heart. Still another sign that a fight impended was provided by Price, who appeared in his "war coat"—a multicolored plaid hunting shirt which he had worn much of the time in Missouri and Arkansas, and at Iuka.[7]

Lovell's division led the advance, followed by Hébert and Maury. The Federals fell back, skirmishing constantly but offering no serious resistance. After about five miles Lovell turned off to the right of the road and Price to the left. Both then formed their men in line of battle and moved towards Corinth's outer defenses, the old Beauregard works. These were manned by sizeable Union forces and protected by a belt of fallen timber four hundred yards wide.[8] As his men moved into assault positions, Price rode along the line, exposed to a heavy fire that killed one of his staff officers. He was his customary calm self but wore an expression of profound concern. He had ordered the field batteries to support the attack, but his chief of artillery had reported that the horses were being shot down too fast for a gun to be planted. In addition, Price was worried about the Mississippi regiments who had "fled ignominiously" at Iuka. But on seeing these regiments standing shoulder to shoulder with the other units, determined to redeem their honor, his lips relaxed into a smile.[9]

When they came to the fallen timber, Price's troops paused briefly

[6] *Ibid.*, 160, 166-67; Rosecrans, "The Battle of Corinth," 743–44.

[7] Bevier, *First and Second Missouri Confederate Brigades*, 337; Anderson, *Memoirs: Historical and Personal*, 198. The reference to earth tremors is from Victor M. Rose, *Ross's Texas Brigade* (Louisville, 1881), 72.

[8] *Official Records*, XVII, Pt. 1, pp. 378–79, 385–86.

[9] Tyler to Yancey, October 15, 1862, in Western Historical Collection.

to dress ranks. Then they rushed forward under a hail of rifle and cannon fire, jumping over and dodging around the trees, and losing all semblance of a regular military line. Once through to the open ground immediately in front of the fortifications, no one waited for those behind; all began climbing up the steep dirt embankment in groups of three or four. The field officers even tried to ride their horses up the parapet, but most of them slid ingloriously back into the ditch and had to dismount and continue on foot. The Federals, astonished by this wild onrush and heavily outnumbered, hastily gave way and re-treated in some disorder to a new position about one mile from Corinth. A shout of triumph went up from Price's men, which soon afterward was echoed by Lovell's troops on the right. Losses in the assault were amazingly light, and two cannons had been taken.[10]

The Confederates completed their occupation of the outer works about noon. By that time Rosecrans had finally concluded that Van Dorn actually was making an all-out effort to capture Corinth. Ac-cordingly, he sent more troops to bolster the small force which so far had been opposing the rebel advance. His plan was to hold Van Dorn in check as long as possible before retiring behind the inner ring of fortifications. Meanwhile, he would seek an opening for a counterattack. To this end he kept half of his total force in reserve.[11]

Price's men pursued the retreating Federals for half a mile before he ordered them to halt and rest. The temperature was in the nineties, canteens were empty, and many soldiers had fallen from sunstroke and sheer exhaustion. They spent about an hour recuperating and reorganizing, then resumed the advance. About 3:30 they again made contact with the enemy; almost immediately the "serpent hissing" of bullets filled the air.[12]

This time the Federals put up a far stronger resistance, tenaciously contesting every position and falling back only in the face of superior numbers. The battle raged with greatest fury along the Chewalla Road. Here Maury's troops found themselves opposed by Brigadier General Thomas A. Davies' division, tough veterans of Fort Donelson and

[10] Bevier, *First and Second Missouri Confederate Brigades*, 148–49.
[11] *Official Records*, XVII, Pt. 1, pp. 167–68; Rosecrans, "The Battle of Cor-inth," 744–46.
[12] *Official Records*, XVII, Pt. 1, pp. 386–87; Tyler to Yancey, October 15, 1862, in Western Historical Collection.

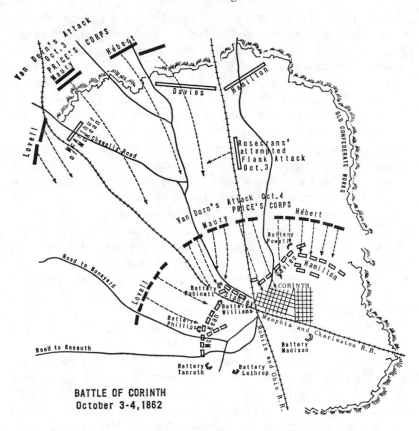

BATTLE OF CORINTH
October 3-4, 1862

Shiloh. Hébert, to Maury's left, likewise encountered a stubborn defense and had to fight for every inch of ground. As a result Confederate progress was slow, and the sun was beginning to sink below the horizon when the Union forces finally withdrew into Corinth's inner line of fortifications.[13]

Scores of Price's followers then sank down exhausted from heat and thirst. Price rode among them, sympathizing with their suffering, praising their courage, and declaring that the enemy were on the run. Cheers followed him, the wounded threw up their caps, and even

[13] *Official Records*, XVII, Pt. 1, pp. 167–68, 379–80, 386–87, 433, 456–57; Bevier, *First and Second Missouri Confederate Brigades*, 149–50; Calkins, "Fauntelroy's Diary," 34.

dying men waved to him. He sent his entire bodyguard with canteens to bring water and dispatched courier after courier to hurry up the surgeons and ambulances.[14]

Van Dorn, who had spent most of the day with Price, asked him whether in his opinion the attack should be continued. Price replied that his men could take Corinth, provided Lovell's division, which had done very little fighting, supported them. However, since it was not known that this would be the case, he believed it would be prudent to postpone the final assault until morning. Van Dorn agreed and ordered the battle broken off. Price's soldiers fell back a short distance to bivouac for the night.[15]

Many of the Confederates afterwards declared that by not pressing ahead with the attack when, so they believed, the Yankees were defeated, Van Dorn threw away a golden opportunity—perhaps his only real chance—of capturing Corinth.[16] And Van Dorn himself subsequently averred that if he had had only one more hour of daylight he would have carried all before him.[17] But in fact neither supposition seems warranted. Rosecrans had approximately ten to twelve thousand fresh troops in reserve and almost certainly would have been able to beat back the weary Confederates, who (in so far as Price's corps was concerned) already had committed their entire battle strength. Moreover, if Van Dorn desired an extra hour of daylight, so did his Union counterpart. All through the afternoon Rosecrans had attempted to deliver a crushing attack on the Confederate left flank (Hébert's division), but largely because of his own poorly worded orders had been frustrated. Even so, in the gathering dusk one of his brigades slipped through a gap in Hébert's line, took eighty prisoners, and threatened much greater damage before being forced to retire for lack of artillery support.[18]

Both commanders looked forward eagerly to grasping in the morning the victory which supposedly had eluded them in the evening. Rosecrans wrote Grant that if the Confederates "fight us tomorrow I

[14] Tyler to Yancey, October 15, 1862, in Western Historical Collection.
[15] *Official Records*, XVII, Pt. 1, pp. 379–80, 386–87, 433, 456–57.
[16] Bevier, *First and Second Missouri Confederate Brigades*, 150; *Official Records*, XVII, Pt. 1, pp. 415, 456–57; Tyler to Yancey, October 15, 1862, in Western Historical Collection.
[17] *Official Records*, XVII, Pt. 1, p. 379.
[18] Rosecrans, "The Battle of Corinth," 746–48; Williams, *Lincoln Finds a General*, IV, 88–89.

think we shall whip them."[19] And Van Dorn sent a dispatch to Richmond stating: "We have driven the enemy from every position. We are within three-quarters of a mile of Corinth. The enemy are huddled together about the town, trying to hold the position. So far all is glorious, and our men behaved nobly. Our loss, I am afraid, is heavy. It is near night. Lovell's and Price's troops have our thanks."[20]

During the night Van Dorn issued his orders for renewing the battle. They called for three batteries posted on a ridge west of Corinth to open fire on the town at 4 A.M. Then, at daybreak, Hébert would attack the Union right and try to outflank it. As soon as he was "heavily engaged" Lovell was "to move rapidly to the assault" against the enemy left, which he was to roll up by forcing his way "inward across the low grounds southwest of town." At the same time Maury would strike Rosecrans' center near the railroad junction. Thus the Federals would be assaulted simultaneously all along their line, and their flanks turned. Once driven from their works, they would have to retreat either to the east or to the south. But no matter which way, they would run into Armstrong's and Jackson's cavalry, which had been sent to block escape in those directions. If all went well, Rosecrans would be destroyed.[21]

Whether or not Van Dorn explained this plan to his generals and obtained their approval of it is not known; apparently he did not. Some of his brigade commanders later accused him of rashness in launching a frontal attack against strongly held fortifications, the exact character and location of which had not been ascertained.[22] But Van Dorn believed that Rosecrans had only fifteen thousand troops on hand and that it was absolutely necessary to engage him before he received reinforcements and the Confederates lost their numerical advantage. In other words, if Rosecrans were not defeated at once, he probably could not be defeated at all. As for the fortifications, it was impossible to reconnoiter them in the dark, the reports of spies had proved of little value, and in any case they could not be any more formidable than the ones so easily carried that morning.[23]

[19] *Official Records*, XVII, Pt. 1, p. 161.
[20] Quoted in Washington (Ark.) *Telegraph*, October 22, 1862. This message probably was the foundation for the subsequent allegation that Van Dorn announced that he had captured Corinth at the end of the fighting on October 3.
[21] *Official Records*, XVII, Pt. 1, p. 379.
[22] *Ibid.*, 415–16, 429, 431, 457.
[23] *Ibid.*, 433, 456–58.

As the night wore on, the Confederates heard the sounds of trains rolling and troops marching in Corinth. This caused some to say that the Federals were evacuating, others that they were reinforcing.[24] Actually, both guesses were wrong: Rosecrans was merely moving men and equipment into position to meet the expected Confederate onslaught. He himself remained awake, issuing orders and supervising their execution, until 3 A.M.[25]

He did not sleep long. Shortly after four, the Confederate batteries opened up. However, they did insignificant damage, and the far more powerful Union artillery, which included siege guns, speedily silenced them and subjected Van Dorn's troops to a harassing bombardment.[26] Even more injurious to Southern plans, Hébert's division failed to advance at the appointed time. Van Dorn, waiting nervously at his headquarters near the center of the line, sent a staff officer to inquire why; but the officer could not find Hébert. A second and a third messenger went, with no better luck. Finally, about seven o'clock, Hébert appeared and announced that he was sick. Price, who had joined Van Dorn, immediately ordered General Martin Green to assume command of the left wing. Green, one of his officers later testified, was "hopelessly bewildered, as well as ignorant of what ought to be done," and so another hour passed before Hébert's division was ready to attack.[27]

Meanwhile, a portion of Maury's division became engaged with enemy sharpshooters. As so often happens, this skirmishing rapidly developed into a full-fledged battle. Without waiting, as planned, for the left wing to attack, Maury's troops began moving forward. At almost the same time Green finally advanced. By 9:30 Price's entire corps was in action.[28] Only Lovell remained out of contact with the

---

[24] *Ibid.*, 396, 431, 433–35; Bevier, *Missouri Confederate Brigades*, 152. At the time Van Dorn was one of those who believed that the Federals were evacuating —an example of his tendency towards wishful thinking, another fatal defect in a general. See Earl Van Dorn to Sterling Price, 1 A.M., October 4, 1862, *Official Records*, XVII, Pt. 2, pp. 719–20.

[25] *Official Records*, XVII, Pt. 1, pp. 168–69.

[26] *Ibid.*, 387; Bevier, *First and Second Missouri Confederate Brigades*, 152–53; Rosecrans, "Battle of Corinth," 748–49.

[27] *Official Records*, XVII, Pt. 1, pp. 379, 387; Bevier, *First and Second Missouri Confederate Brigades*, 340.

[28] *Official Records*, XVII, Pt. 1, pp. 379, 387, 394; Bevier, *First and Second Missouri Confederate Brigades*, 152–53; Anderson, *Memoirs: Historical and Personal*, 235–37.

enemy. His division, after slowly and cautiously advancing a short distance, halted well beyond musket range of the Union line. Brigadier General John S. Bowen, whose brigade had been designated as the storming column, sent three separate couriers to Lovell urgently requesting his presence at the front. But Lovell did not appear nor did he issue any orders to attack.[29] Thus Price was left to fight the battle alone.

Price's men advanced shoulder to shoulder in columns of brigade strength. To a newspaper correspondent in Corinth it seemed as if a "prodigious mass, with gleaming bayonets, suddenly loomed out, dark and threatening" beneath the harsh Mississippi sun. When about three hundred yards from the Federal line they halted briefly to reform, then with a wild cheer swept forward on the double. A terrific fire hit them, but still they charged on, "their faces averted like men striving to protect themselves against a driving storm of hail."[30] At practically the same instant Green's Missourians and Maury's Arkansans and Texans struck Davies' division, which—badly battered in yesterday's fighting and poorly entrenched—broke and fled in confusion, uncovering the Union center. The exultant Southern infantry promptly poured through the gap and penetrated into the very streets of Corinth, reaching the railroad junction and capturing Rosecrans' reserve artillery.

Victory, gallantly won, seemed to be in Confederate hands. But now the lack of coordination in the attack produced its fatal effect. The Union divisions on either side of Davies, not being hard pressed, turned their cannons about and raked the Confederates with murderous crossfire. At the same time they detached large forces to bolster Davies, who rallied his troops and brought up reserves. Beset on front and flank, and unsupported because of the failure of Maury's reserve brigade to come up in time, the storming columns reeled backward. Then, as one of Van Dorn's staff later reported, they melted "like snow in thaw" under the deluge of Federal fire. The remnants either fled back across the fields over which they had so heroically advanced, or else by the hundreds threw up their hands in surrender. Farther to the left, the First Missouri Brigade desperately tried to hold

[29] *Official Records*, XVII, Pt. 1, 422.
[30] Quoted in Horace Greeley, *The American Conflict* (Hartford, 1864 and 1867), II, 228.

the redoubt it had captured but had to retreat when its ammunition gave out. Ordered to retake it, Brigadier General William L. Cabell wept as he led his Arkansas troops forward. Screaming fiercely, they reached the parapet, then broke, leaving behind one-third of their number dead, wounded, or captive.[31]

The attack east of the Mobile and Ohio Railroad had failed, but on the west side it continued with unabated fury. Here Moore's brigade of Maury's division, consisting of one Alabama regiment, one Mississippi regiment, two Arkansas regiments, and the Second Texas Sharpshooters, fought as hard as any Confederate troops anywhere fought during the whole war. Once already they had advanced across the level, tree-studded plain between the Chewalla Road and the Memphis and Charleston tracks, and they had been repulsed with heavy losses. Now they set forth on a second assault. Heading it, astride his horse, was Colonel William P. Rogers of the Second Texas. Marching in perfect formation, his men drove toward Battery Robinett, a redoubt on a slight hill just to the north of the railroad tracks. Rifle fire and canister ripped their ranks, but they stepped over the fallen and kept going. About a hundred yards from the battery they encountered a row of logs and sharpened stakes. At this point they broke into a run, and the straight lines gave way to a seething mass of yelling men. Urging them on, Rogers grabbed up the regimental flag from the third man to fall bearing it. His horse was shot from under him, but he scrambled to his feet, still carrying the flag, and climbed up the parapet, followed closely by scores of his soldiers. The defenders fled, abandoning their cannons, and Rogers lifted the flag in triumph—only to tumble backward from a bullet fired by a drummer boy. And as in the center, strong Union reserves hastened up to seal off the breakthrough. Soon Moore's troops

---

[31] *Official Records*, XVII, Pt. 1, pp. 379–80, 386–87, 396; Bevier, *First and Second Missouri Confederate Brigades*, 153–55, 341–42; Anderson, *Memoirs: Historical and Personal*, 237–39; Rosecrans, "The Battle of Corinth," 748–52: Williams, *Lincoln Finds a General*, IV, 92–94; Washington (Ark.) *Telegraph*, October 22, 1862. A soldier of the Fifth Missouri wrote the following description of the charge: "We advanced through open hilly ground on which there was not a single bush to screen a person from the terrible storm of shot and shell from their heavy siege guns, which were in full view for over a mile, and looked like if hell had been let loose. Shells bursting all around you; round shot plowing the ground everywhere; grape and cannister sweeping down the hill almost by the bushel; it is a miracle how anyone escaped." Thomas Hagan to Father, October 12, 1862, in Civil War Papers, Missouri Historical Society, St. Louis.

were pinned down by a withering fire from the front and on both flanks. Frantically waving handkerchiefs on sticks and bayonets, they cried "For God's sake, stop!" Almost the entire 45th Alabama fell captive, and those who did not surrender or manage somehow to escape were shot or bayoneted. The Federals found Rogers' dust-covered body lying in the ditch beneath the ramparts. Pinned inside his coat was a note telling whom to notify in case he was killed.[32]

Price's two divisions had fought magnificently; both had been cut to pieces. Out of approximately four thousand troops Maury took into battle, over two thousand were dead, wounded, or captured—and nearly half of these belonged to Moore's brigade. As for Hébert's division, it had lost fifteen hundred out of seven thousand, of which nearly one thousand came from the two Missouri brigades.[33]

Price was shocked when he saw his men—for the first time—retreat in utter rout. "My God!" he exclaimed, "my boys are running!" Then, with tears filling his eyes, he added, "How could they do otherwise—they had no support—they are nearly all killed." Van Dorn tried to console him by praising their courage and declaring that the failure of the attack was not their fault. But Price merely pointed toward Corinth and continued to weep.[34]

As the shattered remnants of Price's corps streamed back in defeat, Lovell's division still stood motionless. Finally Lovell responded to Bowen's messages and came to the front. He surveyed the Union positions through his binoculars but issued no orders to advance. One of his staff officers, however, asked General Bowen's opinion of the practicality of carrying the enemy works by storm. Bowen replied that he considered it a questionable enterprise under any circumstances. The officer then said, "Suppose General Lovell orders you to take it?"

[32] *Official Records,* XVII, Pt. 1, pp. 248, 398; Rosecrans, "The Battle of Corinth," 750–51; E. A. Pollard, *Southern History of the War* (New York, 1866), I, 519–20; F. T. Miller (ed.), *The Photographic History of the Civil War* (New York, 1912), II, 140–41, 146–47, 156, 160. This last work contains several photographs of Battery Robinett taken shortly after Rogers' charge. They show the bodies of Rogers and many of his men (see pp. 141, 145). They are among the most gruesomely fascinating photos of the Civil War. These and other photographs provided much of the basis for the description of Corinth and the battlefield.

[33] *Official Records,* XVII, Pt. 1, 382–83.

[34] Bevier, *First and Second Missouri Confederate Brigades,* 155; Maury, "Campaign against Grant," 299.

To this Bowen answered, "My brigade will march up and be killed." Shortly after this strange colloquy, Lovell received orders from Van Dorn to cover the retreat of the rest of the army. His division thereupon turned around and marched away.[35] It had engaged only in what the Union commander opposite described as some "heavy skirmishing," and most of its troops had not "burst a cap."[36]

At noon the Confederates began falling back on the same road over which they had advanced, leaving behind hundreds of wounded to be cared for by the enemy. Some of the harder-hit units were completely demoralized, there were hundreds of stragglers wandering about with glazed eyes, and only Lovell's division was capable of serious battle. Had the Federals counterattacked or pursued immediately, heavy losses, if not utter destruction, probably would have resulted. But Rosecrans was physically and psychologically exhausted by the two days of fighting, and although he had relatively fresh troops available was himself incapable for the time being of further action. Not until the next day did he begin pursuit, and then he bungled the job by jamming up his forces on the Chewalla Road, and neglecting to use a parallel road which offered a splendid opportunity, even with a late start, to intercept Van Dorn.[37]

The Confederate retreat continued until it reached Chewalla, where Van Dorn ordered a halt for the night. Price and the other generals were puzzled by this action, for the Tuscumbia River was only four miles away and it seemed mere common sense to place it between themselves and the Federals. Then that night the matter was explained: Van Dorn issued orders for a march against Rienzi in the morning! Instead of retreating, he proposed to turn about, capture Rienzi, and then attack Corinth again, this time from the south! It was, Maury remarked later, a plan worthy of Charles XII of Sweden (a leader known to his contemporaries as "Ironhead").

Price was amazed by Van Dorn's orders. They came, he felt, from

[35] *Official Records*, XVII, Pt. 1, p. 422.
[36] *Ibid.*, 338.
[37] Williams, *Lincoln Finds a General*, IV, 94–95, 101–102, 105; Tyler to Yancey, October 15, 1862, in Western Historical Collection. Rosecrans gave as his reason for not pursuing at once the exhaustion of his troops—as if they were any more fatigued than the Confederates! Actually it was Rosecrans who was exhausted; his fatal flaw as a commander was that battle left him physically, mentally, and emotionally depleted; this weakness ruined him at Chickamauga.

a mind rendered desperate by misfortune. Along with Maury and several other generals he at once went to Van Dorn. He told him that the troops were in no condition to fight another battle and that if they attempted a march to Rienzi the wagon train would almost inevitably be lost. Maury seconded these arguments; then speaking as a personal friend he added:

"Van Dorn, you are the only man I ever saw who loves danger for its own sake. When any daring enterprise is before you, you cannot adequately estimate the obstacles in your way."

Van Dorn was silent a moment, then replied: "While I do not admit the correctness of your criticism, I feel how wrong I shall be to imperil this army through my personal peculiarities. . . . I will countermand the orders and move at once on the road to Ripley."[38]

Price and Maury prevailed on Van Dorn to change his mind just in time. For as soon as Grant knew definitely that the Confederates were attacking Corinth, he had sent five thousand men from Bolivar under Major General Stephen A. Hurlbut to Rosecrans' relief. Hurlbut, after first marching to Pocahontas, early on the morning of October 5 was heading straight for Davis' Bridge on the Hatchie. If he reached it before Van Dorn, the Army of West Tennessee's retreat would be blocked, and it would be in dire peril of being crushed against the river by Rosecrans' pursuing forces.[39]

The Confederates began marching towards the Hatchie at sunrise. Van Dorn had no serious apprehension of encountering any opposition and so posted Maury's decimated division in front, while Lovell continued to cover the rear. At about 10 A.M. a courier from Wirt Adams, whose cavalry brigade had been left to guard Davis' Bridge, galloped up. "The enemy in heavy force," he reported to Van Dorn, "is moving from Bolivar to oppose the crossing of the Hatchie." Van Dorn turned to Maury, who was riding by his side, and said cheerfully, "Maury, you are in for it again today. Push forward as rapidly as you can and

---

[38] Dabney H. Maury, "Van Dorn, The Hero of Mississippi," in Miller, *A Soldier's Honor*, 294–95; Maury, "Campaign against Grant," 302; Tyler to Yancey, October 5, 1862, in Western Historical Collection.

[39] *Official Records*, XVII, Pt. 1, p. 305. Grant sent Ord to assume command of Hurlbut's column, which he did. But when Ord was wounded early in the fighting Hurlbut resumed command. In order to avoid confusion and unnecessary detail the Union force from Bolivar is referred to throughout as Hurlbut's.

occupy the heights beyond the river before the enemy can get them."[40]

As fate would have it, the survivors from Moore's brigade were in the van. Leading them at the double quick, Maury reached and crossed the bridge before Hurlbut arrived. But before he could form a line the Federals struck with overwhelming numbers. Quickly they routed Moore, took two hundred prisoners and four cannons, and seized the bridge. They then moved down the Chewalla Road, threatening thereby to capture the Confederate wagon train parked nearby. Ross's Texans and Cabell's Arkansans fought valiantly to stem their advance, but the ill-starred Mississippi brigade once more broke in the face of the enemy. Then, at the critical moment, Green's Missourians came panting up, and along with Maury's division succeeded in checking the enemy. The bridge, however, was irretrievably lost and Van Dorn's army appeared hopelessly trapped. In mingled despair and disgust a Missouri soldier declared, "We all thought Van Dorn had played hell at Elkhorn—but *now* he has done it, sure enough!"[41]

Fortunately for the Confederates, there was another way across the Hatchie. Branching off to the south from the Chewalla Road was a dirt trail that led to Boneyard, where it picked up the Jonesboro Road, which in turn crossed the Hatchie at Crum's Mill, where there was a dam that could be used as a makeshift bridge. Early in the morning Van Dorn had sent General Frank C. Armstrong to guard the Jonesboro Road and to destroy the dam. Armstrong had begun the work of destruction when he heard the sounds of battle at Davis' bridge. Realizing at once the situation now facing the army, he sent a courier to Van Dorn with word that a crossing could be made at Crum's Mill. Van Dorn, who subsequently claimed that he had planned from the first to go by way of Crum's Mill in case the bridge was blocked, ordered the wagon trains to move off on the Boneyard Road. At the same time he assigned Price the mission of holding Hurlbut at bay until the train had safely passed.[42]

Price's troops remained in action until 3:30, when they were relieved by Rust's brigade of Lovell's division. They then marched to

[40] Maury, "Campaign against Grant," 302–303.
[41] *Official Records*, XVII, Pt. 1, pp. 305–307, 380, 388, 394–95; Maury, "Campaign against Grant," 302–303; Bevier, *First and Second Missouri Confederate Brigades*, 158–60; Anderson, *Memoirs: Historical and Personal*, 241–42.
[42] *Official Records*, XVII, Pt. 1, pp. 300–301, 388, 396; Maury, "Campaign against Grant," 304; Anderson, *Memoirs: Historical and Personal*, 243–44.

Crum's Mill, reaching it at 9 P.M. The last of the wagon train was still crossing a bridge which Armstrong's cavalry had hastily constructed out of logs and puncheons found at the mill. It was so rickety that it had to be constantly repaired, a task to which Price gave his personal attention. Once, when a wagon knocked loose some of the puncheons, he helped replace them, employing his giant's strength to throw heavy rocks upon them to keep them in place. "His whole soul," wrote one of his followers, "appeared to be in the work, and when it was done, he straightened himself from his stooping posture and remarked, 'Well done, boys; now stand back and let the train pass.' "[43]

By 1 A.M. the entire army had crossed. In the morning it resumed its retreat, marching beneath incessant rain to Ripley, and from there to Holly Springs, where on October 13 it finally halted to recuperate, reorganize, and refit. Grant, believing it impossible to subsist large forces on the sparsely populated countryside, broke off the Union pursuit at Ripley.[44] Thus, two weeks after it started, the Corinth campaign ended. Confederate losses came to nearly 5,000 killed, wounded, and missing, or about a fourth of the original strength of the Army of West Tennessee; Union casualties were 2,500.[45]

[43] Bevier, *First and Second Missouri Confederate Brigades*, 161–63. Bevier cites "Covell's Diary," presumably the diary of an officer under Price, to the effect that when Van Dorn found himself trapped he relinquished command of the army to Price and entrusted him with the task of finding an escape route, and that Price did find the way out. Perkins, "Davis and Price," 475, implies the same. However, Price made no such claim in his report and there is no confirming evidence from a non-Missouri source. Van Dorn in his report does not mention either Price or Armstrong in this respect, but immediately after the campaign one of his staff officers declared in a letter to General Beauregard that Armstrong "saved the army" during the retreat (see *Official Records,* XVII, Pt. 1, 396). Unfortunately there is no report by Armstrong or any other cavalry commander on the Corinth campaign. Hartje, *Van Dorn,* 234–36, ignores this whole problem.

[44] *Official Records,* XVII, Pt. 1, p. 381; Anderson, *Memoirs: Historical and Personal,* 244; Williams, *Lincoln Finds a General,* IV, 102–105. Rosecrans wished to continue to pursue the Confederates, and after the war declared that Grant threw away a chance to destroy the remnants of Van Dorn's army and capture Vicksburg in the fall of 1862. (See Rosecrans, "The Battle of Corinth," 755–56). Lamers, *Edge of Glory,* 170–71, 178–80, supports this view, while Williams, *Lincoln Finds a General,* IV, 102–106, defends Grant's decision and heaps criticism on Rosecrans. Maury, "Campaign against Grant," 305–306, states that "a vigorous pursuit immediately after our defeat at Corinth would have . . . effectually destroyed our whole command."

[45] *Battles and Leaders,* II, 760. Slightly over 2,000 of the Confederate loss were prisoners.

News of the disaster at Corinth produced a fierce public outcry against Van Dorn. Editors and politicians throughout the South denounced him as a rash incompetent who had squandered the lives of his men in a "mad and hopeless" assault against an impregnable fortress. Some even declared that he had been drunk during the battle. But the most serious attack came from one of his own officers, General Bowen, who formally accused him of gross neglect of duty and "cruel and improper treatment" of his men. Van Dorn responded by asking for and obtaining a court of inquiry to investigate these charges. Price served as president of the court, which met at Abbeville, Mississippi, in late November. Van Dorn, who skillfully conducted his own defense, was able to demonstrate that Bowen's allegations were either untrue or unjust. Among those who testified in his behalf was Price himself. Indeed, when Van Dorn concluded a moving speech, Price openly wept. The proceedings terminated with the court unanimously acquitting the defendant on all counts.[46]

Van Dorn, in his report and at the court of inquiry, blamed his defeat on three occurrences, all of which, he contended, were beyond his control to prevent or remedy: (1) the exhaustion of his troops at the end of the first day's fighting, which along with the advent of darkness made it impossible to clinch the victory with a final push into Corinth; (2) the arrival of Union reinforcements during the night of October 3; and (3) Hébert's sudden illness, which resulted in the attack on the second day being late and uncoordinated.[47] To this list Price and his soldiers added Lovell's failure to attack. Had he done his duty, they bitterly asserted, the assault would have succeeded.[48]

The first of Van Dorn's reasons has already been shown to be of extremely doubtful validity; even if the Confederate infantry had been fresh and the sun high, Van Dorn probably could not have captured Corinth on October 3. The second one, like the first, derived from Van Dorn's miscalculation of Rosecrans' strength, a miscalculation on which his entire campaign floundered. Van Dorn, as previously stated, planned to strike at Corinth before Rosecrans could concentrate his forces—

[46] *Official Records*, XVII, Pt. 1, pp. 381–82, 414–59; Washington (Ark.) *Telegraph*, October 22, 1862; Miller, *A Soldier's Honor*, 319–20.

[47] *Official Records*, XVII, Pt. 1, pp. 378–81, 452–58.

[48] *Ibid.*, 434; Bevier, *First and Second Missouri Confederate Brigades*, 154; Anderson, *Memoirs: Historical and Personal*, 239; Tyler to Yancey, October 15, 1862, in Western Historical Collection.

exactly the same strategy he had attempted against Curtis in Arkansas. Since he knew that this offered his only real chance of victory, and since he was desperately anxious to win a victory, he deluded himself into thinking that his plan had succeeded and that he had a four-to-three numerical superiority over Rosecrans. Therefore, when on the second day of the battle the Federals threw in heavy reserves, it was both natural and inevitable that he erroneously concluded that the sounds of trains and marching men heard in Corinth during the night had marked the arrival of reinforcements. In brief, the battle of Corinth provides a classic example of wishful thinking leading first to defeat and then to an incorrect evaluation of the causes of that defeat.

As for Hébert and Lovell, their cases are apparently different but in essence are the same: Neither participated in nor cooperated with the attack on the second day. The former became, at a time and in a manner that are extremely suspicious, "ill"; the latter simply refrained from issuing any orders. Although there is no positive evidence to support such a view, probably both had concluded that an assault on Corinth was hopeless, and therefore decided to have no share in it. If this was the case, then like Longstreet at Gettysburg they probably were correct in their assessment of the tactical situation, but also like Longstreet on that occasion they were guilty of betraying the confidence of their commanding general.[49]

[49] No information is available as to the exact nature of Hébert's alleged "illness." Inevitably the question arises, why did he not immediately report this "illness" and arrange for Green to assume command of the division? Maury, writing in 1872, stated, "I have never understood the reason for so much delay" on the part of Hébert's division (see Maury, "Campaign against Grant," 296). Since Maury must have known of Hébert's "illness," it is obvious that he did not regard it as an adequate explanation or even believe that Hébert was really ill. In addition, Bevier, *First and Second Missouri Confederate Brigades*, 150, indicates that Hébert was guilty of not properly executing his orders on the first day of the battle. It is significant, too, that Hébert did not file a report on Corinth. Therefore, until and unless more evidence comes to light, it must be assumed that Hébert, like Lovell, simply declined to participate in the attack on Corinth. Van Dorn probably was aware of this attitude on the part of Lovell and Hébert but dared not make an issue of it because it would reflect on his own ability as a general (it is just possible that Lovell, a member of his class at West Point, had some sort of personal hold over him, too). And the Confederate authorities most likely took no action regarding Lovell and Hébert because it would not do to admit that Southern generals had refused—or failed —to carry out a direct order to assault the enemy. Both Lovell (who was already under a cloud for surrendering New Orleans without a fight) and Hébert were soon relieved of their commands and shunted to the sidelines.

There is, of course, no way of knowing for certain that the assault on Corinth would have succeeded if Hébert had advanced on schedule and Lovell had attacked according to plan. All that can be said definitely is that without a prompt advance on Hébert's part and without the support of Lovell, the assault, after initial victory, utterly failed. Or, to put it in a slightly different fashion, whatever slim chance the Confederates did have of taking Corinth was ruined by Hébert's "illness" and Lovell's inaction.[50]

However, in the final analysis the fundamental reason for the Southern defeat was an inadequacy in manpower and resources which not even the magnificent bravery of Price's soldiers could overcome. Rosecrans alone outnumbered Van Dorn, and Grant overall possessed at least a two-to-one superiority. To have had a better than even chance of capturing Corinth, Van Dorn's army should have been twice as large as it was. Indeed, what with the odds against them, the surprising thing is not that the Confederates were defeated, but that they came so close to victory. "We gave you," said a wounded Southern prisoner to Rosecrans after the battle, "the best we had in the ranch."[51] That best was very good—but it simply was not enough.

From the strategic standpoint, Van Dorn's Corinth campaign had two objectives: the direct one of opening the way for the recovery of west Tennessee, and the indirect one of aiding Bragg's army in Kentucky. The first obviously was not achieved; instead, Grant soon moved deeper into Mississippi in his first attempt to capture Vicksburg. As regards Bragg, the battle at Corinth probably had little or no effect on his operations, although he subsequently cited Van Dorn's defeat as one of the reasons he retreated from Kentucky.[52] In any case, the great

[50] Maury, "Campaign against Grant," 298, stated that "it is altogether probable that had the attack with the right wing been pressed by the centre and left, Van Dorn would have captured Corinth and the enemy's army."

[51] Rosecrans, "Battle of Corinth," 751–52.

[52] Bragg in a letter to his wife, quoted in Stanley F. Horn, *The Army of Tennessee* (Indianapolis and New York, 1941), 188. Even if Van Dorn had won at Corinth, Bragg would have retreated from Kentucky, forcing Van Dorn either to fall back also or else preventing him from advancing northward. There had not been the mass uprising of Kentuckians in favor of the Confederacy that Bragg had expected, and his army was in danger of being overwhelmed by much larger Union forces. On the other hand, supposing Bragg's strategic position had been good in Kentucky, Van Dorn's defeat would have, in all probability, forced him to abandon his northward thrust and fall back southward.

Confederate counteroffensive in the West ended in failure on both fronts, and the Union armies once more began to push southward.

Price's performance during the Iuka-Corinth operations apparently did not enhance his reputation,[53] but certainly it did nothing to impair it. In fact, his record was quite commendable. He acted prudently in carrying out Bragg's instructions, and if he failed to accomplish his mission it was mainly because of insufficient strength and Van Dorn's uncooperative attitude. In view of the outcome, he was probably right in advising Van Dorn to wait for the exchanged prisoners before attacking Corinth. He helped save the Army of West Tennessee by joining with Maury in opposing Van Dorn's proposed movement against Rienzi. And of paramount importance, the troops under his command fought with a gallantry, endurance, and determination that marked them as among the best in the entire Southern army. His only serious mistake was lingering too long at Iuka, and even here he was essentially the near-victim of Bragg's long-distance orders and Van Dorn's failure to obey those orders promptly. All in all, the judgment of the rank and file was sound. As an Alabama soldier wrote to his wife soon after Corinth: "Our army blames Van Dorn, but no one utters a syllable of censure for Price."[54]

Although the court of inquiry exonerated Van Dorn of Bowen's charges, it could not restore to him the confidence of the government, the public, and the troops. Bragg in particular was harsh in his criticism of the Mississippi Hotspur—harsh but correct. Writing to Davis on October 25, he stated: "I regret to add that there has been a want of cordial co-operation on the part of General Van Dorn since his department was merged with mine. No return or report is ever received from him unless I demand it specifically, and generally I have to send a staff officer to execute my orders. . . . The general is most true to our cause and gallant to a fault, but he is self willed, rather weak minded and totally deficient in organization and system. He never knows the state of his command and wields it only in fragments."[55]

In November, as part of a general reorganization of military affairs

[53] Reynolds, "Price and the Confederacy," 40.

[54] Quoted in Hudson Strode, *Jefferson Davis: Confederate President* (New York, 1959), 317. There is nothing in Strode's biography of Davis about relations between the Confederate President and Price.

[55] Braxton Bragg to Jefferson Davis, October 25, 1862, quoted in Ellsworth Eliot, *West Point in the Confederacy* (New York, 1941), 131–32.

in Mississippi, Van Dorn was relieved of command and assigned a cavalry division. This proved more suitable to his talents and temperament. Early in December he led a dashing raid that destroyed Grant's main supply depot in Mississippi and forced him to abandon his first campaign against Vicksburg. On the strength of this achievement, he became chief of cavalry in Bragg's army and won several more notable victories. But just as it seemed that his luck had turned, a civilian who accused him of seducing his wife murdered him at Spring Hill, Tennessee on May 7, 1863.[56]

---

[56] Williams, *Lincoln Finds a General*, IV, 196–202; Miller, *A Soldier's Honor*, 246–55, 349–54. Van Dorn's friends denied the charge of adultery and contended that the murder was the result of a personal grudge arising out of political reasons. The assassin, who carefully planned his crime, escaped into the Union lines. Hartje, *Van Dorn*, 307–23, presents all the available evidence on the matter but does not come to any specific conclusions.

7

RICHMOND

Immediately following the Corinth campaign Price renewed his efforts to return with his Missourians to the Trans-Mississippi. With reason he believed that they had contributed their full share to the defense of Mississippi—of the eight thousand men he had brought from Arkansas more than half were now dead or lying in hospitals. It was time, therefore, that the survivors be allowed to fight once again for their own homes on their own soil.

Price made his feelings known to Lieutenant General John C. Pemberton, who had superseded Van Dorn as commander of the Department of Mississippi. Pemberton responded by recommending to Secretary of War Randolph that both the Missouri and Arkansas regiments be transferred.[1] He did so, however, in the belief that Price's troops were of such poor quality as to constitute a military liability, a notion which derived from exaggerated reports of their demoralization at Corinth and from a statement by Lovell to the effect that "Price's army was an armed mob, without drill or discipline, unsoldiery in appearance and equipments, and withal a disgrace to the service."[2] But when, a few days after writing Randolph, he inspected the Army of the West at Holly Springs, he withdrew his recommendation of transfer—"I have just witnessed a review [of Price's troops] and am much pleased with them."[3] Ironically, the Missourians, having learned of Lovell's slander, had gone to extra lengths to make a good showing during the inspection. From the standpoint of realizing their desire to getting back to the other side of the Mississippi, they would have done better to have reverted temporarily to their Cowskin Prairie days.[4]

Early in November the Confederate forces in Mississippi fell back before Grant to Abbeville. From there on November 15 Price addressed a long and impassioned letter to Secretary Randolph. He began

[1] *Official Records*, XVII, Pt. 2, p. 739.
[2] Bevier, *First and Second Missouri Confederate Brigades*, 164–65.
[3] *Official Records*, XVII, Pt. 2, p. 740.
[4] Bevier, *First and Second Missouri Confederate Brigades*, 164–65.

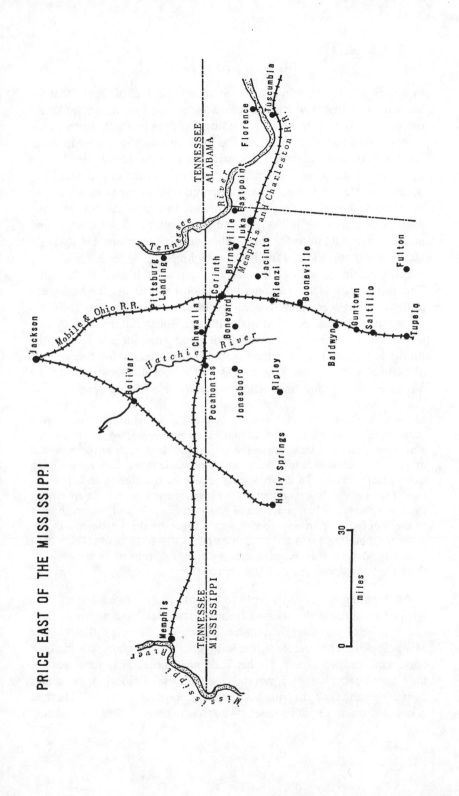

PRICE EAST OF THE MISSISSIPPI

by quoting Randolph's June promise, made in behalf of Davis, that the Missouri contingent would be returned "so soon as it can be safely spared," the time of transfer depending "on the possibility of throwing troops across the river . . . or on the military operations now in progress." He then pointed out: "Nearly five months have passed since that promise was made. The military operations then in progress have been completed. The troops can be spared with as much safety at this as at any time in the immediate future, and the possibility of throwing them across the river is likely to diminish daily, and the officers and men . . . are clamorous for the fulfillment of your promise. I do hope that you will not delay its fulfillment any longer."

Price continued with additional arguments for immediate transfer. The appearance of his veterans in Missouri would inspire heavy enlistments; they were now so sadly reduced in numbers that their absence from Mississippi could make little military difference; they had joined the Confederate army with the understanding, based on the President's assurance, that they would be used solely for the defense of their own state; and, finally, Missouri's "peculiar position" in the war made their return an absolute necessity. He further observed:

The State is and has been for nearly a year in the actual military possession of the enemy, and it is but natural that her people should begin to fear that a treaty of peace will leave her in the Union and drive such of them as take up arms into exile. It is that belief which prevents them from entering the Confederate service. To do so is only to devote themselves and theirs to ruin. They believe, however, that if the Government would make an earnest effort to achieve the independence of Missouri it would succeed and bind it to the Confederacy in any contingency. Those of them who are in the army are therefore anxious that such an effort should be made. They insist that they at least may be permitted by the Government to make it. Is there anything unreasonable in this request?

Anticipating the obvious reply to this question, Price added: "It is not just to say that the soldiers from other States have as much right to ask to be sent to their own States. The case is entirely different. The Mississippian, wherever he fights, knows that he is fighting for his own home and his own liberty, for his State must necessarily form part of the Confederacy; but this is not the case with the Missourian; he cannot fight under any such cheering belief except upon his own soil." He then concluded on an ominous note: "The troops here . . . are . . . clamoring to be led back to Missouri; their terms of service begin to expire next month; they do not admit the right of the Government to conscript them; they will claim their discharges. The Government may choose to force them to continue in the service. I confide in its wisdom not to do so. It will be far better to act justly, and in a spirit of conciliation to order myself and the troops under my command back to Missouri in accordance with your and the President's promises."[5]

Davis' reaction to this letter, with its imputation of bad faith on his part and its implied threat of mutiny, can be readily imagined. Moreover, it scarcely could have been written at a less opportune time. Grant, at the head of a powerful host, was driving on Vicksburg, and Pemberton, far from being disposed to give up any of his badly outnumbered army, was calling for all the troops he could get. On November 26 Randolph's newly appointed successor, James A. Seddon, transmitted a copy of the letter to Pemberton, whom he authorized to retain Price's men if they were deemed essential to military operations in Mississippi. Pemberton, of course, so deemed them. Not only that, but acting on further instructions from the War Department, he ended the meaningless existence of "The Army of the West" as a separate command and reconstituted it as the "Second Corps, Department of Mississippi and East Louisiana."[6]

In December disaffection reached such proportions among the Missouri troops, who had been consolidated into one brigade under General Bowen, that one company, its term of enlistment having expired, threatened to desert and return to Missouri. Price personally assembled it, declared it under arrest, and then roared out: "All of you who want to re-enlist, step forward; all of you who want to be shot, stand still." There was an instant shuffling of feet as all the men moved forward.[7]

Following this incident Price issued a special order warning the Missourians against desertion and assuring them that he was making every effort to secure their return to the West. They had, he admitted, "seeming cause to believe that the Government has designedly entrapped them into its service," but while "the Government may have erred," it has not "willfully or intentionally wronged" them. "If the major-general commanding believed . . . that the Government had acted . . . basely,

[5] *Official Records*, XVII, Pt. 2, pp. 759–61.
[6] *Ibid.*, 757, 759, 787.
[7] William L. Webb, *Battles and Biographies of Missourians* (Kansas City, Mo., 1900), 283; Reynolds, "Price and the Confederacy," 66.

he would place himself at your head and lead you back to the State of your devotion and his love, and no obstacle should prevent him."[8]

Shortly after Price issued this order—which in effect declared that under certain circumstances he would lead a military uprising—President Davis visited Mississippi on an inspection tour. On Christmas Eve he reviewed the Missouri troops (who cheered him as they marched past), and Price took the opportunity to bring up again the question of transfer. But the answer remained the same: The Missourians could return west as soon as they could be spared in the East. Finally, in late January, following Grant's retreat and the end of any immediate threat to Vicksburg, Price again secured leave of absence and accompanied by Snead headed for Richmond, resolved to secure a transfer or else resign his commission and go back to "bushwhack it" in Missouri.[9]

By now Davis and his cabinet were thoroughly exasperated by what they considered to be Price's unreasonableness, obstinate pertinacity, and near insubordination. Furthermore, two recent developments had intensified their doubts about his loyalty and trustworthiness. The first involved his oldest son Edwin W. Price. Familiarly known as "Stump" Price because of his short stature, Edwin had served as a brigadier general in the state guard during the 1861 campaigns. In February, 1862, while on a recruiting expedition, he had been captured by the Federals under circumstances which seemed to indicate that he had wanted to be taken prisoner. Early in October, through the official intervention of President Davis, he had been exchanged for a Union general and had rejoined his father in Mississippi. But instead of remaining, he had promptly resigned his commission and returned to Missouri, where he soon obtained, at the behest of Governor Hamilton Gamble, a pardon from Lincoln. In addition, he had publicly renounced the Confederacy, and the St. Louis *Republican* had predicted in a leading editorial that the elder Price would soon follow his son's example.[10]

The other development had to do with the so-called "Northwest Confederacy." This concerned a scheme to detach the northwestern states from the Union and to form a separate nation which would form an alliance with the Confederate States of America. Among the states

[8] *Official Records*, XVII, Pt. 2, pp. 794–96.

[9] *Ibid.*, XXII, Pt. 1, p. 906; Bevier, *First and Second Missouri Confederate Brigades*, 166–67, 348–55; Reynolds, "Price and the Confederacy," 41–44.

[10] Reynolds, "Price and the Confederacy," 38–39; *Official Records*, Series II, Vol. IV, pp. 642–43; 742; St. Louis *Missouri Republican*, October 23, 1862. The case of Edwin Price will be examined later in a different context.

to be included was Missouri, and rumor had it that Price was the military head of the movement, a rumor which derived support from the fact that J. W. Tucker's newspaper, *The Argus*, now at Jackson, Mississippi, and commonly regarded as Price's organ, had published a number of articles favorable to the Northwest Confederacy. This same journal, incidentally, constantly criticized Davis for his "injustices" to Price and the Missouri troops.[11]

All in all, the prospects were that Price's second trip to Richmond would produce an explosion far exceeding the first one: that it did not owed largely to the timely intercession of Thomas Reynolds. In April, 1862, after being rebuffed by the Missouri congressional delegation in Richmond, who told Reynolds he was meddling in their affairs, he had retired to his family estate at Winnsborough, South Carolina.[12] There, late in December, he received word that Claiborne Jackson had died near Little Rock on the sixth and that he was now the governor of Confederate Missouri. Reynolds assumed the office without joy, but with a strong determination to establish and maintain his authority. As always he was sustained by a belief in his own superior capabilities, and he was confident that his personal friendship with President Davis would prove a valuable asset to both himself and Missouri.[13]

Early in January he journeyed to Richmond. Price was still in Mississippi, but the "Price embroglio," as Reynolds later termed it, was at its peak. At first he joined the Missouri delegation in urging the immediate return of Price and his troops to the Trans-Mississippi. But as soon as he became aware of Davis' feelings in the matter he adopted a different course. The very existence of Missouri as a Confederate state, he believed, depended on establishing "cordial relations" with the President so as to forestall a peace treaty which would leave Missouri under Union rule. To this all-important end he was prepared to sacrifice a great deal—his "personal feelings and interests," if need be, and certainly the aspirations of General Price.[14]

[11] Reynolds, "Price and the Confederacy," 39–40. As with Edwin Price, the Northwest Confederacy and Price's connection with it will be taken up later.
[12] *Ibid.*, 34–36.
[13] Thomas C. Reynolds to John B. Clark, December 27, 1862, and Thomas C. Reynolds to James T. Thornton, February 17, 1863, in Thomas C. Reynolds Papers, Library of Congress.
[14] Reynolds to Thornton, February 17, 1863, Thomas C. Reynolds to Thomas L. Snead, May 26, 1864, Thomas C. Reynolds to James A. Seddon, January 31, 1863, all in Thomas C. Reynolds Papers, Library of Congress.

Therefore, he devoted himself to seeking an accommodation between the government and its disgruntled general. As regards Price,
who arrived in the capital at the end of January, he endeavored to induce him to agree to return to Arkansas without the Missouri brigade,
on the condition that it would be sent to join him as soon as possible.
Price was very reluctant to consent to this arrangement; he wanted his
veterans as the nucleus for the new army he proposed to raise in Missouri. He feared that they might mutiny if he left them in Mississippi,
and he did not trust the Confederate authorities to keep their word.
However, when it became apparent that it was this or nothing and that
Reynolds would not revive the state guard for his benefit, he agreed.[15]

This accomplished, Reynolds had little difficulty obtaining the concurrence of Davis and Secretary of War Seddon; although Price's troops
could not be spared at present in Mississippi, Price himself could be—
and quite happily! On February 5 Seddon directed the new commander
of the Trans-Mississippi Department, Lieutenant General Edmund
Kirby Smith, "to arrange with General Pemberton for exchange of
troops from your command on the west of the river for the command
of General Price, whom it is the desire of the [War] Department to
transfer as soon as existing necessities will allow."[16] Reynolds showed
a draft of Seddon's letter to Price, who declared that he was satisfied
with it—provided, however, that "instructions equally strong and explicit" were sent Pemberton, who was "anxious to retain troops so
valuable" as the Missourians. Seddon, on Reynold's advice, did as
Price wished, writing General Pemberton on February 6 that the War
Department hoped it would be possible to return "General Price, with
his Missouri troops, to the Trans-Mississippi Department . . . without
delay." Yet, in his instructions to both Kirby Smith and Pemberton,
Seddon emphasized that the Missourians were to recross the river only
if they were replaced by an equal force from the Trans-Mississippi and
only if their departure would not jeopardize the safety of Vicksburg.
This obviously fell far short of the unconditional order for an immediate transfer that Price desired. But, just as obviously, it was the most
he could hope for. Therefore he accepted it, and on February 10 started back for Mississippi.[17]

15 Reynolds, "Price and the Confederacy," 46–48.
16 Reynolds to Seddon, January 22, January 31, 1863, in Thomas C. Reynolds Papers, Library of Congress; *Official Records*, XXII, Pt. 2, pp. 780–81.
17 *Official Records*, XXII, Pt. 2, 781–84; Reynolds to Seddon, February 5,
16, 1863, Reynolds to Thornton, February 17, 1863, in Thomas C. Reynolds

While Price was still in Richmond, Reynolds had questioned him about his relations with Davis and the Northwest Confederacy scheme. Price had disclaimed all knowledge of a movement to overthrow the President in the summer of 1862, had denied that he had any connection whatsoever with the Northwest Confederacy, and had declared that the *Argus* was not his organ—that indeed he had written Tucker requesting him to modify the anti-Davis tone of the paper, only to have the "Deacon" reply that he would edit his journal according to his own notions. For reasons of delicacy, Reynolds had not asked Price about his son Edwin, but from other sources he had learned that angry remonstrances and deep groans had been heard coming from Price's tent as he unsuccessfully tried to dissuade his son from deserting the Confederate cause.[18]

Reynolds was satisfied with Price's statements about Davis and the proposed new Confederacy, and he was disposed to dismiss the case of Edwin Price as simply an unfortunate event. But, shortly after Price left Richmond, Reynolds had a conversation with Dr. Montrose A. Pallen, a Missourian and until recently Price's medical director. Pallen asserted that Price had told him, during the course of a social evening, that Edwin was still loyal to the Confederacy, that he had gone back to Missouri in order to keep alive the Southern spirit and to recruit troops, and that he was merely pretending to accept Union rule as a means to this end. Price, Pallen added, had not asked him to keep secret this revelation of Edwin's mission.

Reynolds was greatly alarmed by Pallen's testimony, the truthfulness of which he could not doubt. Why, he wondered, had not Price informed either the Confederate government or himself (the Governor of Missouri and a friend) that his son was acting as an undercover agent? Could it be that the two Prices were in collusion for some object hostile to the Confederacy? Or were they working for a goal hostile to both the Union and Confederate governments, such as the formation of a Northwest Confederacy? In any case, the fact, apparent at least, that neither Price saw anything immoral in such a course, involving as

---

Papers, Library of Congress; Reynolds, "Price and the Confederacy," 47–51. In addition to Reynolds and the Missouri delegation, the Arkansas congressmen and Governor Flanagin of Arkansas urged Price's transfer to the West. Price, according to Reynolds, had hoped to be named commander of the Trans-Mississippi Department.

[18] Reynolds, "Price and the Confederacy," 42–46.

it did gross deception of the Federal authorities and insubordinate concealment from the Confederate officials, spoke extremely ill of their personal integrity and moral sense.

Reynolds advised Pallen to keep quiet about Edwin Price, then pondered what steps he should take in regard to the father. At first he thought of compelling him to resign, but he quickly decided that this would be inexpedient. The Confederacy needed men, and Price's presence in the West would attract recruits. On the other hand, if forced out of the army, Price might join the Unionists; or go to Missouri and "bushwhack it" on his own as he had threatened; or perhaps even proclaim himself the revolutionary governor of the state. Furthermore, using an alleged intrigue on the part of his son to dismiss him would cause great controversy and create sympathy for him as an innocent victim of personal vindictiveness on Davis' part, thus strengthening the antiadministration faction in the South. Finally, he doubted if Price was capable of any overt act of separation from or opposition to the Confederacy; he reflected, too, that no matter how reprehensible the means, Edwin Price might serve to advance the Confederate cause in Missouri. He was confident that Price's ambition was gratified by sending him on an independent command to Missouri, and that he would abandon any desire, real or suspected, of going it alone, and would be of use to the Southern war effort. Reynolds even considered the possibility that after liberating Missouri Price might lead an expedition into Illinois, authorized and controlled by the Richmond government, in aid of a Northwest Confederacy!

For all of these reasons (and also probably because he had absolutely no proof to offer) Reynolds decided not to mention Pallen's story to Davis or any of his cabinet. He did, however, feel obligated to take precautions against Price's doing anything in the West which might endanger or embarrass the Confederacy. Therefore, he went to Davis and proposed that he, Reynolds, confer with Secretary of State Judah P. Benjamin, the President's closest advisor, on "Missouri and North West affairs." Davis agreed, and Reynolds and Benjamin soon afterwards met; their topic was Price.

Benjamin "earnestly and with evident sincerity declared that neither the President nor any of his advisers had the slightest prejudice against General Price; that they had every inclination to afford him the amplest scope for patriotic ambition." But, unfortunately, "his restlessness, the dictatorial tone of his friends in urging his advancement, their habit of threatening if their demands were not at once granted, and bringing congressional and newspaper 'Pressure' to bear in his favor," along with "his propensity to get into quarrels with both his superior officers, his associates and subordinates, had done him great injury." Moreover, "the connection of his name with the proposed prununciamento against the President in the spring of 1862, and with the suspicious 'North West' move, coupled with the other facts before stated, and the doubts of military men concerning his military capacity, made it the duty of the government to look carefully to eventualities in assigning him to a sphere of action."

Reynolds, who agreed with Benjamin's assessment, suggested that Richmond follow a "generous policy" toward the Missouri general "in the way of giving him commands affording legitimate spheres for a patriotic ambition," and promoting him for "any *real* success"; but that it place "*under* him officers of such unquestionable fidelity and subordination, as well as capacity for controlling their troops, that should he even attempt any insubordinate or independent movement, he would find himself without support, and either quickly abandon it, or be easily crushed." Benjamin accepted this advice "as at once just and even generous to General Price, at the same time securing the government and the cause against danger." He also stated that "the perfect confidence" Davis had in Reynolds "induced him to apprehend little or no danger from General Price's restless ambition," for Reynolds "should be constantly near him."

As the result of his talk with Benjamin and of subsequent ones with Davis and Seddon, when Reynolds left Richmond for the Trans-Mississippi late in February, he carried unofficial letters from the President to Kirby Smith and Holmes (the latter now commander of the District of Arkansas) placing him "on a confidential footing with them"—in fact constituting him as "a kind of unofficial adviser" to the two generals. In addition he solicited and obtained a promise from Davis "that no appointment or promotion of a general officer in the Missouri Confederate troops" would be made without first consulting him.[19]

The only source of Reynold's part in "smoothing over" the "Price

[19] *Ibid.*, 54–61.

embroglio" is Reynolds himself. However, his account is supported in general by the *Official Records* and by other indications, and so can be regarded as substantially true. Whether his suspicions of Price in connection with Edwin, the Northwest Confederacy, and so forth, had any foundation in fact will be considered subsequently in a more appropriate context. Without doubt—and this for the present is the only important point—he held such suspicions, and this, along with desire to foster good relations with Richmond and his penchant for manipulation, led him to take measures that had the effect of placing Price's future career in his custody. Price at the time probably had no inkling of Reynolds' arrangements with the Confederate authorities, but he did resent the governor's influence and distrusted his friendship with the President. Thus, on returning to Mississippi, he spoke disparagingly of Reynolds as a Confederate office-holder (Reynolds held a commissionership which he had not yet resigned), and expressed skepticism that he would ever leave Richmond. These indiscreet remarks were soon relayed to Reynolds, naturally producing resentment and further suspicion of the general on his part.[20]

As could have been predicted, Kirby Smith and Pemberton failed (in fact did not even try) to work out an exchange of troops between their respective departments, and Pemberton continued to insist that the Missouri Brigade was absolutely essential to the safety of the fortress he was destined to lose so ingloriously. However, on February 27, per instructions from Richmond, he relieved Price of his command and ordered him to report for duty in the Trans-Mississippi Department.[21] The following day Price bade the men of the Missouri Brigade farewell. With tears in his eyes he told them that he was leaving them only to seek the liberation of their state and that the Secretary of War had promised that they would soon follow. But, as one of the Missourians later recalled, "the hearts of the men were sad, for they truthfully apprehended, notwithstanding his cheering words, that it might be a long time ere they would again follow the banner under which they had endured so much and had gained so many successes."[22]

For awhile Confederate military and civil officials feared that Price's departure would lead to mass desertions, perhaps mutiny, among the Missouri troops. Indeed, he himself had often warned that this might

20 *Ibid.*, 62–63.
21 *Official Records*, XXII, Pt. 2, p. 791.
22 Bevier, *First and Second Missouri Confederate Brigades*, 167–68.

happen. But nothing of the sort occurred, and when Reynolds visited the men in May on his way to the Trans-Mississippi, he found that while they still hoped to return to Missouri, they wanted to do so via New Madrid or Kentucky, not through Arkansas, of whose cold and barren mountains they had only the most bitter recollections. In fact, according to Reynolds, rather than go to Arkansas again, they preferred to remain in the East.[23] And, as the fortunes of war had it, so they did. They fought at Vicksburg and became prisoners with its fall; exchanged, they served in the Atlanta campaign; then under Hood they marched into Tennessee, where at Franklin they were decimated; and in April, 1865, the last remnant, four hundred men, were overwhelmed and captured in a hopeless defense of Mobile.[24] They were undoubtedly one of the elite units of the Confederate army, fighting with consistent gallantry from the banks of the Missouri River to the coast of the Gulf of Mexico.

Price, accompanied by his staff and a bodyguard of cavalry, crossed the Mississippi on March 18 and a week later arrived in Little Rock. On April 1 he took command of an infantry division in the District of Arkansas.[25] The division consisted of a brigade of Arkansas troops under Brigadier General D. H. McRae and a Missouri brigade commanded by Brigadier General M. Monroe Parsons, formerly of the state guard. To the Missourians Price distributed a number of beautiful battle flags he had received from a group of New Orleans ladies. However, Parsons' men refused to use the flags, which had a red cross on a white field, on the grounds that they were Catholic! Price thereupon told them that the colors were those of the Crusaders and that they were the crusaders of this age. Their Protestant prejudices thus placated, they henceforth carried the banners proudly.[26] Price's return was hailed by the Western press and did much to dispel the gloom which had settled among the troops as a result of recent defeats in Arkansas.

[23] Thomas C. Reynolds to Waldo P. Johnson, May 26, 1863, in Thomas C. Reynolds Papers, Library of Congress; Reynolds, "Price and the Confederacy," 66–69.

[24] Bevier, *First and Second Missouri Confederate Brigades*, 252, 254, 268; Anderson, *Memoirs: Historical and Personal*, 396–99.

[25] Calkins, "Fauntelroy's Diary," 42; Diary of John T. Appler (MS in Civil War Papers, Missouri Historical Society, St. Louis).

[26] "Paper by Capt. McNamara," St. Louis *Missouri Republican*, December 5, 1885.

8
HELENA

During Price's absence much had happened in Arkansas, but little had changed. In June, 1862, Brigadier General Thomas C. Hindman took command of the state's defense. Vigorous and efficient, he proceeded to requisition supplies, draft men, and create a new army practically from scratch. The citizenry of Arkansas, unaccustomed to vigor and efficiency in public officials, denounced him as a "military tyrant." However, they might conceivably have forgiven his transgressions of frontier laissez faire had he been successful in repelling the Yankees, who once again invaded the northwestern part of the state. But as it was, he was resoundingly defeated on December 7 at the Battle of Prairie Grove, only a few miles from Pea Ridge. The victorious Federals then advanced and occupied Fort Smith and Van Buren, and the army which Hindman had so quickly raised even more quickly melted away from disease and desertion. In addition, Union forces seized Helena and Arkansas Post, thus opening the state to attack from the east.

These setbacks resulted in discontent and even disaffection among the people of Arkansas, produced a storm of angry criticism of Hindman (who, at his own request, was transferred to the East), and led to the appointment of Kirby Smith as commander of the Trans-Mississippi Department, superseding Theophilus Holmes who assumed command of the District of Arkansas. At the time of Price's arrival, Holmes's entire army consisted of only 12,500 men, most of whom were low in morale, poorly equipped, inadequately fed, and (according to the report of a Union spy) "without shoes or hats, and clothed in rags."[1] Attempts to bolster their ranks by means of the hated conscription laws met with little success, and deserters were so numerous that eventually it was necessary to promise them a pardon if they returned voluntarily to the army. But few came back; instead many joined the Federal army or else formed guerrilla bands which terrorized the populace and defied all efforts to suppress them.[2]

---

[1] *Official Records*, XXII, Pt. 2, p. 225.
[2] *Ibid.*, 796–97, 802, 810–12, 872; Thomas C. Reynolds to William Preston Johnston (aide to Jefferson Davis), August 27, 1863, in Thomas C. Reynolds

Holmes, while in command of the Trans-Mississippi, had lost the confidence and respect of civilians and soldiers alike. Although an experienced professional and possessed of many estimable personal qualities, he was elderly, ailing, half deaf, weak willed, vacillating, and devoid of energy. Newspapers called him an "old fogy," his troops referred to him as "granny Holmes," and in the opinion of several medical men he suffered from "softening of the brain" and was in his dotage. Yet, despite the public scorn, of which he must have been aware, and even despite the fact that he vaguely sensed his own inadequacy, he persisted in remaining on active service in a top command. And Davis, out of friendship and regard for Holmes's devotion to the Southern cause, ignored the well-founded complaints against him and the pleas that he be removed.[3]

Holmes's successor, pious and bespectacled Kirby Smith, was thirty-nine, West Point trained, and had performed well both in Virginia and Kentucky. Although disposed to be somewhat self-righteous, he was brave, hard working, and, if not brilliant, definitely competent. From the first he realized that his post offered little prospect of glory and that his primary task would be administration: The Trans-Mississippi, huge in area and already practically severed from the rest of the South, was as much a semiautomonous nation as it was a military theater, and its problems as much financial and political as strategic. Accordingly it was necessary for him, greatly against his personal inclinations, to leave the actual conduct of operations in the field to the district commanders, exercising himself as a rule only a general supervision.

The sending of Kirby Smith to command in the West represented an attempt by Richmond to compensate for its past appointments in that region. By 1863 the Trans-Mississippi had become the junkyard of the Confederate army. In it were collected the military flotsam and jetsam of the South, men such as Holmes, John B. Magruder (who had been made commander of the District of Texas), and Gustavus W. Smith, all of whom had been found wanting in the East and so sent where pre-

---

Papers, Library of Congress.

[3] Marshall (Texas) *Republican*, January 22, 1863; Washington (Ark.) *Telegraph*, June 24, 1863; John C. Moore to Editor, in St. Louis *Missouri Republican*, April 10, 1886; Diary of Dr. R. J. Bell (MS in Civil War Papers, Missouri Historical Society, St. Louis), August 12, 1863; Reynolds to Johnston, August 27, 1863, in Thomas C. Reynolds Papers, Library of Congress; *Official Records*, XXII, Pt. 2, pp. 856–59; Edwards, *Shelby and His Men*, 107.

sumably they would do the least harm. Moreover, it had been drained of its best fighting men—Hood's and Ross's Texans, Cleburne's Arkansans, Taylor's Louisianians, and Price's Missourians—and those who remained were, with some notable exceptions, not of the same splendid quality. Understandably, therefore, many people in Arkansas, Louisiana, and Texas concluded that since the Confederate government did not regard the Trans-Mississippi as very important to the war, then the war was not very important to the Trans-Mississippi. Besides, cotton was a far more interesting—and profitable—concern than the rather remote battlefronts. As Lee marched towards Gettysburg and Grant invested Vicksburg, a large cotton speculation combine involving army officers openly operated in Texas.[4]

During the spring and summer of 1863 the role assigned to the Trans-Mississippi in Confederate grand strategy was, as always, a supporting one. It was to help in the defense of Vicksburg by creating a diversion which would take some of the pressure off Pemberton. To this end the War Department repeatedly urged Kirby Smith to "throw troops across the river," or to strike at the Union bases in Arkansas and Louisiana, or at least to harass Grant's supply line down the Mississippi.[5] However, April and May passed without any significant action by the Trans-Mississippi forces. It was not so much that Kirby Smith did not try to do something—he did. Rather, it was simply that he lacked the men and material to do anything effective.

Price, upon arriving in Arkansas, predictably proposed an invasion of Missouri for the purpose (so he argued) of drawing off Federal forces from Vicksburg. And, in fact, the time was fairly opportune for such a venture, as the regular Union troops had been stripped from the state to reinforce Grant and for the most part only widely dispersed militia were left. But Holmes refused to sanction a Missouri expedition, maintaining that it would be too hazardous and that it would leave the vital Arkansas Valley open to enemy occupation. In this view he was supported by Kirby Smith, who believed that no movement should be made into Missouri unless with a force strong enough to remain.[6]

Early in June, Price, on orders from Holmes, marched his division to Jacksonport, where he assumed command of all Confederate forces

[4] *Official Records*, XXII, Pt. 2, p. 872.
[5] *Ibid.*, Pt. 1, p. 407; *ibid.*, Pt. 2, pp. 834–35, 852–53.
[6] *Official Records*, XXII, Pt. 2, pp. 308–309, 849, 856, 863, 871; Snead, "Conquest of Arkansas," 454–56.

in northeast Arkansas and moved toward the Missouri border. His first act at this new post was to issue a strong denunciation of lawlessness and plundering by Southern troops in the area. The clearly implied target of this blast was Brigadier General John S. Marmaduke's cavalry division. Marmaduke, who will be remembered as the reluctant leader of the stand of the state guards at Boonville in 1861, had recently made a raid through southeast Missouri. Two Confederate officers, one of them a participant in the raid, had informed Price of the indiscriminate pillaging carried on by Marmaduke's men and the adverse effect this had on the civilian population.[7] The young and proud Marmaduke immediately wrote Price denying the allegations against his division and declaring that they were nothing but "idle tales."[8] Thus originated an animosity between Price and Marmaduke which subsequent events intensified and which ultimately had serious consequences.

Before going to Jacksonport, and after a Missouri campaign had been ruled out, Price urged Holmes to attack the Union garrison at Helena.[9] Secretary of War Seddon suggested the same, and Kirby Smith authorized Holmes to act on the matter "as circumstances may justify."[10] By capturing the town, it was argued, the Confederates would be in a position to block Union riverboats carrying supplies and rein-

[7] Lee Crandall to Thomas L. Snead, May 16, 1863, in *Official Records*, XXII, Pt. 2, p. 840; M. Jeff Thompson to Sterling Price, May 20, 1863, in *ibid.*, 844. Crandall was the officer who participated in the raid. Thompson was the most prominent Confederate leader in southeast Missouri and his testimony that Marmaduke's men were guilty of wanton pillaging in the region can be regarded as conclusive. Furthermore it is backed up by the report of Governor Reynolds' adjutant general, who investigated the matter on orders from Reynolds (see Thomas C. Reynolds to M. Jeff Thompson, June 3 and June 5, 1863, in Thomas C. Reynolds Papers, Library of Congress). Holmes, on learning of the complaints against Marmaduke, telegraphed Kirby Smith that Marmaduke was "not equal" to the command of a division. After failing to get a replacement for Marmaduke, Holmes sent Price to Jacksonport and deprived Marmaduke of two of his four brigades (*Official Records*, XXII, Pt. 2, pp. 846, 851). Edward's account of Marmaduke's "Cape Girardeau Expedition" in *Shelby and His Men*, 151–63, like most of his writings, is merely a fantasy erected on a rickety scaffold of facts.

[8] John S. Marmaduke to Sterling Price, June 6, 1863, in *Official Records*, XXII, Pt. 2, pp. 861–62.

[9] Reynolds, "Price and the Confederacy," 77; Thomas C. Reynolds to E. C. Cabell, July 4, 1863, in Thomas C. Reynolds Papers, Library of Congress. Snead, "The Conquest of Arkansas," 455–56, implies that Price had no part in the decision to assault Helena. But this implication is definitely contradicted by Price to Holmes, June 9, 1863, in *Official Records*, XXII, Pt. 2, p. 863.

[10] *Official Records*, XXII, Pt. 1, p. 407.

forcements to Grant, and if Vicksburg fell they would still have a foothold on the Mississippi. In any event, the operation would have a diversionary value, and the Trans-Mississippi Department at least would have made an attempt to aid Pemberton.

On June 8 Holmes started from Little Rock with the intention of conferring with Price about Helena. But before he reached Jacksonport his ambulance broke down (a characteristic Holmes mishap) and he was obliged to return. However he sent a note asking Price whether the condition of his troops justified an attempt on Helena. Price replied on the ninth that his soldiers were "fully rested and in excellent spirits," and that from "the most reliable information General Marmaduke can obtain, the enemy have not more than 4,000 to 5,000 at Helena, and were a movement conducted with celerity and secrecy . . . I entertain no doubt of your being able to crush the foe at that point."[11]

Holmes at first accepted then rejected Price's advice, but finally on June 15 he telegraphed Kirby Smith: "I believe we can take Helena. Please let me attack it." Then, without waiting for the reply, which was "Most certainly do it," he journeyed (this time without accident) to Jacksonport to make arrangements for the campaign.[12] He still had serious misgivings about it, for on meeting Price he declared: "I risk much in this expedition; you have a great reputation with the public, and if I am blamed for it. I expect you to sustain the propriety of it." Price promised to do so.[13]

On June 22 Price's division set out from Jacksonport. It consisted of 1,227 infantry under McRae, 1,868 under Parsons, and 1,750 cavalry under Marmaduke. Holmes's plan called for Price to march to within a few miles of Helena, where he would be joined by a brigade of Arkansas infantry from Little Rock commanded by Brigadier General James F. Fagan, and by Brigadier General Marsh Walker's cavalry division, which was already operating in the vicinity. Once concentrated, the army would total about 8,000 men. Holmes took the field to lead it in person.[14]

From the start nothing went right for Price. Heavy rains fell day

[11] *Ibid.*, Pt. 2, p. 863.
[12] *Ibid.*, Pt. 1, pp. 407–409.
[13] Reynolds to Cabell, July 4, 1863, in Thomas C. Reynolds Papers, Library of Congress.
[14] *Official Records*, XXII, Pt. 1, pp. 408–409, 413.

General Sterling Price

The Battle of Pea Ridge. Price is the central figure, on horseback, with his arm in a sling. The Elkhorn Tavern is in the right foreground (note elk's head on roof).

Major General Earl Van Dorn

General Edmund Kirby Smith

Major General Benjamin McCulloch

Major General James F. Fagan

Thomas C. Reynolds, Confederate governor of Missouri, 1862–65

Governor Claiborne Fox Jackson of Missouri

Major General John S. Marmaduke

General Jo Shelby

Battle of Big Blue, October 22, 1864

Close Up. Double Quick.

Both of the above scenes were painted by Samuel J. Reader, who served in the Kansas militia against Price in October, 1864.

 Family of General Price after shipwreck while on the way to join Price in
Mexico. Mrs. Price, center; bearded man, rear left, Celsus Price; young woman
at right, Stella Price.

Edwin Price

Confederate generals in Mexico after the Civil War. Front row, seated, left to right: Cadmus M. Wilcox, Sterling Price, Thomas C. Hindman; standing, John B. Magruder, William P. Hardeman.

after day, causing the rivers and swamps to overflow and turning the
region between Jacksonport and Helena into "one vast lagoon." The
foot soldiers slogged along in water to their waists, tormented constantly by swarms of flies and mosquitoes. Much of the way they had
to push, drag, and sometimes even carry the wagons and cannons. And
since there was no pontoon train, numerous bridges had to be constructed or tedious crossings made on rafts. The inevitable result was
that it took Price's column ten days to march sixty-five miles, and it
did not link up with Fagan and Walker until July 3, four days later
than scheduled.[15]

Thus the Confederates failed to gain one of the ingredients named
by Price for a successful assault on Helena—celerity. The other one,
secrecy, likewise was lacking. Even before Price left Jacksonport, the
Union commander at Helena, Brigadier General Benjamin M. Prentiss,
received word that Holmes was planning to make an attack. Subsequent information, plus unusual activity by Confederate cavalry outside the town and the attitude of Southern adherents inside it, seemed
to confirm the report. Hence, Prentiss (who, incidentally, was the general exchanged for Edwin Price) alerted his four thousand troops and
strengthened the fortifications. These last consisted principally of four
2-gun batteries situated on the hills immediately surrounding Helena
and connected by riflepits. Backing them up was a large redoubt, Fort
Curtis, located on level ground west of the town. In addition, Prentiss
obtained the services of a gunboat, which cruised the river, its huge
guns ready to support the land defenses. And finally, in order to forestall a surprise, he instructed the garrison to be up and under arms at
2:30 every morning, and had the roads leading to Helena obstructed
with fallen timber.[16]

On the morning of July 3 Holmes conferred with his generals at the
Allen Polk house five miles west of Helena. Gloomily he announced
that the Union fortifications were "very much stronger" than he had
supposed before undertaking the expedition. Price thereupon proposed
that, instead of assaulting the town, they besiege it and try to starve the

[15] *Ibid.*; Dr. R. J. Bell Diary, June 27, 28, 29, 30, 1863; Edwards, *Shelby
and His Men*, 164; Diary of Dr. W. M. McPheeters (MS in W. M. McPheeters
Papers, Missouri Historical Society, St. Louis), July 1, 1863.
[16] *Official Records*, XXII, Pt. 1, pp. 352, 387–88; Edwin C. Bearss, "The
Battle of Helena," *Arkansas Historical Quarterly*, XX (1961), 258–65.

garrison into surrender. Just how this was to be accomplished with the Federals controlling the river and able to supply themselves at will, he did not explain. Holmes, however, was determined to go ahead with the attack no matter what; indeed, the only practical alternative would have been for his army to march back by the way it came—a humiliation which must have seemed to Holmes at the time worse than defeat. "General Price," he declared, "I intend to attack Helena immediately, and capture the place, if possible. This is my fight. If I succeed, I want the glory; and if I fail, I am willing to bear the odium. At twelve o'clock, tonight, we move towards Helena."[17]

He then issued the attack orders. Price, with McRae's and Parson's brigades, was to drive the Federals from Graveyard Hill due west of the town; Fagan was to seize Hindman Hill directly to the south; and Marmaduke, supported by Walker, was to break through on the north side near the river. All three assault columns were to go into action "at daylight"—a most unprecise designation of time. Holmes's generals agreed to this plan and the conference ended.[18] Before leaving, Price assured Holmes: "As sure as the sun rises, the fort on Graveyard Hill will be ours." Replied Holmes, "That is the way I like to hear a general talk."[19]

At midnight the Confederates began converging on Helena from three different directions. Price's route lay across steep hills and deep ravines, and it was necessary to leave the artillery behind. In addition, his troops experienced much fatigue, particularly in making their way through and around the road obstructions. When within one and a half miles of Graveyard Hill he halted, fearful that he would arrive on the battlefield too early. This, it turned out, proved to be a bad mistake, but Holmes, who accompanied Price's column, made no objection at the time. As day began to break Price resumed the march, only to stop again about a half mile from the Union lines in order to form McRae's and Parson's brigades into assault columns. This necessary maneuver completed, he pushed forward until his skirmishers came under heavy fire. At this point the civilian guides ran away and some confusion and delay ensued until another guide was found. Then, following another

[17] *Official Records*, XXII, Pt. 1, p. 409; Snead, "The Conquest of Arkansas," 456; Edwin A. Pollard, *The Lost Cause* (New York, 1866), 397.
[18] *Official Records*, XXII, Pt. 1, pp. 409–10.
[19] "Paper by McNamara," St. Louis *Missouri Republican*, December 5, 1885.

short advance, Price rested his weary troops in preparation for the charge. At the same time he ordered McRae to take up position on Parson's left, after which both brigades, according to previously issued instructions, would attack simultaneously.[20]

It was now an hour since daylight, and Fagan's brigade, which had gone into action without waiting to make sure that Price would be in support, was suffering severely from enfilade fire from Graveyard Hill. Observing this, Holmes rode up to Price and angrily asked why he had not yet attacked. Price answered by describing the unexpected delays and exhausting toil experienced by his troops while getting into position. He then sent a staff officer to Parsons to ascertain why he was not advancing. Parsons replied that he was waiting for McRae to come up. Actually, however, McRae was in position, but owing to an intervening ridge Parsons could not see him, and apparently he did not think of sending anyone to look for him! Fearful that McRae would attack unsupported, Price immediately ordered Parsons to assault the Federal works without further delay.

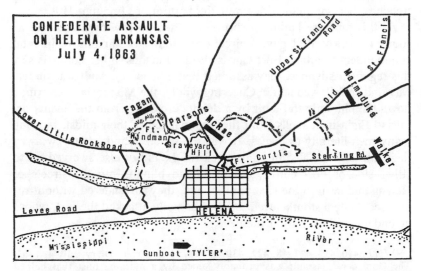

CONFEDERATE ASSAULT
ON HELENA, ARKANSAS
July 4, 1863

Fortunately the order arrived in time and both brigades charged together and in good order, giving a "great shout" as they did so. A storm of bullets, grape and canister ripped their ranks from front and flank

[20] *Official Records*, XXII, Pt. 1, pp. 403–14, 417, 421.

but they did not waver and in one quick rush they carried Graveyard Hill and planted the Confederate flag on its summit. Price's gunners followed close behind the infantry, hoping to turn the captured Union cannons against the town. But the Federals had spiked them before re-treating, and the blocked roads made it impossible for Price to bring up his own artillery. The other commanders experienced the same diffi-culty—only two Confederate batteries managed to take part in the fighting, and the gunboat quickly silenced one and rendered the other harmless.[21]

The charge up the rugged, timber-strewn slopes of Graveyard Hill had thrown Price's troops into considerable disarray. Soon they came under a terrific bombardment from Fort Curtis, the gunboat, and the adjoining Union positions. Unable to reply effectively and suffering heavy losses, they milled about in confusion or else crouched behind the earthworks they had so gallantly taken. Meanwhile, Marmaduke and Walker on the north failed to make any headway whatsoever, and Fagan's Arkansans, after overrunning several lines of outlying trenches, became pinned down at the bottom of Hindman Hill.[22]

At this juncture Holmes, who had ridden up to Graveyard Hill as soon as it was carried, gave a direct order to one of Parsons' regimental commanders to attack Fort Curtis. When Parsons' other colonels saw this regiment advance, they assumed that a general assault was under-way and so followed suit.[23] Cheering wildly, the Missourians swarmed down the hill, only to be hit by a deadly cross-fire from the enemy ar-tillery. Eight-inch shells from the gunboat fell in their midst, blowing many men literally to pieces. It was too much. Hundreds threw away their muskets and fled in panic back up the hill or else swerved off to either side of Fort Curtis and wandered blindly into the streets of Helena and even to the riverbank, where they surrendered without re-sistance. Only a stouthearted handful actually attacked the fort, whose defenders easily repulsed them.[24]

[21] *Ibid.*, 410, 414, 417–18, 421, 430, 435–37; McPheeters Diary, July 4, 1863. The Confederate assault was probably aided by a morning mist that helped conceal their movements from the defenders.

[22] *Official Records*, XXII, Pt. 1, 410–11, 414, 425.

[23] *Ibid.*, 421–22. This according to Parsons. Holmes made no mention of the incident in his report, as he had every reason not to. Probably the regiment ordered by Holmes to advance into Helena was the 10th Missouri.

[24] *Ibid.*, 411, 414–15, 421–22. In his report Holmes stated: "Most of my loss

Holmes, unaware that Price had already issued similar instructions, next ordered Parsons to support Fagan by attacking the rear of the Union works on Hindman Hill. Then, after sending a staff officer to inform Price of this order, he rode back down the hill to his headquarters. On the way he met McRae and, according to his official report, directed him to join his brigade in the captured redoubt.[25] McRae, however, subsequently stated that Holmes ordered him to attack Hindman Hill also.[26] If this is true, then Holmes was guilty of the incredible blunder of giving commands that would have resulted in all the Confederates abandoning Graveyard Hill!

In any event, Holmes's orders were not executed. McRae and Parsons, on conferring with each other, agreed that the latter's brigade, being the stronger, should remain on the hill while the former went to Fagan's aid. Price approved this arrangement, and McRae with only two hundred men—all he could collect—moved around to the north side of Hindman Hill. But when he attempted to charge up the hill, a withering Union fire stopped his troops in their tracks and forced them to take cover in a ravine. Another attack by Fagan, who tried to take advantage of the temporary diversion created by McRae, also failed. Thus the entire front of the Confederate offensive came to a complete and bloody standstill.[27]

Seeing this, Holmes rode back up Graveyard Hill to ascertain if his orders had been carried out. Inside the works he met Parsons, who told him that McRae had gone to Fagan's assistance and that only three hundred to four hundred men remained on the hill. Unable to locate McRae (whom he later unjustly accused of misbehavior in front of the enemy)[28] and noting that Fagan was being pushed back by a Federal counterattack, Holmes at 10:30 A.M. directed his forces to withdraw. They did so in good order, with Prentiss making no attempt to pursue. That night they camped about five miles from Helena, then in the

---

in prisoners resulted from not restraining the men after the capture of Graveyard Hill from advancing into the town, where they were taken mainly without resistance." This, to say the least, is an ambiguous way of describing it!

[25] *Ibid.*, 411, 414.

[26] *Ibid.*, 418.

[27] *Ibid.*, 414–15, 418, 422, 425.

[28] A court of inquiry, after investigating Holmes's charges, declared McRae guiltless (*ibid.*, 438). Price (*ibid.*, 416) praised McRae highly.

morning began a slow and arduous retreat that finally took them to
Des Arc on the White River.[29]

The same day that Holmes attempted to storm Helena, Vicksburg
fell to Grant and Lee retreated from Gettysburg. Thus the Confederate
debacle in Arkansas was overshadowed by these greater disasters, just
as it was far less important in its consequences. Nonetheless it was bad
enough. Out of an army of less than 8,000 Holmes lost 1,636 killed,
wounded, and missing without serving any purpose whatsoever beyond
inflicting slightly over 200 casualties on an enemy protected by trenches
and ramparts.[30] Little wonder, then that in his report on the battle he
stated: "I write this . . . with a deep pain."[31]

The attack on Helena was a blunder in its very conception. In the
first place, as Horace Greeley caustically commented, the only real
hope the Confederates had of taking it was for Prentiss to have been
"a coward, a traitor, or an idiot."[32] Second, if by some chance they
had captured it, they could not have held it more than a day or two
in face of the Union gunboats.[33] And finally, although there was no
way for them to know it at the time, they made the attempt far too
late to help Pemberton in any case.

Holmes's battle plan called for a coordinated converging attack,
and as usual in the Civil War (or for that matter in any war) it did
not come off. In his report Holmes blamed the failure on the indiscipline
of his troops, McRae's alleged misconduct, and Price's delay in attacking Graveyard Hill. As regards the first charge, it need only be pointed
out that troops capable of making an all-night march across rugged
terrain, and of taking Graveyard Hill, and almost carrying Hindman
Hill against such formidable opposition, were not lacking in what is
called battle discipline. As to the second one, McRae's innocence has
already been demonstrated and it was confirmed by a court of inquiry.
And as to the third one against Price, two observations are in order:

(1) Both McRae and Parsons in their reports emphasize the need
for frequent halts in approaching Helena, and in fact indicate that

[29] *Ibid.*, 411, 415.
[30] *Ibid.*, 389, 411–20. Of the Confederate casualties, only 76 were suffered by
Marmaduke's and Walker's cavalry. Price's division suffered 1,078—nearly
two-thirds of the total Confederate loss.
[31] *Ibid.*, 411.
[32] Greeley, *The American Conflict*, II, 320.
[33] Snead, "The Conquest of Arkansas," 456.

they, not Price, originally ordered these halts. McRae is especially outspoken on the subject of the difficulties encountered during the night march and in taking position for the assault: "I must here call . . . attention to the fact that the information concerning the localities, strength of the enemy, &c, was very erroneous. The ground over which we move was almost entirely impracticable; the crest of the [Graveyard] hill so narrow that it would have been murder to have attempted to have assaulted along it; the sides of the hill, full of gulches, with almost perpendicular sides, and that covered with fallen timber, so placed as to most impede an approach . . . ."[34]

(2) Holmes neglected to mention that he accompanied Price's division during its approach march and that tacitly at least he consented to the several halts that it made prior to reaching Graveyard Hill. Moreover, once he saw that Price was going to be late in attacking and that the garrison had not been surprised, he should have ordered Fagan to postpone or suspend his attack until Price was ready to support him. Although it is extremely unlikely that this would have made any difference in the ultimate outcome of the battle, it at least would have given the Confederates a better chance to achieve victory, and have prevented many unnecessary casualties. Finally, it should be noted in Price's favor that his troops were the only ones to carry their objective: perhaps the fact that they were rested before attacking might possibly have had something to do with their success.

Holmes's direct orders to regimental and brigade commanders after the seizure of Graveyard Hill were the acts of a man in a state of panic. In his report he tried to explain his strange conduct by stating that he could not locate Price, but no one else seemed to have had any such difficulty, and Holmes himself stated that he rode up the hill with Price.[35] Possibly he lost confidence in Price's ability to command his division—in which case he should have relieved Price on the spot and announced that he was assuming personal charge. But more likely

[34] *Official Records*, XXII, Pt. 1, p. 419.

[35] Price greatly resented Holmes's assertion that he could not find Price on Graveyard Hill, which implied cowardice on Price's part. According to Reynolds, who states he got his information from Price himself, Price, at the suggestion of Major John Tyler of his staff, let Holmes ride up to Graveyard Hill first so as to allow him the "eclat" of being the first general officer to enter the captured works. Price then followed and remained on the hill until ordered by Holmes to withdraw. See Reynolds, "Price and the Confederacy," 80–83.

he became frantic at the prospect of disaster—a disaster which his ill-advised interference only served to make more certain and much greater. According to Major John Edwards, who participated in the attack on Helena, Holmes deliberately courted death during the fighting, and after the battle "remarked gloomily . . . that to him death upon the field was preferable to disaster and that he had prayed for it earnestly when the attack proved a failure."[36]

Holmes's decision to attack Helena was motivated by a sincere desire to do something to relieve Vicksburg. But it also was undoubtedly the result of either a conscious or unconscious yearning to restore his tarnished reputation with a resounding victory. Naturally the ensuing fiasco had precisely the opposite effect. The people of Arkansas, led by their press, angrily demanded his removal, and—far worse to a professional soldier such as Holmes—the army openly scorned him. Heartsore and humiliated, on July 23 he turned over the command of the District of Arkansas to Price. He gave illness as his reason for doing so.[37]

[36] Edwards, *Shelby and His Men*, 182. For a somewhat different appraisal of the reasons for Confederate defeat at Helena, see Bearss, "Battle of Helena," 293. Williams, *Lincoln Finds a General*, V, 11–18, 289–91, gives essentially the same analysis of the Helena operations as presented here. Holmes's lack of ability to command on the battlefield, as well as his tendency to panic under stress, was demonstrated in the Battle of Malvern Hill during the Seven Days (see Freeman, *Lee's Lieutenants*, I, 581–614). To assign him to an active and important field command in the wake of that performance was an inexcusable blunder on the part of Davis.

[37] *Official Records*, XXII, Pt. 2, p. 942; Reynolds to Cabell, July 20, 1863, in Thomas C. Reynolds Papers, Library of Congress.

9

LITTLE ROCK

The army that Holmes turned over to Price was badly dispirited by the mauling it had received at Helena. An officer from the inspector-general's staff who visited it in August reported that "a great number of desertions . . . have occurred and are daily taking place, particularly in the case of Fagan's and McRae's brigades. . . . With few exceptions, there is too little pride and effort at soldierly bearing among the officers, and too much familiarity between them and the men. . . . The general officers of the command are zealous and competent, but are in a measure paralyzed in their endeavors by a lack of hearty co-operation from their subordinate officers. . . . A lethargy seems to have fallen on the troops of the command."[1] Even in Colonel Jo Shelby's "Iron Brigade," perhaps the best cavalry unit in the West, there was so much dissatisfaction that Shelby predicted "there will in all probability be numerous desertions."[2]

With his forces in this sad condition, Price faced the prospect of a Union expedition against Little Rock. The same day he replaced Holmes (who remained, however, in nominal command of the district), he wrote Kirby Smith that a northern army estimated to be 60,000 strong was gathering to invade the Arkansas Valley from three directions. He would, he declared, endeavor to defend Little Rock because it was the state capital and the key to the Arkansas Valley, but he doubted it would be possible to hold it with the forces presently available to him—"four weak brigades of infantry and 3,000 or 4,000 cavalry, miserably supplied with artillery, and disheartened by repeated defeats."[3]

Price evidently hoped that Kirby Smith would send him reinforcements; if so, he was doomed to disappointment. In the first place, Kirby Smith did not consider Little Rock to be in any immediate danger—the Federals, he predicted, would wait until winter, when the Arkansas River was higher and they could use their gunboats,

[1] *Official Records*, XXII, Pt. 2, p. 1049.
[2] *Ibid.*, 923–24.
[3] *Ibid.*, 941–42; *ibid.*, LIII, 884.

before moving against the town. Second, large Union armies threatened Louisiana and Texas, and Kirby Smith simply had no troops to spare for Arkansas. Finally, he believed that the best strategy for the defense of the Trans-Mississippi was to concentrate his forces in the Red River Valley, thus drawing the Federals deep into the interior where their long communication lines would expose them to disaster. Suspecting that this was his intention, Governor Harris Flanagin of Arkansas and other prominent citizens warned him that failure to hold the state would have calamitous political and military consequences, but he paid them no heed. In fact, he would have preferred to have voluntarily abandoned large areas of his department in order to achieve a concentration of his widely dispersed forces. But since public opinion made this impossible, he looked to enemy pressure to produce the same result.[4]

Kirby Smith's prognosis of enemy action in Arkansas proved wrong. On August 11 a force of six thousand blueclad infantry, supported by thirty-nine cannons, left Helena and marched to Clarendon on the White River, where it linked up with an equal number of cavalry that had moved down from southeast Missouri. Commanding the expedition was tough, determined, and clever Major General Frederick Steele. Its purpose was primarily political—to set up at Little Rock a Union state government which would serve as a rallying point for the numerous Unionists and disaffected Confederates in Arkansas.[5] Steele's army, which included several Negro regiments, had been hard hit by illness, and he disgustedly termed it "the poorest command I have ever seen, except the cavalry."[6] The latter were headed by Brigadier General John W. Davidson, an able and experienced regular army officer.

After crossing the White River, Steele pushed on to Devall's Bluff, then to Brownsville (present-day Lonoke), which he reached August 25. Price's cavalry under Marmaduke and Walker endeavored to delay his advance by burning bridges and obstructing roads; at the

    [4] *Official Records*, XXII, Pt. 2, pp. 945–46, 958–59, 988–90.

    [5] *Ibid.*, Pt. 1, pp. 472–76; Thomas C. Reynolds to George C. Watkins, October 31, 1863, in Thomas C. Reynolds Papers, Library of Congress. Originally Steele's army was organized to halt a thrust into southeast Missouri, which the Federals erroneously thought Price was planning.

    [6] *Official Records*, XXII, Pt. 1, p. 472.

same time, it destroyed cotton and removed slaves lying in the path of the Union army. On August 27 at Reed's Bridge on Bayou Meto, Marmaduke temporarily checked Steele by burning the bridge. But Price, fearful of being outflanked, pulled his forces back, and on September 6 Steele crossed the bayou without opposition at Shallow Ford.[7]

By failing to make an all-out stand at Bayou Meto, Price probably threw away his best chance of turning back the Union drive.[8] But by now Price was more concerned with saving his army than with holding Little Rock. Not only was he faced with Steele's superior forces, but two other Federal columns had seized, respectively, Monroe, Louisiana, and Fort Smith, Arkansas, thus endangering his communications from both the south and west. His sole hope of success, as he saw it, was for Steele to make a frontal attack on the riflepits which had been hastily constructed two and a half miles east of Little Rock on the north side of the Arkansas River. However, it was extremely unlikely that Steele would be so obliging. The Arkansas was fordable in many places, and by crossing to the south bank Steele could easily turn the Confederate entrenchments. Hence, even before the Federals reached Bayou Meto, Price began preparing for an evacuation. He shipped as much of the public stores as transportation permitted to Arkadelphia and threw a pontoon bridge across the river so that his forces could quickly retreat southward. Indeed, Governor Flanagin had already moved his capital to Washington, Arkansas.[9]

In addition to these worries, Price learned at midnight on September 5 that a duel was impending between Marmaduke and Walker! Bad feeling had existed between the two generals ever since the battle at Helena, where according to Marmaduke's official report Walker had been guilty of gross military misconduct.[10] Then, during the operations against Steele, Marmaduke had publicly implied that Walker had displayed cowardice at Reed's Bridge and in a subsequent skir-

[7] *Ibid.*, 473–76, 520–21.

[8] Leo E. Huff, "The Union Expedition Against Little Rock, August—September, 1863," *Arkansas Historical Quarterly*, XXII (1963), 236.

[9] *Official Records*, XXII, Pt. 1, 520–21.

[10] See Marmaduke's report on Helena, *ibid.*, 437, and Edwards, *Shelby and His Men*, 164–68, denouncing Walker. Walker presented his side in *Official Records*, XXII, Pt. 1, p. 433, and he is convincingly defended by Williams, *Lincoln Finds a General*, V, 15.

mish. Walker thereupon challenged Marmaduke to a duel and Marmaduke accepted. Price tried to forestall so disgraceful an affair by ordering both officers to stay in their quarters for the next twenty-four hours. Unfortunately, his order did not reach Walker, and Marmaduke ignored it. The duel, which was fought with revolvers at fifteen paces, took place early on the morning of September 6 near Little Rock. Both men fired and Walker fell mortally wounded. Price immediately placed Marmaduke and his seconds under arrest, but the inconvenience and danger of a complete change in the command of the cavalry while in the close presence of the enemy, coupled with the pleas of Marmaduke's officer, caused Price to suspend the arrests and restore Marmaduke to his command during the pending operations.[11] No subsequent action, however, was taken against Marmaduke. In fact, the young general came out of the Little Rock campaign with an enhanced military reputation, especially among his own men, who earlier had been threatening to desert him *en masse* out of disgust for his ineptitude.[12] But of greater eventual consequence, his misconduct, insubordination, and arrest worsened relations between him and Price.

Steele did as Price had feared. On the morning of September 10 he crossed Davidson's cavalry to the south side of the Arkansas at Terry's Ferry, about ten miles east of Little Rock. Moreover, he showed, in Price's words, "excellent judgment" by selecting a point where the river made a horseshoe loop to the north, upon the sides of which he stationed five batteries of artillery. When Walker's division, now under the command of Colonel Archibald S. Dobbin, attempted to block Davidson's passage, the Federals swept the area with a concentric cross-fire that quickly silenced the Confederate cannons and forced Dobbin to retreat. Davidson then advanced along the south bank while Steele with the Union infantry marched up the opposite side. Price, on learning of the crossing, declared that he was "not going to be trapped in Little Rock like Pemberton was at Vicksburg" and ordered his army to evacuate the town. To cover this movement

[11] *Official Records*, XXII, Pt. 1, pp. 524–26; Edwards, *Shelby and His Men*, 173–86. A detailed account of the Marmaduke-Walker affair is provided in Leo E. Huff, "The Last Duel in Arkansas: The Marmaduke-Walker Duel," *Arkansas Historical Quarterly*, XXIII(1964), 36–49.

[12] Reynolds to Clark, December 12, 1863, in Thomas C. Reynolds Papers, Library of Congress.

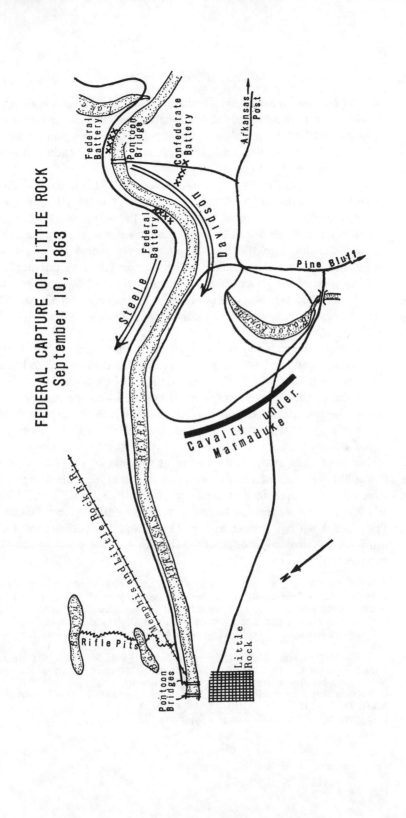

FEDERAL CAPTURE OF LITTLE ROCK
September 10, 1863

he sent Marmaduke to hold Davidson in check. In an engagement at Bayou Fourche, Marmaduke accomplished his mission, although Dobbin, embittered by Walker's death, refused to obey Marmaduke's orders and had to be placed under arrest. But like Marmaduke himself he was soon restored to command.[13]

By 5 P.M. all of Price's troops had pulled out of Little Rock. Before leaving they set fire to the recently completed gunboat *Missouri* (useless because of the seasonal low level of the Arkansas River) but failed to destroy the arsenal. As they marched away from the town, smoke billowing into the late summer sky, General Holmes commented to Marmaduke: "Steele will make no effort to pursue; it is not the wish of his government to disturb us now; *we are an army of prisoners and self-supporting at that*." For once Holmes was right. Price retreated unpursued and undisturbed to Arkadelphia, which he reached September 14.[14]

Losses in the campaign were trifling on both sides: 137 Union casualties, a reported 64 for Price's army. But during and following the evacuation of Little Rock, large numbers of Confederate soldiers, especially in the Arkansas regiments, deserted—so many that Governor Flanagin declared that a pitched battle would have been less costly.[15] Kirby Smith was undisturbed by the fall of Little Rock and wrote Price that they had acted "wisely in saving and keeping together your little army. Unfortunate as the loss of the Arkansas is, it would have been infinitely more disastrous had the little army upon which all our hopes in that area are concentrated been lost."[16] The Washington (Arkansas) *Telegraph* took a similar view: "General Price acted with judgment and gallantry and his course saved the army for the protection of South Arkansas and the good of the Department."[17]

[13] *Official Records*, XXII, Pt. 1, pp. 476–77, 480, 486–87, 522–26. Williams, *Lincoln Finds a General*, V, 113, states that Steele's plan of operations at Little Rock "marks him as a good general," and he compares the "brilliance and boldness" of his performance to some of Stonewall Jackson's moves.

[14] *Official Records*, XXII, Pt. 1, pp. 480, 522; Edwards, *Shelby and His Men*, 186, 248.

[15] *Official Records*, XXII, Pt. 1, pp. 480, 482, 499, 523. The Washington (Ark.) *Telegraph*, September 23, 1863, reported that Price's army at Arkadelphia was "somewhat injured by straggling and desertion."

[16] Kirby Smith to Sterling Price, September 12, 1863, in *Official Records*, XXII, Pt. 2, p. 1014.

[17] Washington (Ark.) *Telegraph*, September 23, 1863.

Others were more critical. According to Missouri's Governor Reynolds, who was now in Arkansas, "General Holmes and *all* the general officers under Price at Little Rock, except General Frost, considered the evacuation a blunder, and that Steele could have been beaten back with great disaster to him."[18] And writing shortly after the war John N. Edwards, an officer in Shelby's brigade, declared dramatically: "the capital of Arkansas was abandoned without a blow . . . to inferior numbers of the enemy and another dark stain left upon the escutcheon of the young Confederacy. . . . History looks in vain for the palliation of the offense; prejudice can find no excuse for the result; and posterity must seek other leaders than those at Little Rock to crown with laurel leaves."[19]

These strictures are probably in part justified. Although Steele began the campaign with 12,000 men which were subsequently reinforced to about 14,000, by the time he reached Little Rock, attrition and illness had reduced his ranks to about 10,500, and he made the final assault with "not more than 7,000 troops."[20] Since Price, according to his report, had 7,749 effectives, the odds against him obviously were not prohibitive, especially since he was close to his base and presumably had access to better knowledge of the countryside. Price, however, also stated in his report that Steele had 20,000 troops— almost a three-to-one superiority.[21] If this was Price's sincere belief at the time, based on the intelligence supplied by his scouts and spies,

---

[18] Reynolds, "Price and the Confederacy," 88–89.

[19] Edwards, *Shelby and His Men*, 185–86. Edwards further stated that: "Nothing could have been more desirable for General Price than the dispositions of Steele, for they involved a separation of forces and a destruction of that unity of action so essential to armies when evenly balanced in numbers. A concentration of his cavalry on the south bank of the river, and the interposition of one brigade of infantry, would have driven Davidson into the Arkansas, and crushed the left wing of Steele's advance." Besides assuming as a certainty what is at least doubtful—that Davidson would have been "crushed"—Edwards was mistaken in asserting that the division of the Union army resulted in a loss of unity of action. Both of Steele's columns remained in view of each other across the shallow, many-forded Arkansas, and Steele, anticipating that the Confederates might try to "crush" Davidson, had heavy concentrations of artillery ready to support him from the other side. See *Official Records*, XXII, Pt. 1, p. 477.

[20] *Official Records*, XXII, Pt. 1, p. 477; Williams, *Lincoln Finds a General*, V, 325. Steele believed that Price had superior numbers and was also apprehensive that Kirby Smith might bring up strong forces to Little Rock.

[21] *Official Records*, XXII, Pt. 1, p. 521.

then he merely exercised common prudence in evacuating Little Rock and can be justly criticized only for failing in his command responsibility of obtaining accurate information about the enemy. But, claimed Reynolds (who it must always be remembered is a source extremely hostile to Price) the divisional and brigade commanders in Price's army did not overestimate Steele's strength, and hence Price's figure of 20,000 was merely an attempt on his part to conceal and excuse the "moral panic" which really caused him "precipitately" to abandon Little Rock.[22]

No doubt greater skill and determination by Price would have made the going much rougher for Steele. But it is doubtful that he could have prevented Steele from ultimately capturing Little Rock. The Federals possessed great superiority in artillery and equipment; the Confederate command was torn by personal dissension; many of the Arkansas contingents were unreliable; and the bayous and rivers about Little Rock offered less an obstacle than an opportunity to a clever, persistent enemy. Given these circumstances, Price (who, whatever his deficiencies as a general may have been, can scarcely be accused of fearing to fight) probably did the *best* thing, if not the *right* thing, in not making a major stand against Steele's column. By so doing he not only saved his "little army" to fight another day, but furthered (unwittingly, to be sure) Kirby Smith's concentration strategy.

A week after Price's forces reached Arkadelphia, Jo Shelby's brigade set forth on a raid into Missouri. Shelby had proposed the enterprise himself, and his purpose, aside from generally "playing hell with the Yankees," was to encourage Southern adherents in Missouri, raise recruits, and obtain the general's commission which Reynolds promised him if he were successful.[23] A native of Kentucky who had operated a hemp business at Waverly, Missouri, prior to the war, Shelby was in his early thirties and was noted for his dash, vigor, and

[22] Reynolds, "Price and the Confederacy," 89. However in a letter of March 27, 1864 (in Thomas C. Reynolds Papers, Library of Congress), Reynolds told Kirby Smith that the Confederates retreated from Little Rock in the face of an enemy army "not much larger than our own because its numbers were misrepresented to us." This would seem to indicate that at the time he believed Price merely the victim of bad intelligence reports and not guilty of deliberate exaggeration of Steele's strength to conceal his ineptitude.

[23] Reynolds to Davis, November 14, 1863, in Thomas C. Reynolds Papers, Library of Congress.

resourcefulness. According to Edwards, his adjutant and the author of his official reports (which were written in the purplest of prose and occasionally interspersed with poetry) he "had a magic power over the hearts and the affections of his soldiers which was as powerful as it was mysterious."[24] Although the tales of his exploits related by Edwards are absurdly exaggerated, even at times utterly fictitious, there can be little doubt that he was a first-rate cavalry leader, a sort of Trans-Mississippi Forrest.[25]

Shelby took 600 men and 2 cannons on the raid. He swung deep into Missouri, reached Boonville, and returned to Confederate-held Arkansas early in November, having ridden fifteen hundred miles in forty-one days. He reported that he had killed 600 Union soldiers, captured and paroled 500 more, destroyed or carried off great quantities of equipment, and garnered 800 recruits, all at the cost of only 125 casualties and the loss of his artillery.[26] The Federals, as to be expected, quoted drastically different figures.[27] Colonel C. Franklin, a prominent Confederate Missourian, wrote President Davis that Shelby boasted he had "gutted Boonville," that the plundering which had accompanied Shelby's and Marmaduke's raids had made the Southern uniform more feared in Missouri than the Northern, and that Shelby had not actually added a single man from Missouri to the army. In addition, Franklin spoke darkly of whisky and drinking in "high places."[28] Nevertheless, Shelby's claims, on the whole, were justified and he soon received his general's stars.[29]

On September 25 Holmes resumed command of the army at Arka-

[24] Edwards, *Shelby and His Men*, 391–93.

[25] Edwards' book on Shelby makes exciting reading, but as a historical source must be used with utmost caution. Oddly enough, Daniel O'Flaherty in his *General Jo Shelby: Undefeated Rebel* (Chapel Hill, 1954) was unaware of the rather obvious fact that Edwards wrote Shelby's official reports. Consequently he stated that the accounts of Shelby's exploits in Edwards' book are confirmed by Shelby's reports!

[26] *Official Records*, XXII, Pt. 1, pp. 670–79; Edwards, *Shelby and His Men*, 188–245.

[27] *Official Records*, XXII, Pt. 1, pp. 628, 632; John F. Snyder, "The Shelby Raid, 1863" (MS in Civil War Papers), 15.

[28] C. Franklin to Jefferson Davis, November 6, 1863, in *Official Records*, XXII, Pt. 2, pp. 1058–60.

[29] J. O. Shelby to Thomas C. Reynolds, March 10, 1865, in Civil War Papers; Reynolds to Davis, March 21, 1865, in Thomas C. Reynolds Papers, Library of Congress.

delphia and Price returned to his division. Early in October Holmes, on orders from Kirby Smith, fell back to Camden, where his army was in better position either to resist a threatened advance by Steele or to cooperate with the Confederate forces in Louisiana under Major General Richard Taylor.[30] Steele, however, remained at Little Rock, so in December Kirby Smith journeyed to Camden with the idea of launching a counteroffensive into the Arkansas Valley. But he found Holmes's army reduced by sickness and desertion to less than seven thousand effectives and Holmes utterly lacking in reliable information about Steele's strength, which on investigation proved much greater than expected. Therefore he decided not to undertake "at this season an expedition so Quixotic and impracticable," and ordered Holmes to go into winter quarters.[31]

"The long winter months," subsequently wrote John Edwards, "broken by alternate snows, freezes, and thaws, were spent in hard drilling when the weather permitted, and upon the most meager and damnable rations imagineable [sic]."[32] In Arkansas as in the rest of the Trans-Mississippi neither side engaged in any significant operations, as both made ready for the spring campaigns. By means of conscription and the addition of Arkansas state troops the strength of Holmes's army was increased to slightly over ten thousand. Moreover, according to an inspector-general's report, its morale, drill, and general efficiency likewise improved.[33] On the other hand, a disproportionate number of the troops consisted of poorly mounted and armed, indisciplined cavalry, and their clothing and camp equipment were so miserable that a rumor that the army might change its base brought a protest from a surgeon in Price's division, who warned that this would inevitably result in heavy loss of life from pneumonia and typhoid.[34] In addition, plundering and marauding by soldiers became such a serious problem that, in February, Price found it necessary to station cavalry patrols around his division's camp.[35]

Personal relations between Price and Holmes, bad ever since Helena, became worse during the fall and winter. Holmes blamed Price for

[30] *Official Records*, XXII, Pt. 2, pp. 1027, 1034–35.
[31] *Ibid.*, 1110–11.
[32] Edwards, *Shelby and His Men*, 248–49.
[33] *Official Records*, XXII, Pt. 2, pp. 1060, 1084, 1130–31.
[34] *Ibid.*, 1125–26.
[35] *Ibid.*, 957.

the July 4 fiasco, and Price complained that Holmes circulated slanders about him.[36] Late in September, when Kirby Smith visited the Arkansas forces, Governor Reynolds informed him of the quarrel and urged that he end it by relieving Holmes from a command in which he had lost the confidence of both the people and the troops. Kirby Smith agreed that the two generals should be separated, but hesitated to relieve Holmes unless he could at the same time replace him with someone besides Price, whose military ability he considered inferior to Holmes's, although possessing "more of the confidence and love of the troops." Furthermore, as he explained to Reynolds, he was reluctant "to take the bold step, especially with an executive as jealous of his prerogative as Mr. Davis, of removing a district commander enjoying the President's special confidence, in order to place the district under a general in whom the President was known to have no confidence at all."

Kirby Smith, nonetheless, did promise Reynolds that he would lay all the facts concerning Holmes's incompetence before Davis and ask authority to relieve him. Reynolds then communicated the substance of this talk to Price, who expressed disappointment but agreed to follow the governor's advice of "keeping perfectly cool until the decision of the President could be had." But it was not until January 20 that Kirby Smith, very cautiously and tactfully, recommended to Davis that Holmes be replaced with a "younger and more energetic officer." In the meantime Davis, who had learned of the Price–Holmes "disagreement," had written Kirby Smith suggesting that Price be sent to operate in "Kansas and West Missouri."[37]

During the summer of 1863 the war in that region had reached a new peak of violence. On August 21 Quantrill, at the head of 450 bushwhackers, had completely destroyed Lawrence, Kansas, and butchered 180 of its citizens. Then, on October 6 at Baxter Springs, Kansas, he had overwhelmed and massacred the 100-man bodyguard of Major General James G. Blunt, Federal commander of the Indian Territory. Following this atrocity, he had marched to the Canadian River in Texas. From there on October 13 he sent—for the first and last time in his career—a written report to Price. In it he gave a disjointed

[36] Reynolds, "Price and the Confederacy," 78–80; Sterling Price to R. W. Johnson, September 27, 1863, in *Official Records*, LIII, 897–98.
[37] Reynolds, "Price and the Confederacy," 90–92; *Official Records*, XXII, Pt. 2, 896, 1035–36, 1072.

account of the Baxter Springs affair and promised a report of his "summer's campaign on the Missouri River" at a future date. He signed himself "W. C. Quantrill, Colonel, Commanding, &c."[38]

Price, through a member of his staff, acknowledged the report on November 2. He complimented "Colonel" Quantrill on his Baxter Springs victory and thanked him and his men for their "gallant struggle" against Northern oppression in Missouri. However, he was anxious to obtain a report on the Lawrence raid so that Quantrill's acts "should appear in their true light before the world." Also, he desired information on the treatment accorded captured guerrillas, so that "the world may learn [of] the murderous and uncivilized warfare" waged by the Federals and "thus be able to appreciate their cowardly shrieks and howls when with a just retaliation the same 'measure is meted out to them.' "[39]

Like most Southerners Price discounted the Northern stories of wholesale, cold-blooded massacre at Lawrence. But obviously he was disturbed by the charges against the guerrillas and also uneasy over their "no quarter" policy. In addition he believed that partisan warfare in Missouri only brought misery to the people and that the bushwhackers would be of greater value both to the state and the South if they served in the regular forces. To this end he joined with Kirby Smith and Reynolds in pressuring Quantrill, who established a camp near Sherman, Texas, to abandon his free-lance war. Ultimately, in March, after conferring personally with Kirby Smith, Reynolds, and Price, Quantrill agreed to give up all but one hundred of his followers to the army.[40] But he himself ignored Reynolds' prophetic warning that "the history of every guerrilla chief has been the same. He either becomes the slave of his men, or if he attempts to control them, some officer or private rises up, disputes his authority, gains the men, and puts him down. My opinion of you is that you deserve a better fate . . . ."[41]

[38] For Quantrill's report, see *Official Records, XXII*, Pt. 1, 700–701. The Lawrence raid and the Baxter Springs massacre are described in detail in Castel, *Quantrill*, 122–43, 149–54.

[39] Castel, *Quantrill*, 154–55.

[40] *Ibid.*, 156–64; *Official Records*, XXII, Pt. 2, p. 855; *ibid.*, LIII, 907–908; Washington (Ark.) *Telegraph,* September 23, 1863; Thomas C. Reynolds to Sterling Price, October 30, 1863, Thomas C. Reynolds to Kirby Smith, October 30, 1863, Thomas C. Reynolds to William C. Quantrill, March 5, 1864, in Thomas C. Reynolds Papers, Library of Congress.

[41] Reynolds to Quantrill, March 10, 1864, Thomas C. Reynolds Papers,

More and more Reynolds was taking—or attempting to take—an influential part in the military and political affairs of the Trans-Mississippi Department. He did so because he was the type of man who simply found it impossible to abstain from active involvement in any situation which interested him; because he was determined to make his authority, even though he was a governor in exile, respected by all parties and especially by the military; and because of his special arrangement with Richmond to "keep things straight" as regards Price.

At first, in his efforts to build up his official and personal powers, he encountered discouraging obstacles. The affairs of the Confederate government of Missouri were in "utter confusion" because of Claiborne Jackson's illness and death. The state archives and other property had been taken to Camden, Arkansas, and when he arrived there in April from Richmond he was forced to "trudge" around town on foot while his subordinate officers rode about on horses and in carriages which they claimed to be "private" but which he suspected of belonging to the Missouri government. Moreover, he immediately got into a dispute with Price over the disbursement of state funds (of which there was only a small amount) to the Missouri troops, and anger and resentment was aroused on both sides.[42]

But by July, writing from Little Rock, he was able to report with obvious pleasure to Seddon: "My position here is satisfactory . . . . A firm but conciliatory course . . . produced a complete alteration in the attitude of General Price and others, and I now have confidence in harmonious action between them and me, in support of the views I expressed in Richmond to you and the President. A system of counterpoises among the military politicians, indispensable to a just exercise of civil authority, will soon be established. The materials for it are ample."[43]

Library of Congress. This prophecy, which was to come true quite soon and quite literally (see Castel, *Quantrill*, 169–72), is just one of many examples of Reynolds' truly superior intellect and knowledge that could be cited if the subject of this book was Reynolds and not Price!

[42] Reynolds, "Price and the Confederacy," 59–61; Reynolds to Cabell, April 27, June 5, 1863, and Reynolds to Price, May 25, 1863, in Thomas C. Reynolds Papers, Library of Congress.

[43] Reynolds to Seddon, July 20, 1863, in *Official Records*, XXII, Pt. 1, p. 935. See also Reynolds to Johnston, July 18, 1863, in Thomas C. Reynolds Papers, Library of Congress, stating that he had established his authority over the army largely because of the belief among its officers that he had the confidence of and support of the President.

Reynolds made sure that all concerned were aware of his confidential relationship with the President and the departmental commander.[44] In addition, as illustrated by the case of Shelby, he employed the control Richmond had given him over promotions to secure the interested support of high-ranking Missouri officers, who now looked to him rather than to Price for preferment. Given the intense ambitions and jealousies characteristic of any officer corps, he could not have conceived of a more effective means (as he no doubt knew) of enhancing his own authority and undermining Price's.

Outwardly Price and Reynolds remained on cordial terms. When Reynolds first visited the Missouri troops in Arkansas, Price's band serenaded him, and the two men called on each other frequently at their respective headquarters. Indeed, according to Reynolds, following the evacuation of Little Rock, Price remarked to him, with some feeling, "Governor, whenever I am in trouble, I feel like coming to you for advice."[45] Also, as has been described, Reynolds supported Price in the Holmes dispute and used his influence with Kirby Smith to have Holmes removed.

Yet, in actual fact, both the general and the governor profoundly distrusted one another, and their relationship steadily deteriorated. Reynolds regarded Price as being impulsive, tactless, and prone to indiscreet and exaggerated language—weaknesses which in his opinion had given rise to Price's difficulties with the administration and which he believed must be guarded against in the interests of the future of Confederate Missouri. And as time went by, he also came to consider Price to be devious, insincere, petulant, and arrogant. Perhaps of more importance, he concluded that Price had little if any military capacity, that his reputation was largely the product of "puffing," and that he lacked both the ability and the desire to maintain proper discipline among his troops. Hence, in backing Price against Holmes, he was motivated not by friendship for the former, but by a belief that Holmes was utterly incompetent, and out of the hope that Price's reputed popularity would attract recruits in the "ever-contemplated" expedition to Missouri. He did not think Price qualified to replace Holmes, and in advising Davis to relieve that general he urged him to

[44] Reynolds to Cabell, June 5, 1863, in Thomas C. Reynolds Papers, Library of Congress; Reynolds, "Price and the Confederacy," 69–70; Perkins, "Davis and Price," 476–77.
[45] Reynolds, "Price and the Confederacy," 91.

promote Simon B. Buckner (the hero of Fort Donelson) to lieutenant general and assign him the District of Arkansas.[46]

Unfortunately, Price's side of the story of his relations with Reynolds is not set forth as fully as the governor's. In fact, apart from a few scattered letters of Price and his friends, most of it has to be deduced from Reynolds' own writings—an extremely awkward and unhealthy situation from a historical standpoint. However, on the basis of the above materials, and with the aid of a little supposition, it is possible to derive the following conclusions. First, Price knew of Reynolds' special connection with Davis and Kirby Smith, and no doubt suspected the purpose to which it was being put. And, secondly, he resented what he deemed to be Reynolds' unwarranted meddling in military affairs and his exaggerated claims to official prerogatives as governor.[47]

As regards the second inference, shortly after Reynolds arrived in Arkansas, he had an interview with Snead, whom he considered Price's "right hand man" and a "prejudiced personal enemy" of himself. Snead began by objecting to a recent proclamation of Reynolds stipulating, in the event of Reynolds' death, the election of a provisional governor for Missouri by means of a popular election in the state. "General Price," Snead (according to Reynolds) declared, "is in effect the State of Missouri," and if it became necessary to elect a provisional governor he would have it done by the Missouri troops, who were the state's "true constituency."

Reynolds took this as a direct challenge. Therefore he replied that he had the "express pledge of the President" to support his authority as governor and that if members of Price's staff attempted to flout it he could and would crush them "like an eggshell in a hand of iron." And by crushing, he explained, he meant that "if General Price's staff should begin a cabal against my legitimate authority, I should on his failing to stop it, ask General [Kirby] Smith to order the offending officers to the Cis-Mississippi country, or assign them to duty on the Rio Grande."[48]

As Reynolds of course intended him to do, Snead reported this warn-

[46] *Ibid.*, 36–91, *passim.*

[47] *Ibid.*, 69–70, 75; Diary of Thomas C. Reynolds (MS in Thomas C. Reynolds Papers, Library of Congress), May 31, 1864; Trusten Polk to Thomas L. Snead, August 11, 1864, in *Official Records*, XLI, Pt. 2, p. 1060.

[48] Reynolds to Cabell, April 27, 1863, in Thomas C. Reynolds Papers, Library of Congress; Reynolds to Price, December 4, 1863, in *Official Records*, LIII, 918; Reynolds, "Price and the Confederacy," 72–75.

ing to Price. Thus Price found his personal military family threatened by a civilian outsider who owed his rather dubious official position solely to accident and who was a friend and ally of his enemy, President Davis. It was a situation which no self-respecting general could be expected to regard with equanimity, least of all one as proud and passionate as Price.

In October, Reynolds obtained another opportunity to assert his power when Robert L. Y. Peyton, one of Missouri's Confederate senators, died and it became necessary to appoint a replacement. Holmes and Senators Robert W. Johnson and Thomas Mitchell of Arkansas advised him to appoint "your big man," meaning Price. The latter two maintained that doing so "would relieve the district of the difficulty arising from the Price-Holmes quarrel," that Price "would from his position and popularity, be a kind of representative of the wants of the whole Trans-Mississippi Department," and that Missouri "should be represented in the Senate by a man of his great prestige in order to prevent a sacrifice of its interests in fixing the northern boundary of the Confederacy."

Reynolds replied that Price was needed for the future Missouri expedition, that the Price-Holmes difficulty could be ended by other means, that Price had no skill as a debater or legislator, that he would strengthen the Congressional opposition to Davis, and that he could speak out against a peace treaty harmful to Missouri more effectively outside of than in the Senate. Reynolds further stated that although he himself had the "highest confidence" in Price, "his lateness in coming into the opposition to Benton, and into the secession movement, the connection of his name with the counter-revolution talk of 1862, and with the North West reconstruction movement of 1862–3 had created distrust among the Cotton State politicians: that the *interests* of Missouri *demanded* the cultivation of the confidence and *good will* of those States and the President who would have the initiative in a treaty of boundary . . . ." Privately, Reynolds suspected that the advocacy of Price by the two Arkansas senators was motivated by a desire to "fasten General Holmes on the district" by "getting rid of General Price," and that Holmes himself had inspired their efforts.

In any event, Reynolds had already decided to appoint Colonel Waldo P. Johnson, a former United States Senator from Missouri, and a friend of Davis, Kirby Smith, and himself. By so doing he not only would improve Missouri's standing with the administration, but would also bolster his own influence in Richmond and among the Missouri "military politicians." He did not announce his choice for several days, and in the meantime E. C. Cabell, now a major on Price's staff, and Major O. M. Watkins, a volunteer aide to Holmes, urged him to select Price, both claiming Price had indicated that he desired the position. But Reynolds received a letter from Price stating that he did not wish to be considered, and in a conversation several months later Price declared that he was not interested in being a Senator, "as he was no debater." Therefore, presuming that Price's statements were sincere, the appointment of Colonel Johnson probably did not increase friction between the general and the governor.[49]

However, the question of a successor, if any, for Missouri's other Senator, John B. Clark, had far different consequences. Clark's term was due to expire on February 22. During his tenure in Richmond he had made himself thoroughly obnoxious, politically and personally, to the administration. Not only had he been a prominent advocate of "counter-revolution," but he was reputed to have described Davis as "a slow-coach," sneered at Benjamin as "a cut-prick Jew," and on one occasion he entered the Secretary of War's office through an open window! In addition he was notorious for hard drinking, heavy gambling, and persistent fornication, having in the last connection supposedly seduced Albert Pike's mistress! Therefore, it is quite understandable that Reynolds, with his overriding desire to maintain good relations with the President, concluded that he was unfit for the office and so decided not to reappoint him. Price, on the other hand, favored his reappointment, for although he had little personal liking for the Senator, Clark had supported him in the course of his altercations with Davis. Furthermore, Clark was highly popular with the Missouri troops, who remembered his gallantry at Wilson's Creek. Hence, during a visit to Reynolds' "capital" at Marshall, Texas, Price advised the governor to rename Clark in order to avoid dissatisfaction and resentment in the army.

But Reynolds ignored the wishes of Price and the army and offered the senatorship to Colonel L. M. Lewis, who at the time was a Union

[49] Reynolds, "Memoranda relative to . . . Confederate Senators," in Thomas C. Reynolds Papers, Library of Congress; Reynolds, "Price and the Confederacy," 92–101.

prisoner of war! At once Clark's friends bitterly denounced Reynolds, and Price and his circle openly sympathized with them.[50] The consequence was that the implicit division among Confederate Missouri politicians now became explicit, with a pro-Clark, anti-Davis faction opposing an anti-Clark, pro-Davis group, and with the first rallying around Price and the second looking to Reynolds for leadership. There was, however, no open break between the general and the governor, who remained on nominally friendly terms.

[50] Reynolds, "Memoranda relative to . . . Confederate Senators," in Thomas C. Reynolds Papers, Library of Congress; Reynolds, "Price and the Confederacy," 104–106; Reynolds to Johnson, May 21, 1864, in Thomas C. Reynolds Papers, Library of Congress.

10

JENKINS' FERRY

The squabble with Holmes and the growing friction with Reynolds were not the only difficulties Price experienced during the winter. He also had a bout of illness, and complained to a friend that "age was coming on him and that he felt his bodily strength affected by the hardships and fatigues of camp-life."[1] In January he obtained a 60-day leave of absence and joined his wife in Washington, Texas, where, like many other Missourians, she had refugeed, taking along the family slaves. He rejoined the army in Arkansas on March 7, looking "well."[2]

During his absence Holmes learned of Kirby Smith's letter asking Davis to replace him. Greatly angered by what he regarded as Kirby Smith's "want of confidence and respect," he requested on February 28 that he be relieved as commander of the District of Arkansas.[3] Kirby Smith, feeling he had no alternative, accepted Holmes's resignation. "A succession of circumstances," he wrote Holmes, "involving a loss of country, loss of confidence, loss of hope approaching almost to despair, necessitates a change in the administration of the district. . . . I know that the District of Arkansas will never have a purer, more unselfish, and patriotic commander."[4]

On March 16, 1864, Price assumed command of the District of Arkansas.[5] Kirby Smith, who believed that he was unequal to the post, looked on him as only a temporary replacement for Holmes.[6] Price himself, at this time, did not want to be district commander, preferring instead to remain "foot-loose" for an expedition into Missouri.[7] For,

---

[1] Reynolds, "Memoranda relative to . . . Confederate Senators," Thomas C. Reynolds Papers, Library of Congress; Reynolds, "Price and the Confederacy," 100.

[2] Reynolds, "Price and the Confederacy," 96, 102, 111; W. M. McPheeters Diary, March 7, 1864.

[3] *Official Records*, XXXIV, Pt. 2, pp. 935, 1021–22.

[4] Kirby Smith to T. H. Holmes, March 11, 1864, in *ibid.*, 1035.

[5] *Ibid.*, 1047.

[6] Kirby Smith to Johnson, January 15, 1864, in *ibid.*, 870.

[7] Reynolds to Johnson, July 14, 1864, in Thomas C. Reynolds Papers, Library of Congress.

as always, the redemption of his home state was uppermost in his mind. Shortly before succeeding Holmes, he had proposed to Kirby Smith that the Arkansas army be reinforced with troops from Texas for a campaign against Steele. "I am sure," he wrote, "that an army of 20,000 men led by yourself would be amply sufficient for the re-occupation of the valley of the Arkansas, and that if you, after taking Little Rock, will either go in person or send me into Missouri with a competent force, such as you might easily spare, we would not only be able to sustain ourselves there, but attract to our army thousands and tens of thousands of recruits."[8] At the same time he declared in a speech to his Missouri soldiers that before the year was over he would be "addressing them from the steps of the Planters' House in St. Louis," provided his counsels were followed.[9]

Kirby Smith, in replying to Price, pointed out that sufficient forces for such a campaign as he proposed simply were not available— Magruder in Texas had only two thousand infantry, Taylor in Louisiana between seven thousand and eight thousand, and both were threatened by large Federal armies. "We can only concentrate in sufficient force to take the offensive . . . by the enemy forcing our columns to within supporting distance of each other, or through the relief obtained by successes east of the river."[10] Meanwhile Price could best serve the cause by dismounting the inefficient and poorly disciplined cavalry units in his district and converting them into sorely needed infantry.

Before answering Price's letter Kirby Smith showed it to Reynolds, who happened at the time to be at Trans-Mississippi headquarters. Its effect was to "considerably impair" the governor's opinion of Price's "candour and military judgment." Furthermore, to Reynolds "it looked . . . rather like a mere maneuvere to enable him to say hereafter that Little Rock could have been retaken if his advice had been followed." Reynolds, however, retained "confidence that in an exclusively Missouri campaign [Price's] local knowledge would compensate for any deficiency in military capacity."[11]

[8] Price to Kirby Smith, March 8, 1864, in *Official Records*, XXXIV, Pt. 2, pp. 1028–29.

[9] Reynolds to Price, April 11, 1864, in Thomas C. Reynolds Papers, Library of Congress; Reynolds, "Price and the Confederacy," 103.

[10] Kirby Smith to Price, March 15, in *Official Records*, XXXIV, Pt. 2, pp. 1043–44.

[11] Reynolds, "Price and the Confederacy," 103.

In truth, Price's proposal of a Missouri expedition was most unrealistic, nor could it have been made at a less opportune moment. Even as he wrote to Kirby Smith, a strong Union army under Major General Nathaniel P. Banks, supported by a gunboat flotilla, was moving up the Red River with the intent of capturing Shreveport. A short time later Steele also began advancing on Shreveport, where he was to form a junction with Banks. Should the two Union pincers meet, organized Confederate resistance in the West soon would come to an end.

To oppose the Union offensive Kirby Smith had barely twenty-five thousand soldiers in his entire sprawling department. The combined enemy strength, on the other hand, he estimated at fifty thousand—a figure substantially correct. Obviously his best chance of making a successful defense was to try to defeat Banks and Steele separately and in turn. Since Banks's column was the more dangerous, he decided to concentrate against it first.[12] Accordingly on March 18 he ordered Price to rush Parsons' and Brigadier General Thomas J. Churchill's infantry divisions, four thousand men in all, to Shreveport, where they would be used to bolster Taylor's army. Price promptly complied, with the result that his command was reduced to about six thousand cavalry under Marmaduke, Shelby, and Fagan, and some fifteen hundred infantry.[13]

In a series of dispatches during the latter part of March, Kirby Smith described to Price the overall Confederate strategy and assigned him his role in it. This, in essence, was to hold Steele in check until Taylor defeated Banks. As soon as this had been accomplished, sufficient forces would be switched northward to dispose of Steele and regain the Arkansas Valley. Kirby Smith believed that, given Price's "immense superiority" in cavalry, "an advance of Steele into our exhausted and impoverished country must be attended with great risk, and should result in the destruction of his command." Therefore he instructed Price to retreat before the invaders and not risk a major engagement unless he possessed a definite advantage. As he fell back, he should make every effort "to embarrass and retard the enemy's advance by throwing cavalry upon his flanks and rear, interrupting his communi-

---

[12] *Official Records*, XXXIV, Pt. 1, p. 483.
[13] *Ibid.*, Pt. 2, pp. 1056, 1059–60. Churchill commanded the Arkansas troops formerly headed by Fagan, who now commanded the cavalry previously under Walker.

cations, and destroying his trains, as well as by opposing him at every point which may afford facilities for making a stand, and by destroying as you fall back all supplies which might be used by him."[14] In brief, he was to trade space for time, in hopes that in time space itself would foil Steele and set the stage for his defeat.

On March 23 Steele's army left Little Rock. It numbered 8,500 of all arms and included an elite cavalry force organized specially for the purpose of dealing with Shelby's feared troopers.[15] Marching slowly over rainsoaked roads it crossed the Ouachita River and occupied Arkadelphia on the twenty-ninth. Here it halted several days to await a column of 5,000 men from Fort Smith under Brigadier General John M. Thayer. But when Thayer, who was delayed by lack of food and forage, failed to arrive as scheduled, Steele on April 1 took up the march again, moving southward on the road to Washington, Arkansas.[16]

Price, per his instructions from Kirby Smith, made no attempt to stand against the Union advance. Instead he ordered Marmaduke to impede Steele in front and sent Shelby to strike from the rear. Shelby was unable to do any appreciable damage, the Federal rear guard beating him off when he attacked near Spoonville on April 2. The next day Steele established a bridgehead on the south bank of the Little Missouri at Elkins' Ferry. Marmaduke, who had expected him to cross the river elsewhere, hurried to this point and on the morning of the fourth delivered a fierce mounted assault. According to his own report he drove the Federals back in rout two miles; according to the Union version he was "repulsed with ease." In any event Steele crossed his entire army over the Little Missouri at Elkins' Ferry, thus surmounting what his chief of engineers considered at the time "a more serious obstacle" than the Confederates.[17]

On April 5 Price, accompanied by all of his remaining infantry, left Camden to take the field in person. It would appear that he acted

[14] *Ibid.*, 1062, 1070, 1095, 1102.
[15] "The Federal Occupation of Camden As Set Forth in the Diary of a Union Officer," *Arkansas Historical Quarterly*, IX (1956), 215.
[16] *Official Records*, XXXIV, Pt. 1, pp. 659, 672–73.
[17] *Ibid.*, 660, 673–74, 779–80, 821–24; Edwards, *Shelby and His Men*, 246–63. Edwards was not with Shelby during the Spring, 1864 campaign in Arkansas and hence obtained his information from another of Shelby's officers. His account of the fighting is, as always, greatly romanticized, but he is useful for movements and analysis.

in accordance with the latest dispatch from Kirby Smith, who telegraphed on April 3 from Shreveport that Steele's objective was Washington, and that consequently Camden was "entirely out of the sphere
of operations."[18] On the seventh he joined Marmaduke at Prairie
d'Ane. Marmaduke had his troops drawn up behind a line of log and
dirt breastworks covering the road to Washington at a point where it
was bisected by the road from Camden. Four days later Steele, who
finally had been reinforced by Thayer, moved against the Confederate
entrenchments. Both sides engaged in a great deal of long-range
cannonading but very little serious fighting. In the evening, with his
outnumbered forces in danger of being flanked, Price withdrew to a
new position eight miles north of Washington. Here he was confident
that "if the [enemy] advanced I could attack him at great disadvantage,
and destroy or capture the greater part of his train." Moreover, the
arrival that night of a thousand Choctaws and Texans under Brigadier
General S. B. Maxey, whom Price had summoned from the Indian
Territory, increased his army's strength and bolstered its morale.[19]

In the morning, however, Steele merely demonstrated in the direction of Washington, then turned off on the road to Camden, which
had been his goal from the first. The ruse was so successful that Price
did not realize that the Federals were moving eastward until the next
day.[20] Immediately he set out in pursuit with Fagan's and Maxey's
troops, at the same time ordering Marmaduke and Shelby to intercept

[18] Lieutenant E. Cunningham (aide to Kirby Smith) to Sterling Price, April
3, 1864, in *Official Records*, XXXIV, Pt. 2, p. 728.

[19] *Ibid.*, Pt. 1, pp. 661, 674–76, 780–81, 824–25, 837–38. In his report Marmaduke stated that the Confederates, by constructing a line of works at Prairie
d'Ane, forced "the enemy to waste his time and keep his army starving in a
barren country for nearly three days." [See *ibid.*, 824–25]. The report of Steele's
chief of engineers (the best Union account of the campaign) makes it clear
however that the Federal delay was caused not by Marmaduke's fortifications
but by difficulty in crossing the Little Missouri, plus the need to wait for Thayer
[*ibid.*, 674–75]. Kirby Smith had not intended Maxey to join Price unless Price
was forced to retreat further, but his chief of staff mistakenly authorized Price
to call on Maxey. Earlier about 500 cavalry from the Indian Territory had
reinforced Price [*ibid.*, Pt. 3, pp. 729, 760–61].

[20] Edwards, *Shelby And His Men*, 266, states that Marmaduke and Shelby
proposed to Price that half the army be deployed so as to cover the road to
Camden, the other half on the Washington road, "so that in whatever direction
Steele moved, troops were upon his front and rear." This arrangement might
have checked Steele; it might also have enabled him to defeat both halves of
the Confederate army in succession.

and block Steele in front. He managed to engage the Union rear guard near Moscow, but his attack, after initial success, was beaten back. As for Marmaduke and Shelby, their men and horses were so worn down from two weeks of constant marching and skirmishing that they could do little more than harass Steele's column, although making what a Northern officer termed a "gallant resistance." On the evening of April 15 the Federals occupied Camden, encountering only token opposition from a small force that Price left there to remove public stores and destroy the bridge across the Ouachita.[21]

Steele, with a minimum of losses, had now reached his first main objective, and his army for the time being was safe from attack behind the strong fortifications which the Confederates had laboriously constructed around Camden during the winter. Furthermore, as in the Little Rock campaign, he had outmaneuvered Price with feints and quick dashes. Nonetheless, the mood of the Federals was less one of exultation than of anxiety. They were deep in enemy territory and far from their base; the sparsely settled, pine-covered countryside was nearly barren of food and forage and already they were on half-rations; and, most disturbing of all, they had heard rumors that Banks had met with disaster in Louisiana.[22]

These rumors, although exaggerated, were essentially correct. At Mansfield on April 8 and at Pleasant Hill the following day Taylor's army attacked Banks (who approached total incompetence as a general) and caused him to retreat after advancing to within thirty miles of Shreveport. Taylor wished to press on in pursuit, but Kirby Smith chose instead to turn against Steele.[23] On April 14 he telegraphed Price, who had been apprised earlier of Taylor's success, informing him that three divisions of infantry (Parsons', Churchill's, and the Texans of Major General John G. Walker) were on the way to his support, and urging him to do everything possible to prevent Banks and Steele from communicating with one another. He also instructed Price, should he be unable to hold Camden, to "throw a sufficient force

[21] *Official Records*, XXXIV, Pt. 1, pp. 675–76, 780–81, 825, 838–39; Edwards, *Shelby and His Men*, 266–70.

[22] *Official Records*, XXXIV, Pt. 1, pp. 661, 676.

[23] For Banks's Red River Expedition and the battles of Mansfield (sometimes called Sabine Crossroads) and Pleasant Hill, see Joseph Howard Parks, *General Edmund Kirby Smith, C.S.A.* (Baton Rouge, 1954), 371–94.

of cavalry across the Ouachita to cut off the enemy's supplies and break up his communications with his rear."[24]

Price, after failing to overtake Steele, established new headquarters at Woodlawn, Arkansas, and disposed his forces so as to cover all the approaches to and from Camden south of the Ouachita. On April 17 Marmaduke's scouts reported that a large wagon train, guarded by over a thousand infantry and cavalry and by four pieces of artillery, had sallied forth from Camden to collect corn from the countryside. At once Price ordered Marmaduke to capture the train, and when Marmaduke stated he needed more men, he sent Maxey to reinforce him.[25]

The following morning, at Poison Spring on the road west of Camden, the Confederates ambushed the train as it was returning, captured all of the wagons and cannons, and killed or wounded 301 of the escort at a cost of only 114 on their side. The Federal loss, Marmaduke claimed, would have been greater had not Maxey, who as senior in rank commanded the operation, stopped the pursuit prematurely. Most of the Union dead were Negro troops of the First Kansas Colored Regiment, which had 117 out of a total strength of 438 killed. The Confederates, by their own admission, showed the Negroes no quarter, slaying the wounded and those who tried to surrender.[26] Maxey's Choctaws took the most prominent part in this slaughter: "You ought to see Indians," recalled an Arkansas soldier who was present, "fight Negroes —kill and scalp them." Efforts by the more humane and responsible Southern officers to restrain their men were of little avail.[27]

That same day Kirby Smith arrived at Woodlawn to take personal charge of the operations against Steele. Much to his irritation he found that Price had not yet thrown cavalry across the Federal communications as instructed. Therefore he promptly organized a special task force of 3,500 cavalry under the command of Fagan. He ordered Fagan to destroy the Union depots at Little Rock, Pine Bluff, and Devall's Bluff, after which he was to place himself between the enemy and Little

[24] Kirby Smith to Price, April 11, 1864, in *Official Records*, XXXIV, Pt. 3, p. 759; Kirby Smith to Price, April 14, 1864, in *ibid.*, 766.

[25] *Official Records*, XXXIV, Pt. 1, p. 781.

[26] *Ibid.*, 676, 680, 743–46, 818–20, 825–26, 841–44; Edwards, *Shelby and His Men*, 271–76.

[27] C. T. Anderson, "Campaigning in Southern Arkansas: A Memoir," ed. Roman J. Zorn, *Arkansas Historical Quarterly*, VIII (1949), 243.

Rock. The destruction of these depots, Kirby Smith reasoned, would "insure the loss of Steele's entire army," for neither "man nor beast could be sustained in the exhausted country between the Ouachita and White Rivers." Before Fagan set out he impressed on him the importance of his mission, promised him promotion if successful, and told him to "move rapidly and *stop for nothing*."[28]

Fagan crossed the Ouachita on April 12 at Eldorado Landing, where he was joined by five hundred more troopers under Shelby, and struck northward. On the twenty-fourth Shelby's scouts reported that a large Union wagon train protected by a strong escort was on the road ahead. Fagan, ignoring or forgetting Kirby Smith's instructions to "stop for nothing," decided to attack the train, even though he knew that it consisted only of empty wagons returning to Pine Bluff after having delivered supplies to Steele at Camden. Making a rapid march of forty-five miles, he came upon the Federal column near Marks' Mills at daybreak on the twenty-fifth. A hard, desperate battle ensued, with both sides losing heavily. Finally, after the Union commander had been wounded, the Confederates routed the escort, capturing in the process 1,100 prisoners, 6 cannons, and seizing or burning all of the wagons. Once again the Southern troops got out of hand and massacred a large

[28] Kirby Smith to Jefferson Davis, June 11, 1864, in *Official Records*, XXXIV, Pt. 1, p. 481; William R. Boggs, *Military Reminiscences* (Durham, N. C., 1913), 78. There is no copy of Kirby Smith's instructions to Fagan in the *Official Records* [or in the National Archives]. Fagan's description of the instructions differs from Kirby Smith's. They were, he stated, "to cross to Ouachita, interrupt the enemy's line of communications toward the Arkansas River, destroy his supplies, &c." [*Official Records*, XXXIV, Pt. 1, p. 788]. Most significantly he did not mention what Kirby Smith stated was his primary mission: destruction of the Union depots at Little Rock, Devall's Bluff, and Pine Bluff. Price's report seems to support Fagan, as it states "On April 19, Brigadier-General Fagan received orders to cross the Ouachita . . . and to attack and cut off all trains of the enemy he might find on that side of the river" [*ibid.*, 781]. Price did not say who issued these orders to Fagan, although the ordinary implication would be that they came from himself. Fagan stated that his orders came from "district headquarters"—which would mean Price. However, Kirby Smith did not assume formal command of the Army of Arkansas until April 26; therefore he may have issued the orders to Fagan via Price or through Price's headquarters, although his letter to Davis and Boggs's account seem to make it clear that he gave them in person to Fagan. Kirby Smith's version of the orders is supported, in addition to Boggs, by Edwards, *Shelby and His Men*, 290, and by Lieutenant Cunningham, aide to Kirby Smith, in a letter written on June 27, 1864 to his uncle in Virginia (*Official Records*, XXXIV, Pt. 1, p. 555). Possibly Fagan received contradictory orders from Price and Kirby Smith.

number of Negroes and Arkansas Unionist refugees who were accompanying the train. Moreover, according to Reynolds, the troopers who were detailed to escort the captured wagons back to the Confederate lines sold them for personal gain to the local farmers![29]

Although Marks' Mills was a stinging defeat for the Federals, Fagan had departed from his primary mission in fighting the battle, and his force was so reduced by attrition, casualties, and the need to provide guards for the prisoners that he was left with only fifteen hundred effectives—not enough to overcome the strong Union garrisons at Pine Bluff and Little Rock. Shelby, therefore, urged him to turn back towards Camden and block Steele's retreat. But Fagan answered that his orders required him to continue northward and accordingly he did so.[30]

Meanwhile Steele's position had become most precarious. His food supplies were nearly exhausted, he had received definite word of Banks's failure, and he knew that Kirby Smith had joined Price with a large force of infantry. Hence, when he learned of the disaster at Marks' Mills, he ordered an immediate retreat to Little Rock. To advance to Shreveport or to stay at Camden would be equally suicidal. By daybreak on April 27 his entire army had pulled out of Camden and was on the other side of the Ouachita.[31]

The Confederates reoccupied the town that afternoon, but could not cross the river until late on the morning of the following day because, owing to a mix-up at Shreveport headquarters, they lacked pontoons and had to construct a raft bridge.[32] While work proceeded on this, Kirby Smith sent Marmaduke's cavalry to head off Steele, but since Marmaduke had to cross the Ouachita at Miller's Bluff, forty miles to

[29] *Official Records*, XXXIV, Pt. 1, pp. 712–16, 788–89; Edwards, *Shelby and His Men*, 280–85. Reynolds to Johnson, July 14, 1864, in Thomas C. Reynolds Papers, Library of Congress, refers to the selling of wagons to local farmers.

[30] *Official Records*, XXXIV, Pt. 1, p. 790; Edwards, *Shelby and His Men*, 290–91. The figure of 1,500 is close to incredible. From the standpoint of manpower Fagan could not have been much worse off after Marks' Mills if he, rather than the Federals, had been smashed!

[31] *Official Records*, XXXIV, Pt. 1, pp. 662–63, 668, 671–72, 677, 680. Steele's quartermaster reported to him on April 25 [*ibid.*, 683] that it would be impossible to secure sufficient forage for 1,000 mules and horses, not to mention the nearly 9,000 men in the Union army.

[32] The Federals claimed that Kirby Smith did not discover their evacuation until the afternoon. Edwards, *Shelby and His Men*, 291–92, made the same assertion. He also stated that Kirby Smith failed to patrol the roads about Camden, thus enabling Steele to slip away unobserved.

the east, the assignment was "an utter impossibility," and he found himself behind the Union army when he finally reached Princeton on the road to Little Rock.[33]

As soon as he got his infantry across the makeshift bridge, Kirby Smith strove desperately to catch up with Steele. Marching almost incessantly through rain and over muddy roads, and stimulated by the sight of large quantities of abandoned enemy equipment and plunder, the Confederates reached Tulip at nightfall on the twenty-ninth, having covered fifty-two miles in forty-six hours. Here they learned that Steele had passed through at eight o'clock that morning. Nevertheless they remained optimistic about their chances of at least overtaking his train and rear guard at Jenkins' Ferry on the Saline River, fourteen miles distant. It had been raining heavily for days and the Saline bottom had been turned into a quagmire five miles wide. Under such circumstances Steele was bound to encounter considerable delay in crossing the river. In addition, Kirby Smith hoped that Fagan had learned of Steele's flight and so would throw himself across the Union front.[34]

This hope, however, was doomed to disappointment. Following the victory at Marks' Mills, Fagan endeavored to cross the Saline in order to attack a supply train reported to be en route from Princeton to Little Rock. But he was unable to ford the rain-swollen river, and the information concerning the train proved erroneous. He then swung westward in quest of food and forage for his men and horses, who were beginning to suffer acutely from hunger. On the way, ironically, he unknowingly passed over the road to Jenkins' Ferry just a few hours ahead of Steele's column. Not until he reached the vicinity of Arkadelphia on the night of the twenty-ninth did he receive word of Steele's retreat. He at once set out for Jenkins' Ferry, hoping to reach it before the Federals, but already he was much too late.[35]

---

[33] W. M. McPheeters Diary, April 28, 1864. Edwards, *Shelby and His Men*, 296–97, criticizes Kirby Smith for not pursuing Steele on the direct road to Pine Bluff instead of going by way of the longer road through Princeton taken by the Federals. Most likely Kirby Smith did not take the Pine Bluff route for the same reason that Steele did not—because rain had made it so muddy as to be practically impassable (see *Official Records*, XXXIV, Pt. 1, pp. 668–69).

[34] *Official Records*, XXXIV, Pt. 1, pp. 556, 782.

[35] *Ibid.*, 556, 669, 790. Edwards, *Shelby and His Men*, 290–91, states that the ford on the Saline was "deep, but by no means dangerous or impracticable" and that some of Shelby's command actually crossed. He also asserts that Fagan marched to Arkadelphia "after Shelby's scouts brought in prisoners from the

Kirby Smith rested his army at Tulip until midnight, then resumed the pursuit in "a vague hope of being able to overtake the enemy's rear guard." All through the night the Confederates marched, soaked to the skin by a driving rainstorm. Churchill's Arkansas troops headed the column, followed by Parsons' Missourians and Walker's Texans, in all about eight thousand men. Early in the morning Marmaduke's cavalry, riding far in advance, contacted Union pickets about two miles from Jenkins' Ferry. Instead of a mere rear guard, the bulk of the Federal army and a large portion of its wagon train were still on the west bank of the Saline, waiting to cross on a long pontoon bridge. Aware that the Southern army was close behind, Steele had established a defense perimeter around the crossing and manned it with four thousand infantry. He and his troops had only one desire—to escape. But to escape they knew they had to fight.[36]

As soon as he learned (somewhat to his surprise) that he had Steele at bay, Kirby Smith ordered Price, who now commanded Parsons' and Churchill's divisions, to attack immediately. Price deployed Churchill to the right of the road and held Parsons in reserve; both he and Kirby Smith thought that only a small Union rear guard confronted them and that hence one division would suffice to crush it. The ground was swampy and covered with dense woods and undergrowth. It continued to rain heavily, and in many places the troops had to wade through water up to their knees and even their waists. Churchill found the Federals drawn up behind a belt of timber fronting an open field, with their left flank protected by an impassable swamp and their right, by a creek. His men advanced to the attack but quickly came to a halt under the

retreating army." Available sources offer no way of denying or confirming these statements, which if true mean that Fagan lied mightily in his official report. Shelby did not report on events following Marks' Mills—an omission that may or may not be significant. Kirby Smith, writing to Davis, June 11, 1864, in *Official Records*, XXXIV, Pt. 1, p. 482, stated that Fagan's "taking the road to Arkadelphia after the battle of Marks' Mills was one of those accidents which are liable to befall the best of officers." According to a letter [probably written by one of Kirby Smith's staff] to the Richmond *Whig* [reprinted in the Washington (Ark.) *Telegraph*, March 22, 1865], Kirby Smith after the fall of Camden sent dispatches to Fagan to intercept Steele at the Saline, but the dispatches did not reach him in time. This contradicts Edwards' story, in *Shelby and His Men*, 290–91, that after Marks' Mills Fagan sent a courier to Kirby Smith's headquarters to obtain further instructions, but that the courier was ignored and no new orders provided.

[36] *Official Records*, XXXIV, Pt. 1, pp. 481, 556, 669–70, 677, 782.

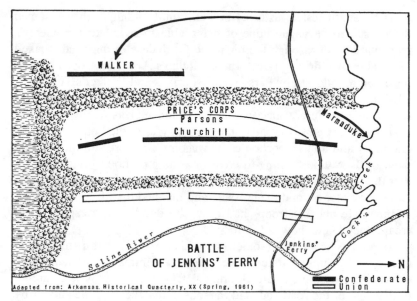

WALKER

PRICE'S CORPS
Parsons
Churchill

Marmaduke

Creek

Cock's

Saline River

BATTLE
OF JENKINS' FERRY

Jenkins'
Ferry

→ N

■ Confederate
▭ Union

Adapted from: Arkansas Historical Quarterly, XX (Spring, 1961)

withering fire of the Union troops, who fought behind the cover of bushes and fallen logs. After about two hours he was forced to fall back and Price, belatedly realizing that the Federals were present in strong force, ordered Parsons to his support. Both divisions then renewed the attack but without success. An attempt by dismounted cavalry under Marmaduke to flank the Union right by crossing the creek likewise failed, and the muddy terrain made it impossible to employ more than a few scattered pieces of light artillery. One battery pushed too far forward and was captured by soldiers of the Second Kansas Colored Regiment, who bayoneted three of the cannoneers after they surrendered, in retaliation for Poison Springs.[37]

By 11:30 A.M. Churchill's and Parsons' troops were fought out and their ammunition exhausted. Kirby Smith ordered them to retire and Walker's Texans took over the battle. But they were no more successful in breaking the stubborn enemy defenses than the Arkansans and Missourians, and two of their brigadiers fell dead and another was badly wounded urging them onward. The Confederate soldiers were hungry and weary, and in the opinion of one of Kirby Smith's staff

[37] *Ibid.*, 556, 669–70, 677, 782, 799–800, 809, 813; W. M. McPheeters Diary, April 30, 1864.

officers "did not fight well." Furthermore, the rain and terrible ground caused much confusion in their ranks, and "it was impossible for their officers, most of whom are of no earthly account, to do anything with them."[38]

The fighting continued in a rather desultory fashion until early afternoon, when Steele, having gotten his wagons across, withdrew his rear guard. The Confederates, being "in great disorder," made no attempt for two hours to follow—a good indication that they had gotten the worst of the battle. When they advanced to the river, they found the entire Union army on the other side and its pontoon bridge lying half submerged in the water, punctured and useless. With no way to cross and his men running low on food, Kirby Smith decided to abandon further pursuit. Three days later Steele's battered and depleted column reached the safety of Little Rock. The "Camden Expedition," as the Federals called it, was over.[39]

Confederate casualties at Jenkins' Ferry were slightly over a thousand, those of the Union, considerably less.[40] For the campaign as a whole, however, the Southern forces lost only about twelve hundred, as compared to twice that number for Steele, and they captured or burned six hundred wagons in addition to acquiring large quantities of military booty.[41] Thus the Confederates inflicted a serious setback on the Union forces in Arkansas, one that altered the balance of military power in the state in their favor.

Little if any blame can be attached to Steele for this outcome. From the first his success depended on Banks's movements, and when Banks fell back it became not only impossible but pointless for Steele to continue advancing. For this reason General Richard Taylor, the able but rather emotional son of Zachary Taylor, bitterly criticized Kirby Smith for transferring the infantry divisions of Parsons, Walker, and Churchill to Arkansas after the battles of Mansfield and Pleasant Hill. Had

[38] *Official Records*, XXXIV, Pt. 1, pp. 556, 670, 677, 782. The staff officer of Kirby Smith quoted was Lieutenant Cunningham, who wrote a long letter to his uncle in Virginia candidly describing the Red River and Camden campaigns. The letter was intercepted by the Federals.

[39] *Ibid.*, 556–57, 669–70, 677–78, 782–83. Edwards, *Shelby and His Men*, 294–96, provides a good account of the Battle of Jenkins' Ferry, but includes a number of implausible incidents and is excessively critical of Kirby Smith.

[40] *Official Records*, XXXIV, Pt. 1, pp. 691, 787–88; Edwards, *Shelby and His Men*, 297.

[41] *Official Records*, XXXIV, Pt. 1, pp. 684, 786–88.

he retained these forces, Taylor asserted, he would have "certainly de-stroyed" Banks's entire army and altered the course of the war. As it was, the Confederates had achieved nothing decisive either in Louisiana or Arkansas, and the campaign as a whole was "a hideous failure."[42]

It is outside the scope of this work to go into the ramifications of the Kirby Smith–Taylor controversy. Suffice it to say that Kirby Smith had four main reasons for deciding to concentrate against Steele after Banks retreated. First, he considered Banks no longer an immediate danger, whereas he feared that Steele, whom he characterized as "bold to rashness," might push on and destroy the vital factories and military installations at Jefferson, Louisiana, and Marshall, Texas, if the Con-federates pursued Banks. Second, he did not agree with Taylor that Banks's destruction was certain if the Confederates continued to press him with their full strength. In attacking at Pleasant Hill they had been bloodily repulsed, and only Banks's lack of aggressiveness and his ob-session with retreating saved them from utter rout. They could hardly expect greater success farther from their base, and with Banks support-ed (as he was not at Pleasant Hill) by the powerful Union gunboats. Third, Kirby Smith felt that he had an excellent chance of bagging Steele's entire army—a much better one, in fact, than was the case with Banks's army. Banks had a secure line of retreat and supply on the Red River, Steele's could be easily cut. Moreover, Banks heavily out-numbered Taylor's army even with the support of Parsons, Churchill, and Walker; these same divisions added to Price's force gave the Con-federates superiority over Steele. And finally, Kirby Smith believed that more was to be gained strategically by defeating Steele than Banks. If the Confederates by some miracle did smash Banks, they would merely be able to advance to the Mississippi, where the Federal warships would block their further progress, and where eventually they would be assailed by overwhelming forces. On the other hand, by knocking out Steele the Confederates would not only regain the Arkansas Valley and break up the Union's puppet government at Little Rock, but they would also be in a position to invade Missouri, thereby creating a strong, perhaps decisive, diversion in behalf of Lee and Johnston in the East.[43]

[42] *Ibid.*, 541–43, 546–48.
[43] *Ibid.*, 480–82, 485–87. Parks, *Kirby Smith*, 394–95, 403–14, ably discusses the Kirby Smith–Taylor quarrel and decides in favor of the former.

All of Kirby Smith's reasons were sound except his fear of Steele's seizing Jefferson and Marshall. As already indicated there was no actual danger of this happening once Banks started to retreat. Kirby Smith's unwarranted fear probably in part stemmed from his extreme lack of confidence in Price's military ability. Throughout the campaign he bombarded Price with highly detailed, frequently repetitious instructions, and quite obviously he took it for granted that Price would be unable to defeat Steele, much less keep him from reaching the Red River. No doubt he would have decided to concentrate against Steele for the other reasons described even if Robert E. Lee himself had commanded in Arkansas, but had he possessed greater faith in Price he would not have been so concerned about Steele.

It is difficult to evaluate Price's performance in the Camden campaign. His own report is often ambiguous and sometimes ingenuous, and there are many gaps and deficiencies in the reports of his subordinates and associates. A correspondent of the Houston *Daily Telegraph* praised him for the "coolness and courage" he displayed in personally leading Parsons' and Churchill's divisions into battle, but he had never lacked in those qualities.[44] During the campaign Kirby Smith commended him for his "prompt and unselfish behavior" in relinquishing Churchill and Parsons and also for the "skill and judgment" with which he had conducted operations against Steele, but subsequently criticized Price for failing to hold Camden and for not executing orders to cut Steele's communications to Little Rock and Pine Bluff.[45] In addition, some officers declared that he was negligent in investing the Federals at Camden.[46]

The first of the above criticisms, failure to hold Camden, was unfair, for Kirby Smith himself had stated that Camden was entirely out of the area of operations and had repeatedly cautioned Price against risking his army in a major engagement. Nor does there seem to be much substance to the one about the investment of Camden, in view of Poison Springs. As to the charge that Price did not carry out Kirby Smith's orders regarding the Union communication line, this is supported by

[44] Houston *Daily Telegraph*, May 11, 1864.
[45] *Official Records*, XXXIV, Pt. 1, pp. 481–82, 486, 531–32; *ibid.*, Pt. 2, pp. 1145–46.
[46] Reynolds, "Price and the Confederacy," 120–21; Houston *Daily Telegraph*, May 18, 1864.

the testimony of two members of Kirby Smith's staff,[47] and by Reynolds and Edwards.[48] Ordinarily this would be considered conclusive. However, in his report Price at least implied that he gave instructions to Fagan to raid the Federal rear independent of Kirby Smith, and Fagan stated in his report that his orders came from "district headquarters," e.g., Price. Moreover, in a personal letter from Snead to Price, Snead expresses great indignation over stories being circulated that Price did not carry out Kirby Smith's orders in the Camden campaign and states that "whoever charges you with disobeying or failing to obey any order of General Smith . . . lies."[49] Such a statement can be ignored only if we are to assume that Snead and Price were in the habit of lying to each other in private correspondence about matters of mutual knowledge. Therefore this allegation must be put down as, at the least, not fully proved. In fact, the evidence would appear to indicate that Price probably was preparing to send Fagan on a raid against Steele's communications when Kirby Smith arrived in Arkansas, with the result that both Price and Kirby Smith issued (without knowledge of each other's action) orders to Fagan. If so, this would help explain Fagan's seeming violation of Kirby Smith's instructions to head straight for Little Rock and the other Union depots.[50]

The records make it clear that Price, to the best of his ability, did carry out Kirby Smith's instructions to delay and harass Steele's advance from Little Rock. And, given the fact that Steele possessed a much stronger army and enjoyed the advantage in maneuvering that goes with being on the offensive, he performed adequately. By the time the Federals reached Camden they were already in a weakened condition, and it is doubtful that they could have pushed much farther south, even against Price alone, without suffering heavy losses: Poison Springs would have been repeated manifold. Indeed, so great was Steele's logistical problem that it would appear that his only real chance of accomplishing his mission was for him to have decisively defeated the

[47] *Official Records*, XXXIV, Pt. 1, p. 555; Boggs, *Military Reminiscences*, 78.
[48] Reynolds, "Price and the Confederacy," 120; Edwards, *Shelby and His Men*, 271. See also Houston *Daily Telegraph*, May 18, 1864, quoting extracts from the notebook of a member of the Third Texas, Walker's Division.
[49] Snead to Price, July 20, 1864, in *Official Records*, XLI, Pt. 2, p. 1017. Snead wrote the letter from Richmond, Virginia, but he was with Price during the Camden campaign.
[50] See footnote 28, this chapter.

Confederate army in Arkansas. Consequently, instead of engaging in clever flanking marches, he could have made every effort to bring Price to bay in an all-out battle. The smashing of Price would not have changed, because of Banks's defeat, the ultimate outcome of his expedition, but it would have saved him from the nearly disastrous predicament he found himself in first at Camden and then at Jenkins' Ferry.

Kirby Smith was greatly disappointed by the failure to destroy Steele's army. He blamed it on Fagan, the lack of pontoons, the flooding of the Saline, and the physical exhaustion of his troops. However, he rightly believed that on the whole his strategy of luring the enemy deep into the interior and concentrating his own forces had worked well. "With a force of 25,000 men, all told, in the entire department," he proudly wrote President Davis, "I drove back whence they came armies 60,000 [sic] strong, supported by an enormous fleet, inflicting immense loss in both men and material."[51] Moreover, Banks's army had been rendered impotent and Steele's badly crippled forces had been cooped up behind the fortification of Little Rock, from which they dared not venture. Thus the Trans-Mississippi was for the time being safe from attack; thus, too, the way was free for an invasion of Missouri.

[51] *Official Records*, XXXIV, Pt. 1, pp. 481–82, 486.

11

ACROSS THE ARKANSAS

Two days after the Battle of Jenkins' Ferry the Missouri troops turned their attention from bullets to ballots and acting as their state's electorate voted for members of Congress. Among the candidates chosen were Snead and ex-Senator John Clark. The latter's friends hailed his victory as a "popular rebuke" to Reynolds for not reappointing him to the Senate. Reynolds thought otherwise but had to recognize that the pro-Price, anti-Davis faction had been strengthened. He also noted that Clark received most of his votes from units directly under Price's command, and that Price had openly backed him.[1]

About two weeks after the election Representative George G. Vest, leader of the Missouri House delegation, arrived from the East and spent three days with Reynolds at his Marshall, Texas, "capital." In the course of their conversations Vest related the following story. During the winter a letter came to Richmond from Washington. It was addressed by Unionist Congressman James S. Rollins of Missouri to Senator Clark and covered a letter from Edwin Price to President Davis. In the letter Edwin Price stated that he wished to visit Texas in order to see his mother and attend to some family business; that President Lincoln had given his consent to the visit and to his return to Missouri; and that he desired a safe conduct from Davis for the same purpose. Rollins' letter to Clark requested him to present Edwin Price's letter to Davis and to use his influence to obtain the safe conduct. It also urged Clark to abandon the Confederate cause, assuring him of a cordial reception should he return to Missouri.

The packet containing the letter came sealed but was opened in the Confederate prisoner exchange office (to which such communications came) and the letter to Davis forwarded to him. On reading it, Davis summoned Vest, had him read it, then asked him, "What do you advise me to do about it?" Vest answered, "I decidedly advise you, Mr. Presi-

[1] Reynolds to Davis, May 10, 1864, in Thomas C. Reynolds Papers, Library of Congress; Reynolds, "Price and the Confederacy," 104–107. The Missouri troops east of the Mississippi also voted for members of Congress at this time.

dent, not to grant the request." Said Davis, "Then, I have no further hesitation; I shall refuse it." Davis' manner was "peculiar and expressive, as if the letter had seemed to him extraordinary and suspicious."

Sometime later Vest left Richmond for the Trans-Mississippi. On the way, at Selma, Alabama, another of Price's sons, Major Thomas Price, gave him a letter which he placed with a number of others he was carrying. When he reached Camden he distributed all the letters except one, which he found sealed and without an address. Presuming that it was for himself, he opened it and commenced reading—only to discover that it was a letter from Edwin to Thomas Price intended for the perusal of their father. In it Edwin denounced Vest and the rest of the Missouri delegation for having, as he believed, prevented Davis from giving him the safe conduct to Texas he had asked.

Much embarrassed, Vest at once delivered the letter to Price, who accepted his explanation of how he came to open it. However, knowing Price "to be devoted to his sons, and rather vindictive," he thought it best to make an effort to counteract the effect of the letter on his mind. Therefore, he related his action in regard to Edwin's application and stated that it was in the best interests of both Price and his son. Price replied that he had "done perfectly right" in advising the President as he did. "I have," he continued, "suffered myself and my son to be maligned and injured by the reports about his return to Missouri, because I could not break silence without exposing his life to the enemy. But it was I who advised him to go home. He was exchanged in 1862, and came to me saying that he was willing to enlist as a private in the Confederate army, but thought he could do more good in Missouri, as Gamble had offered to let him return to his farm, without entering into any obligation; that the Southern men in his neighborhood were without leaders, as all the prominent men were either exiled, in prison, or under bond; that he could keep up the Southern feeling and secretly organize men to join me on [my] return to the State. I accordingly told him to go, to tell our friends that I would certainly return with an army in the ensuing Spring, and Edwin thought he would be able to join me with from 1,000 to 2,000 men. I was disappointed in my expectations, but can assure you that Edwin is a true Southern man."

Price concluded that so far he had patiently borne the implications against his son and the suspicions of himself, but felt now that he should no longer do so. Hence, although he did not wish his explanation of Edwin's conduct to be generally circulated, lest it should become the subject of camp gossip or get into the newspapers, he authorized Vest to communicate it to Davis and such other persons he thought proper.

Reynolds listened to Vest with acute interest. Price's explanation of why he, Edwin, had returned to Missouri, he noted, squared with the version he had earlier received from Dr. Pallen in Richmond. When Vest finished, Reynolds told him that he had acted wisely in counseling Davis to withhold the safe conduct pass, for if Edwin had gone to Texas, he would have been there at the same time as his father, "and as General Price was known to have been very doubtful last fall of our independence, the conjunction might have been commented on." To this Vest replied that Davis' "prejudice against Price is still violent," and related the following incident as an illustration: In the spring of 1863, following Price's visit to Richmond, Senator George Pugh of Alabama said to Davis, "Mr. President, I saw for the first time lately this great popular leader, General Price, and on acquaintance with him I must say I fully concur in your opinion that he is one of the greatest humbugs in existence." In response Davis said nothing, but he did smile.

The two Missouri politicians then discussed the Edwin Price case. Vest stated that all of his information about Edwin's course in Missouri indicated that he had become a zealous Unionist and was regarded as such by all parties in the state. Reynolds said that this was also the uniform tenor of the intelligence he had received. Neither, however, expressed an opinion as such on the veracity of Price's explanation of his son's conduct.[2]

The conversations with Vest strengthened Reynolds' long-standing doubts about Price's devotion to the Confederacy and his intentions regarding Missouri and the West. He recalled that, on his return from Texas, Price had spoken at length concerning the prospects of a campaign in Missouri, but "had made not even the most distant allusion to his son." This, with his previous silence on the subject, seemed to

[2] The above account of the Edwin Price, Vest, et al affair is based on, and all quotes are from, Reynolds, "Price and the Confederacy," 107–11, which in turn appears to have been in large part based on Reynolds, "Memoranda relative to . . . Confederate Senators," in Reynolds Papers, Library of Congress, a document he wrote at the time of the affair.

indicate that whatever plans the Prices had were not such as they cared
to reveal to the Confederate executive of Missouri. Furthermore, his
authorization to Vest to explain the matter to Davis showed that even
the President had been kept in the dark. In Reynolds' opinion Edwin
Price's asking permission to visit his mother, and not so much as hint-
ing at a meeting with his father, was nothing but a "clumsy effort to
conceal the design to confer with the latter."

Just what Price and his son were up to, Reynolds could not exactly
decide. But he was inclined to suspect that it had something to do with
the Northwest Confederacy scheme. For Price "was universally regarded, and even mentioned in the Southern press, as the destined and
perhaps already selected leader of a military movement for a 'North
West' republic, united to or at least allied with, the Confederacy." According to Reynolds' information, the object of this conspiracy (which
was being carried out by a secret organization known as the O.A.K.—
the Order of American Knights) was the "reconstruction of the old
Union on a pro-slavery basis," and hence was "as much opposed as
Mr. Lincoln himself . . . to acknowledge the independence of the Confederacy." And while many public men in the South expected and even
desired at least a partial reconstruction of the Union as an eventual
result of the war, a premature attempt, especially a military one, to
achieve that end would, Reynolds believed, only dilute and weaken the
Confederacy. Consequently he decided that the "profound mystery of
[Price's] operations through his son, without the sanction, or even the
knowledge of his military superiors, or the Confederate governments,
State or general, demanded attention," or, in other words, steps must
be taken to forestall any plot Price might be hatching which would be
injurious to the Southern cause.

But, reflected Reynolds, what steps? If he used his influence with
Davis and Kirby Smith to have Price transferred to a command distant
from Missouri, the result would be a serious "fuss" on the part of the
general and his friends. On the other hand, to place him under the command of another general during the proposed Missouri expedition
would produce the same effect, besides irritating Price at the very moment when it would be in his power to do mischief and perhaps even
commit some dangerous act of military insubordination. In the end
Reynolds concluded that it would be best to let Price head the Missouri
campaign, but "at the same time to surround him with subordinate gen-

erals exclusively devoted to the Confederacy." In this manner the arrangement he had made with Benjamin would be continued, Price would render a service to the common cause and gratify his legitimate ambition, the Richmond authorities would be spared a revival of the "Price question," and reliable safeguards would be provided against any abuse by Price of his opportunities as an independent commander.[3]

Having thus resolved on what he termed "this policy of generosity and confidence," Reynolds on May 17 wrote the following to Price:

My Dear General:

Mr. Vest yesterday related to me a conversation he had had with you, and which you authorized him to communicate to your friends, in reference to General Edwin Price. It removed a feeling of delicacy I have heretofore felt about speaking to you on the subject, and leaved [sic] me free to mention a circumstance, which I trust will give pleasure to you, as his father, and show you that, whatever may have been, or hereafter be our differences about public men or measures, you have in me a *warm personal friend.*

Governor Jackson never received the resignation by General E. Price of his position in the Missouri State Guard. On my succession to the Governorship I learned that General Parsons had it, but I determined not to accept it, but to leave him still on the State Roster as Brigadier of the Third District. Harsh constructions, as you are aware, had been put upon his course, but as your friend I determined to show by my executive action, that I had confidence in his justifying it when the proper occasion should arrive, or that at least, unlike some others of your friends, (and his neighbors,) I would not condemn him unheard. He is an able, gallant officer, and I trust yet to see him leading Missourians on Missouri soil to victory in our cause.[4]

The object of this letter, Reynolds subsequently explained, "was to exhibit my disposition to trust and oblige [Price], to elicit a frank explanation [of his plans for Missouri] in return, and . . . by apprizing him of the fact that his son was still an officer of the Missouri State Guard, attract his attention to the fact that any real adherence to the Federals might, in the event of our recovery of Missouri, make his son amenable to my jurisdiction for the punishment of his desertion. . . ." Price did not answer the letter, and Reynolds took his silence as "an

[3] Reynolds, "Price and the Confederacy," 111–13.
[4] Reynolds to Price, May 17, 1864, in Reynolds Papers, Library of Congress.

indication that there was much he wished to conceal in his relations with his son.''[5]

There can be no doubt that Vest's revelations led to a widening of the breach between Reynolds and Price. Given the governor's fervent devotion to the Confederacy and Davis, his suspicious nature, and his low opinion of Price, it is quite understandable that he would distrust Price's intentions, whatever they were, and feel called upon to take countermeasures. Also it is probably safe to assume that Price resented Reynold's letter concerning Edwin, which at best must have seemed to him officious meddling in his private affairs, at worst, implicit blackmail. The question is, were Reynolds' suspicions concerning Price justified in fact? Was Price actually playing a tricky double game with the aim of establishing a separate Northwestern Confederacy and/or reconstructing the Union along proslavery lines?

On the basis of the ascertainable facts the answer can neither be yes nor no, because the facts are very skimpy. First, there was an organization, or at least the semblance of one, known as the Order of American Knights. Its founder and leader was an obscure individual named Phineas Wright, and its avowed objective was the establishment of a Northwest Confederacy, consisting of the states of Ohio, Indiana, Michigan, Illinois, Wisconsin, Minnesota, and Iowa, which would be in alliance with the Confederate States of America. It claimed hundreds of thousands of members throughout the North, and at least some Federal officials attributed great strength to it, but in the opinion of all historians it was basically a sham and never constituted a real threat to the Union.[6]

Second, Price was, for what little it was worth, its designated military commander. Evidence for this is to be found in contemporary Southern newspapers (as mentioned by Reynolds), the testimony of O.A.K. members, and in various documents of the Order.[7] In addi-

---

[5] Reynolds, "Price and the Confederacy," 113–14.

[6] "The John P. Sanderson Report on the O.A.K." (Microfilm, Missouri Historical Society, St. Louis); Joseph Holt to E. M. Stanton, October 8, 1864, in *Official Records*, Ser. II, Vol. VII, pp. 930–53; J. W. Tucker to Jefferson Davis, March 14, 1864, in Rowland, *Jefferson Davis, Constitutionalist*, VI, 204–206; Frank M. Klement, *The Copperheads in the Middle West* (Chicago, 1960), 178–205.

[7] "The John P. Sanderson Report"; John A. Logan, *The Great Conspiracy: Its Origin and History* (New York, 1886), 559; *Official Records*, XLI, Pt. 2, p. 1085; *ibid.*, Pt. 3, pp. 975–76.

tion, it is significant that editor J. W. Tucker wrote a confidential letter, dated March 14, 1864, from the Spottswood Hotel, Richmond, Virginia, to President Davis, in which he outlined the nature and purpose of the O.A.K. ("the most perfect and the most secret [organization] the world has ever known") and requested that $100,000 be sent to Lieutenant General Leonidas Polk for disbursement to its agents in support of their sabotage activities against Union transports, factories, and military installations. Tucker, despite Price's denial, was one of Price's cohorts, and General Polk also was on friendly terms with the Missouri general.[8]

Third, Price did have strong personal reasons to be dissatisfied with the Richmond government and its policies respecting Missouri and the West; in particular, as noted earlier, he feared that the Confederacy might make a peace settlement in which Missouri would be conceded to the North. Therefore it is easy to see why the formation of a Northwest Confederacy, to which Missouri could attach itself in case it was excluded from the Confederate States of America, would attract his interest.

And finally, Representative James S. Rollins of Missouri did contact Lincoln regarding Price, writing to him as follows on July 26, 1863:

Major Genl Sterling Price is no smarter than he ought to be, or he never would have been caught in this rebellion.

He started out a Union man, and I have every reason to believe, his vanity and his ignorance, induced him to drift into the whirlpool of treason.

Now that the State of Missouri is about fixed—I am inclined to the opinion that Price would be glad to quit—lay down his arms, and come home. . . . Rest assured (altho' I have no respect for the intellect or the intelligence of the man) it would be a great point to get him back. Can't you offer him a free pardon if he will return? If you will say so—I'll try

[8] Tucker to Davis, March 14, 1864, in Rowland, *Jefferson Davis, Constitutionalist*, VI, 204–206. Tucker stated that the O.A.K. had 490,000 men in Michigan, Minnesota, Wisconsin, Iowa, Illinois, Indiana, and Ohio, and that out of this vast membership "only two individuals have ever shown a disposition to betray the secrets of the order; and these two men disappeared mysteriously." Tucker did not mention Price, but Davis knew of the connection between the editor and the general. There is no record of Davis' replying to Tucker's fantastic letter.

and induce some of his particular friends—to go and have an interview with him.[9]

Since nearly a month later Edwin published a letter in the St. Louis *Missouri Republican* denying reports that his father was "penitent" and wanted to abandon the Confederacy, presumably the initiative for this proposal was Rollins', although of this one cannot be certain. In any case, Lincoln responded favorably and Edwin received a safe conduct, only to be denied permission to go to Texas by Davis acting on the advice of Vest.[10]

These facts lend themselves to at least two interpretations. One is that, as Reynolds suspected, Price and his son were engaged with the O.A.K. in a conspiracy to establish a Northwest Confederacy to which Missouri would or could attach itself; that this conspiracy involved deliberate deception of the Federal authorities and secret activities contrary to the interests of the Confederate cause; and that Edwin's attempt to visit his mother in Texas early in 1864 was somehow connected with the conspiracy. The other is that Price regarded the O.A.K. (which according to Tucker had a thousand adherents in St. Louis alone) as mainly if not solely a potential source of aid in redeeming Missouri from Federal rule and did not take seriously its talk of a Northwest Confederacy; that Edwin was sincere in professing allegiance to the Union and that he attempted to visit Texas at the behest of Rollins to induce his father to renounce the Confederacy and/or transact certain family business; and that Price's explanation of Edwin's conduct, as given to Dr. Pallen and to Vest, was merely a clumsy yet understandable attempt to conceal the embarrassing fact of his son's defection.

Of these two explanations, the first could well be true, but the latter is the more likely one. This conclusion derives in part from a judgment of Price's character but is based mainly on the known facts of

[9] James S. Rollins to Abraham Lincoln, July 26, 1863, in Roy P. Basler (ed.), *The Collected Works of Abraham Lincoln* (New Brunswick, 1953), VI, 360.

[10] St. Louis *Missouri Republican*, August 21, 1863; Lincoln to Rollins, August (?), 1863, in James S. Rollins, "Letters and Speeches" (Binder, Missouri Historical Society, St. Louis). Perhaps more could be learned of the dealings between Edwin Price and Rollins, and Edwin and his father, if the James S. Rollins Papers at the Missouri State Historical Society, Columbia, were presently open to scholars.

his entire career and is supported by the testimony of Charles L. Hunt, leader of the O.A.K. in St. Louis. Hunt stated that Price formed the organization in Missouri during the summer and fall of 1863, and that his principal object in doing so was to unite Confederate adherents for the purpose of rising up when he invaded the state and to recruit for his army in the meanwhile.[11] Consequently Reynolds' suspicions of Price probably were not justified, although he cannot be blamed for entertaining them in view of the general's failure to confide in the Confederate government or himself. However, until more evidence comes to light, the whole matter of Price, the O.A.K., and the Northwest Confederacy will remain essentially what it was then and it is now—a minor yet intriguing mystery.

Immediately following the Battle of Jenkins' Ferry, Kirby Smith hurried back to the Red River with Parsons', Walker's, and Churchill's divisions in hopes of inflicting further damage on Banks. But when he found that Banks had retreated beyond effective striking range, he again turned his attention northward. As previously noted he believed that Federal naval power made a movement against New Orleans impractical. Therefore he proposed to concentrate his forces in Arkansas, destroy Steele's army, and invade Missouri. Such a campaign, in his opinion, was the only feasible way in which the Trans-Mississippi Department, given its material weakness and geographical isolation, could make an important contribution to the overall Confederate war effort.[12]

Accordingly on May 19 he directed Price to accumulate supplies and gather intelligence about the enemy in preparation for a northern offensive.[13] However, despite these instructions, he did not intend for Price to lead the campaign. Price, he wrote President Davis, was capable neither of "organizing, disciplining, nor operating an army," although his "name and popularity would be a strong element of success

[11] "Sanderson Report," Missouri Historical Society, St. Louis. Hunt, who was the Belgian consul in St. Louis, was arrested and made a confession in the fall of 1864. Sanderson, a Federal army officer in St. Louis, made a report on Hunt's confession and other findings concerning the O.A.K. The report contained many exaggerations and even fabrications and was designed to present the O.A.K. as something it definitely was not–a serious threat to Union security. However, if used cautiously, it does provide some useful information about the O.A.K., and Hunt's testimony regarding Price is confirmed by other evidences and appears inherently plausible.

[12] *Official Records*, XXXIV, Pt. 1, pp. 486–87; *ibid.*, XLI, Pt. 4, pp. 1068–69.

[13] *Official Records*, XXXIV, Pt. 3, pp. 828–29.

in an advance on Missouri."[14] His choice as commander was Richard Taylor, whom he regarded as the ablest general in the department. Although Taylor was primarily interested in his native state of Louisiana, he accepted the assignment and even outlined a plan of operations. But early in June, after picking a quarrel with Kirby Smith over the conduct of the Red River campaign, he asked to be transferred east. This of course made him unavailable for the Missouri expedition, but for the time being Kirby Smith did not decide on a replacement.[15]

During May, Jo Shelby moved into northeast Arkansas with orders from Kirby Smith to attack the Union supply line between Little Rock and Devall's Bluff and to recruit men for the forthcoming campaign. This region abounded in slackers, deserters, and bandits, and all previous attempts to obtain any large number of recruits there had failed. But the energetic Shelby succeeded in conscripting thousands of men into service, forming them into battalions and regiments, and equipping some of them with captured arms. In addition he routed several Federal detachments, took hundreds of prisoners, and destroyed miles of railroad tracks and even several steamboats. These exploits further enhanced his reputation as the best cavalry leader in the West.[16]

Kirby Smith's intention was to launch the Missouri expedition about mid-August. Not until then, he believed, would the troops and horses involved in the operations against Banks and Steele be fully rested and refitted, sufficient wagons collected, and the corn crop in Missouri be ripe enough to provide food and forage.[17] Price, on the other hand, wished to move at once. He was anxious to exploit the opportunity provided by Steele's defeat to liberate Missouri, and feared that if Kirby Smith waited too long, the Federal armies in Arkansas and Missouri would be heavily reinforced.[18] Also he was apprehensive (with good reason) that Kirby Smith might supersede him as commander of the District of Arkansas with either Magauder or Major General Simon B. Buckner (who had recently been assigned to the Trans-Mississippi). Also, he resented the fact that Kirby Smith had not given him any pub-

[14] Kirby Smith to Davis, May 5, 1864, in *ibid.*, XLI, Pt. 1, p. 478.
[15] *Ibid.*, 533, 544–47.
[16] *Ibid.*, XLI, Pt. 1, pp. 191–92; *ibid.*, Pt. 2, pp. 1027–28; *ibid.*, Pt. 4, p. 1068; Edwards, *Shelby and His Men*, 317–18.
[17] *Official Records*, XLI, Pt. 2, pp. 1011, 1052; *ibid.*, Pt. 4, p. 1028.
[18] Thomas L. Snead to Sterling Price, July 20, 1864, in *Official Records*, XLI, Pt. 2, 1019; Reynolds, "Price and the Confederacy," 103–104.

lic credit for his part in defeating Steele and that Congress had not voted a resolution of thanks to him as it had to Taylor.[19]

In a letter of June 9 to Reynolds, who had requested his views on the Missouri expedition, he expressed these feelings:

I have but little encouragement to form opinions or plans for our future military movements. None have [sic] been adopted that have been suggested by me. I, however, do not complain. Perhaps it was best that they were not adopted; nobody will ever know. And my plans are to attract the less attention in the future, for the reason that I am being thrown farther from the chief in command of the department by the promotion of my juniors over me; but let that be as it may, I shall go on and endeavor to discharge my duty to my country, to my command, whatever it may be, and to myself. I shall hope to deserve the approbation of my country, and if I get it I should surely be satisfied.[20]

He added that "we have just closed a brilliant campaign in my district," that "the cavalry is entitled to the credit for our successes," and that if he had not been deprived of his infantry he would have bottled up Steele in Camden and "made another Lexington affair of it."

When Snead went to Richmond to take his seat in Congress, he endeavored to secure Price's promotion to lieutenant general with a view to maintaining him in his position as commander of the District of Arkansas.[21] In interviews with Davis, Seddon, and Bragg (now the President's chief of staff) he "explained to them fully the condition of affairs in the Trans-Mississippi" and gave them "a faithful account of the campaign in Arkansas," all the while being "careful to avoid the appearance of partisanship" for Price. He soon discovered that Davis was not recommending anyone for promotion in the West unless first endorsed by Kirby Smith—and this in itself sufficed to dispose of Price's prospects, which were nil in any event.[22]

Price's failure to obtain increased rank must have become all the more galling to him when departmental headquarters announced in July that Marmaduke had been promoted to major general. Not only

[19] *Official Records*, XLI, Pt. 2, pp. 1015, 1017.

[20] Reynolds to Price, June 2, 1864, in *ibid.*, LIII, 998; Price to Reynolds, June 9, 1864, in *ibid.*, 999–1000.

[21] Reynolds, "Memoranda relative to . . . Confederate Senators," Thomas C. Reynolds Papers, Library of Congress.

[22] Snead to Price, July 20, 1864, in *Official Records*, XLI, Pt. 2, pp. 1015–17.

had Price opposed Marmaduke's promotion, but during the Camden campaign had also tried to persuade Kirby Smith to relieve him of command. In Price's opinion Marmaduke was incompetent, a source of dissension in the cavalry, and an intriguer who exercised an unfortunate influence with Kirby Smith. For his part Marmaduke had a "very low opinion of Price's military capacity," and believed Price and his staff to be "malignantly hostile to him."[23]

Despite his personal disappointments, Price busied himself through the hot summer months preparing for the pending campaign. Starting in June he sent numerous agents into Missouri to gather intelligence, raise recruits, and circulate propaganda. One of these men, Captain John Chestnut, carried special instructions to the guerrillas, who were to soften up the Union defenders by raiding outposts, ambushing patrols, cutting telegraph wires, burning bridges, and tearing up track. Chestnut met with the principal partisan leaders early in August, and soon afterwards the bushwhackers were riding rampant through the northern and western counties.[24] In addition, Price got into touch with the O.A.K., whose leaders promised a mass uprising when the Confederate army entered the state.[25]

As June gave way to July the Missourians in Arkansas became greatly concerned that the whole summer and perhaps fall were to pass without a movement into their state. Should this happen, they feared that the pro-Confederate population of Missouri would lose hope and so reconcile itself to Yankee rule, and that it might thus become impossible to secure a peace treaty incorporating the state into the Confederacy. These considerations prompted Reynolds, who believed that the army was "shamelessly inactive," to write Price on July 18 proposing a cavalry raid into Missouri as an alternative to a major offensive. Davis and Seddon, he stated, were "impatient for an advance into Missouri," which even if unsuccessful would provide a useful diversion. And if successful, "the cavalry might be re-enforced by infantry from Arkansas and by recruiting within our State." Did Price, he asked, approve of such an expedition, and would he be "willing to take command of it (which is especially desirable), . . . ?"[26]

[23] Ibid., 1017, 1041; Reynolds, "Price and the Confederacy," 116–17, 121–22.
[24] John N. Edwards, Noted Guerrillas, or, The Warfare of the Border (St. Louis, 1877), 283; Castel, Quantrill, 173–83.
[25] Official Records, LIII, 999; ibid., XLI, Pt. 2, p. 1085.
[26] Ibid., XLI, Pt. 2, p. 1011.

Price, who himself had earlier suggested a cavalry raid,[27] replied four days later that he considered Reynolds' proposal both practicable and desirable. He commented: "If it is not General Smith's purpose to concentrate the troops and take possession of the Arkansas Valley I would like to take command of the expedition. . . . My opinion is that the people of Missouri are ready for a general uprising and that the time was never more propitious for an advance of our forces into Missouri."[28]

Stirred to action by Reynolds' letter, Price the following day addressed Kirby Smith in a similar vein. Federal forces in Missouri, he asserted, consisted mainly of unreliable militia. Large guerrilla parties were operating, and "the Confederate flag floats over nearly all of the principal towns of North Missouri." The people feared that a "negotiation for boundaries" would take place without the Confederacy being in possession of any part of the state. Even the "least sanguine" predicted that an invasion would produce no less than thirty thousand recruits. Moreover, Steele's army at Little Rock and Pine Bluff was reportedly on half-rations and so constituted no serious obstacle. In conclusion he urged an early movement into Missouri and requested a meeting with Kirby Smith to discuss the matter.[29]

Kirby Smith, who received a letter from Reynolds also calling for a cavalry raid into Missouri,[30] asked Price to visit him at his headquarters. Although "quite sick" from an attack of "chills and fever," Price left Camden on August 1 and journeyed to Shreveport. There he spent several days conferring with Kirby Smith, Reynolds, and Senators Johnson and Mitchell of Arkansas. The eventual outcome was an order, dated August 4, in which Kirby Smith instructed Price to "make immediate arrangements for a movement into Missouri, with the entire cavalry force of your district."[31]

Kirby Smith's sudden decision to abandon his plan for a full-scale northern offensive stemmed only in part from the solicitations of Price and Reynolds. At the same time he received their letters, an order

[27] *Ibid.*, LIII, 999–1000.

[28] *Ibid.*, XLI, Pt. 2, p. 1020.

[29] *Ibid.*, 1023.

[30] Reynolds to Kirby Smith, July 25, 1864, in Thomas C. Reynolds Papers, Library of Congress.

[31] Reynolds, "Price and the Confederacy," 127–28; *Official Records*, XLI, Pt. 2, pp. 1040–41.

arrived from the War Department directing him to transfer immediately all of the infantry in Louisiana and Arkansas to the other side of the Mississippi, and urging him to create a diversion in favor of the Confederate armies in Georgia and Alabama. The first part of this order left him without sufficient forces to drive Steele from the Arkansas Valley; by the same token, the only practical way in which he could comply with the second part was to make a cavalry raid into Missouri. Hence, sheer necessity gave him no choice except to agree to Price's and Reynolds' proposal. However, apart from its primary diversionary purpose, he was encouraged by the optimistic reports and predictions of the Missourians to hope that a raid into Missouri would inflict severe damage on the enemy and produce sizable numbers of recruits.[32] And last, but perhaps subconsciously not least in his mind, by sending Price off to Missouri he most conveniently solved the problem of obtaining a more satisfactory commander for the District of Arkansas. On the same day that Price got his orders to make the raid, Shreveport headquarters announced that John Magruder had been assigned to Arkansas and that Price henceforth would command only the cavalry of the district.[33]

Indeed, for awhile there was a distinct possibility that Price might not even head the Missouri expedition. Reynolds, doubtful of Price's generalship and distrustful of his intentions, would have preferred either Buckner or Kirby Smith himself as commander, with Price coming along in a nominal position of second-in-command (obviously his declaration to Price that it was "especially desirable" that he be the commander was hypocritical). But Kirby Smith had more important duties, and Buckner was not interested. Reynolds then considered Fagan, Marmaduke, and Shelby. Selection of the first, however, would create resentment among the Missouri troops because he was from Arkansas; the naming of Marmaduke would invite a disruptive protest from Price's friends; and Shelby, otherwise the best suited of all for a quick, slashing cavalry raid, was without the necessary rank.

Consequently when Kirby Smith asked for his views on the subject of a commander for the Missouri campaign, Reynolds advised him to employ Price, "but to send with him the best division and brigade commanders and an unusually efficient staff." Kirby Smith expressed strong reluctance to adopt this plan and in reference to Price's military ability

[32] *Official Records*, XLI, Pt. 4, pp. 1068–69.
[33] *Ibid.*, Pt. 1, pp. 92–93; *ibid.*, Pt. 2, pp. 1039–40.

declared "he is good for nothing." To support this contention he related
a number of incidents from the recent operations against Steele, among
them Price's alleged neglect of orders at Camden. Reynolds readily
agreed that Price was deficient in military talent, but pointed out the
lack of an acceptable alternative to him, and also called attention to
Davis' desire to avoid another "Price embroglio." Finally Kirby Smith
agreed to give Price the command under the arrangement suggested by
Reynolds.[34]

Kirby Smith then briefed Price. He was to organize his army into
three divisions headed by Marmaduke, Fagan, and Shelby, but to leave
in Arkansas Colonel Colton Greene and "other regimental commanders whose mutinuous conduct has already proved them unfit for command." St. Louis was to be the objective point of his movement, "which
if rapidly made, will put you in possession of that place, its supplies,
and military stores, and which will do more toward rallying Missourians to your standard than the possession of any other point." The rais-
ing of new forces was to be his principal endeavor, and if compelled
to retreat from Missouri he was to do so by way of Kansas and the
Indian Territory, "sweeping that country of its mules, horses, cattle,
and military supplies of all kinds," and bringing back as many recruits
as possible. Finally, throughout the campaign he would "scrupulously
avoid all wanton acts of destruction and devastation," restrain his men,
and impress on them that "their aim should be to secure success in a
just and holy cause and not to gratify personal feelings and revenge."[35]

To these military objectives Price privately added another, the political one of gaining control of enough territory in Missouri, at least
temporarily, to hold an election for a new governor and a legislature.
In this way not only would the Confederate Missourians keep alive
their claim to authority in the state, but (equally desirable from Price's
personal standpoint) Reynolds would be removed from the scene, or
at least prevented, as Snead put it, from exercising "without control all
the powers of the executive and legislative departments."[36] Reynolds,

[34] Reynolds, "Price and the Confederacy," 116–27.
[35] Kirby Smith to Price, August 4, 1864, in *Official Records*, XLI, Pt. 2, pp.
1040–41.
[36] Snead to Price, July 20, 1864, in *ibid.*, 1018. In this letter Snead also stated
that unless there were an election, Reynolds would hold on to office and "continue to exercise, after the expiration of his present term of office, what will
then be an autocratic, despotic, and illegal authority." He then added, quite

who suspected this latter intention, at first opposed an election, but under pressure from Price and former governor Trusten Polk, reluctantly consented.[37] Not without reason he feared that an election would result in "legitimate civil authority" (his own) being superseded by an "army council" (Price).[38] Indeed, so discouraged was he at this prospect that he even sent feelers to Richmond in regard to obtaining an appointment as a Confederate judge.[39]

Price planned to begin the campaign by crossing the Arkansas River below Little Rock. In order to cover this movement he ordered Shelby, who was still in northeast Arkansas, to attack Devall's Bluff and the railroad between Little Rock and the White River. Shelby carried out the assignment brilliantly, capturing six small forts and several hundred prisoners, inflicting heavy casualties, and destroying ten miles of track.[40] Simultaneously Brigadier General Stand Watie's Indian Brigade further diverted Federal attention by threatening southern Kansas.[41]

Originally Price hoped to be north of the Arkansas by August 20, but owing to a delay in receiving needed ordnance stores from Shreveport he was unable to leave Camden until the twenty-eighth. He then traveled to Princeton, where the following day he assumed command of Marmaduke's and Fagan's divisions. On the thirtieth he began marching northward. Fearful that his belated start had alerted the enemy of his intentions, he decided to cross the Arkansas above Little Rock rather than below. Therefore, after feinting toward Little Rock, he swung off to the northwest and forded the Arkansas at Dardanelle

unnecessarily: "Don't understand me as advocating Governor Reynolds' re-election." Because of Claiborne Jackson's death, the death of Josiah Chilton (President of the Missouri Senate in 1861), and the legal expiration of the Missouri House of Representatives elected in 1860 (and thus of the office of its Speaker), Reynolds was, from the Southern viewpoint, the sole representative of the sovereignty of Missouri. To forestall the Confederate Missouri government becoming extinct in case of his death, Reynolds on March 20, 1863, issued a proclamation stating that if he died he would be succeeded by the following in this order: Waldo P. Johnson, Trusten Polk, and Sterling Price.

[37] Reynolds to Price and Polk, June 27, 1864, in *ibid.*, XXXIV, Pt. 4, p. 696.
[38] Reynolds to Seddon, August 6, 1864, in Thomas C. Reynolds Papers, Library of Congress.
[39] Reynolds to Johnson, July 14, 1864, in Thomas C. Reynolds Papers, Library of Congress.
[40] *Official Records*, XLI, Pt. 1, pp. 625, 650.
[41] *Ibid.*, Pt. 2, pp. 1095–96; *ibid.*, Pt. 3, p. 235.

on September 7. A week later, moving by way of Batesville, he reached Pocahontas in northeast Arkansas, only a few miles south of the Missouri line.[42]

Thus Price successfully executed the first phase of his expedition by penetrating Steele's lines and gaining a jump-off point for the invasion of Missouri. In so doing he was aided greatly by the fact that Steele lacked sufficient troops and transport to guard all crossings on the Arkansas River. Moreover Steele believed that it was impossible for a large force to sustain itself in northern Arkansas and southern Missouri, and hence was convinced that Price intended to attack Little Rock, an attitude which was further encouraged by an advance by Thomas Churchill and Monroe Parsons from Camden. When he learned that Price was across the Arkansas and obviously heading for Missouri, he organized a pursuing force, but it was too late to accomplish anything.[43] In brief, this time Price outmaneuvered Steele.

At Pocahontas, Price was joined by Shelby, who brought with him approximately eight thousand recruits gathered during his summer's operations in that area. Price now organized his army, per Kirby Smith's instructions, into three divisions under Fagan, Marmaduke, and Shelby, and distributed the recruits, who had been formed into brigades and regiments, among them, with Fagan receiving the most. In all he had about twelve thousand troops. It was the largest force he had commanded since 1862, and on paper appeared formidable. However it was afflicted with a number of serious weaknesses which greatly reduced its military potential. Many of the men were ill-clad and in poor health. Four thousand of them—recruits raised by Shelby—had no weapons. The train contained an inordinate number of "wheezy, rickety wagons," and although indispensable for carrying the food and forage required in a barren country, was a serious encumbrance. Approximately half of the armed troops were untrained to fight on foot and the other half were mounted infantry equipped with long-barreled muskets and so practically useless on horseback. About a thousand men lacked mounts, which meant that the army could not move with

[42] *Ibid.*, Pt. 1, pp. 625–26, 712; *Ibid.*, Pt. 4, pp. 1068–69. The Arkansas River was so low that Price did not have to use the pontoons he had brought from Camden for crossing. Therefore they were converted into wagons. John C. Darr, "Price's Raid into Missouri," *Confederate Veteran*, XI (1903), 359.

[43] *Official Records*, XLI, Pt. 3, pp. 82, 89–94.

the rapidity normally associated with cavalry. All of the fourteen cannons were small caliber, only a few were rifled, and several were crude
"home-made" pieces. Most of Shelby's recruits were conscripts and deserters whose overriding desire was to return home to "Sarah and the
children," and who were in the opinion of one of Price's officers "almost worthless as soldiers." Discipline was extremely slack, especially
among the recruits and unarmed men, a situation largely caused and
certainly compounded by the utter inefficiency of the majority of the
line officers.[44]

By far the best fighting outfit in the army was Colonel David Shanks's
brigade of Shelby's division. Formerly Shelby's own command ("The
Iron Brigade"), it was made up of veteran, battle-hardened Missourians, each of whom carried several revolvers in addition to a carbine or
rifle (they had long-since discarded the sabre as worthless). Shelby's
other brigade, commanded by Colonel Sidney Jackman, contained
mainly recent recruits from Missouri and only five hundred of its fifteen
hundred men possessed arms. The division as a whole was supported
by the four-gun Parrott battery of Captain Richard Collins, a hell-for-
leather officer who believed in working his cannons on the front line if
not ahead of it. *Esprit* was high, and although the men were not well
disciplined, they were, to quote one of Price's staff officers, "reliable
in battle." Throughout the ensuing campaign they would be the main-
stay of Price's army.[45]

Less formidable, yet battle worthy, were Brigadier General William
L. Cabell's brigade of Fagan's division, and Brigadier General John B.
Clark, Jr.'s brigade of Marmaduke's division (General Clark was the
son of the ex-Senator). These were both veteran units and competently
commanded. Cabell's men and horses were in "extra trim" for the
campaign, and only a small number of his troops were unarmed. The
efficiency of Clark's brigade, however, was impaired by widespread

[44] *Ibid.*, Pt. 1, pp. 626–27, 651, 662, 671, 702–26; *ibid.*, Pt. 2, pp. 1067, 1071;
ibid., Pt. 3, pp. 940, 954; Edwards, *Shelby*, 478; Darr, "Price's Raid," 359; Paul
B. Jenkins, *The Battle of Westport* (Kansas City, Mo., 1906), 144. Despite
Kirby Smith's instructions to the contrary, Colton Greene's regiment formed
part of the army, being in Clark's brigade of Marmaduke's division. However,
according to Clark, Greene was "pre-eminent" for his services during the succeeding campaign. See *Official Records*, XLI, Pt. 1, p. 685.
[45] *Official Records*, XLI, Pt. 1, pp. 670, 678, 718. Edwards gives the impression that Shelby's men were better equipped than they were. But he would have
had them wearing curaisses in his descriptions if he had dared.

illness. As for the other brigades in Marmaduke's and Fagan's divisions, they consisted almost entirely of the recruits rounded up by Shelby.[46]

Accompanying the army were a goodly number of Missouri politicians, including Reynolds. Initially Reynolds had declared that he would not join the expedition until its success was assured, as he did not care to participate in a "farce" similar to the inauguration of a Confederate government in Kentucky during Bragg's 1862 invasion.[47] Several considerations changed his mind. He was sensitive to the criticism voiced by some Missourians that he did not spend enough time with the army. He could better keep an eye on Price and would be on hand when and if an election for a governor and legislature took place. And finally, influenced apparently by optimistic reports and predictions about conditions in Missouri, he hoped and even expected to be installed in the governor's office in Jefferson City, if only temporarily. Accordingly he joined Price at Camden early in August, and on arriving at Pocahontas he attached himself to Shelby as a volunteer aide.[48]

Price and his circle had not expected the governor to accompany the expedition and so reacted to his decision to do so with something approaching alarm. Major Cabell, who had replaced Snead as Price's confidential secretary, promptly wrote Snead, who was in Mississippi, urging him to rejoin "the old hero" and go with him to Missouri.

I am particularly anxious for you to go [Cabell explained] since Governor Reynolds is going. You know he is likely to be a marplot, assumes to possess and wield autocratic powers, and in all probability will at least interfere with, impede, and embarrass the operations and movements of General Price and the army, if, indeed, he does not absolutely check or counteract them. You are fully aware how much damage opposition and hostility, or even a want of harmony, on the part of even Governor Reynolds would produce. You also know what are his notions about his duty

[46] *Ibid.*, Pt. 4, pp. 1068–69; William L. Cabell, *Report of Gen. W. L. Cabell's Brigade in Price's Raid in Missouri and Kansas in 1864* (Dardanelles, Texas, 1900), 3. This work is a brief account written by Cabell long after the war. A brigade of Louisiana cavalry, 1,500 strong, had been ordered by Kirby Smith to join Price for the raid, but for some reason it did not come up in time.

[47] Reynolds to Kirby Smith, July 25, 1864, in Thomas C. Reynolds Papers, Library of Congress.

[48] Reynolds to Seddon, August 6, 1864, Reynolds to Price and Polk, June 27, 1864, and Thomas C. Reynolds Diary, May 31, 1864, all in Thomas C. Reynolds Papers, Library of Congress; Edwards, *Shelby and His Men*, 383.

and mission to protect the people there, &c., and also of his own immense powers to effect that thing, and the vigor and extremity with which he has announced it to be his purpose to do so.[49]

Snead had already written Price expressing his profound regret over their separation—"it would have been better," he stated, "had I kept by your side to the end of the war."[50] Most likely, moreover, he had the danger from Reynolds in mind when he expressed this sentiment. But the advent of a new session of Congress made it impossible for him to act on Cabell's plea, supposing even that it arrived in time for him to do so. During the months ahead Price was to have frequent need for the counsel of his former adjutant general.

"The Army of Missouri," as Price named his forces, spent four days at Pocahontas organizing, shoeing mules and horses, distributing ammunition, and completing all the other necessary preparations. Then, on the morning of September 19, it set forth, marching in three parallel columns—Shelby on the left, Fagan in the center, and Marmaduke on the right—in order to facilitate the collection of forage and to keep the Federals guessing as to its objective. That same day it crossed into Missouri.[51] After two years and seven months Price had returned.

[49] W. L. Cabell to Thomas L. Snead, August 4, 1864, in *Official Records*, XLI, Pt. 2, p. 1041.
[50] Snead to Price, July 20, 1864, in *ibid.*, 1014.
[51] *Ibid.*, Pt. 1, p. 627.

12

PILOT KNOB

He was not unexpected. The Union commander in Missouri was Price's old adversary at Iuka and Corinth, Rosecrans, who had been transferred there after his defeat at Chickamauga. Since spring Rosecrans had been hearing rumors that Price was on the way, and he had taken due note of the increased activity of the guerrillas and other pro-Confederate elements. "Rebel agents, amnesty oath-takers, recruits, sympathizers, O.A.K.'s, and traitors of every hue and stripe, had warmed into life at the approach of the great invasion," he subsequently related. "Women's fingers were busy making clothes for rebel soldiers out of goods plundered by the guerrillas; women's tongues were busy telling Union neighbors 'their time was coming.' "[1] His only uncertainty was when and where the blow would fall. To defend against Price he had only eleven thousand troops, mostly militia, scattered throughout the state in small detachments chasing bushwhackers.[2] If he concentrated them prematurely along the Arkansas border, not only would Price be able to outflank him, but the guerrillas would overrun large areas in the interior, spreading terror and devastation. Therefore, in the beginning all he could do was wait until Price's intentions became clear, meanwhile hoping that Steele would intercept the Confederates before they reached Missouri.[3]

Early in September, after learning that Shelby planned to join Price with a large force in northeast Arkansas, Rosecrans obtained permission from Washington to employ Major General A. J. Smith's division, then en route down the Mississippi to reinforce Sherman. He posted Smith's command, which consisted of 4,500 veteran infantrymen, near St. Louis.[4] In the subsequent campaign only a few of its

[1] *Official Records*, XLI, Pt. 1, pp. 308–309.
[2] *Ibid.*, Pt. 2, p. 967.
[3] Grant criticized Rosecrans for not promptly concentrating his forces to meet Price at the Arkansas border, a view most historians have taken also. However, where Rosecrans was concerned Grant always found fault. Given the situation in Missouri, it is hard to see how Rosecrans could have done other than he did.
[4] *Official Records*, XLI, Pt. 1, pp. 308–309.

troops saw action, but these few played a vital part, and the division as a whole proved invaluable to the Union defense of Missouri.

On September 23 Rosecrans received the first reliable intelligence that Price had eluded Steele and was north of the Arkansas. Certain now that Missouri faced invasion, he began concentrating his forces at Springfield, Jefferson City, Rolla, and St. Louis, Price's most likely targets. However, at none of these places did he have sufficient strength to be sure of withstanding the Confederates; thus all depended on getting prompt and accurate warning of where Price intended to make his main thrust. On September 24 a report came in that Shelby's cavalry were below Pilot Knob, eighty-six miles south of St. Louis on the Iron Mountain Railroad. If this were true, then it probably meant that Price planned to take St. Louis, the loss of which, even temporarily, would be a staggering blow to the Union cause, not merely in Missouri but in the nation as a whole. Hence Rosecrans immediately ordered Brigadier General Thomas Ewing, Jr., commander of the St. Louis District, to make a reconnaissance in force to Pilot Knob. In addition he sent two brigades under Smith down the railroad to De Soto, called out the St. Louis home guard, and obtained the services of several one-hundred-days regiments from Illinois to help defend the Missouri metropolis.[5]

Rosecrans assessed the situation correctly. Price's plan of operations called for his three columns to regroup at Fredericktown in southeast Missouri, then move against St. Louis. In company with Fagan's division he reached Fredericktown on September 24, having been preceded by Shelby. Marmaduke's division, which had been assigned the longest route, was still two days' march away. Shortly after arriving at Fredericktown, Price received word from spies that Smith with eight thousand troops was encamped south of St. Louis. At the same time he heard that there was a Union garrison of fifteen hundred infantry at Pilot Knob—a potential threat to his rear. Both items of information caused him to have second thoughts about St. Louis.[6]

On the night of September 25, Marmaduke having arrived, Price conferred with his division commanders on the army's future course of action. Shelby as the junior officer present expressed his opinion

[5] *Ibid.*, 309–10.
[6] *Ibid.*, 627–28; *ibid.*, Pt. 2, pp. 943, 954.

first. He favored going straight on to St. Louis. There was no need, he argued, to worry about the Pilot Knob garrison. Being infantry it offered no threat to a mounted force. Furthermore his scouts had reconnoitered Pilot Knob and it contained nothing which would justify the probable cost of an assault. "What we want is men, and to reach St. Louis."

Marmaduke and Fagan, on the other hand, urged that the Pilot Knob garrison be disposed of before advancing on St. Louis. Price dismissed the meeting without issuing any orders. However, later during the night he decided to follow Marmaduke and Fagan's advice. Ostensibly he did so because he was afraid to leave the Pilot Knob garrison in his rear. But in all likelihood he had concluded that it was no longer possible to seize St. Louis; whereas by attacking Pilot Knob he could obtain badly needed arms and other equipment and gain an easy victory that would stimulate the morale of his troops and arouse the spirits of Confederate sympathizers throughout the state.[7]

Early on the morning of September 26 Price sent Shelby galloping northward with instructions to destroy the tracks and bridges of the Iron Mountain Railroad so as to prevent Smith from aiding the Pilot Knob garrison. Simultaneously he moved out with Fagan's and Marmaduke's divisions on the road to Arcadia, a village twenty-one miles due west of Fredericktown and about two miles south of Ironton, which was located two miles below Pilot Knob. Late in the afternoon Fagan's troops, leading the advance, reached Shut-In Gap, a strategically important mountain pass several miles east of Arcadia. After some severe skirmishing with Union pickets they seized the gap and pressed on towards Arcadia with the intention of swinging northward and occupying Ironton. However, they encountered stiff opposition from reinforced Federals who drove them back to the gap with heavy casualties. Rain and darkness, plus an order from Price to Fagan not to attack Ironton unless he was confident he could take it without serious loss, put an end to the day's fighting.[8] The fact

[7] *Official Records*, XLI, Pt. 1, p. 628; Jo Shelby to Major C. C. Rainwater, January 5, 1888, quoted in Cyrus A. Peterson and Joseph M. Hanson, *Pilot Knob, The Thermopylae of the West* (New York, 1914), 99–100. Norman Potter Morrow, "Price's Missouri Expedition, 1864" (M.A. thesis, University of Texas, 1949), 76, also concludes that Price as early as September 25 had abandoned any serious intention of taking St. Louis.

[8] *Official Records*, XLI, Pt. 1, pp. 447, 628–29, 706–707; Peterson and Hanson, *Pilot Knob*, 101–47.

that a few companies of Union infantry had beaten back the advance of Fagan's entire division boded ill for the Confederates.

Commanding the garrison was General Ewing, who it will be recalled had been sent to Pilot Knob by Rosecrans to conduct a reconnaissance in force. Ewing had arrived that noon by train, bringing with him two hundred Iowa soldiers from Smith's division. It was these veterans who had spearheaded the counterattack against Fagan, and they were to be the core of the Union defense throughout the subsequent fighting. In all Ewing had fewer than one thousand troops (not the fifteen hundred reported to Price), some of whom were civilian volunteers from the vicinity. Nonetheless he was determined to hold on to Pilot Knob as long as possible, both to establish definitely the whereabouts and movements of Price's army (he was not sure that its main body was in the area) and to delay the Confederate northward march in order to give Rosecrans more time in which to strengthen the defenses of St. Louis.[9] In addition, it is quite possible that he hoped to promote his political career with a brilliant military exploit, for he was a prominent Kansas Republican and had a driving ambition to become United States Senator.

At sunrise on the twenty-seventh Fagan, now closely supported by Marmaduke, renewed the attack. More hard fighting ensued, but the superior Southern numbers told and by 10 A.M. the Union forces had been pushed through Arcadia and Ironton to Pilot Knob, where they took refuge inside of Fort Davidson. This was an "ugly, angular fort" with a nine-foot dirt parapet topped with sandbags. It mounted four 32-pounder siege guns, three 24-pounder howitzers, and three 12-inch mortars, and had been bolstered by six field guns. Surrounding its eight sides was a ditch ten feet wide and six feet, four inches deep, which was partially filled with water from the rain of the night before. The outer slope of the parapet had been badly eroded and was so gradual that it was quite easy for a man to spring into the ditch and run up it to the crest. The fort's field of fire was excellent, for a level plain extended from it in all directions, broken only by a dry creek bed about 150 yards to the south and east. However, commanding the works on three sides were several high hills, the most prominent of which were Pilot Knob to the southeast and Shepherd's Mountain to the southwest. Both heights were within musket range of the fort, and well-served artillery firing from them could soon render

[9] *Official Records*, XLI, Pt. 1, pp. 446–48.

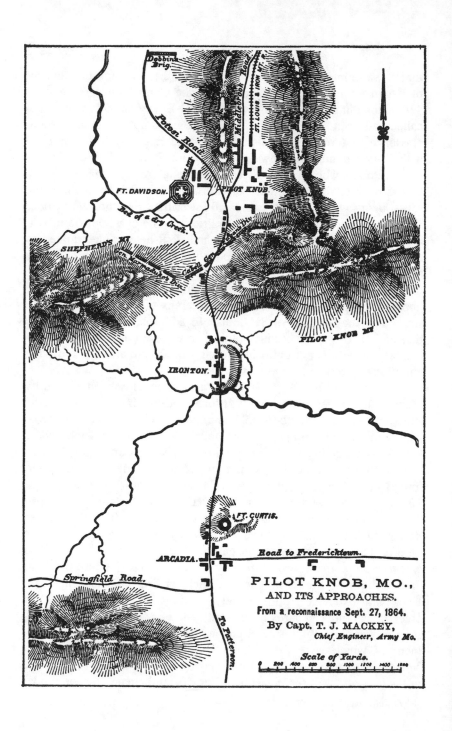

PILOT KNOB, MO.,

AND ITS APPROACHES.

From a reconnaissance Sept. 27, 1864.

By Capt. T. J. MACKEY,

Chief Engineer, Army Mo.

Scale of Yards.

it untenable. Acutely aware of this fact, Ewing had the trails leading up to Shepherd's Mountain and Pilot Knob obstructed and the hillsides facing the fort cleared of timber. He also had two rifle pits dug, one running southwest to the dry creek bed, the other north towards the Potosi Road. He did not expect to hold out in the fort more than one day.[10]

On the advice of his chief of engineers, Captain T. J. Mackey, Price at first planned to bombard the garrison into submission with artillery planted atop Shepherd's Mountain. But, just as he was about to give the necessary orders, some local civilians came to him and pleaded that the fort not be shelled. The Federals, they stated, were holding prisoner a number of Southern adherents, including old men and boys, who would be killed as a result. This information, which apparently he did not check out, made Price more receptive to the views of Marmaduke and Fagan, both of whom advocated a direct assault. Fagan (whose ability Price regarded highly) declared that his division alone could take the fort in twenty minutes. And Marmaduke stated that with the support of two cannons on Shepherd's Mountain he would carry it in even less time. In the end, after some hesitation, Price told them to do as they proposed.[11]

Marmaduke's division, some three thousand strong, deployed on the north slope of Shepherd's Mountain, and Fagan, with about four thousand men, lined up on Marmaduke's right at the base of Pilot Knob and facing northwest. Both were about nine hundred yards distant from the fort. While these dispositions were being made, the two cannons Marmaduke said he needed were manhandled to the crest of Shepherd's Mountain, and Dobbin's brigade of Fagan's division, fifteen hundred in number, took up a position on the north side of Fort Davidson near the Potosi Road, the garrison's only practical avenue of retreat. Fearful of a repetition of the fiascos at Corinth and Helena, Price personally impressed on Marmaduke's and Fagan's staff officers the need for coordination in the assault—both divisions, he stated, must move simultaneously and in line.[12]

[10] *Ibid.*, 446–48, 707–709.

[11] *Ibid.*, 707–708, 713–14. These citations refer to testimony under oath by Mackey.

[12] *Ibid.*, 629, 707, 709–10. The figures on the strength of Marmaduke and Fagan are derived from Mackey's testimony. Obviously many of these men were unarmed. Whether or not unarmed troops participated in the actual attack is not stated. This is true of all subsequent battles, making it difficult to assess effective Confederate strength.

Before ordering the attack Price twice called on the garrison to surrender, but, each time, Ewing staunchly refused.[13] Besides believing that his troops could hold the Confederates at bay, the Kansas general had compelling personal reasons for not wanting to become a prisoner. In August, 1863, while commanding the District of the Border with headquarters at Kansas City, and following Quantrill's raid on Lawrence, he had issued the famous Order No. 11 requiring the entire population of four counties in west Missouri to leave their homes. The order resulted in great suffering among the people affected, and Missouri Confederates bitterly denounced Ewing's "barbarism" and vowed vengeance.[14] Should he fall into their hands there was a strong possibility that they would kill him. They had already killed one of his officers, Major James Wilson, whom they held responsible for outrages in the Pilot Knob area.[15] Furthermore, his second in command, Colonel Thomas C. Fletcher, was the Republican candidate for governor of Missouri, and he too would have been a prize captive. Indeed, although none of the Confederate accounts mention the matter, it is conceivable that one of Price's motives in pressing the attack against Pilot Knob was to capture Ewing and Fletcher.

Shortly after 2 P.M. the two cannons on Shepherd's Mountain opened up. But they were so situated that their muzzles could not be depressed sufficiently to hit the fort with accuracy, and deadly Union counterbattery fire quickly silenced them. A little later Marmaduke's and Fagan's troops moved forward on foot to attack. They at once encountered a storm of shell and shot that strewed the hillsides and gullies with dead and wounded. In addition their ranks were broken and thrown into disarray by rocks and timber, and despite Price's warning the two divisions did not keep in line. As a consequence

---

[13] Peterson and Hanson, *Pilot Knob*, 155–56.

[14] Castel, *Frontier State at War*, 142–53.

[15] During the early stages of the second day's fighting men of the Fifteenth Missouri Cavalry, attached to Fagan's division, captured and then murdered Major Wilson and six Union privates. They held Wilson and his men responsible for looting, burning, and other outrages against Southern adherents in the area. In retaliation the Union authorities in St. Louis executed six Confederate prisoners of the rank of private, but did not carry out their original intention of executing a Confederate major. See W. M. McPheeters Diary, September 20, 1864; Cabell, *Report of Cabell's Brigade*, 4–5; St. Louis *Missouri Republican*, October 31, 1864; John T. Scharf, *History of St. Louis City and County from the Earliest Period to the Present Day* (Philadelphia, 1883), I, 444.

Fagan debouched onto the plain first, with Marmaduke well behind. And after advancing scarcely a hundred yards, and before experiencing material loss, Fagan's entire right wing broke in a "disgraceful manner" and fled back up the side of Pilot Knob. Only Cabell's veteran brigade on the left continued to charge forward at the double, stopping occasionally to fire and reload. Since it was closer to the fort than Marmaduke's division, the defenders concentrated their fire against it. Nonetheless it pushed on bravely, losing men at every step, until it reached the ditch. Here it stopped, wavered, then fled in great disorder back towards Pilot Knob, leaving the ground in front of the ditch literally heaped with the fallen. Cabell, who had opposed making the attack, had his horse shot out from under him while leading his men.

Meanwhile, Marmaduke's troops advanced about two hundred yards across the plain, suffering only slight losses. Then, just before Cabell's brigade broke, the new men recruited by Shelby halted and lay down in the creek bed. Cursing and imploring, Marmaduke's staff officers tried to get them moving again, but to no avail. Clark's brigade alone kept going, and the Federals, no longer concerned about Cabell, turned their full fire against it, inflicting heavy losses. On reaching the ditch it too hesitated, then fled in confusion back to the creek bed where it joined the rest of the division in seeking shelter from the guns of Fort Davidson. Marmaduke made no further attempt to attack, and most of his men remained in the creek bed until darkness fell and it was safe to withdraw.[16]

Price helped rally Fagan's retreating soldiers, who eventually reformed their ranks. Fagan, angered and humiliated by his failure, pleaded for permission to renew the assault. Another charge would succeed, he declared, and he even asked Price to throw in his personal escort. But Price, shaking his head sadly, stated that he would not make another attack that day. This, commented Cabell, "was a damned wise decision."[17]

[16] The above account of the Confederate assault on Ft. Davidson is based on the following sources: *Official Records*, XLI, Pt. 1, pp. 448, 629, 679–80, 709; Peterson and Hanson, *Pilot Knob*, 165–210; W. M. McPheeters Diary, September 27, 1864; Cabell, *Report of Cabell's Brigade*, 5–6; Diary of an officer in Cabell's Brigade, in Washington (Ark.) *Telegraph*, November 30, 1864; Darr, "Price's Raid," 360.
[17] *Official Records*, XLI, Pt. 1, p. 715.

The dispirited Confederates bivouacked for the night. While they rested, Price instructed Mackey's engineers to prepare scaling ladders for use in a new assault in the morning. Also he sent a courier riding northward with an urgent message for Shelby to hasten to Pilot Knob— Shelby's tough young cavaliers and Collins' well-served battery were desperately needed to capture the fort! Unfortunately, for some unknown reason, Shelby did not receive this order, nor an earlier dispatch from Price instructing him to rejoin the main army. Hence, unaware that Price wanted him, he proceeded with his mission against the Iron Mountain Railroad, destroying three bridges and "miles and miles" of track. By nightfall he was at Potosi, some twenty-five miles to the northwest of Pilot Knob.[18]

Ewing had won an amazing victory. With no more than nine hundred men—but with sixteen cannons—he had repulsed an enemy force of seven thousand and inflicted well over a thousand casualties while losing only seventy-three himself.[19] The field south of Fort Davidson was littered with Confederate dead and wounded, and the groans and screams of the latter made the night hideous. Also, according to a Federal account, Price's men had "filled up pretty well" with whisky at Ironton before attacking, and after their dead had lain on the battlefield during the afternoon "the stench was fearful, smelling like an overcrowded grog-shop."[20]

Meanwhile, Ewing's situation remained extremely perilous. In two day's fighting he had lost a fourth of his tiny command, and he knew it would be impossible to hold out another day. Therefore, after consulting with his officers, he decided to evacuate the fort and retreat by way of Potosi to Mineral Point, where according to his last information two regiments of Smith's division were stationed. At 3 A.M. his troops slipped silently out of the fort and began marching up the Potosi road. An immense pile of burning charcoal at the north base of Pilot Knob made the entire valley "as light as noonday," yet Dobbin's men camped along the road did not attempt to stop them. They must have seen the Union column but in Colonel Fletcher's opinion they mistook it for a body of their own forces moving to a new position. "They gave no evidence whatever of seeing or hearing us."

[18] *Ibid.*, 629, 653; *ibid.*, Pt. 3, p. 960.
[19] Peterson and Hanson, *Pilot Knob*, 210, 213, 215, 320–23.
[20] *Ibid.*, 180–81.

Thus through sheer boldness Ewing made a seemingly impossible escape.[21]

One hour after the garrison evacuated the fort, a slow fuse left burning in the powder magazine sputtered to an end and there was a terrific explosion that shook the hills for miles around. But even then the Confederates remained quiescent: they thought that an accident had occurred in the fort and that the surviving Federals would surrender in the morning! Not until 8 A.M. did Price, who was staying at a house in Arcadia, learn that Ewing had given him the slip. At once he ordered Marmaduke to remount his men and overtake the fleeing enemy. However, it was almost noon before Marmaduke got under way.[22]

As the Confederates made ready to pursue, the head of Ewing's column entered Caledonia, some ten miles north of Pilot Knob. Here it met and routed the advance guard of Shelby, who was heading south to rejoin Price. From a prisoner Ewing ascertained that Shelby had occupied Potosi the evening before and that Smith's troops at Mineral Point had retreated. This of course meant that his intended escape route was no longer practicable. Accordingly, he turned off the Potosi Road and marched westward on the road to Rolla. Several hours later Marmaduke and Shelby linked forces at Caledonia and with the former in command continued the pursuit. But although their men were mounted and the Federals on foot, they were unable to overhaul Ewing, who was further slowed by the numerous refugees that accompanied him. Paralleling the road on either side were steep cliffs that made it impossible for them to attack his flanks or cut him off in front; and the Iowans in the rear guard, supported by a battery of artillery, valiantly beat back all attempts to charge up the narrow road.

All through the day, the night, and into the next day the chase went on. Finally, on the evening of September 29, Ewing halted at Harrison (present day Leasburg), where he decided to make a stand

---

[21] *Official Records*, XLI, Pt. 1, pp. 448–49; Peterson and Hanson, *Pilot Knob*, 218–20. None of the Confederate accounts attempts to explain the strange failure of Dobbin's brigade to intercept Ewing. There is no report in the *Official Records* by either Dobbin or Fagan.

[22] Peterson and Hanson, *Pilot Knob*, 220–23; *Official Records*, XLI, Pt. 1, pp. 449, 629, 710; John C. Moore, "Missouri," in Clement A. Evans (ed.), *Confederate Military History* (Atlanta, 1899), Vol. IX, Pt. 2, p. 181.

while waiting for help to arrive from the Union forces at Rolla, thirty-five miles away. His weary but still resolute troops threw up breastworks of rails and ties and prepared for a desperate fight. The Confederates, however, did not attack. Marmaduke's division had long since dropped out of the pursuit from exhaustion (!), and only Shelby's men remained. After considerable discussion Marmaduke and Shelby agreed that an assault would be pointless. Not only would it probably cost more than an uncertain success would justify, but Ewing's command could no longer be a factor in the campaign. Hence, in the morning they withdrew, leaving behind only a small body to put on the appearance of a siege. This force tried to bluff Ewing into surrender with threats of massacre if he did not, but failed to frighten the Kansas general. Then it too left to rejoin Price. Ewing, who had marched sixty-six miles in thirty-nine hours with a motley force over poor roads in rough country, had made good his escape.[23]

Once again Price had thrown his soldiers against a strong and well-defended enemy fortification, and once again they had been bloodily repulsed. According to Confederate sources Fagan suffered approximately 350 killed and wounded (of whom about 250 were in Cabell's brigade), and Marmaduke lost 94, mainly in Clark's brigade.[24] The Federals, on the other hand, stated that they inflicted 1,500 casualties on Price's army during the two days of fighting at Pilot Knob— a claim they backed with a great deal of convincing evidence.[25] In any case, the fighting edge of Fagan's division was badly blunted for the remainder of the campaign, Marmaduke's division was exposed as unreliable in battle, and the morale of the Army of Missouri as a whole (except for Shelby's command) seriously impaired. As soon

[23] The account of Ewing's flight and escape is based on the following sources: *Official Records*, XLI, Pt. 1, pp. 449–51, 629–30, 653; *ibid.*, Pt. 2, pp. 964–65; Peterson and Hanson, *Pilot Knob*, 253–96, 311.

[24] Peterson and Hanson, *Pilot Knob*, 210, 213, 215, 317–19; *Official Records*, XLI, Pt. 1, pp. 451, 709; Cabell, *Report of Cabell's Brigade*, 5–6; "Diary of an Officer," in Washington (Ark.) *Telegraph*, November 30, 1864. Ordinarily the Confederate figure would be accepted as being most likely correct. However, in the case of Pilot Knob the Confederates had unusually strong reasons to minimize their losses. Also, owing to the slack organization of Marmaduke's and Fagan's divisions, many of the units that participated in the attack did not make any casualty returns or else sent in incomplete ones. Colonel Morrow, "Price's Expedition," 83, estimates the Confederate loss at Pilot Knob at about 1,000.

[25] Peterson and Hanson, *Pilot Knob*, 247–48.

as the fighting ended, large numbers of deserters began wending their way back to Arkansas or headed for homes in Missouri.[26]

Captain Mackey subsequently testified that Fort Davidson could have been forced to surrender in fifteen or twenty minutes by eight or ten cannons firing from Shepherd's Mountain.[27] But, as has been described, Price refrained from ordering a heavy bombardment because he had been told that the garrison was holding Southern civilians and because Marmaduke and Fagan expressed complete confidence in their ability to take the fort by a frontal assault. However, neither Ewing nor any of the other Federal participants mentioned hostages in their accounts; they did, on the other hand, report the presence of a large number of Union refugees, many of whom took part in the fighting (which explains the dead civilians the Confederates found when they occupied the fort). Most likely, therefore, Price was the well-meaning victim of erroneous information either innocently or deliberately conveyed to him by the local inhabitants. What he should have done, on being told of the alleged hostages, was to have gone ahead with the massing of his cannons atop Shepherd's Mountain. Then, when they were ready to open fire, he should have informed Ewing that if any civilians were found in the fort after it fell, the entire garrison would be killed. In this way the matter of the hostages would have been definitely settled, the fort attacked in proper fashion, and heavy losses avoided. But the easy-going Price was incapable of such harshness; besides, Marmaduke and Fagan assured him that they could take the fort easily by assault, and even Mackey, while advising a bombardment, told him that the fort's ditch was "slight."[28]

Following the battle Mackey personally tested the fort's ditch and parapet. He found that a man carrying a rifle could easily run up and over them. They were not, he concluded, "a serious obstacle to a successful assault." In his opinion if Marmaduke's and Fagan's columns had kept going and properly supported each other, they would have carried the Union works in their first rush.[29] And, in all likelihood, if

[26] *Ibid.*, 319.
[27] *Official Records*, XLI, Pt. 1, p. 709.
[28] *Ibid.*, 707. In his report (see *ibid.*, 629) Price did not refer to the alleged hostages or to Marmaduke's and Fagan's urgings, but explained the repulse simply by stating that "the information I received in regard to the strength of the fortifications proved totally incorrect."
[29] *Official Records*, XLI, Pt. 1, p. 715.

Price's troops had been of the same quality as those that stormed Corinth or captured Graveyard Hill, the charge would have succeeded. But such troops he did not have. Instead, he had poorly disciplined cavalry who lacked the training and equipment for assaulting fortifications, and whose ranks were filled with retrieved deserters and reluctant conscripts. Marmaduke, Fagan, and Price (who of course must bear the main responsibility) should have realized the weakness of their forces and hence not sent them to be mowed down by the determined defenders of Fort Davidson.

However, two things must be noted, one in fairness to Price, the other in fairness to his men. First, the ease with which the far superior Federal artillery drove away the two cannons that did open fire from Shepherd's Mountain, and the difficulty these cannons had in finding the range while they were in operation, casts some doubt on Mackey's assertion that the garrison could have been forced to surrender by a fifteen or twenty minute bombardment from that height. Certainly it would have required all of Price's available artillery, and far more accurate aiming, to have achieved that result. Second, although it was no doubt a simple matter for a man who was fresh and unafraid to spring up the sides of Fort Davidson when no one was shooting at him, it must have been a far different matter for men who had been charging a half mile under terrific artillery and rifle fire and suffering heavy losses. To Cabell's and Clark's panting and excited soldiers the ditch no doubt seemed most formidable and the high, smoke-shrouded parapet looming above it utterly impregnable.[30] Finally, it is significant that Price's plans for renewing the attack called for another direct attack, this time with scaling ladders. Quite obviously he believed that the ditch was the main reason the first attempt failed, and apparently he still did not intend to shell the fort, either for fear of injuring the hostages said to be in it, or because he did not believe his artillery capable of doing the job.

---

[30] John Darr, a member of Cabell's brigade, stated ["Price's Raid," 360] that the troops were surprised by the order to charge the fort, as they thought it would be bombarded into surrender. Cabell, writing long afterwards, stated [*Report of Cabell's Brigade*, 5–6] that the ditch was so "steep and so wide" his men could not scale it without ladders, and one of his officers, in a diary written during the campaign, declared that the Confederates "could scarcely have got in [the fort] had there been no one inside." [Washington (Ark.) *Telegraph*, November 30, 1864]. All of these men, however, had a reason to justify the failure of Cabell's troops to storm the fort.

Ewing's escape from Fort Davidson was an incredible exploit. But only equally incredible carelessness on the part of the Confederates made it possible. For this Price personally cannot be held responsible. He anticipated that Ewing might try to flee by the Potosi Road and so stationed Dobbin's brigade across it, as well as ordering Shelby to hasten back to the army. Yet Dobbin's men failed in this simple assignment and the dispatches to Shelby miscarried. Ewing then eluded pursuit by a combination of luck, fortitude, and favorable terrain.

Of course the greatest Confederate blunder was to attack Pilot Knob in the first place. As Shelby pointed out, its small garrison of infantry was no threat to the invaders, and the flour, bacon, blankets, and unusable cannons that the Confederates found in the fort were small compensation for the terrible cost of capturing it. In the opinion of Shelby, Edwards, and other critics, Price should have ignored Ewing's force and pushed on from Fredericktown to St. Louis, which they contend he could have easily seized.[31] This last, however, is extremely doubtful. Most likely any attempt to enter St. Louis, defended as it was by Smith's hard-fighting infantry, would have produced an even greater debacle than Pilot Knob. Price, therefore, probably did the right thing in abandoning the St. Louis enterprise.[32] And he should have done the same as regards Fort Davidson instead of letting himself be swayed by Marmaduke and Fagan. By attacking the fort he not only seriously crippled his army but wasted valuable time. For in addition to the two days spent in the actual assault, another three days were used up in chasing Ewing and regrouping the army.

Price remained at Pilot Knob until September 29. Then, after sending some of Shelby's cavalry in a feint towards St. Louis, he began marching in the direction of Jefferson City.[33] The second phase of the great raid was under way.

---

[31] Edwards, *Shelby and His Men*, 479–80; Peterson and Hanson, *Pilot Knob*, 45, 100.

[32] Morrow, "Price's Expedition," 74, is of the same opinion. Indeed, Colonel Morrow holds that Price had lost whatever chance he had of taking St. Louis even before he left Camden (see *ibid.*, 67).

[33] *Official Records*, XLI, Pt. 1, p. 630.

13
WESTPORT

During the early days of October, Price's columns wended their way across the rolling prairies of central Missouri. Rain fell and the weather began to turn just a little cold, but resistance was slight and the countryside offered abundant supplies. Ranging far and wide the Confederate troopers scooped up hundreds of hapless militiamen, "liberated" dozens of small towns, tore up long sections of the Pacific Railroad, and "exchanged" tired horses for fresh ones.[1]

They also plundered. They began doing so when they reached Arcadia and they continued to do so from that point on. Governor Reynolds later wrote:

It would take a volume to describe the acts of outrage; neither station, age, nor sex was any protection. Southern men and women were as little spared as Unionists; the elegant mansion of General Robert E. Lee's accomplished niece and the cabin of the negro were alike ransacked; John Deane, the first civilian ever made a State prisoner by Mr. Lincoln's Government, had his watch and money robbed from him in broad day, as unceremoniously as the German merchant at Frederickstown [sic] was forced, a pistol at his ear, to surrender his concealed greenbacks . . . the clothes of a poor man's infant were as attractive spoil as the merchant's silk and calico or the curtain taken from the rich man's parlor; ribbons and trumpery gee-gaws were stolen from milliners, and jeweled rings forced from the fingers of delicate maidens whose brothers were fighting in Georgia in Cockrell's Confederate Missouri brigade.[2]

Before leaving Arkansas, Price had issued strict orders against pillaging and established a special court martial to punish offenders. Later while at Pilot Knob, he appointed Lieutenant Colonel John P. Bull provost marshal general of the army. Bull proceeded to organize a provost guard of fifty picked men for each brigade, which he deployed along the line of march to prevent straggling. Furthermore, in

[1] *Official Records*, XLI, Pt. 1, pp. 630–31, 653–54; W. M. McPheeters Diary, October 1, 2, 3, 1864.
[2] Reynolds quoted in Edwards, *Shelby and His Men*, 471.

many instances Price himself directed the arrest of men with stolen goods in their possession. Thus on October 3 he had Lieutenant Colonel C. H. Nichols and two other members of Jackman's brigade arrested for looting at Potosi. And when Colonel Thomas R. Freeman of Marmaduke's division personally shot two soldiers for stealing, Price commended him and declared that if it were in his power he would promote him to brigadier general.[3]

Although these efforts produced some improvement, straggling and marauding persisted. Because the army was living off the countryside, the line officers permitted their men to range about on private foraging expeditions, despite Price's repeated orders to end this practice. And, since the troops were constantly on the move and widely dispersed, there was neither time nor opportunity to remedy their basic lack of discipline. In addition, the army stretched out five or six miles along the road and it "proved difficult" for Bull's provost guards to maintain order or to prevent unauthorized departures from the column. According to Reynolds, Bull was inadequate to his duties, being a "youthful officer of amiable disposition, who had been recently wounded and being thus disabled from riding his horse, was compelled to make the rest of the campaign in a buggy." Most of the line officers, on whom in the last analysis the task of enforcing discipline fell, were generally incompetent and indifferent, or else actively engaged in committing depredations themselves! And finally, and perhaps basically, a large proportion of the army, as has been noted, were conscripts and returned deserters—in short, military riffraff.[4]

One other reason for the prevalence of straggling and plundering was the slowness of Price's advance—an average of only fifteen miles a day. This pace, which would have done little credit to infantry, much less cavalry, was mainly attributable to poor management in marching and to the cumbersome wagon train. Large to begin with, the train had now swollen to over five hundred wagons and extended several miles along the road. Accompanying it was a "rabble of deadheads, stragglers and stolen negroes on stolen horses," who gave the army

---

[3] *Official Records*, XLI, Pt. 1, pp. 648, 720, 722, 724–25; *ibid.*, Pt. 3, pp. 943, 980; St. Louis *Missouri Republican*, September 28, October 2, 7, 10, November 4, 1864; Darr, "Price's Raid," 360; Peterson and Hanson, *Pilot Knob*, 232–33, 236.

[4] *Official Records*, XLI, Pt. 1, pp. 719–20, 722–26; St. Louis *Missouri Republican*, October 7, 1864.

the appearance of a "Calmuck horde."[5] Many of the soldiers believed, probably with reason, that the wagons contained the private loot of staff officers and camp-followers. They also became apprehensive that "the odious train would occasion disaster to the army."[6]

On October 6 Shelby, as always leading the advance, forced a passage across Moreau Creek, a branch of the Osage six miles from Jefferson City. In the fighting Colonel David Shanks was mortally wounded. To replace him Price named Brigadier General M. Jeff Thompson, the colorful, courageous, and capable officer who earlier in the war had gained fame as the "Swamp Fox" of southeast Missouri.[7] The next day, at noon, the Confederates occupied the hills overlooking Jefferson City on the south. In plain sight was the capitol, the stars and stripes waving atop its dome. But also visible were five forts and long lines of connecting rifle pits, all heavily manned and protected by palisades and *chevaux-de-frise*. During the preceding days the Federals had worked frantically to strengthen the town's defenses, and at the same time had rushed all available units there and armed civilian volunteers. In all there were seven thousand regulars, militia, and home guards holding the place.

The Confederates deployed, then advanced as if to attack, their artillery booming away in support. But after only a few rounds they fell back and bivouacked in the hills. Price hesitated to order an assault because of the attitude of his troops, who were fearful of another Pilot Knob and had convinced themselves that Jefferson City could not be taken. Then, that night, a spy reported to him that the garrison numbered twelve thousand and that three thousand more Federals were on the opposite bank of the Missouri River. This information caused Price to conclude that he was outnumbered two to one in armed strength and hence it would be suicidal to attack. Shelby and Mackey, on whose advice he principally relied from Pilot Knob onward, concurred in this view. Therefore he abandoned the idea of seizing the capital.[8]

[5] Edwards, *Shelby and His Men*, 471.

[6] Henry C. Luttrell, "Diary of the Price Raid," St. Louis *Missouri Republican*, March 6, 1886.

[7] *Official Records*, XLI, Pt. 1, pp. 630–31, 655. Thompson, who had been recently exchanged after being in a Union prison, joined the expedition without any command. His commission was in the Missouri state guard.

[8] *Ibid.*, 311, 345, 395, 418–19, 631.

Although based on false intelligence, it was a wise decision, as even the hypercritical Edwards subsequently admitted.[9] However, it should be noted that the major portion of the Jefferson City garrison arrived there after October 3 and that the most effective part of it, 8 cannons and 2,400 cavalry from Rolla, did not reach the town until October 6, or just one day before the Confederate army.[10] Thus if Price had marched from Pilot Knob at a faster pace—as he could and should have done—he would have found Jefferson City practically defenseless. His failure to do so meant frustration for the political objective of the campaign, namely the installation of a Confederate state government.

Early on the morning of October 8 Price ordered the Army of Missouri to take up the march again, this time for Boonville. He now had no hopes of remaining for any appreciable length of time in the state or of bringing about a mass uprising against Federal domination. Henceforth his primary desire was to recruit as many men as possible from the strongly pro-Confederate river counties of west Missouri, and then, in accordance with Kirby Smith's instructions, retreat southward by way of Kansas, devastating it as he passed through.[11]

As Price moved westward, Major General Alfred Pleasonton arrived in Jefferson City to take command of the forces gathered there. Formerly chief of cavalry of the Army of the Potomac, he was a hard-driving fighter capable of inspiring great enthusiasm in his men, but with a tendency towards independent-mindedness that bordered on insubordination. On learning that the Confederates were heading for Boonville, he ordered Brigadier General John Sanborn with a force of four thousand cavalry to follow them, report on their movements, and keep them within the great bend of the Missouri River. No attempt, however, was to be made to bring Price to battle until reinforcements came up from St. Louis and Springfield. Pleasonton himself remained at Jefferson City for the time being to organize additional troops and arrange plans with Rosecrans.[12]

The Army of Missouri entered Boonville on October 10. The pro-Southern townspeople cheered the ragged troopers as they paraded

[9] Edwards, *Shelby and His Men*, 395.
[10] *Official Records*, XLI, Pt. 1, pp. 418–19.
[11] *Ibid.*, 631.
[12] *Ibid.*, 311, 340, 395–96.

through the streets, and blushing young ladies handed bouquets to Price and the other generals. During the next several days between twelve hundred and fifteen hundred men, mostly unarmed, joined Price at Boonville. He had already collected large numbers of volunteers and conscripts, and in the days to come he added many more. All of them, except those fortunate enough to have some sort of weapon, were assigned to an unarmed brigade commanded by Colonel Charles H. Tyler, and they usually accompanied the train. In addition, a considerable body of civilian refugees attached themselves to the army, a source of further delay and confusion.[13]

Besides the recruits, about one hundred bushwackers under "Bloody Bill" Anderson rode into Boonville. Two weeks earlier Anderson's gang had, in conjunction with other guerrilla bands, wiped out a force of 150 Union militia near Centralia, Missouri. Many of his followers were psychopathic killers, and several of them, including Anderson himself, had bedecked the bridles of their horses with human scalps. Shocked and disgusted, Price refused to talk with Anderson until these ghastly trophies were thrown away. He then accepted a brace of silver-mounted pistols from the partisan leader, declared that if he had fifty thousand men such as his he could hold Missouri forever, and assigned him the mission of destroying certain key bridges on the North Missouri Railroad. Anderson, however, failed to do any material damage, and on October 26 Federal troops killed him near Albany, Missouri, cut off his head and mounted it atop a telegraph pole.[14]

Price also sent an order to Quantrill to operate against the Hannibal and St. Joseph Railroad. He did not know that Reynolds' prediction of the spring had come true and that Quantrill had been supplanted by his former lieutenant, George Todd, and now had only a handful of followers. In any case Quantrill never received the order and took no part in the campaign except to engage in a little freelance plundering.[15]

Several authors have severely criticized Price for seeking to employ the services of Anderson and Quantrill, feeling that he thus countenanced vicious murderers.[16] Their reaction is understandable, but

[13] *Ibid.*, 631–32, 700–701; W. M. McPheeters Diary, October 10, 1864; Edwards, *Shelby and His Men*, 401–403; Peterson and Hanson, *Pilot Knob*, 55, 239, 242; Darr, "Price's Raid," 361.

[14] Castel, *Quantrill*, 196–99.

[15] *Ibid.*, 196–97.

[16] Peterson and Hanson, *Pilot Knob*, 57–58; Jay Monaghan, *Civil War on the Western Border* (Boston, 1955), 323.

it should be borne in mind that Price, like other Missouri Confederates, believed that the guerrillas were merely retaliating against Union outrages and that their alleged crimes had been greatly exaggerated by enemy propaganda. Furthermore, in his desperate desire to shake Union control of Missouri he no doubt was ready to use any tool that came handy, and the bushwhackers promised to be quite useful. This promise, as already indicated, was not fulfilled.

Despite the friendly reception of the citizens, the Army of Missouri continued to display a predilection for plunder while at Boonville. "What was done and not done there," later reminisced Jeff Thompson, "I do not propose to relate as I had only to try to control my own Brigade, to save their reputation from the demoralization which was seizing the army. The plunder of Boonville nearly completed this demoralization for many officers and men loaded themselves, their horses and wagons with 'their rights' and now wanted to turn Southward and save what they had."[17] Moreover, according to Reynolds, "the hotel occupied as General Price's own headquarters was the scene of public drunken revelry by night."[18]

On October 11 General Sanborn with the Union cavalry from Jefferson City pressed to within a few miles of Boonville, causing the Confederates to sally forth and drive him back.[19] Two days later Price pulled out of the town and headed west to Chouteau Springs. From there he sent Clark's brigade, supported by Shelby in command of Sidney Jackman's brigade, on a raid against Glasgow. After a hard fight on the fourteenth Clark and Shelby captured the 550-man garrison, plus a large number of muskets and much other valuable military booty. The following day, in another foray, Jeff Thompson forced the Federal militia at Sedalia to surrender.[20]

Meanwhile the main column moved on to Marshall, where on the seventeenth the side expeditions rejoined it. Most of Shelby's and Clark's troopers came from this region, and many of them, usually

[17] M. Jeff Thompson, "Reminiscences of M. Jeff Thompson" (MS in M. Thompson Papers, Southern Historical Collection, University of North Carolina Library, Chapel Hill, North Carolina), 31. See also Thompson's report, *Official Records*, XLI, Pt. 1, pp. 663–64, and St. Louis *Missouri Republican*, October 20, 22, 1864.
[18] Quoted in Edwards, *Shelby and His Men*, 471.
[19] *Official Records*, XLI, Pt. 1, pp. 632, 711.
[20] *Ibid.*, 632–33, 656–57, 664–65.

without official leave, took time off to visit their homes.[21] As a consequence, Price's effective force was reduced and his advance slowed;
had the Federals been able at this time to attack him in strength they
probably would have destroyed the entire expedition.

While the Missouri troops thus, in effect, enjoyed a holiday, the
Arkansas contingents were suffering from hunger and sickness. Wrote
Brigadier General James Fagan to Price on October 18:

I beg leave to call your attention to a want of breadstuffs for my division. My men are much dissatisfied and complain a good deal. They deem
it strange that in such a plentiful country as the one in which we are now
operating breadstuffs cannot be supplied at least while we are moving so
leisurely. Being totally unacquainted with the country and its resources,
and not knowing one day where my command will be the next or even the
direction it will take, I am unable myself to make any arrangements to
supply my command, and must rely on the proper officers of the staff of
the army to do so.

Enclosed with Fagan's letter was a statement by his chief surgeon
to the effect that "catarrh, bronchitis, pneumonia, rheumatic affections, and glandular swellings" were rampant in the Arkansas division,
that the men were poorly clad and lacking blankets, and that their
daily ration of one-half pound of flour, "even if it were regularly supplied," was inadequate to maintain good health.[22]

The army reached Waverly, Shelby's home town, on the eighteenth.
Near there, George Todd with Quantrill's old gang reported for duty.
Price assigned the guerrillas to Shelby's division, where they served
as scouts.[23]

Price's slow rate of march along the Missouri gave the Federals
extra time in which to mobilize their forces. In his rear Rosecrans had
taken the field with an army of about 4,500 cavalry under Pleasonton
and some 9,000 infantry commanded by A. J. Smith, who had been
reinforced by Major General Joseph A. Mower's division up from
Arkansas.[24] To his front, General Samuel R. Curtis, his antagonist at

[21] *Ibid.*, Pt. 4, p. 1012.
[22] *Ibid.*, 1003–1004. There is no record of a reply or action on the part of
Price in regard to Fagan's complaint.
[23] Castel, *Quantrill*, 197.
[24] *Official Records*, XLI, Pt. 1, pp. 311–12.

Pea Ridge and now commander of the Department of Kansas, waited near Kansas City with 15,000 regulars and militia. Rosecrans hoped to trap the raiders in a pocket formed by the Missouri River, Pleasonton's cavalry, and Curtis' army, then crush them with Smith's infantry, but he had been unable to communicate with Curtis and knew nothing of his plans and dispositions. Curtis, on the other hand, was equally ignorant of Rosecrans' intentions and movements. In addition, he was having trouble with the Kansas militia, who threatened to mutiny when he ordered them to march into Missouri. As a consequence he was able to send only 2,000 troops under Major General James G. Blunt across the state line to Lexington—a force utterly inadequate to block the Confederate advance.[25]

Price left Waverly on the 19th and marched for Lexington, scene of his greatest military exploit. On the outskirts Shelby encountered Blunt's scouts and drove them through the streets and beyond the town. The appearance of Federal troops in front was ominous. Along with increased pressure from Pleasonton, it caused Price to move faster. On the twentieth he covered twenty miles, and the following day he pushed towards Independence. Several miles east of there, at the crossing of the Little Blue, Blunt disputed his advance. Initially, John S. Marmaduke's division, which was in the van that day, attacked alone. But Blunt's Kansans and Coloradans, veterans armed with repeating rifles, fought so stubbornly from behind the shelter of stone walls that Marmaduke (who had three horses shot from under him) was unable to dislodge them. Price then threw Shelby into the fray, whereupon the Federals, in danger of being surrounded, retreated to the other side of Independence. In later years Shelby remarked that for his division, at least, the campaign up to this time had been a "walkover," but that on reaching the Little Blue this ceased to be the case.

[25] *Ibid.*, 462–75. Kansas at this time was rent by a bitter political fight between the supporters and opponents of Senator Jim Lane, boss of the state Republican party and "king" of Kansas politics. Since no authentic word of Price's whereabouts had reached the state for some time, Lane's enemies began to suspect that there was no real danger of invasion and that the mobilization of the militia was a trick to prevent their voting on election day (Curtis with some reason was regarded as subservient to Lane). The militia, commanded by anti-Lane politicians and stirred up by anti-Lane propaganda, came to believe the same, and some of them actually headed for home. Lane had a record of trickery that made such an attitude on the part of his foes quite understandable. See Castel, *A Frontier State at War*, 186–92.

Price's men were now tired and hungry, their ammunition was beginning to run low, and their horses were thin and nearly exhausted. Many miles and many days lay between them and the Arkansas.[26]

Following the battle at the Little Blue the Federals took up new positions behind the Big Blue, a steep-banked stream flowing south to north several miles east of Kansas City. Curtis, who so far had merely sought to delay the Confederate advance, proposed to make an all-out stand along this line, which his engineers had bolstered with rifle pits and other defensive works. His army now included the Kansas militia who, finally convinced that their homes indeed were in danger, had consented to cross into Missouri. Also he had succeeded in contacting Rosecrans and informing him of his plans.[27] Rosecrans, assuming that Curtis would be able to hold Price at the Big Blue and so force him to turn southward, thereupon advised Pleasonton to pursue the Confederates with only one of his brigades and send the other three to join Smith's corps at Lone Jack, from which point it would be easy to intercept Price. But Pleasonton, who had no confidence in Curtis' ability to stop Price, disregarded Rosecrans' suggestion and continued to press the raiders with his entire division.[28]

Price camped on the night of the twenty-first at Independence. In the morning he began moving westward again, with Shelby in the lead, Marmaduke following, and Fagan in the rear. His strategy called for Jackman's brigade to feint in the direction of Kansas City while Shelby with the "Iron Brigade" forced a passage across the Big Blue at Byram's Ford to the south.[29] It is not clear at this point whether he intended to turn southward after crossing the Big Blue or else attempt to seize Kansas City and perhaps even Leavenworth. Many of his officers had been urging the first course for several days, but his instructions from Kirby Smith contemplated the latter. Quite likely he had not yet made

[26] *Official Records*, XLI, Pt. 1, pp. 476–78, 634; Castel, *A Frontier State at War*, 193–94. The Union troops were armed with Martin-Henry rifles that fired sixteen shots without reloading. Had they been properly supported by the Kansas militia, probably they could have checked the Confederate advance. See George S. Grover, "The Price Campaign of 1864," *Missouri Historical Review*, VI (1912), 174. Grover served in the Federal army at the Little Blue.
[27] *Official Records*, XLI, Pt. 1, pp. 476–79.
[28] *Ibid.*, 312–13.
[29] *Ibid.*, 634.

up his mind on the matter but was waiting for developments to clarify the situation. As always he was most reluctant to retreat and not in the least alarmed because he found himself in a tight spot.

Shelby's scouts reported that Byram's Ford was blocked by a belt of fallen timber some five hundred yards wide and defended by a large body of enemy troops. Price thereupon rode to the front and ordered a portion of the "Iron Brigade" to dismount. Then, under his personal direction, this force splashed across the Big Blue, scaled the opposite bank, and drove the Federals, who made little effort to resist, from their position. As soon as this had been accomplished Price ordered Mackey's pioneer detachment to remove the obstacles at the ford, an operation which took about an hour and a half. The rest of Shelby's force then crossed, engaged the enemy, routed several regiments of Kansas militia, and captured numerous prisoners. Curtis, his line breached and many of his troops in danger of being cut off, fell back to Westport. The failure of the Union army to hold at the Big Blue was mainly the fault of Colonel Charles Jennison, the infamous jayhawker leader, whose brigade had been stationed at Byram's Ford.[30]

Price did not attempt to follow up his easy victory by pursuing the Federals into Westport. His primary object was to get his train across the Big Blue, and this he succeeded in doing, with Shelby standing guard, ready to fend off a Union counterattack. During the fighting the bushwhackers, whose leader Todd had been killed by a sniper the day before, murdered some of the captured Kansans. When informed of their deeds Price immediately ordered them to leave the army. They did so, except for a number who joined Shelby.[31]

But while the van of the Confederate army achieved success, the rear experienced defeat. Pleasonton crossed the Little Blue on a hastily constructed bridge, mauled Cabell's brigade, took four hundred prisoners and two cannons, and occupied Independence. Marmaduke's division then attempted to halt him two miles west of the town but without success. The Federal cavalry, reported General Clark, "rushed

[30] *Ibid.*, 478–84, 634–35, 658, 666–67, 710; Castel, *A Frontier State at War*, 193.

[31] Castel, *A Frontier State at War*, 228–29; Castel, *Quantrill*, 198–200. While Price's army was at Lexington, Todd's guerrillas plundered the town, according to a correspondent of the St. Louis *Missouri Republican*, November 2, 1864.

upon us with a reckless fierceness that I have never seen equalled . . . .[32] The Southern troops, on the other hand, Pleasonton noted, "seemed to be in haste," and with the instinct of a true fighting man he drove onward relentlessly, pushing Marmaduke back almost to the Big Blue before breaking off his pursuit at 2 A.M. in order to rest his men and horses.[33]

Shortly after nightfall Price, who established his headquarters at a farmhouse near Byram's Ford, received a message from Shelby urging that the army retreat southward immediately. At the same time he learned from intercepted Union dispatches and other sources that strong enemy units were concentrating to the south. This information, coupled with the presence of Curtis' army at Westport and Pleasonton's onslaught, left no possibility of doubting that the Army of Missouri was in dire peril of being trapped and destroyed. Therefore he abandoned all lingering notions of capturing Kansas City and Leavenworth and issued an order for the train to proceed southward in the morning on the State Line Road leading to Fort Scott.[34] It was a wise decision, indeed the only sensible one under the circumstances. However, he should have made it at least a day sooner; furthermore, he should have started the train in motion at once instead of waiting until morning. But, ruefully remarked a Conferedate officer later, "that was not Price's *style*."[35]

Sunday, October 23, dawned clear and cold. To cover the movement of the train Price sent Shelby, supported by two of Fagan's brigades (Dobbin's and Colonel W. F. Slemons') to attack the enemy at Westport. The Federals under Blunt also advanced, and during the next two hours the rolling, wooded country along Brush Creek to the south of Westport raged with what Edwards termed "the hardest battle of the campaign." Both sides charged and countercharged repeatedly and both suffered severe losses. At one point Colonel James

[32] *Official Records*, XLI, Pt. 1, p. 683.

[33] *Ibid.*, 340, 635, 683. Moore, "Missouri," p. 189, states that Cabell's brigade was routed and lost its cannons at Independence because it was run over and thrown into disarray by a large mob of fleeing Confederate stragglers and camp followers, who stampeded when the Federals attacked.

[34] *Official Records*, XLI, Pt. 1, pp. 624, 635; *ibid.*, Pt. 4, p. 1012; Edwards, *Shelby and His Men*, 428–30.

[35] Edwards, *Shelby and His Men*, 436.

McGhee's regiment of Dobbin's brigade made a wild assault in close order down a narrow lane and was slaughtered by Union artillery. On another occasion one of Collins' Parrotts burst from constant firing. All the while, fresh masses of militia poured onto the field, threatening

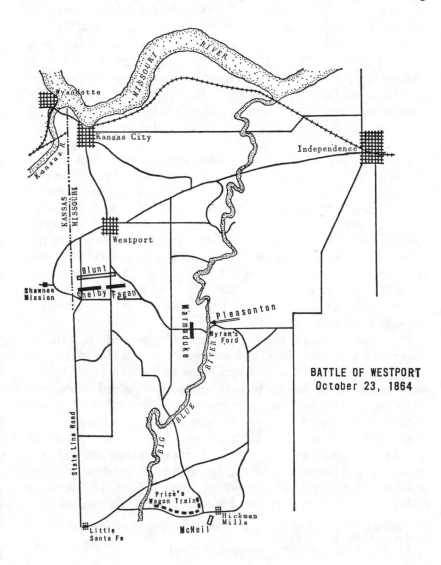

BATTLE OF WESTPORT
October 23, 1864

the Confederate flanks. Yet, despite the odds, Shelby eventually drove
the enemy back and occupied their positions. He then halted to reform
his ranks and wait for badly needed ammunition to be brought up.[36]

At this juncture disaster struck the other wing of Price's army.
Urging his men onward with cries of "Rebels! Rebels! Fire! Fire! you
damned asses!" Pleasonton hurled a savage assault against Marmaduke, who was endeavoring to hold Byram's Ford. Marmaduke's men
fought desperately, beating back charge after charge. Then, having
suffered heavy losses and with their ammunition spent, they crumpled
and fled, scattering in utter rout across the prairie. Howling in triumph,
the blue-clad cavalry pursued them, riding them down and taking many
prisoners. For the time being, Marmaduke's division ceased to exist
as a fighting organization.[37]

While this was occurring, another and even worse blow threatened
the Army of Missouri. Before attacking Marmaduke, Pleasonton had
sent Brigadier General John H. McNeil's brigade on a flanking march
south toward Little Santa Fe. Price, who was observing the battle in
front of Westport, learned of McNeil's movement just as Marmaduke
gave way at Byram's Ford. A great fear clutched his heart, for the
train also was heading toward Little Santa Fe, protected only by the
remnants of Cabell's brigade and Tyler's unarmed recruits. At once
he ordered Shelby and Fagan to disengage and hasten to its rescue.
He then galloped off, accompanied by his bodyguard, to organize a
stop-gap defense.

He found the long column of wagons, refugees, and cattle toiling
along the Harrisonville Road a short distance west of Hickman Mills.
Ordering it to leave the road, which followed the crest of a ridge, so
as to escape enemy fire, he formed his escort, Cabell's brigade, and
Tyler's recruits in line of battle, prepared for a desperate stand against
McNeil, whose squadrons could be seen deploying to the east. Fortunately, McNeil mistook Tyler's command, which now numbered
over five thousand, for the main body of the Confederate army! Hence,
much to the subsequent disgust of Pleasonton, he merely engaged in
some tentative skirmishing and did not attack in force. In fact, when
Cabell's troops advanced and set fire to the prairie grass, he fell back

[36] *Official Records*, XLI, Pt. 1, pp. 485–90, 575, 635, 658, 667; Edwards,
Shelby and His Men, 430.
[37] *Official Records*, XLI, Pt. 1, pp. 341, 635, 684.

half a mile and made no further movements. As a result the train
passed safely by, followed by Cabell, Tyler, and, sometime later,
Marmaduke.[38]

The collapse of Marmaduke's division at the Big Blue exposed the
flank and rear of Shelby and Fagan to Pleasonton. At the same time
Blunt, reinforced by thousands of militia, launched a massive counterattack. Fagan's two brigades, which were posted on Shelby's right,
soon faltered. At Fagan's urgent plea Jackman's brigade went to their
support. Jackman repulsed the Federal waves, then fell back with the
Arkansans toward Little Santa Fe.

Shelby and the Iron Brigade also began to retreat—not because of
Price's order to disengage, which apparently never was delivered, but
because of the overwhelming enemy pressure to his front and the
threat to his rear. Suddenly he found his path blocked by Pleasonton's
cavalry bearing in from the east. There was only one thing he could
do—attack. With a wild cheer his veterans charged, smashed into
Sanborn's brigade, "shook it considerably" (to quote Pleasonton's
report), and broke through. However, a second Union line came up,
and as the Missourians attempted to reform for a second assault, six
of Pleasonton's cannons, double-shotted with canister, raked them
with deadly enfilade fire. In addition Blunt's columns approached in
hot pursuit. Thus there was nothing to do, Shelby later frankly stated,
"but to run for it." The Federals, seeing the renowned Iron Brigade
flee, gave chase, yelling and shooting. Shelby's men, "every one on
his own hook," would turn, fire, and then gallop away again, being
incapable of an organized stand. Their flight continued to Little
Santa Fe, where the enemy abandoned the pursuit. Shelby and Thompson then rallied their troops, after which they rode on until they caught
up with the rest of the army, now in full retreat down the Fort Scott
Road.[39]

From the standpoint of numbers Westport was the greatest battle
of the Civil War in the West, with approximately forty-five thousand
Northern and Southern troops being either directly or indirectly involved. Strategically Price achieved his main objective of saving his

[38] *Ibid.*, 341, 372, 635–36; Luttrell, "Diary of the Price Raid," St. Louis
Missouri Republican, March 6, 1886; Frank Robertson, "The Price Raid,"
Houston *Daily Telegraph*, December 3, 1864.
[39] *Official Records*, XLI, Pt. 1, pp. 337, 390, 485–91, 636, 659, 667–68, 676.

train and escaping south, but tactically he took another bad licking. Persons who toured the fields about Westport after the fighting ended described it as being strewn with dead horses, saddles, blankets, rifles, cannon balls, and bodies. Many of the Confederate slain, they noted, were boys sixteen or seventeen years old. In all Price probably suffered about a thousand casualties, and the already low morale of his army was further reduced.[40]

Yet his losses could have been far worse. Not only was he outnumbered in effective fighting strength more than two to one by Blunt and Pleasonton, but all that saved the train, and with it the entire Confederate army, from destruction, was luck, a bluff, and McNeil's incompetence. Also it could be argued that Price was most fortunate that Pleasonton decided to pursue him with his full force rather than send the major portion of it to Lone Jack where it would have been in position to cut off the retreat from Westport. But since it was in large part Pleasonton's attacks that forced Price to turn south, and since it was scarcely Pleasonton's fault that McNeil did not intercept the train near Hickman Mills, probably judgment should be reserved on this point. Pleasonton, however, did commit one blunder for which there can be little excuse. On the night of October 23, after driving Marmaduke across the Big Blue, Pleasonton asked Rosecrans to order Smith's column to Independence, alleging as he did so that Price's whole army confronted him. Rosecrans reluctantly agreed to this request, with the result that Smith's corps was taken completely out of the following day's battle. Had Smith been at Lone Jack, as Rosecrans originally intended, in all likelihood he would have been able to

---

[40] *Ibid.*, 491; Richard Josiah Hinton, *Rebel Invasion of Missouri and Kansas and the Campaign of the Army of the Border Against General Sterling Price in October and November, 1864* (Chicago and Leavenworth, 1865), 179–80; Leavenworth (Kansas) *Daily Times*, October 26, 1864. There are no Confederate figures on losses at Westport, and the figure cited in the text is the approximation of one of Cabell's officers ["Diary of an Officer," Washington (Ark.) *Telegraph*, November 30, 1864]. Edwards, *Shelby and His Men*, 435, states that Shelby's division alone lost over 800 men, but this figure is contradicted by the official returns which indicate that this division did not lose that many men in the entire campaign [see *Official Records*, XLI, Pt. 1, pp. 670, 676, 678]. Incredible as it may seem some of the Confederates [see *ibid.*, 715, and Edwards, *Shelby and His Men*, 437] looked upon Westport as a victory! This probably was because they had achieved their objective of escaping from the Union trap.

strike the Confederates as they retreated from Westport with the devastating power of his nine thousand veteran infantry and five batteries of artillery.[41]

Price, in brief, owed his escape from the trap into which he had led his forces less to his own skill than to the mistakes of his opponents, although he must be given some credit for saving the train by his prompt and gallant action in deploying Tyler's unarmed recruits. As for Rosecrans, he was truly an ill-starred general, for with any luck he would have smashed Price's expedition and in part at least regained the reputation lost at Chickamauga.

[41] *Official Records*, XLI, Pt. 1, pp. 312–13; Howard N. Monnett, *Action Before Westport, 1864* (Kansas City, Mo., 1964), 92–93.

14

MINE CREEK

O n October 24 Price continued to retreat in the direction of Fort Scott. Curtis pursued him with Blunt's and Pleasonton's cavalry, in all about seven thousand men. Rosecrans, realizing that Smith's infantry would never be able to catch up, ordered them back to St. Louis, and himself ceased to take an active part in the campaign. The Kansas militia went home.[1]

Curtis had no trouble following Price's trail. It was marked by broken wagons and caissons, discarded rifles and blankets, bits of harness and debris, and by sick, wounded, and exhausted Confederates lying by the roadside waiting to be captured.[2] In addition, up ahead the Union troops saw long columns of smoke twisting into the air. For the Army of Missouri was now in Kansas—the only regular Southern force ever to enter the state—and Shelby's troopers were taking advantage of the fact to extract revenge for jayhawker depredations against their friends and relatives. "Haystacks, houses, barns, produce, crops, and farming implements," boasted Major Edwards, "were consumed before the march of his squadrons, and what the flames spared the bullet finished."[3] Infuriated Kansans in turn murdered and maltreated Confederate prisoners.[4]

At the end of the day on the twenty-fourth, Price halted near Potosi on the banks of the Marais des Cygnes River. During the night Marmaduke, whose division was in front, sent word that the Federals were threatening his pickets. After consulting with the bespectacled young general, Price decided that Curtis was marching along a parallel road to the west, undoubtedly with the intention of striking him on the right flank or blocking his line of retreat. A captured dispatch, plus

[1] *Official Records*, XLI, Pt. 1, pp. 313, 341, 491–93.
[2] Hinton, *Rebel Invasion of Missouri and Kansas*, 183–90.
[3] Edwards, *Shelby and His Men*, 447–48; Hinton, *Rebel Invasion of Missouri and Kansas*, 183–90.
[4] Diary of Samuel J. Reader (MS in Kansas State Historical Society, Topeka), October 25, 26, 27, 1864.

the testimony of some newly arrived recruits that they had not seen any enemy forces to the north, confirmed Price in this opinion.[5] Hence, he paid no heed to Cabell, who reported that the Federals were probing his lines along the Marais des Cygnes at the rear of the army, and urged that the retreat be resumed at once—a view in which, apparently, Marmaduke also joined.[6]

Once again, however, Price was the victim of erroneous intelligence, or rather of a poor evaluation thereof. Union forces indeed were on his right flank, but they consisted only of a small cavalry brigade sent by Samuel Curtis to protect Mound City and Fort Scott from raids. Blunt's and Pleasonton's divisions still were following and had gained considerable ground. In fact, only darkness and unfamiliarity with the terrain prevented Sanborn's brigade from making a full-scale assault at the Marais des Cygnes.[7]

At daybreak the Federals did attack the Confederate rear, causing some of the Confederates to flee in confusion.[8] But Price, who was several miles to the south at the time, either was unaware of this action or else chose to ignore it.[9] Still expecting to encounter the enemy in front or on the right, he deployed Jackman's brigade to the immediate front, Thompson's to the right front of the train, Tyler's to the right center of the train, and Marmaduke's and Fagan's divisions to the rear. He himself rode in a carriage at the head of the train.[10]

At noon, after a march of about fifteen miles, the Confederate van crossed the Little Osage River. At this point Price ordered Shelby to capture Fort Scott, where a thousand Negro troops were reported stationed. Obviously he still believed there was no danger in the rear and just as obviously he no longer was concerned about an attack on the front or right flank. However, as he was issuing Shelby's instruc-

[5] *Official Records*, XLI, Pt. 1, p. 636.
[6] Edwards, *Shelby and His Men*, 440; Darr, "Price's Raid," 361; Moore, "Missouri," p. 192; Reynolds, quoted in Edwards, *Shelby and His Men*, 472.
[7] *Official Records*, XLI, Pt. 1, p. 493. Blunt proposed doing what Price thought the Federals intended to do but was overruled by Curtis.
[8] *Ibid.*, 493–95. One of Cabell's officers claimed that Cabell's brigade repulsed the attack ["Diary of an Officer," Washington (Ark.) *Telegraph*, November 30, 1864].
[9] Price did not mention the Federal attack at the Marais des Cygnes in his report. In fact there are almost no Confederate references to the action.
[10] *Official Records*, XLI, Pt. 1, p. 636.

tions, a message arrived from Marmaduke: The enemy, estimated to be three thousand strong, were in sight in the rear! Immediately Price ordered Shelby to hasten with his division to the support of Marmaduke and Fagan. He then mounted his large, white horse and galloped to the rear, accompanied by his staff and escort. After riding several miles and passing the rear of the train he drew rein in utter horror and amazement. Fleeing towards him across the prairie like a "herd of stampeded buffaloes" were the troops of Marmaduke and Fagan![11]

What had happened was this: As the end of the train was crossing Mine Creek, a deep, high-banked stream some three miles north of the Little Osage, the ford became jammed with the wagons, buggies, and teams of the refugees, completely blocking it. At the same time two of Pleasonton's brigades under Colonel John F. Phillips and Lieutenant Colonel Frederick W. Benteen, about twenty-five hundred men, pressed to within six hundred yards of the rear guard. In order to protect the train and check the enemy, Marmaduke and Fagan decided to turn about and make a stand on the north side of Mine Creek; in fact, with the crossing blocked, they had no other choice. Since the Federals were so close, they did not, as customary when giving battle, dismount their troops but formed them on horseback, three ranks deep, with Fagan's division to the west of the road, Marmaduke's to the east. This line was about eight hundred yards long and ran across the open prairie. Supporting it were eight cannons, four in the center and two on either flank. These pieces promptly opened up with a heavy but ineffective fire.[12]

[11] *Ibid.*, 636–37; W. M. McPheeters Diary, October 25, 1864; Edwards, *Shelby and His Men*, 450.

[12] Luttrell, "Diary of the Price Raid," St. Louis *Missouri Republican*, March 13, 1886; Darr, "Price's Raid, 361; Cabell, *Report of Cabell's Brigade*, 12. General Clark referred to the creek as a "ravine" in his report (*Official Records*, XLI, Pt. 1, p. 684). Moore, in his contribution to Evans (ed.), *Confederate Military History*, IX, Pt. 2, p. 192, stated that on coming to Mine Creek, Marmaduke "was surprised to find the wagon train on his side of the creek, the teamsters dismounted and lying on the grass talking with each other, and about one wagon crossing the creek every five minutes." Moore, who was on Marmaduke's staff, but who did not participate in the Missouri expedition of 1864, cites no source for this story, which like many of his statements is demonstrably in error. For instance, in this particular case several independent sources establish that the bulk of the train was south of Mine Creek when the rear guard arrived.

The Union cavalry hesitated before the Confederate mass, which outnumbered them at least two to one. Benteen, however, concluded that the rebels had made a "fatal blunder" in the placing of their artillery, and he resolved to exploit it. Calling on Phillips to support him, he ordered his brigade to attack. With bugles sounding the Federals charged at a gallop. A ragged Confederate volley emptied some saddles but failed to stop the charge. Benteen's brigade crashed into Marmaduke's center and Phillips struck the left flank of Fagan. Marmaduke's front rank bolted, breaking the lines behind and spreading panic and confusion. In the close quarter fighting that ensued, the long-barreled, muzzle-loading rifles of the Southern troops were no match for the revolvers, carbines, and sabers of the enemy. It was practically impossible to reload them on plunging, rearing horses, and little short of suicidal even to make the attempt.[13] After a brief but fierce melee the Confederates fled in wild disorder, most of them throwing away their useless weapons. Hundreds, finding their escape barred by the creek, threw up their hands in surrender, but most somehow managed to scramble across. In all the Federals killed and wounded three hundred, captured the eight cannons, and took nine hundred prisoners. Among the latter were Marmaduke and Cabell; the former yielded to Private James Dunlavy of the Third Iowa Cavalry, whom he nearsightedly mistook for one of his own soldiers, many of whom were wearing blue Union jackets.[14]

"The scene after the battle," recalled a local Kansas resident years later, "was terrifying. Fully 300 horses horribly mangled were running and snorting and trampling the dead and wounded. Their blood

[13] *Official Records,* XLI, Pt. 1, pp. 331, 351–52, 495–98, 501, 646, 684, 687, 691, 694, 696–97; "Diary of an Officer," Washington (Ark.) *Telegraph,* November, 30, 1864; Luttrell, "Diary of the Price Raid," St. Louis *Missouri Republican,* March 16, 1886; R. L. Brown Army Journal (MS in Missouri Historical Society, St. Louis), October 25, 1864; Edgar Langsdorf, "Price's Raid and the Battle of Mine Creek," *Kansas Historical Quarterly,* XXX (1964), 295–96. It should be noted that some of the Federal troops also were equipped with infantry rifles and so fought on foot (*Official Records,* XLI, Pt. 1, p. 361). But the great majority of Phillips' and Benteen's men were regularly equipped cavalry.

[14] *Official Records,* XLI, Pt. 1, pp. 331, 352, 498, 684, 691; Cabell, *Report of Cabell's Brigade,* 12–14; St. Louis *Missouri Republican,* November 4, 1864.

had drenched them and added to the ghastliness of it all."[15] Union casualties, in one of the most spectacular cavalry charges of the war, were a mere 150.[16]

Price, after recovering from the initial shock, took the disaster with his usual calm. Meeting an officer retreating from Mine Creek he stopped him and asked, "Where is General Marmaduke?" The officer replied that he was probably captured. Price reflected a moment, then as if speaking to himself said, "A bad state of affairs, a very bad, a very annoying mishap. But—" and his voice, as he swept the scene with his binoculars, rose—"but we will soon set things to rights again." Soon he was galloping ahead to rally the fleeing remnants of Marmaduke's and Fagan's troops.[17]

However he found the men "deaf to all entreaties or commands." Only Shelby, it was obvious, could save the army from destruction. In response to Price's urgent order, Shelby moved with the Iron Brigade to a hill one mile north of the Osage. Following his standard tactics for a rear-guard action, he formed his troops in three lines. The first line was to fire, then retreat beyond the second and third, who in their turn would repeat the same procedure.[18] In his official report (written by Edwards) Shelby gave this dramatic account of the subsequent fighting:

The enemy advanced in overwhelming numbers and with renewed confidence at the sight of the small force in front of them. . . . The fight lasted nearly an hour, but I was at last forced to fall back. . . . Elliot, Gordon, Slayback, Hooper, Smith, Blackwell, Williams, and a host of other officers seemed to rise higher and higher as the danger increased, and were always where the tide of battle rolled deepest and darkest. It was an evening to try the hearts of my best and bravest, and rallying around me they even

[15] Quoted in Langsdorf, "Mine Creek," 297.

[16] *Official Records*, XLI, Pt. 1, p. 344. Price reported [*ibid.*, 637] a loss of 300 to 400 men captured and 5 pieces of artillery. However these figures do not even pretend to be complete, and probably are only for Marmaduke's division, as neither Fagan or any of his officers filed reports on Mine Creek. One of Fagan's officers ["Diary of an Officer," Washington (Ark.) *Telegraph*, November 30, 1864] unofficially estimated the total Confederate loss at Mine Creek at between 1,500 and 3,000; this is probably too high.

[17] Luttrell, "Diary of the Price Raid," St. Louis *Missouri Republican*, March 13, 1886.

[18] *Official Records*, XLI, Pt. 1, pp. 637, 659–60.

surpassed all former days of high and heroic bearing. . . . Pressed furiously,
and having to cross a deep and treacherous stream, I did not offer battle
again until gaining a large hill in front of the entire army. . . . It was a
fearful hour. The long and weary days of marching and fighting were
culminating, and the narrow issue of life or death stood out all dark and
barren as a rainy sea. The fight was to be made now, and General Price,
with the pilot's wary eye, saw the storm cloud sweep down, growing larger
and larger and darker and darker. They came upon me steadily and calm.
I waited until they came close enough and gave them volley for volley,
shot for shot. For fifteen minutes both lines stood the pelting of the leaden
hail without flinching, and the incessant roar of musketry rang out wildly
and shrill, all separate sounds blending in a universal crash. The fate of
the army hung upon the result, and our very existence tottered and tossed
in the smoke of the strife. The red sun looked down upon the scene, and the
redder clouds floated away with angry, sullen glare. Slowly, slowly my old
brigade was melting away. The high-toned and chivalric Dobbin, formed
on my right, stood by me in all that fiery storm, and Elliott's and Gordon's
voices sounded high above the rage of the conflict: "My merry men,
fight on."[19]

However, a Union officer who took part in the battle later commented sarcastically in regard to Shelby's account that "nobody was
'tossed in the smoke' of battle, and nobody on our side, in so far as
I heard, was either killed, wounded, or turned up missing. It was
simply a lively skirmish." And according to another Federal soldier,
following Mine Creek "the enemy made several stands as we pursued
him, but was easily driven."[20] Thompson's report provides a more
sober and no doubt more accurate description of Shelby's rear-guard
action:

We were ordered to dispute the passage of the enemy [across the Little
Osage] and delay his approach. . . . Our first line, composed of Elliott's
and Williams' regiments, cooly witnessed the formation and advance of
the enemy, and when within range commenced firing. The impossibility of

[19] *Ibid.*, 660.
[20] The first quote is from Samuel J. Crawford, *Kansas in the Sixties* (Chicago,
1911), 167. Crawford was the Republican candidate for governor of Kansas in
1864 and was serving as a volunteer aide on Curtis' staff. He was an experienced
soldier. The second quotation is from the Diary of Fletcher C. Pomeroy (MS
in Kansas State Historical Society), October 25, 1864. Pomeroy was an officer
in the Seventh Kansas Cavalry, Pleasonton's division.

loading Enfield rifles on horseback now became apparent again, for after one discharge the horses became excited, and when the enemy charged . . . there was nothing to do but retreat. The men held their horses well in hand and could have been controlled, but upon approaching our second line it commenced firing before we reached and broke before we passed through. There was a third line . . . that had the advantage of a ditch, which covered the road, and had it not been for the check that [it] gave the enemy very many of the brigade would have been killed or captured. We soon passed out of immediate danger, and the men formed again very readily, although all regimental organization was lost.[21]

During the remainder of the afternoon Shelby's troopers continued to fall back before the oncoming Federals, stopping now and then for a short stand. "All ran," further wrote the realistic-minded Thompson, "yet none were [sic] frightened, and as there was no discipline I found a quiet voice and ordinary remark attracted more attention than the vehement language that some use. Our lines were formed and broken several times this day, but our loss was small. Each colonel retained a part of his command about him, but the brigade was not formed together after the first line was broken."[22]

While Shelby thus endeavored to slow down the Union pursuit, the rest of Price's army streamed southward in demoralized flight. Late in the afternoon, about two miles from the Marmiton River, the train again had difficulty crossing a ford and once more the army was obliged to make a stand in order to save it. Price, assisted by Fagan and Clark (who now commanded Marmaduke's division), managed to rally about a thousand troops. These, plus the unarmed recruits, he posted behind a stone wall in support of Shelby. Two of Pleasonton's brigades under the command of McNeil came up, but they did not attack with their customary impetuosity. Their horses were so tired that they could move only at a walk, and as at Hickman Mills, McNeil mistook the unarmed men for real troops and so thought he was heavily outnumbered and in danger of being outflanked. After two hours of skirmishing, during which Tyler's brigade made a gallant charge, Price withdrew, Shelby still bringing up the rear. It was now dark and McNeil made no attempt to pursue. Moreover, Pleasonton with the rest

[21] *Official Records*, XLI, Pt. 1, p. 668.
[22] *Ibid.*, 668–69.

of his division marched to Fort Scott for food and rest, ignoring Curtis' pleas to remain on the field. Curtis then directed Blunt, whose troops had seen no action during the day, to attack Price, but through some mix-up Blunt also went to Fort Scott. Thus the Confederates were able to make their retreat without further fighting.[23]

As soon as he was across the Marmiton, Price ordered the destruction of all superfluous wagons and those with broken-down teams. In a short time the night sky was ablaze as a third of the train was put to the torch.[24] At two A.M. the army again began trekking southward. The debacle at Mine Creek had wrecked it, and except for Shelby's division it was now little more than a mob. Probably only the fear of death at the hands of the enemy, who were shooting all Confederates wearing Northern uniforms, prevented a mass surrender.[25]

Through the rest of the night and all the next day Price's followers trudged wearily but steadily along. By nightfall they reached Carthage, Missouri, having covered sixty miles since leaving the Marmiton. It had been, wrote one soldier in his diary, "a fatal day for horse flesh."[26] At Carthage they obtained desperately needed food—many men had not had any bread for six days—and rested briefly. The following day, October 27, they moved another twenty-two miles to Shoal Creek. Their morale, noted Major Lauchlan A. Maclean in his official campaign journal, was beginning to improve, but there were "many desertions among the Arkansas troops."[27] On the 28th they passed through Granby and went into camp four miles south of Newtonia. Here Price held a council of his generals on whether to remain there three or four days or march on immediately for Arkansas. Shelby advocated the first alternative. "It is much better to lose an army in actual battle, than to starve the men and kill the horses." All the others disagreed and wished to continue retreating, but the condition of the army was so bad that Price decided it must have a rest. Besides, there had

[23] *Ibid.*, 373, 502–504, 637, 701–702; W. M. McPheeters Diary, October 25, 1864; Luttrell, "Diary of the Price Raid," St. Louis *Missouri Republican*, March 13, 1886.

[24] *Official Records*, XLI, Pt. 1, p. 637; *ibid.*, Pt. 4, pp. 1013–14.

[25] *Ibid.*, Pt. 1, pp. 352, 637, 646; Cabell, *Report of Cabell's Brigade*, 15–16; W. M. McPheeters Diary, October 25, 1864.

[26] Diary of J. H. P. Baker (MS in Missouri Historical Society, St. Louis), October 25, 26, 1864.

[27] *Official Records*, XLI, Pt. 1, pp. 637–38.

been no sign of Curtis since the Marmiton, and he assumed that the pursuit had been left far behind.[28]

But as so often during this campaign he was mistaken. Curtis, with Blunt's division and McNeil's and Sanborn's brigades, was close on his heels. As the Confederates began gathering corn in the fields near their camp, some of Fagan's men galloped up crying "Yanks! Yanks!" Marching toward them was Blunt at the head of a thousand cavalry. Price, thinking that Curtis' entire army was upon him, ordered instant retreat. At the same time he sent Shelby, supported by the remains of Cabell's brigade, to hold the Federals at bay. Blunt, a general with a damaged reputation to restore, did not wait for the rest of the Union forces to come up but rashly attacked alone. Shelby counterattacked and drove him back, then threatened to envelop his flanks with superior numbers. Only the opportune arrival of Sanborn's brigade saved the Kansas general from the consequence of his folly. Shelby thereupon withdrew, and, with night approaching, Blunt and Sanborn made no attempt to pursue. Both sides claimed victory in this "Battle of Newtonia," but the Confederates fought only to protect their retreat, and the Federals, because of Blunt's incompetence, missed an excellent opportunity to finish off Price's army.[29]

The Confederate flight went on, day after day, through the desolate hills and fields of southern Missouri and northern Arkansas. The weather became bitterly cold, with rain, sleet, and finally snow falling. The poorly clad troops suffered greatly, and many succumbed to pneumonia. Much straggling took place, and hundreds of men either fell by the wayside or else slipped off for home. Shelby's division alone retained a semblance of discipline and fighting spirit.[30]

[28] Edwards, *Shelby and His Men*, 455.

[29] *Official Records*, XLI, Pt. 1, pp. 507–509, 638, 647, 661; "Diary of an Officer," Washington (Ark.) *Telegraph*, November 30, 1864; Edwards, *Shelby and His Men*, 455–59. Blunt, who had been credited with the Union victory at Prairie Grove in December, 1862, and who had defeated the Confederates in the Indian Territory and been made a departmental commander, had lost much of his prestige as a result of the Baxter Springs massacre and at the start of the compaign against Price was operating against Indians in the west with only a battalion-sized command. During the campaign he fought hard to re-establish his reputation, doing good service at the Little Blue and Westport, but at Newtonia he overreached himself. See Castel, *A Frontier State at War*, 160–65.

[30] *Official Records*, XLI, Pt. 1, pp. 638, 647, 670; J. H. P. Baker Diary, October 28, 1864; Edwards, *Shelby and His Men*, 461.

On November 1 the wretched column staggered into the little village of Cane Hill, Arkansas. Here Price ordered a halt, and many of his men now received the first corn and salt for themselves and their animals since leaving Independence. Contact again had been lost with Curtis, but word arrived that a Confederate force was besieging the Union garrison at Fayetteville, thirty miles to the southwest. Fagan thereupon requested and obtained permission to take five hundred of Shelby's men and Collins' battery and assist in its capture. This detachment moved off in a snowstorm and on November 2 joined in an attack on Fayetteville. The troops, however, had so little enthusiasm for the enterprise that they refused to advance within range of the garrison's rifles, despite the pleas and threats of their officers. Then, hearing that Blunt was approaching, Fagan abandoned the futile assault and returned to Cane Hill. Apparently Fagan's purpose in this otherwise senseless operation was to enable a portion of his division to make its way, by Fayetteville, to their homes in Arkansas.[31] In any case it was, appropriately enough, the last action fought by the Army of Missouri.

The stay at Cane Hill merely accelerated the disintegration of Price's forces. Entire regiments, even brigades, of the Arkansas conscripts disbanded. Riding in small parties, they headed for their homes and families. Faced with a situation he was powerless to remedy, Price instructed the Arkansas commanders "to return [with] such of their men as still remained with their colors" to the places where they had been recruited and to "collect the absentees together and bring them within our lines during the month of December, if possible." In addition, all of Jackman's brigade and one of Thompson's regiments were allowed to leave the army for the purpose of "visiting their friends in Northern Arkansas." As a result of these dispersions the army was reduced to Shelby's old brigade, Clark's brigade, Cabell's and another Arkansas brigade, and Tyler's recruits.[32]

On November 4 Price left Cane Hill. Fearful of being intercepted if he tried to cross the Arkansas between Little Rock and Fort Smith, he

[31] R. L. Brown's Army Journal, November 1, 5, 1864; *Official Records*, XLI, Pt. 1, pp. 638, 661; Edwards, *Shelby and His Men*, 461.

[32] *Official Records*, XLI, Pt. 1, pp. 639, 647, 661, 677. The regiment detached from Thompson was Slayback's, which had been recruited during the summer in northeast Arkansas and was only "attached" to the brigade.

headed for the Indian Territory, which also promised to be a better route from the standpoint of food and forage than the barren Boston Mountains.[33] Curtis did not reach Cane Hill until two days afterwards, his progress having been delayed by the temporary detachment of McNeil and Sanborn from his command by Rosecrans, who considered the campaign at an end, but he pushed onward, still hopeful of over-hauling Price. On November 7 he came upon a carriage, said to be Price's own, broken and abandoned along the road. He observed, too, that the "elm trees for miles had been stripped to furnish food for the starving [rebel] multitude." At 11 A.M. on November 8 his advance rode up to the banks of the Arkansas at Pheasant's Ford and found that the Confederates had crossed the day before. Feeling that it would be useless and dangerous to go on, he at last called off his long pursuit. Had he been properly supported by Pleasonton and Rosecrans, and if Blunt had not been such a glory-seeker, he would have completed the work begun at Westport and Mine Creek.[34] Wrote Edwards:

After crossing the Arkansas the worst stage of misery came upon the army, and the sufferings were intense. Horses died by thousands; the few wagons were abandoned almost without exception; the sick had no medicines and the healthy no food; the army had no organization and the subordinate officers no hope. Bitter freezing weather added terrors to the route and weakness to the emaciated, staggering column. Small-pox came at last, as the natural consequence, and hundreds fell out by the wayside to perish without help and be devoured by coyotes without a burial.[35]

Desperate men ate killed horses or even consumed the carcasses of mules and wolves; those who wished to preserve a valued mount stayed up nights guarding it. On the evening of November 8 Price's headquarters had to post sentinels to protect against a threatened charge by sol-

[33] *Ibid.*, 638–39.
[34] *Ibid.*, 510–17. After Mine Creek, Pleasonton decided it would be best not to pursue the Confederates, and also he quarreled with Curtis over the credit and spoils of the victory. Pleading ill health he withdrew from the campaign on October 26, taking Phillips' and Benteen's brigades with him. Then, after the Battle of Newtonia, Rosecrans recalled Sanborn and McNeil, leaving Curtis with only Blunt's small division. However Grant, who had instructed Curtis to keep after Price, countermanded Rosecrans' order. But in the meantime three days had been lost in the pursuit.
[35] Edwards, *Shelby and His Men*, 462–63.

diers who mistakenly believed that the staff officers were hoarding enormous quantities of food. In the morning twenty famished privates actually came to the staff's table, where they received equal shares of the meager breakfast that had been prepared. The horses had to feed on dead prairie grass, and as they gave out even generals, among them Thompson and Fagan, were forced to trudge along on foot.[36] Clark's brigade subsisted on wild game alone for twenty days,[37] and Colonel John W. Burbidge of that command later declared that during the march through the Indian Territory "severe starvation . . . completed the demoralization of my regiment."[38] One Missourian expressed in his journal the opinion that "No campaign in this country equals this for suffering,"[39] and another likened the army to the children of Israel wandering through the wilderness. "But alas!" he added, "We have no Moses to lead us."[40]

In his report Price admitted to heavy losses among the stock, but declared that the troops never approached starvation.[41] Several of his generals expressed the same opinion,[42] and Edwards pointed out that most of the units which suffered real privations had only themselves to blame, for the prairies abounded with game.[43] Furthermore most of the sickness occurred in the ranks of the new recruits, who were unaccustomed to hardship and lacked experience in camping and making proper sanitary arrangements. Nevertheless there can be no doubt that the march through the Indian Territory was the crowning horror of the expedition. And, as was to be expected, the soldiers blamed their miserable plight on their commander: "God Damn Price!" was frequently heard.[44]

On November 10 Price furloughed Cabell's and the other remaining

[36] Luttrell, "Diary of the Price Raid," St. Louis *Missouri Republican*, March 19, 1886; W. M. McPheeters Diary, November 8, 9, 1864.
[37] *Official Records*, XLI, Pt. 1, pp. 694–95.
[38] *Ibid.*, 697.
[39] R. L. Brown's Army Journal, November 10–17, 1864.
[40] William A. Hazen to Alex R. Hazen, December 21, 1864, in Missouri State Historical Society, Columbia, Missouri. For accounts of the retreat, see also J. H. P. Baker Diary, November 1–5, 1864, and "Diary of an Officer," Washington (Ark.) *Telegraph*, November 30, 1864.
[41] *Official Records*, XLI, Pt. 1, p. 639.
[42] *Ibid.*, 669, 677, 685.
[43] Edwards, *Shelby and His Men*, 462–64.
[44] Hazen to Hazen, December 21, 1864, in Missouri State Historical Society.

Arkansas brigade. The following day he granted Shelby's request to be allowed to camp on the Canadian River for awhile in order to rest his men and horses. Now with only the remnants of Clark's brigade and Tyler's recruits, Price moved on into Texas. At Clarksville on November 30 an order arrived from Magruder instructing Price to establish his headquarters at Laynesport, Arkansas. Two days later he did so.[45] Thus, slightly over three months after it began, the Missouri expedition officially ended.

In his official report Price claimed that it had been a success.

I marched 1,434 miles; fought forty-three battles and skirmishes; captured and paroled over 3,000 Federal officers and men; captured 18 pieces of artillery, 3,000 stand of small arms, 16 stand of colors . . . , at least 3,000 overcoats, large quantities of blankets, shoes, and ready-made clothing for soldiers, a great many wagons and teams, large numbers of horses, great quantities of subsistence and ordnance stores. I destroyed miles upon miles of railroad, burning the depots and bridges; and taking this into calculation, I do not think I go beyond the truth when I state that I destroyed in the late expedition to Missouri property to the amount of $10,000,000 in value. On the other hand, I lost 10 pieces of artillery, 2 stand of colors, 1,000 small arms, while I do not think I lost 1,000 prisoners, including the wounded left in their [the enemy's] hands and others than recruits on their way to join me, some of whom may have been captured by the enemy.

I brought with me at least 5,000 new recruits, and they are still arriving in large numbers daily within our lines, who bring the cheering intelligence that there are more on their way to the army. After I passed the German settlements in Missouri my march was an ovation. The people thronged around us and welcomed us with open hearts and hands. Recruits flocked to our flag in such numbers as to threaten to become a burden instead of a benefit, as they were mostly unarmed. In some counties the question was not who should go to the army, but who should stay at home. I am satisfied that could I have remained in Missouri this winter the army would have been increased 50,000 men.[46]

[45] *Official Records*, XLI, Pt. 1, pp. 639, 647–48.
[46] *Ibid.*, 640. Dr. W. M. McPheeters in a memorandum written in 1879 and to be found in the W. M. McPheeters Collection, Missouri Historical Society, St. Louis, endorsed Price's report as being a correct account of the expedition, saying that he personally had witnessed almost all the battles. However the report has many significant omissions, and I agree with Colonel Morrow, "Price's Expedition," 166, that the report is "so full of distortions and evasions as almost to defy analysis."

Kirby Smith also took a favorable view of the raid. In transmitting Price's report to the War Department he commented: "The movement of General Price accomplished all the objects for which it was inaugurated by me. A concentration of the enemy's forces in Missouri was compelled; at least 30,000 of his soldiers were employed there, and troops en route for Sherman's army were diverted from that destination and sent to operate in that State. A large number of recruits were obtained, and but for the losses incident to the retreat the results of the expedition would have been most brilliant."[47] Kirby Smith also held that the expedition, by drawing off Union troops intended for the East, helped prevent the fall of Mobile, weakened Thomas' army in its campaign against Hood, and enabled Forrest to raid Tennessee.[48]

However, neither Price's nor Kirby Smith's evaluations can be accepted as valid. In the first place both generals had an obvious interest in presenting the Missouri expedition in the best possible light: Price because he led it, Kirby Smith because he ordered it, and also because it was the only important military operation carried out by the Trans-Mississippi Department during the critical summer and fall of 1864. In addition, both men greatly exaggerated its achievements and either ignored or glossed over its failures.

Thus, Price's statistics about railroads and bridges destroyed, prisoners taken, and war material captured are essentially meaningless. The railroads and bridges were quickly repaired; the prisoners were mostly home guards who in any event were paroled; and the Confederates lost far more in material than they acquired. Indeed, according to Magruder, the Army of Missouri returned with fewer arms than it started with—undoubtedly an accurate assessment in view of the large number of rifles thrown away at Westport and Mine Creek.[49]

Equally misleading was Price's claim to "at least 5,000 new recruits." Although he did bring back that many, and although one or two thousand more came in later, they were unorganized, untrained, and unarmed—and, as Confederate officials frequently complained, the great lack in the Trans-Mississippi was not men but weapons. Fur-

[47] *Official Records*, XLI, Pt. 4, pp. 1068–69.
[48] *Ibid.*, XLVIII, Pt. 1, pp. 1419, 1428.
[49] *Ibid.*, XLI, Pt. 1, p. 721; *ibid.*, Pt. 4, p. 1098. On November 29 Price informed Magruder that he had only enough arms in his army for guard duty (*ibid.*, 1083).

thermore, their accession was more than offset by the heavy losses the Army of Missouri suffered from battle, desertion, and disease. No overall casualty returns are available, for none were ever made, but in all likelihood Price lost two-thirds of his original force—half from fighting and sickness, half from desertions and "furloughs." As late as December 15 he had only 3,500 troops "in hand," of whom no more than a third possessed arms. Moreover they were so ill, exhausted, and demoralized that in Magruder's opinion they were "not in a fit condition to fight any body of men."[50]

True, the expedition did deprive the Federals of the services of Smith's and Mower's divisions east of the Mississippi during the summer and fall of 1864. But these units comprised only nine thousand soldiers; their absence did not prevent Sherman from taking Atlanta or do more than postpone the fall of Mobile, and Smith arrived at Nashville in time to help Thomas crush Hood's army. The rest of the Union forces opposing Price would have served in Missouri and Kansas in any case.

Finally, neither Kirby Smith nor Price mentioned that the expedition failed to seize St. Louis or occupy Jefferson City and install a Confederate government, failed to bring about a mass uprising of Southern sympathizers, failed to influence the state elections except probably to increase the Republican vote, and failed to do any damage to the Union military installations in Kansas. In fact Price failed to achieve a single one of his objectives other than obtain recruits, and he did this only in the imperfect fashion described.

From a strategic standpoint the most that can be properly claimed for Price's thrust into Missouri is that it employed troops who otherwise would have stood idle; that after Kirby Smith had been obliged to scrap his original plan for a full-scale northern offensive, it was the only practical military option open to the Trans-Mississippi Department; and that it alarmed and embarrassed the Federals in Arkansas, Missouri, and Kansas. In this last connection it is interesting to note

---

[50] *Ibid.*, 112–13, 1076. On November 24 Price wrote Magruder that his troops were exhausted, less than one-half mounted, over two-thirds unarmed [*ibid.*, 1076–77]. An officer in Cabell's brigade, whose diary has been frequently cited [Washington (Ark.) *Telegraph*, November 30, 1864], assessed the campaign as follows: "We certainly captured many strong places, and many prisoners, all whom were parolled, but in doing so, we lost many men and valuable officers, arms, artillery, ordnance, wagons, mules, horses, &c."

that immediately after the raid Grant dismissed both Steele and Rosecrans—the first for allowing Price to cross and then recross the Arkansas River, the second for permitting him to remain so long in Missouri and to escape with his army still intact. Probably Grant was justified in his action against Steele, but in the case of Rosecrans he was motivated largely by personal prejudice.[51]

Who, if anyone, was to blame for the disastrous outcome of the Missouri expedition? Mainly Price himself, asserted Edwards. Price had "the roar of a lion but the spring of a guinea-pig." He was too old and lacked the experience and physical vigor to lead cavalry successfully. "Hard as he tried he could not handle cavalry. They would get away from him in spite of his efforts, or tangle themselves up, or stampede, or fall back without fighting, or become demoralized by plunder." Furthermore, he "had no fixed plan . . . or rather no fixed purpose" while in Missouri, and his "speed was on the wrong end of the line, and commenced when there were no fresh horses to be gained and no enemy at its terminus." His greatest single mistake, aside from attacking Pilot Knob, was fighting at Westport. "The avoidance of this battle and a march of fifty miles from Independence without halting would have placed it in his power to fall back leisurely through an extremely fertile country west of Fort Scott, [and] cross the Arkansas river [sic] west of Fort Gibson, thereby sacrificing but few horses and fewer men. Westport was the turning point in the expedition. While up to this time nothing of consequence had been accomplished, after it were the horrors of defeat, hunger, and the pestilence."[52]

Allowing for obvious prejudice and exaggerations, Edwards' strictures were on the whole justified. In particular, his comment about Price's lack of fixed purpose deserves attention. There can be little doubt that the underlying reason for the failure of the campaign was its contradictory aims. Kirby Smith's instructions to Price called essentially for a diversionary cavalry raid, with gathering up recruits and destroying Union military facilities as important subsidiary objectives. But it is evident that Price himself was primarily interested in reestablishing Confederate rule in Missouri, if only temporarily.[53] This

---

[51] Lamers, *Edge of Glory*, 433–44, 437–39. Rosecrans left himself open to removal by failing to cooperate with Curtis—a failure inspired by personal prejudice on his part. See *Official Records*, XLI, Pt. 1, pp. 547–49.

[52] Edwards, *Shelby and His Men*, 465, 482–84.

[53] Wrote one of Shelby's officers to a woman in Missouri on September 12,

political motive was at cross-purposes with the military goals. Furthermore it doomed the campaign at the outset. At least in part it caused
Price to take into Missouri the large numbers of unarmed, recalcitrant,
and worse-than-useless Arkansas conscripts. And it probably explained
his insistence on dragging along the huge and cumbersome wagon train,
the occasion of so many delays and disasters. Thus his army, by its
very composition, was incapable of marching, maneuvering, and fighting well enough to achieve its military objectives and, ironically, lacked
sufficient strength to realize its leader's political hopes. Finally, this
motive helped produce the hesitancy and indecisiveness in Price which
proved so fatal at Pilot Knob and Westport. As the Southern historian,
Pollard, wrote in respect to Price, "the breadth of the [Missouri] campaign, its indefiniteness, and the failure to concentrate on important
points, ruined him."[54]

It would have been best for Price and the Confederate cause in the
West if he had conceived of the expedition strictly as a large-scale raid
and had entered Missouri only with the veteran brigades of Shelby,
Clark, and Cabell, without a large wagon or artillery train. But Price
would not have been Price had he done other than he did. He was first
of all a politician and a Missourian, then a general and a Confederate.
Thus it was only natural, perhaps inevitable, that he placed political
considerations over military, and that he was more interested in redeeming his state than in furthering Confederate grand strategy. And
as from the beginning of the war, wishful thinking led him to overestimate pro-Confederate sentiment in Missouri and to believe, no
doubt quite sincerely, that merely by marching into the state he could
ignite a mass uprising against Union rule.

However, it is very unlikely that even if he had devoted himself
exclusively to the military side and employed a smaller but more effective force the outcome of the expedition would have been materially

---

1864: "He [Price] means to go through and stick this time." [Quoted in *Missouri
Historical Review*, XXII (1928), 106]. Soldiers in Price's army generally declared that he intended to stay in Missouri and Confederate newspapers stated
the same.

[54] Pollard, *The Lost Cause*, 554. Morrow, "Price's Expedition," 58, arrived at
basically the same conclusion, stating that Price thought primarily in political
terms, "and by aiming beyond his means, failed to take out of Missouri with
him the tangible results that were at one time in his possession."

different. At most, some of the worse disasters and suffering would
have been avoided, and the minimal effect it had on the Federals,
achieved at less cost. The plain fact of the matter was that the Confederate Trans-Mississippi was too isolated and too weak to inflict significant damage on the Northern enemy or to influence in any important way the course of the war. Price's autumn raid into Missouri was
the last military effort of the South in the West. After its failure, the
Trans-Mississippi waited supinely and impotently for the war to be
decided in Virginia. Wilson's Creek was the first great battle of the war
west of the Mississippi, and Mine Creek the last. Between these events
is the story of a lost cause. After Mine Creek came limbo.

15
SHREVEPORT

Governor Reynolds returned from the Missouri campaign feeling quite proud of himself. Throughout it he had ridden with Shelby in the van, and when Price had suggested a safer position he had answered that "in an army endeavoring to restore him to the executive chair the proper place of the Governor of Missouri is in the front."[1] At Potosi he had patrolled the streets at night with sword and pistol in hand to protect the women against pillaging soldiery, and at Boonville had "in strong language censored" Anderson's bushwhackers for taking and carrying scalps. During the crossing of the Big Blue he had borne himself with "conspicuous bravery" and at Mine Creek he had helped rally the fugitives of Marmaduke's and Fagan's commands. He had, in his own words, "been among the bullets on the battlefield, shared mule meat with the starving, and walked in the retreat"; as a result he had become "almost an idol to the troops."[2]

He also returned with a fierce determination to destroy Price. He deemed the expedition "a weak and disgraceful plundering raid" which had seriously damaged the Confederate cause in Missouri. He blamed Price for the army's lack of discipline and held him responsible for the disasters at Westport and Mine Creek and for the misery of the long retreat through Arkansas and the Indian Territory. But above all he was angry at the failure of Price to seize Jefferson City and install him in the governor's chair, a failure which he found inexcusable. In the past he had tried to overlook Price's deficiencies, believing that his name would prove a valuable asset in liberating Missouri. But no more —he would not rest until Price had been driven in disgrace from the army and from public life itself.[3]

Reynolds had signaled his final and complete break with Price dur-

[1] Reynolds to Price, October 2, 1864, *Official Records*, XLI, Pt. 3, pp. 976–77.
[2] Thomas C. Reynolds to E. J. Merrick, January 19, 1865, to E. H. Cushing, January 23, 1865, and to Colonel Harrison, March 25, 1865, in Thomas C. Reynolds Papers, Library of Congress; Edwards, *Shelby and His Men*, 424, 453.
[3] Thomas C. Reynolds to G. G. Vest, January 24, 1865, and to Johnson, March 2, 1865, in Reynolds Papers, Library of Congress.

ing the raid. On October 10, at Boonville, he wrote him complaining that "in an expedition designed to re-establish the rightful government of Missouri, the Governor of the State cannot even purchase a horse or blanket, while stragglers and camp followers are enriching themselves by plundering the defenceless families of our poor soldiers in Confederate service."[4] Later, when the army reached Texas, he left for Marshall, at the same time writing Kirby Smith that the expedition had been "*disgracefully* managed" and requesting him not to take any action regarding Price until he conferred with him.[5] After he reached Marshall he became further incensed against Price on reading newspaper accounts that pictured the raid as a success and hearing that Price's "strikers" were circulating "base slanders" about Marmaduke and Cabell. Earlier he had planned either to issue a formal address to the people of Missouri denouncing Price or else send an account of the campaign to Davis. Now, however, he decided to attack the general in the guise of vindicating Marmaduke and Cabell. Another reason for adopting this course, he subsequently claimed, was that prior to the expedition Marmaduke had expressed fear that Price's circle would try to make him the scapegoat for any disaster that might occur, and he had promised the young cavalry general to defend him if this should happen.[6]

During early December the governor's facile pen covered page after page. The result appeared in the December 23 Marshall *Texas Republican* as a long letter entitled "Generals Price, Marmaduke, and Cabell in the Missouri Campaign," and was addressed to the public.[7] In it Reynolds, after denying that Cabell was responsible for the rout of his brigade at Independence and that Marmaduke was drunk at Mine Creek, condemned Price for causing unnecessary loss of life at Fort Davidson; charged him with gross mismanagement in marching and deploying his army; accused him of lacking accurate geographical

[4] *Official Records*, XLI, Pt. 3, pp. 1000–1001.

[5] Reynolds to Kirby Smith, November 19, 1864, in Thomas C. Reynolds Papers, Library of Congress.

[6] Thomas C. Reynolds to Henry Ewing, January 16, 1865, to Vest, January 24, 1865, and to M. M. Parsons, January 28, 1865, in Thomas C. Reynolds Papers, Library of Congress. See also Reynolds, "Price and the Confederacy," 116–17, concerning Marmaduke's telling Reynolds prior to the Missouri expedition that he feared a plot against him by Price's circle.

[7] The only known copy of this letter appears in Edwards, *Shelby and His Men*, 467–74.

knowledge and of making no effort to remedy his ignorance; declared that he had neither the ability nor the desire to maintain discipline and prevent plundering; denounced him for being confused in his strategy and indecisive on the battlefield; and portrayed him as lazy, drunken, and callously indifferent to the sufferings of his troops. Respecting this last Reynolds wrote (and this selection serves as a good sample of the whole):

His [Price's] regular course was to sit in his ambulance at the head of his train on the march, rarely mounting his horse; to sip his copious toddy immediately after going into camp, and in view of the soldiers passing by, and soon after generally to take a nap—a mode of life entirely virtuous, but not precisely in accordance with established conceptions of the kind of hero needed to free an oppressed people. His somnolency was marked; although his practice was to make no halts for rest in the day's march, yet one day on the road from Camden to Dardanelle, he stopped the whole command for about half an hour and took a nap on a carpet spread out under a tree. On the whole campaign, as far as I observed or could learn, he never reviewed or personally inspected even in a cursory manner, any portion of his army, its camps, or even its sick and wounded, or its hospitals. On the field of battle his movements and countenance unmistakably indicated, not the activity or fire of genius, or even the calm of routine generalship, but only puzzled bewildered anxiety. His outfit was on a scale that even Federal generals dare not adopt. Three vehicles with fourteen mules carried him and the personal effects and camp equipage of his mess. Of course his staff imitated, though to a far less extent, this ill-timed luxury; and that bold and hardy cavalry, accustomed to leaders who sleep in storms under trees, and cook their simple, scanty rations on sticks and boards, gazed with unconcealed wonderment on a pomp and circumstance which to their shrewd minds foreboded anything but glorious war.

Reynolds closed the letter by declaring that he was "perfectly willing to take General Price, if he desires it, before his own troops, and, freely discussing his campaign, call out from among his own officers and soldiers, witnesses of what has here been stated, and much more besides."[8]

[8] This challenge to a public trial before Price's own troops, Reynolds explained privately, was necessary to make his attack effective and to gain the respect of the soldiers. In other words, he knew it was mere demagoguery. See Thomas C. Reynolds to E. H. Cushing, January 23, 1865, in Thomas C. Reynolds Papers, Library of Congress.

No one reading and believing Reynolds' tirade could form any other conclusion than that Price was an imbecilic and pusilanimous incompetent who had blithely led his army to destruction, thereby ruining a golden opportunity to redeem Missouri and alter the course of the war. It was without doubt one of the most vicious assaults ever made in print on a military commander.

Nor did Reynolds content himself with public villification; he also resorted to private blackmail. On December 24 he sent Price a copy of the previous day's *Texas Republican* and with it the following letter:

General: The inclosed publication I have deemed necessary to vindicate Generals Marmaduke and Cabell against injurious charges and to place the late Missouri campaign in a proper light before the public. In performing my imperative official duty in reference to that expedition I desire to avoid giving unnecessary pain to any one. I herefore frankly state to you that, believing myself fully acquainted with all the facts in relation to the return of your son, General Edwin Price, by your advice, within the Federal lines in 1862, his subsequent course, and the communications between you and him, I design to make a memoir of those facts to the President of the Confederate States, and on it and the management of the late expedition to ask from him an order that you cease to be an officer in the provisional army of those States. Such a request (and still more such an order) would perhaps necessitate the giving of more or less publicity to that memoir. With a disposition to enable you to avoid the disagreeable discussions it would occasion, I propose that if you will at once resign your commission in that army and your position of Missouri bank commissioner (assigning, if you think proper, whatever reasons for those steps you may judge best, and such as will not necessitate controversy), and abstain hereafter from any interposition, directly or indirectly, in the military or political affairs of the Confederate States or the State of Missouri, that memoir will be sent as a paper to remain in the secret archives of the Government and not used unless necessary to meet such an interposition, or an attack by yourself, or any of your friends, on the Confederate authorities or myself for the action of any of us in this matter. I presume it will be in accordance with your own feelings, as it is with mine, that any future intercourse between us shall be only in writing, confined to indispensable official business and an answer to this letter.[9]

Price did not answer this letter, nor did he bow to Reynolds' threat and resign from the Confederate army and as Missouri bank commis-

[9] *Official Records*, XLI, Pt. 4, p. 1123.

sioner. Either he felt he could cope with any attack via Edwin, or else
he believed that Reynolds was bluffing. But whatever his reasons he
acted wisely. Although Reynolds wrote to various persons at this time
seeking further information on the Edwin Price affair, he did not mention Edwin in his letter to Davis about the Missouri expedition, and he
never tried to use Edwin against Price in their subsequent controversy.[10] Not until after the war did he write down his suspicions concerning Price and his son, and then he did it in a manuscript (the one
so frequently cited in these pages) that was never published and which
did not become known until long after both he and Price were dead.
Most likely he failed to carry out his threat to "expose" the Prices because he was not fully sure of his case, feared that the attempt might
backfire against him by creating sympathy for Price, and did not want
to embarrass the Davis administration with another Price embroglio.

Price also at first ignored Reynolds' letter in the *Texas Republican*.
His only reply to it was an implied one in his official report on the Missouri campaign. Far from condemning Marmaduke and Cabell he
praised them for their courage, efficiency, and devotion to duty. Indeed, he practically went out of his way to extol Marmaduke and excuse the failures of his division at Pilot Knob, Byram's Ford, and Mine
Creek. Obviously he hoped to undercut Reynolds' charge that he was
trying to make Marmaduke and Cabell scapegoats.

However the governor's attack created such a sensation in the army
and among the public that Price was obliged to resort to more direct
rebuttal. Early in January he obtained leave of absence and journeyed
to Shreveport. There, on the sixth, he addressed the following letter
to Kirby Smith:

Herewith I inclose to you a copy of the Texas Republican containing a
lengthy communication from one Thomas C. Reynolds filled with the most
gross and violent charges against myself as the commanding officer of the
late expedition to Missouri. Were this but the malignant effusion of a
simple individual it would be but of passing moment, but as Mr. Reynolds
pretends to be the governor of the State of Missouri, and so describes himself in the communication, it assumes a grave and public character, and

[10] See Thomas C. Reynolds to Robertson Moore, January 24, 1865, and to
Caleb B. Stone, January 28, 1865, and to Davis, January 18, 1865, in Thomas
C. Reynolds Papers, Library of Congress.

the interests of the State demand that the matter should be investigated. If the charges made in the communication are true, I am unfit to be intrusted with any command in the Army, and action should be had accordingly. If they are untrue, the interests of the service as well as justice to myself require that my character as an officer should be vindicated. I therefore respectfully solicit that you request Governor Reynolds, as he styles himself, to prefer charges against me, and that you order a court-martial to be convened to try the same at as early a date as the exigencies of the service will possibly admit.[11]

Price next published "A Card" in the Shreveport *News* of January 10. It read:[12]

In the Texas Republican of the 23d of December, there appears a communication over the signature of one Thos. C. Reynolds, who pretends to be, and styles himself in it, the Governor of the State of Missouri.

The communication purports to defend two gallant and distinguished officers against charges alleged to have been made against them, but which I had never heard made by either officer or soldier. In reality it was intended to be a violent and malignant attack upon myself, as the officer in command of the late expedition to Missouri.

So far as the communication pays tribute to the gallantry displayed by the officers and soldiers engaged in that expedition, I heartily concur in it. So far as it relates to myself, however, I pronounce it to be a tissue of falsehoods.

Reynolds, who had been struck in a most sensitive spot by the doubt cast on his legitimacy as Governor of Missouri, responded with a public letter as follows:

In the card published by General S. Price in the Shreveport News of the 10th inst., after his departure from that city for Central Texas, he silently declines my offer in letter of 17th of December last to "take him before his own troops and call out from among his own officers and soldiers witnesses of what has there been stated, and much more besides." After such a shrinking, his coarse general denial will have less weight with thinking men, than a specific answer to even any single allegation in that detailed statement of his campaign, and is in fact merely a specimen of the

[11] *Official Records*, XLVIII, Pt. 1, p. 1318.
[12] Edwards, *Shelby and His Men*, 474.

bluster by which he has been accustomed to keep down discussion of his public acts.

That farce is about played out.

As to the existence of the slanders on Generals Marmaduke and Cabbell [sic], I refer to their staff officers.

He concurs in my tribute to the gallantry of his officers and soldiers. It was made at his expense; I am glad he bears it cheerfully.

General Price describes me as one who "pretends to be Governor of the State of Missouri." The Federals take the same view of my position; but he has the distinction of being the first man in our lines to publish his concurrence with them in it.

As the Missouri executive recognized by the Confederate Government I have deemed it both my right and my duty officially to publish, in reference to the late campaign in that State, a statement of facts which are admitted to have shocked the public conscience. I reaffirm it. To the Confederate authorities it belongs to determine whether a truculent denial by the accused is, in their system, an acquittal, or whether they will take any action on it.[13]

Kirby Smith agreed that Price deserved a chance to clear his name, but stated that instead of a court-martial he would order a court of inquiry, since Reynolds, not being a Confederate officer, could not present formal charges. Price objected to this arrangement, for a court-martial, although a more serious affair, gave the accused a completely purified reputation if acquitted, whereas a court of inquiry was generally regarded in the army as a mere "whitewashing tribunal." However, he accepted the court of inquiry on the condition that he be allowed to choose its members so as to assure himself a thorough hearing by qualified officers. Kirby Smith granted his wish and his subsequent selections proved acceptable even to his enemies.[14]

Reynolds was delighted that Price, "like any ordinary mortal, [was] to go before a military court." His denunciation of Price, he believed,

---

[13] *Ibid.*, 474–75. Reynolds was now suffering from such "dire pecuniary necessity," to use his own words, that he had to reduce his official staff drastically and to sleep in the office of a friend when he visited Shreveport. See Thomas C. Reynolds to J. F. Howes, February 28, 1865, and to Roland Jones, February 25, 1865, in Thomas C. Reynolds Papers, Library of Congress.

[14] Edwards, *Shelby and His Men*, 518; *Official Records*, XLVIII, Pt. 1, p. 1415.

had already done much good by producing a reaction in favor of greater discipline and order in the army, "without which our cause may be lost."[15] Until recently, he wrote a friend, "every petty subaltern thought himself safe in plundering citizens under the very noses of our courts; now the haughtiest of our military chieftains begs to have an investigation of his acts on the distant banks of the Missouri." Price, he was confident, was "played out" in Missouri, and "will not again be *assigned to command troops.*"[16]

The meeting of the court was postponed until Price returned from his furlough, which he spent at Washington, Texas, with his wife. During his absence one of his friends, the Reverend M. Kavannaugh, published a letter in which he described the Missouri expedition as a success and referred to Reynolds as a "deadhead" who stuck with the train "and therefore knew nothing of the campaign." This attack occasioned much indignation in the army, and Shelby answered with a testimonial to Reynolds' courage and "untiring energy for good."[17] According to Reynolds only the Houston *Daily Telegraph* attempted to defend Price,[18] but it would be more accurate to say that most newspapers adopted the neutral attitude of the Washington (Arkansas) *Telegraph*, whose editor stated in regard to the general and the governor: "We are personally acquainted with both these high dignitaries, and cannot doubt the honesty of motives, or purity of intention of either."[19] Moreover, as news of the fall of Savannah, the destruction of Hood's army at Nashville, and other military disasters in the East

[15] Reynolds to Parsons, January 28, 1865, in Thomas C. Reynolds Papers, Library of Congress.

[16] Reynolds to Merrick, January 19, 1865, in Thomas C. Reynolds Papers, Library of Congress. Reynolds was somewhat wrong in his confident prediction that Price would never be given another command. On March 7 Department headquarters assigned Price to the command of the "Missouri Division of Infantry" (Parsons' and Mitchell's brigades) of the District of Arkansas. However, he was not to assume actual command (or be assigned to duty) until after the court of inquiry completed its work. See *Official Records*, XLVIII, Pt. 1, pp. 1413, 1416.

[17] Edwards, *Shelby and His Men*, 475. Edwards is the only source that could be found for Kavannaugh's letter.

[18] Reynolds to Merrick, January 19, 1865, in Thomas C. Reynolds Papers, Library of Congress. This defense apparently led Reynolds to write the editor of the Houston *Telegraph* justifying his attack on Price. See Reynolds to Cushing, January 23, 1865, in Thomas C. Reynolds Papers, Library of Congress.

[19] Washington (Ark.) *Telegraph*, February 1, 1865.

reached the Trans-Mississippi, the public and troops lost interest in the Reynolds-Price controversy, which now seemed to be of no practical consequence.[20]

On April 21 the court of inquiry convened in Shreveport. It was composed of two brigadier generals and a colonel. Major Oscar M. Watkins, a friend of both Reynolds and Price, served as judge-advocate (the military equivalent of a prosecutor). Price, at his request, was assisted by Colonel Richard H. Musser, described by Edwards as "a scholar of extensive erudition, a man eminent for attack and defense; a cool, wary, skillful diplomatist—versatile in the cabinet and in the field."[21] The first and principal witness was Captain T. J. Mackey, who had been recommended by Reynolds, but whose testimony proved favorable to Price, as did that of the other witnesses. On April 26 the court invited Reynolds, who had sneered at military tribunals in his *Texas Republican* article, to testify, but he refused, and because he was a civilian there was no way to require him to do so. Shelby was scheduled to appear before the court, and the army awaited his testimony with much anticipation. However on May 3 Kirby Smith (for reasons which will be explained later) ordered the court to adjourn to Washington, Arkansas, and because of the termination of the war it never met again.[22]

Price protested the early suspension of the inquiry, but at the same time claimed that he had been vindicated.[23] He was, to a degree, justified in this view. Testimony before the court, especially that of Mackey, rebutted Reynolds' accusations pertaining to the attack on Fort Davidson, ignorance of geography, incompetency in troop deployments, lack of energy and decision, and willful slackness in maintaining discipline. On the positive side, it also brought out many of the problems and handicaps that Price had to cope with during the campaign—problems and handicaps which if they did not always excuse his failures at least helped explain them. And above all the evidence

---

[20] Edwards, *Shelby and His Men*, 475.

[21] *Official Records*, XLVIII, Pt. 1, p. 1415; Edwards, *Shelby and His Men*, 518.

[22] The proceedings of the court of inquiry appear in *Official Records*, XLI, Pt. 1, pp. 701–29. The statement regarding Shelby is from Edwards, *Shelby and His Men*, 519. Reynolds recommended that Mackey be the first witness, which he was. See Thomas C. Reynolds to O. M. Watkins, April 10, 1865, in Thomas C. Reynolds Papers, Library of Congress.

[23] *Official Records*, XLI, Pt. 1, pp. 727–28.

gave full support to the judgment rendered on the expedition by Shelby in his official report: "General Price had elements in his command so weak, so helpless, so incongruous that no human hand could control them."[24]

The court, however, did not consider the overall conduct of the campaign; it failed to produce much evidence on individual battles other than Pilot Knob; and it made no attempt to investigate Reynolds' allegations against Price's personal character. As Colonel Norman Morrow has remarked in his excellent study of Price's Missouri raid, it was "quite chary of probing sensitive issues" of this sort.[25] Nevertheless the fact remains that in the areas which were covered none of Reynolds' charges was substantiated and many were positively contradicted. Moreover, except for Price's military mistakes and the army's lack of discipline, there is little in all the other sources pertaining to the Missouri campaign that bears out Reynolds' diatribe. And finally it is significant that Reynolds refused to testify before the court, where Price and his legal aide, Colonel Musser, would have had a chance to cross-examine him.

At this point the question naturally arises, did Reynolds in his attack on Price either consciously or unconsciously engage in exaggeration and falsification? In answering it certain observations are in order. Although there is no reason to doubt Reynolds' basic integrity, he was a man who tended to transform political differences into personal animosities and then carried these animosities to extreme lengths. In 1856 he dueled and wounded B. Gratz Brown; a little later he challenged the editor of the St. Louis *Republican*; and nearly ten years after the war, when he was fifty-some years old, he sought "satisfaction" from another partisan opponent. Furthermore, he deliberately and cold-bloodedly resorted to such tactics. In 1864, following his refusal to reappoint Clark to the Confederate Senate, he wrote George G. Vest to warn Clark that if Clark "made any publications" against

[24] *Ibid.*, 662. Edwards, certainly no friend to Price, stated that "General Price was in no manner responsible for the lawlessness of the soldiers. . . . No man more condemned the wholesale plundering than General Price, and his failure to apply the remedy arose from the fact that he knew no remedy to apply" (Edwards, *Shelby and His Men*, 481). Mackey's testimony was quite favorable to Price, and since Reynolds himself recommended Mackey as the person best qualified to provide evidence on Price, this fact is most significant.

[25] Morrow, "Price's Expedition," 170.

him, "he must expect a skinning, both as to his public life and private habits as he had never had in all his career. . . . Clark ought to know that my system in such warfare was to pile on abuse, and give satisfaction at ten paces if asked."[26] Probably he applied this "system" to Price, bolstering it for the occasion with blackmail; perhaps, although this is unlikely, he hoped to provoke Price to a duel.

Also, Reynolds was not above underhanded tactics if he believed circumstances warranted. Thus, when in November 1863 an Arkansas preacher named Gantt publicly declared that the war was lost for the South, Reynolds proposed to Colonel J. R. Eakins, editor of the Washington (Arkansas) *Telegraph*, that a false letter, allegedly written by an "abolitionist" to Gantt and then intercepted, be printed in order to discredit the defeatist preacher. Eakins, however, refused to have anything to do with this scheme and Reynolds therefore dropped it.[27]

In addition, on January 16, 1865, Reynolds wrote Fagan, Shelby, and Major Henry Ewing, Marmaduke's adjutant, requesting comments on his *Texas Republican* letter. Both Fagan and Ewing declined to provide them, whereupon he excused Shelby from doing so.[28] Ewing's refusal is significant in view of the fact that earlier Ewing had written Reynolds thanking him for defending Marmaduke against stories that he had been drunk at Mine Creek.[29] As for Shelby, he was under obligations to Reynolds, who at his request wrote Davis urging his promotion and denying that Shelby's troops had been guilty of committing depredations during their 1863 raid into Missouri.[30] However—and this too is significant—Edwards, in describing the reaction in the army to Reynolds' letter, carefully limits himself to saying that "Shelby's divi-

[26] Reynolds, "Memoranda relative to . . . Confederate Senators," in Reynolds Papers, Library of Congress.

[27] Thomas C. Reynolds to J. R. Eakins, November 9, 1863, in Thomas C. Reynolds Papers, Library of Congress. Benjamin Franklin, it might be pointed out, used essentially this same device with good effect against the British during the American Revolution.

[28] Reynolds to Ewing, to Fagan, to Shelby, all on January 16, 1865, and to Shelby, February 18, 1865, in Thomas C. Reynolds Papers, Library of Congress.

[29] Ewing to Reynolds, December 8, 1864, in Thomas C. Reynolds Papers, Missouri Historical Society, St. Louis.

[30] Reynolds to Davis, March 21, 1865, in Thomas C. Reynolds Papers, Library of Congress. See also Shelby to Reynolds, March 10, 1865, in Civil War Papers, Missouri Historical Society, St. Louis, requesting a testimonial from Reynolds regarding Franklin's charges.

sion" (i.e., Shelby) believed the statements contained in it were true in so far they referred "to the military movements," implying thereby that the personal allegations were not so regarded.[31]

And last but far from least, we have Reynolds' own postwar confession about his attack on Price. Writing in 1887 in response to an inquiry by Snead, he admitted that he was led into a controversy with Price about the Missouri expedition of 1864 by "my extreme irritation at the campaign's results." He then added that the statements in the *Texas Republican* letter "were, of course, largely on the authority of others than myself. It is against all the canons of history that, made in a heated controversy, they should be used, or even referred to, in stating *facts* of that campaign itself."[32]

No more need be said.

While the court met, the Confederacy fell. Lee, then Johnston, surrendered, and Union forces dominated all of the South except the Trans-Mississippi. There the die-hards and the romanticists called for continued war, but their words were hollow. Public confidence in victory had long since evaporated. Confederate currency was worthless and men everywhere engaged in a frenzied scramble for specie and United States greenbacks. Except for a few units such as Shelby's, the morale of the army was at a new low: as early as February four hundred men deserted in one day from a division in Arkansas. The highways and forests, the swamps and the hills crawled with deserters and guerrillas. Only the unquenchable speculation in cotton thrived, and it was based on the idea that defeat, by ending the blockade, would open the way for enormous profits in foreign markets. So great was the cotton mania that many farmers neglected to plant sorely needed wheat, corn, and oats. Edwards afterwards reflected that as a consequence "starva-

---

[31] Edwards, *Shelby and His Men*, 475. Shelby could not have joined in the attack on Price regarding plundering without leaving himself open to the same accusation, for his men were far from innocent of such activities themselves during the expedition.

[32] Reynolds to Snead, February 16, 1887, in Thomas L. Snead Papers. In another letter written June 2, 1886 to Snead (in *ibid.*), Reynolds stated the same, explaining that he attacked Price because of his "poignant regrets for the meager results" of the Missouri expedition, and because of his "great irritation about it." Both of these letters are in Reynolds' handwriting and there can be no doubt as to their authenticity.

tion might have been a probability for the army to consider, had the war lasted another year."[33]

Price was among those who favored fighting on; if he had been reluctant to begin the war, he proved just as reluctant to end it. He shared this attitude with his fellow Missourians, including Reynolds. The prospect of returning defeated and in rags to a Missouri dominated by their enemies, to be persecuted and perhaps imprisoned as traitors, was more than they could face. Rather than do that they preferred to struggle to the last, then seek refuge in Mexico.

News of Lee's surrender and the flight of the Confederate government from Richmond reached Shreveport at the end of the third week of April. On April 29 a mass meeting took place in the town square. Price, Kirby Smith, Governor Henry Watkins Allen of Louisiana, and General Simon B. Buckner (now Kirby Smith's chief of staff) were present but did not speak. Orators representing the Trans-Mississippi states urged continued resistance; Colonel L. M. Lewis, spokesman for Missouri, declared that he would never surrender.

At the close of the meeting Governor Allen invited Price, Colonel Musser, Major Watkins, General A. T. Hawthorne, and Colonel George Flournoy to his office. Flournoy, a member of Kirby Smith's staff, announced to the astonishment of all that a truce boat had arrived bearing dispatches from the Federals; that Colonel John T. Sprague, chief of staff to Union General John Pope, was waiting at the mouth of the Red River with a demand for the surrender of Confederate forces in the Trans-Mississippi; and that Kirby Smith intended meeting Sprague for that purpose. Flournoy further stated that Kirby Smith had placed several million dollars worth of cotton aboard the boat, and that he had arranged to take himself and family from the country, leaving the Confederacy to its fate. Flournoy added that he derived his information from documents he had seen bearing Kirby Smith's signature, and Allen vouched for his statements. The officers present then discussed Flournoy's charges and Kirby Smith's career in the department, but did not agree on a course of action.

Sometime later, however, Allen in company with Reynolds called on Kirby Smith and advised him that prudence required his presence in Shreveport and that he should send a staff officer to treat with Colo-

---

[33] Washington (Ark.) *Telegraph*, January 13, 1865; *Official Records*, XLVIII, Pt. 2, pp. 400–403; Edwards, *Shelby and His Men*, 509–14.

nel Sprague. Kirby Smith, who had no intention at this time of surrendering, quickly agreed. Needless to say, the story about the cotton
and his fleeing the country was merely the product of Flournoy's excited imagination.[34]

Meanwhile Price, who apparently did not know of Allen's and
Reynolds' visit to Kirby Smith, held a meeting at his house in Shreveport with five other officers, among them Colonel Musser and Colonel
Lewis. He proposed arresting Kirby Smith "should he prove trouble-
some" by attempting to confer with Sprague. Would the troops, he
asked, support such a move? To this question no one had an answer,
but later in the day Price visited a Missouri brigade stationed in Shreveport and commanded by Lewis. Shortly thereafter Lewis (who had
personal and political obligations to Reynolds) went to Kirby Smith
and told him that an officer of "the highest rank" had formed a conspiracy with the object of overturning the government and seizing the
authorities of the department. Kirby Smith replied that his secret service had already informed him of the plot and that he knew Price was
its leader. He added that his agents kept him fully posted on Price's
movements and intentions and that he had taken measures to forestall
any *coup*. One of these measures was the ordering on May 3 of the
court of inquiry to Washington, Arkansas, thus removing Price from
Shreveport.[35]

By then there probably was no danger of Price's attempting to arrest
Kirby Smith (if there ever was), because such action was premised on

[34] Edwards, *Shelby and His Men*, 519–22. Unfortunately, Edwards is practically the only source providing details on what took place in the Trans-
Mississippi during the spring of 1865. However his account for once appears to
be generally accurate and, allowing for his prejudices and exaggerations, can be
used with fair confidence.

[35] *Ibid.*, 522, 539; Kirby Smith to Governor [?], May [?], 1865, in Edmund
Kirby Smith Papers, Southern Historical Collection, University of North Carolina Library. This letter was almost surely addressed to Reynolds, who learned
of the meeting at Price's house and, seeing in it further evidence of Price's "rule
or ruin" disposition, warned Kirby Smith of the "plot" against him. In this letter
Kirby Smith related Lewis' earlier warning and his reply to Lewis. According to
Edwards, Kirby Smith also told Reynolds that while he could have been killed
he could not have been arrested. Lewis' obligations to Reynolds lay in the fact
that Reynolds had helped bring about his release from a Union prison camp and
had offered to appoint him to the Confederate Senate. See Reynolds, "Price and
the Confederacy," 113, and Thomas C. Reynolds to L. M. Lewis, February 22,
1865, in Thomas C. Reynolds Papers, Library of Congress.

Kirby Smith's making an immediate capitulation of the department, and this he had no intention of doing. The news of Johnston's surrender in North Carolina had not yet arrived, the Trans-Mississippi forces numbered over fifty thousand, and Kirby Smith believed that it was his "supreme duty" to hold out at least until Davis reached the department or until he received definite orders from the fugitive President.[36] On May 8 at Shreveport he met Sprague, who informed him of Johnston's surrender and presented Pope's terms for the Trans-Mississippi. He discussed the terms with Sprague, but before making a final reply obtained permission to consult the governors of Texas, Louisiana, Arkansas, and Missouri, whom he had summoned to a conference at Marshall. At Marshall the governors decided that further resistance was futile and advised him to arrange a surrender. Reynolds concurred in this view with great reluctance and afterward asked Kirby Smith to delay the surrender as long as possible in order to give the Missourians time to prepare for flight into Mexico. With this in mind, and in hopes of getting better terms, Kirby Smith on May 15 handed Sprague a letter rejecting Pope's surrender demand. He knew, though, that he was merely postponing the inevitable. Every day brought more reports of companies and even entire brigades disbanding, of troops pillaging government stores, and of a complete breakdown of the will to fight.[37]

There was one soldier, however, who had visions of more battles—Shelby. At a meeting of generals (Price was not among them) at Marshall while the governor's conference was taking place, he declared that the army had lost confidence in Kirby Smith and proposed replacing him with Buckner, then continuing the war until driven across the Rio Grande, after which the Confederates would "re-instate Juarez or espouse Maximillian." The generals, at least for the moment, were swayed by the fiery young cavalry leader, and Buckner agreed to take the command if Kirby Smith gave it up voluntarily. Shelby then went to Kirby Smith and bluntly told him of the decision his generals had made. Tears in his eyes, Kirby Smith promised to relinquish command of the army to Buckner on returning to Shreveport.

But what he did instead was to depart on May 18 for Houston, leaving Buckner in charge at Shreveport. As a result an ambiguous situ-

[36] Edwards, *Shelby and His Men*, 523; Kirby Smith to John Pope, May 9, 1865, in *Official Records*, XLVIII, Pt. 1, p. 189; Memorandum by Kirby Smith to Colonel J. T. Sprague, n. d., in *ibid.*, 192–93.
[37] Parks, *Kirby Smith*, 464–66, 470.

ation was created, with Buckner commanding the army (or what was left of it), and Kirby Smith still heading the Department![38]

Meanwhile, Price at Washington learned through a friend that the order requiring his presence there for the court of inquiry was merely designed to remove him from Kirby Smith's immediate vicinity. At once he started for Shreveport. On the way he received, but ignored, a new order from Kirby Smith directing him to remain at Washington. He reached Shreveport soon after Kirby Smith left for Houston. Going to departmental headquarters he demanded that Colonel S. S. Anderson, the adjutant general, turn over to him all the papers relating to the court of inquiry. When Anderson objected, he intimated that he would employ force if necessary. Anderson thereupon delivered the documents and the matter ended.[39] Price presumably resorted to this high-handed action out of a desire to have the court proceedings available to answer any future attacks by Reynolds and other enemies.

If Shelby expected Buckner to make a desperate last-ditch stand, he was doomed to disappointment. "The troops," later wrote Buckner, "were deserting by divisions and were plundering the people as well as the government property. The troops who adhered to me had no desire to prosecute the struggle, and were, in fact, powerless to do so. . . . The people were suffering [and] the army would soon be in a starving condition."[40] Accordingly, acting in Kirby Smith's name, but on his own initiative, Buckner went in person to New Orleans where on May 26 he signed a surrender treaty. With him he took Price, a maneuver probably designed to reconcile the Missouri contingents to the idea of ending the war.[41] Shelby, on getting word of Buckner's mission, saddled up his division and made a forced march towards Shreveport with the intention, so says Edwards, of seizing command and resuming military operations. But rain and muddy roads held him back, and when he reached Corsicana he learned that he was too late.[42]

---

[38] Edwards, *Shelby and His Men*, 524–25, 533–34, 540. Edwards gives more details on this affair in his later book, *Shelby's Expedition to Mexico*, to be found in Mary V. Edwards (comp.), *John N. Edwards: Biography, Memoirs, Reminiscences, and Recollections* (Kansas City, Mo., 1889), 235–37, hereinafter cited as *Shelby's Expedition*.

[39] Edwards, *Shelby and His Men*, 539–40.

[40] Simon Buckner to wife, August 1, 1865, in Arndt M. Stickles, *Simon Bolivar Buckner, Borderland Knight* (Chapel Hill, 1940), 273.

[41] *Official Records*, XLVIII, Pt. 2, 600–602; Parks, *Kirby Smith*, 476–77.

[42] Edwards, *Shelby's Expedition*, 238.

On June 2 Price announced the surrender terms to the Missouri troops at Shreveport. He then thanked them for their service and declared that he had been privileged to command the best soldiers that had ever taken the field. The war, he continued, had been especially difficult for him as he had not favored secession and had espoused the Confederate cause only because of the coercive measures taken against the South and because he opposed abolishing slavery. He concluded by advising the men to return to their homes and remain law-abiding citizens. But as for himself, he was obliged to leave the country, probably never to return. Then, with tears in his eyes and in a quivering voice, he ordered his chief of staff to dismiss the troops.[43] "Some of the men," wrote one of their officers that evening in his journal, "jump for joy, while others curse and swear and gnash their teeth in frantic rage, and yet again others are cast down, silent and dejected, sighing as if their hearts are broken."[44]

The Civil War in the West had ended.

[43] Ralph R. Rea, *Sterling Price, The Lee of the West* (Little Rock, 1959), 166–67. Rea does not cite his source for this speech by Price, but presumably he obtained his information from his grandfather, George Rea, who was a soldier with Price. It has the ring of authenticity.

[44] Luttrell, "Diary of the Price Raid," St. Louis *Missouri Republican*, March 19, 1886.

16

CARLOTA AND ST. LOUIS

On the night of June 2, 1865, Price, accompanied by his son, Captain Heber Price, and some members of his personal escort, set out for the Rio Grande. En route he stopped briefly at Washington, Texas, to arrange future plans with his family.[1] He then went on to San Antonio, which was the designated rendezvous for all Confederates intending to migrate into Mexico. Soon a large party was formed, including Kirby Smith, Reynolds, John B. Magruder, Governor Allen, and Shelby. The latter had with him several hundred veterans of the Iron Brigade who like their commander preferred exile to surrender.

Late in June the refugees began their long journey. On July 4 they crossed the Rio Grande at Eagle Pass, pausing while Shelby's troopers buried their battle flag in the river. In northern Mexico they had several bloody encounters with guerrillas and almost fought a battle with French forces. Finally they reached Monterrey and from there went on to Mexico City. Maximilian welcomed them, gave them badly needed money, and assigned them lands for colonies. However, he declined Shelby's offer of the services of the Iron Brigade out of fear of United States reaction.[2]

The largest of the Confederate colonies was Carlota, named in honor of Maximilian's beautiful wife and situated in the Cordova Valley about seventy miles west of Vera Cruz. Price helped select the site and was recognized as the leader of the settlement—evidence that Reynolds' attack had done little to impair his standing. He and about 250 other Southern colonists laid out a town, began constructing houses, and with the aid of Mexican laborers planted coffee, corn, and tobacco. Shelby did not join the colony, but set himself up in a nearby hacienda and established a freighting business. Reynolds remained in Mexico City, where he became a railroad commissioner and unofficial

---

[1] Rea, *Sterling Price*, 167. Rea's grandfather accompanied Price from Shreveport to Washington.

[2] Edwards, *Shelby and His Men*, 545–50; Carl C. Rister, "Carlota, a Confederate Colony in Mexico," *Journal of Southern History*, X (1945), 33–41.

advisor to the Emperor. Governor Allen established a newspaper, the *Mexican Times*, with John Edwards (who was hard at work on his biography of Shelby) as typesetter. Later, on Allen's death, the major became publisher and editor of the paper. As for Kirby Smith, he soon returned via Cuba to the United States, where in time he became a college professor.[3]

Toward the end of 1865 Price sent for his family. At about the same time a correspondent of the New York *Herald* visited Carlota. He found it to consist of "a few tents scattered here and there, and a . . . cluster of a dozen unfinished houses pleasantly situated along a brook lined with a row of trees and plants." Price, he reported, probably with exaggeration, passed most of his time seated in a "cool and inviting retreat" amongst a grove of mango trees, "entertaining his numerous guests, giving advice to the settlers, cracking jokes with old companions in arms, or giving orders respecting the cultivation of his plantation." His *casa*, which he shared with former Governor Isham Harris of Tennessee, was a straw-roofed, bamboo cottage that still needed plastering. He had made the furniture himself: "General Price is not a little of a Yank, and is about as ingenious and handy as any New Englander."

The correspondent had a five-hour interview with the "old soldier," during which Price extolled the future of Carlota in a style reminiscent of Mark Twain's Colonel Sellers:

I have been here four or five months, and all I have seen and heard goes to convince me that this is really the land of promise. I have here 640 acres which I would not exchange for any 1,200 acres in any part of the United States. What you have seen already must convince you that I do not exaggerate. Where will you find a richer soil, a healthier climate than this? Not in any part of the world. The Patriarchs alone could boast of such advantages. Here a man can live under his tent from the wool of his sheep and from the fruit of the earth without being compelled to lift up either the shovel or the hoe; but as we are in an age of civilization and as we have contracted habits of luxury and all sorts of fictitious wants, we must plough, hoe and turn the sod upside down, for we have not only the appetites of our nature to satisfy, but we have to work for others and to create wealth the effect of which benefits the whole world.

Price discounted any danger from the *Juaristas* and expressed confidence that the French would not abandon Mexico: ". . . the Na-

[3] Rister, "Confederate Colony in Mexico," 41–45; Parks, *Kirby Smith*, 482–83.

poleon family is not in the habit of backing down in the accomplishment of its schemes." In addition he showed the reporter a trunk containing 460 pounds of documents concerning the Confederate army in the Trans-Mississippi and stated that he should like to have a historian use them to write the story of his campaigns. "With them," he declared, "I can raise, I think, an eternal monument to the memory of the gallant soldiers who fought under my orders, and whose deeds, sufferings and endurance are still buried under the shadow of silence."[4]

In the spring Price's family (his wife, daughter, and son Celsus) joined him after being delayed by a shipwreck in which they lost most of their belongings. Not long afterwards a large band of guerrillas claiming to be *Juaristas* raided Carlota, destroyed some buildings and crops and carried off thirty settlers. Shelby negotiated the release of the prisoners, and Price went to Mexico City where he obtained the aid of a detachment of Imperial troops who "scourged" the robbers and killed their chief. Nevertheless many of the colonists became discouraged as a result of the attack and began to leave for Cuba, Brazil, or the United States.[5] Price, however, remained cautiously hopeful. In a letter written on July 2 to his son Edwin at Keytesville, he stated:

Every month I live in Mexico, satisfies me more and more that it is the best climate, the most productive soil and with a stable government would be the most desirable country I have ever seen. With regard to the stability of the government, you occupy as good a standpoint to determine as I do. The Emperor becomes impatient and fretted when it is even doubted that this government is not a fixed and permanently established government; he should know better than outsiders; my opinion is that one year will develop the fact.[6]

During the Missouri expedition Price had met with Edwin's wife.[7] What transpired is unknown, but possibly any tension that existed between father and son over the latter's defection was then resolved. In

[4] Quoted in George D. Harmon, "Confederate Migration to Mexico," *Hispanic American Historical Review*, XVII (1937), 472–75.

[5] Rister, "Confederate Colony in Mexico," 46–50.

[6] Sterling Price to Edwin Price, July 2, 1866, in Thomas C. Reynolds Papers, Missouri Historical Society, St. Louis. Why this letter is in the papers of Reynolds is puzzling, but probably it indicates that Reynolds continued after the war to take a strong interest in the affairs of the Prices.

[7] W. M. McPheeters Diary, October 15, 1864.

any case Edwin took care of his mother and other members of the family while Price was establishing himself in Mexico. In his letter of July 2 Price thanked Edwin for his assistance and also transferred to him "in fee simple" all his land holdings. Since the Federal District Court of Western Missouri had ordered the confiscation of all of Price's property, he probably did this in order to circumvent such action.

During the summer more colonists quit Carlota, the French evacuated their forces, and Maximilian's artificial regime began to crumble. At the same time both Price and Heber became ill with fever induced by the rainy season and hard labor. Price's family moved from the still unfinished *casa* to the town of Cordova, from where on August 29 Mrs. Price wrote to relatives in Missouri:

Words are inadequate to convey an idea of my feelings upon seeing him (General Price) return from his work with not a dry thread of clothing. He labored very hard to get his house done before the rainy season set in; but failed. That brought on his sickness; all the work had to be done by hand. It will be several years before we can realize anything upon wild land, such as we settled upon. We must economize at every point. We have been living in Cordova, and it is very expensive. Rent high; provisions enormous. My little means left from the wreck almost expended. I found General Price out of funds; but what now distresses me most of all is the state of his health. It will be months before he will be fit for business, if ever, and Heber, poor boy, will not be able to do anything for some time to come.[8]

Finally Price himself was forced to abandon his plantation, and Carlota returned to the jungle.

By then it was obvious that to remain much longer in Mexico was to risk death, either from disease and privation, or else at the hands of the triumphant *Juaristas*, who regarded the Confederates as enemies. Therefore, after corresponding with Snead and others in the United States, Price and his family took a ship to New Orleans, then traveled up the Mississippi to St. Louis, where they arrived early in January, 1867.[9] As Price passed by Vicksburg, Helena, and Memphis he must have experienced certain emotions, but they could not have equaled the intensity of his feelings on setting foot in St. Louis—the city he had

[8] Quoted in Jefferson City (Mo.) *Peoples' Tribune*, October 3, 1866.
[9] *Ibid.*, January 9, 1867.

last seen on that June evening in 1861 when with Jackson and Snead
he had hurried back on the train to Jefferson City after the futile conference with Lyon and Blair at the Planter's House—the city he had
so long and vainly sought to capture in the months and years that
followed.

Legally Price was still a rebel, barred from voting and holding office.
However, although he probably could have readily obtained a presidential pardon, he refused to request one. "I have done nothing," he
declared, "that I am dissatisfied with; nothing I would not do again
under similar circumstances. Thus I have no pardon to ask."[10]

An acquaintance who called on him shortly after he returned found
him looking thin and old, his head partially bald.[11] The Jefferson City
Tribune reported that "his once powerful frame" was "a mere wreck
of its former self," and proposed that the general's friends raise
$50,000 to buy him a home in St. Louis and provide for his mainte-
nance through life.[12] The St. Louis *Times* endorsed this idea, and also
urged his pardon.[13] Scores of old friends and veterans of his army
hastened to welcome him back, and it was apparent that to most Confederate Missourians he remained the personification of their cause
and struggle.[14]

In the spring he opened up the offices of "Sterling Price & Co., Commission Merchants," at the corner of Commercial and Chestnut Streets,
with Celsus as one of his partners. However, early in July he became
ill and was bent and feeble looking. In August Mrs. Price took him to
the spa at Baden Springs, Indiana, where at first he improved, but then
experienced an attack of dysentery. He returned to St. Louis, again
rallied, and early in September even took a trip to St. Ferdinand to visit
General Daniel Frost. Then on September 20, he complained of acidity
of the stomach, and three days later cholera symptoms appeared. The
family called in a physician, but his condition steadily worsened, and he
had periods of delirium during which he imagined himself on the battle-

[10] Mrs. Celeste Thompson, granddaughter of Price, citing letter by Price to
Snead, in Columbia (Mo.) *Missourian*, May 31, 1924.
[11] Diary of W. B. Napton (Typescript in Missouri Historical Society, St.
Louis), 382.
[12] Jefferson City (Mo.) *Peoples' Tribune*, January 9, 1867.
[13] St. Louis *Times*, January 10, 1867.
[14] Anderson, *Memoirs: Historical and Personal*, 262; Bevier, *First and Second
Missouri Confederate Brigades*, 292.

field and gave orders "for a prompt flank movement." On the twenty-sixth he seemed to improve, and when a female friend of the family, thinking he was asleep, kissed him, he at once said to his wife, "Ah, I wish I was young again." And, that same day, when Mrs. Price asked him if he could turn over, he replied, "Oh yes, a somersault, if necessary."

But the improvement was only temporary. On Sunday morning, September 29, a minister baptized him—he had never been a church member—and at 2:15 that afternoon he died. The following day, after lying in state at the Methodist Church at the corner of Eighth Street and Washington Avenue, he was buried in Bellefontaine Cemetery beside Celsus' wife and her infant son, both of whom had died a short time before. Scores of Price's soldiers marched in the funeral procession, following Old Pap for the last time.[15]

The news of Price's death reached Reynolds in Mexico City. Abruptly he broke off writing his lengthy exposé of Sterling Price—there was now no point in finishing it.[16] He lingered on in Mexico, determined not to return to Missouri until he could do so as a member of "the ruling class." Finally, in 1869, he ended his exile and took up residence again in St. Louis, where he engaged in law, politics, and more controversies. In 1871 at a Confederate reunion he praised Price as "Missouri's foremost soldier," and subsequently joined an association to erect a monument to him in St. Louis.[17] However he retained the manuscript of "Sterling Price and the Confederacy" and as late as 1880 was writing Jefferson Davis requesting, apparently in vain, more information about Price's activities in 1861.[18] His law practice prospered, he served in the legislature, and was a United States trade commissioner to

[15] "Last Hours of General Sterling Price," newspaper clipping in Reynolds Papers, Missouri Historical Society, St. Louis. See also Bevier, *First and Second Missouri Confederate Brigades*, 168.

[16] This is a supposition, but it would seem to be a reasonable one. The manuscript is dated Mexico City, March 10, 1867 (presumably the day Reynolds began writing it), and it stops abruptly at the point when the Missouri expedition of 1864 is about to begin.

[17] Reynolds to Snead, February 16, 1887, in Thomas C. Reynolds Papers, Missouri Historical Society. In a letter to General Frost, January 11, 1882, in the Daniel Marsh Frost Collection, Reynolds referred to Price's 1861–62 campaign as "brilliant" and called Price "that distinguished officer."

[18] Reynolds to Davis, January 20, 1880, and November 13, 1880, in Thomas C. Reynolds Papers, Missouri Historical Society.

South America during Cleveland's first administration. Then, on March 30, 1887, he threw himself down an elevator shaft in the St. Louis Custom House. On his body was a note stating that he had decided to commit suicide because he feared he was losing his mental powers.[19] Life without his greatest pride was intolerable to the ex-Confederate Governor of Missouri.

[19] St. Louis *Missouri Republican*, March 31, 1887.

17

"OLD PAP" PRICE

News that a movement was underway in Missouri to raise $50,000 for Price had reached Shelby while he was still in Mexico, and caused him to snarl, "They had better a damn sight appropriate that fifty thousand dollars to the orphans and widows that were made by his damn blunders."[1] However the majority of Confederate Missourians took a much different view of Price. As one of his former officers stated immediately after the war, "He is today looked upon proudly by the mass of [Missouri's] people, and loved, honored and admired by every one of her true hearted sons that marched under his command."[2] And declared another of his soldiers in 1879, "Sterling Price . . . was personally the most popular and best-loved man in Missouri. To the day of his death he remained so."[3] Even Reynolds, as noted, found it expedient to praise him, and Shelby himself ruefully confessed in later years that it was considered treason in Missouri for anyone to criticize "Old Pap."[4]

Price's admirers did not claim for him "a brilliant mind or genius," or "any great strategic ability." Instead, they emphasized his "practical sense and judgment," his patriotism and integrity, his courage and benevolence, and above all his ability to "evoke all the reckless belligerency of the Missourians." Declared one Missouri editor in a eulogy on Price's death: "Among ten thousand ordinary men you could, without any previous knowledge of the man, single him out as the chief. No one has ever seen him preside over a deliberative assembly with the firm tone and calm dignity that distinguished him, or at the head of his army, with that stern look and gallant bearing, without feeling that he was born to command."[5]

---

[1] J. O. Shelby to R. J. Lawrence, February 2, 1867, in Civil War Papers, Missouri, 1865–1900, Missouri Historical Society.

[2] Anderson, *Memoirs: Historical and Personal*, 262.

[3] Bevier, *First and Second Missouri Confederate Brigades*, 292.

[4] Statement of W. E. Connelley, September 19, 1908, in W. E. Connelley Papers, Kansas State Historical Society.

[5] Jefferson City (Mo.) *Peoples' Tribune*, October 1, 1867.

Indeed, practically all accounts agree that Price was able to win and hold the enthusiastic devotion of his men. Witness this entry in the diary of Dr. R. J. Bell, surgeon of Parson's brigade, describing Price at a review on August 13, 1863, at Little Rock: "He is six feet high, heavily made and gracefully proportioned, has white hair, grey eyes, a stern, yet amiable countenance, and is extremely handsome. . . . His presence among his soldiers awakens a thrill of joy and confidence. No general, in the history of revolutions, ever had, in my opinion, more influence in his army, either in camp or battle."[6]

William E. Connelley, a Kansas historian of the turn of the century, talked to many of Price's veterans, and they all spoke of "Old Pap" with great and sincere affection, and stated that they would rather have died under his leadership than fight under any other man.[7] And it is told that if the troops of Price's army were asked what they were cheering about, the reply would be: "It is either a rabbit, or General Price moving along the line."[8]

Price's popularity resulted mainly from the great bravery he so often displayed in battle, his distinguished yet fatherly appearance, and the strong personal interest he took in the welfare of his men. In this last connection it is worth noting that even Union soldiers who were held prisoner by the Confederates praised him for his kindness. They related that he frequently visited the hospital wards of the Northern wounded, and never failed to inquire closely about the care and food they were receiving. He often gave such commands as "Get this man something more to eat," or "This man must have different treatment," or "This man must have a different diet."[9]

McCulloch, Reynolds, and other unfriendly critics accused Price of pandering to his troops through laxity of discipline, and no doubt he was a poor disciplinarian. But on this score several observations are in order: (1) The level of discipline was, by professional standards, never high in any of the Confederate armies, and this was especially so in the

[6] Dr. R. J. Bell Diary, Missouri Historical Society.

[7] John T. Hughes Journal, 45 n.

[8] Stella M. Drumm (ed.), *Down the Santa Fe Trail and into Mexico: The Diary of Susan Shelby Magoffin, 1846–1847* (New Haven, 1920), 118 n.

[9] Footnote supplied from John T. Hughes Journal, 45. William Watson, whose Third Louisiana regiment served with and under Price during the first half of the war, stated that Price was "exceedingly careful and attentive to the wants of his men, and was very popular." See Watson, *Life in the Confederate Army*, 364.

West, where in the words of Edwards "the worst ideas of the most democratic form of liberty" prevailed, and where men were "opposed, from the very nature of their hearts, to all restraints or discipline." (2) Had Price tried to impose a harsh and rigid discipline on his Missourians, probably many if not most of them would have deserted, particularly in 1861. (3) The only time that Price had the proper facilities and support in training his soldiers—in Mississippi in 1862— they became one of the finest units in the Southern army, whose drill and soldierly appearance won even the approval of the martinet Bragg. (4) The troops which, under Price's command, stormed the fortifications of Corinth and Helena definitely possessed battle discipline, and certainly were not a mere mob. (5) The only times that lack of discipline seriously effected Price's operations were during the Missouri campaigns of 1861 and 1864. As regards the first campaign, it is difficult to imagine how it could have been otherwise; as to the second, the blame scarcely rests on Price alone.

Perhaps the fairest assessment of Price's leadership was made by, of all people, Jefferson Davis. Writing long after the war the ex-President stated: "General Price possessed an extraordinary power to secure the personal attachment of his troops, and to inspire them with a confidence which served in no small degree as a substitute for more thorough training. His own enthusiasm and entire devotion to the cause he served were infused throughout his followers and made them all their country's own."[10]

And to this evaluation must be added that of General Dabney Maury, an officer who was well qualified to judge Price and who did not hesitate to criticize his mistakes:

A braver or a kinder heart beat in no man's bosom; he was wise in counsel and bold in action, and never spared his own blood on any battlefield. No man had greater influence over his troops; and as he sat on his superb charger, with the ease and lightness of one accustomed all his days to ride a thoroughbred horse, it was impossible to find a more magnificent speci-

---

[10] Davis, *Rise and Fall*, I, 429. Davis also referred to Price as a man "ever characterized [by] magnamity, self-denial, and humanity"—words that have a curious and ironic ring in view of the wartime relations between the two. Or was Davis being sarcastic?

men of manhood in its prime than Sterling Price presented to the brave Missourians, who loved him with a fervor not less than we Virginians felt for Lee.[11]

But although Price had the ability to win the devotion of his troops, he had absolutely no talent for maintaining friendly relations with superiors and associates. Without exception he quarreled with, harbored resentments against, or was disliked, by every commanding general he served under or with—McCulloch, McIntosh, Van Dorn, Pemberton, Marmaduke, Holmes, and Kirby Smith—not to mention his controversies with such civilian leaders as Davis, Seddon, and Reynolds. Although the fault in no case was exclusively his, and indeed in several cases he was the aggrieved party, such a record speaks for itself.

Price and his friends blamed his difficulties on the prejudices and jealousies of the "West Point clique," who in fact did have a critical and sometimes unfair attitude towards him. But the main sources of these difficulties were, first of all, an enormous self-pride bordering on arrogance, that caused Jefferson Davis to declare that Price was "the vainest man he had ever met"; and, second, his persistent preoccupation with Missouri, which automatically and inevitably put him into conflict with leaders having other and broader considerations to take into account. He was not, by any means, always or entirely wrong in pursuing his obsession, but had he exercised proper patience, tact, and judgment in dealing with such men as McCulloch and Davis, he probably would have accomplished more both for himself and Missouri than he did. His worse enemy was not Reynolds; it was Price.

Because of Wilson's Creek and above all Lexington, Price acquired a very high reputation as a general during the early phases of the war, both North and South. However, involvement, even though as a subordinate, in the defeats at Pea Ridge, Corinth, and Helena dulled his fame, and obviously Little Rock, Jenkins' Ferry, and the Missouri expedition of 1864 did nothing to refurbish it. Furthermore, as we have seen, all the commanders under whom he served expressed low opinions of his competence, Kirby Smith being especially contemptuous.

Detailed criticisms of Price's generalship have been made already and they will not be repeated. Suffice to say that his strategic thinking

11 Maury, "Elkhorn Campaign," 184.

usually was vague and impractical, his battlefield tactics clumsy and (except for Lexington) unimaginative, that he was very poor in obtaining and evaluating intelligence about the enemy, and that he had a tendency to be either over-bold or over-cautious. The blunt fact of the matter was that he did not possess the intellect—or that quasi-substitute for intellect, training and experience—to exercise successfully a top command against a competent opponent. This is why he was so dependent on Little, and after Little, Snead. It explains, too, his constant consulting of Mackey, Shelby, Fagan, and even Marmaduke during the Missouri expedition, for he no longer had Snead and he obviously realized his deficiency. Davis was right in not entrusting him with the Trans-Mississippi command, and Kirby Smith cannot be blamed for not wanting him in charge of the District of Arkansas (although he was, Kirby Smith's opinion to the contrary notwithstanding, superior in ability to Holmes). His proper level of command was at most that of a division, where his personal qualities and ability to inspire troops in battle would have maximum effectiveness. And it should have been an infantry division, for Edwards was quite correct in stating that he lacked the requisites of a good cavalry leader. Significantly, at the end of the war his assignment was the command of the Missouri Division of infantry in the District of Arkansas.

Price's basic objective in the war, to repeat, was to "redeem" Missouri. This also represented his basic error, the tragic yet natural miscalculation of his entire career. For in all likelihood there never was more than a very slim chance of the Confederate cause triumphing in the state—at least after the excitement aroused by the Camp Jackson Massacre had subsided. The hard truth of the matter is that secession did not attract more than minority support among Missourians, and that the vast majority of them favored the Union or at least remained neutral. Thus, while some 35,000 Missourians served in the Southern army, over 150,000 entered the Federal. And as Edward Conrad Smith has observed, throughout the war Missouri was largely defended against the Confederates by its own militia, voluntarily enlisted.[12]

Given this situation, the only way the Confederates could ever have seized and held Missouri would have been to muster decisively superior military power in the West—and this they never came close to

[12] Smith, *The Borderland in the Civil War*, 260–61.

doing. Yet Price, perhaps out of sincere conviction, but perhaps simply out of sheer desperation and because he could not admit even to himself that he had been so terribly mistaken, insisted to the very end that Missouri was held down against its will by Northern armies and that the people were merely waiting for him to enter the state at the head of a large army before rising up to overthrow their oppressors and win the war for the South.

Nonetheless, despite his defects and mistakes, the fact remains that Price challenged the Union control of the key to the West, and that with the exception of Taylor's defeat of Banks in 1864, Wilson's Creek and Lexington were the only important engagements won by the Confederacy in the Trans-Mississippi. Moreover, in practically all the battles in which he served as a subordinate whatever success was realized by the Confederates was won by that part of the army led by him: Pea Ridge, Iuka, Corinth, and Helena. He of course does not deserve all of the credit for these achievements: most of it belongs to his men for their superb courage and fighting qualities. But they fought well under him, and in part at least fought so well because they fought *for* him.

The scene of Price's military career was remote from the main arena of the Civil War. It was confined territorially to the region from the Missouri River on the north, to Mississippi in the east, to the Kansas border on the west, and the lower portion of Arkansas to the south. Within this vast area the Confederate armies were small in numbers, poorly equipped, badly officered, and rarely victorious. Furthermore they could at no time decisively influence the overall course of the war, whereas at all times they were subject to what happened elsewhere. Under these limitations, and to the best of his ability, Price fought for Missouri and for the South. The story of his successes and failures is the story of the Confederacy's war in the West.

BIBLIOGRAPHY

This bibliography contains only items actually cited, not all sources examined.

I. MANUSCRIPTS

John T. Appler Diary. Civil War Papers, Missouri Historical Society, St. Louis, Missouri

J. H. P. Baker Diary. Missouri State Historical Society, Columbia, Missouri

Dr. R. J. Bell Diary. Civil War Papers, Missouri Historical Society, St. Louis, Missouri

James O. Broadhead Papers. Missouri Historical Society, St. Louis, Missouri

R. L. Brown, Army Journal. Missouri Historical Society, St. Louis, Missouri

Civil War Papers, Missouri, 1865–1900. Missouri Historical Society, St. Louis, Missouri

Thomas A. Coleman Letters. Missouri State Historical Society, Columbia, Missouri

W. E. Connelley Papers. Kansas State Historical Society, Topeka, Kansas

Daniel Marsh Frost Collection. Missouri Historical Society, St. Louis, Missouri

Thomas Hagan to Father, October 12, 1862. Civil War Papers, Missouri Historical Society, St. Louis, Missouri

William A. Hazen to Alex R. Hazen, December 21, 1864. Missouri State Historical Society, Columbia, Missouri

W. M. McPheeters Collection. Missouri Historical Society, St. Louis, Missouri

W. B. Napton Diary (Typescript). Missouri Historical Society, St. Louis, Missouri

Fletcher C. Pomeroy Diary. Kansas State Historical Society, Topeka, Kansas

Price Family Papers. Missouri Historical Society, St. Louis, Missouri

Samuel J. Reader Diary. Kansas State Historical Society, Topeka, Kansas

Thomas C. Reynolds Papers. Library of Congress, Washington, D.C.

Thomas C. Reynolds Papers. Missouri Historical Society, St. Louis, Missouri.

Thomas C. Reynolds, "Gen. Sterling Price and the Confederacy" (Typescript). Missouri Historical Society, St. Louis, Missouri

James S. Rollins, "Letters and Speeches" (Binder). Missouri Historical Society, St. Louis, Missouri

The John P. Sanderson Report on the O.A.K., Microfilm. Missouri Historical Society, St. Louis, Missouri

Edmund Kirby Smith Papers. Southern Historical Collection, University of North Carolina Library, Chapel Hill, North Carolina

Thomas L. Snead Papers. Missouri Historical Society, St. Louis, Missouri

John F. Snyder Collection. Missouri Historical Society, St. Louis, Missouri

M. Jeff Thompson, "Brig. Gen. M. Jeff Thompson: His Story" (Edited by his daughter, Marcie A. Bailey). Missouri State Historical Society, Columbia, Missouri

M. Jeff Thompson, "Reminiscences," M. Jeff Thompson Papers. Southern Historical Collection, University of North Carolina Library, Chapel Hill, North Carolina

John Tyler to William L. Yancey, October 15, 1862, Western Historical Collection, University of Missouri, Columbia, Missouri

Earl Van Dorn Collection. Alabama State Department of Archives and History, Montgomery, Alabama

Wilson Family Papers, Western Historical Collection, University of Missouri, Columbia, Missouri

II. NEWSPAPERS

Columbia (Mo.) *Missourian*

Columbia (Mo.) *Statesman*

Elwood (Kansas) *Free Press*

Glasgow (Mo.) *Weekly Times*

Houston (Texas) *Daily Telegraph*

Jefferson City (Mo.) *Peoples' Tribune*

Kansas City (Mo.) *Daily Western Journal of Commerce*

Kansas City (Mo.) *Weekly Western Journal of Commerce*

Leavenworth (Kansas) *Daily Times*

Liberty (Mo.) *Tribune*

Marshall (Texas) *Republican*

St. Louis *Democrat*

St. Louis *Missouri Republican*

St. Louis *Times*

Shreveport (La.) *News*
Washington (Ark.) *Telegraph*

III. BOOKS

Abel, Anna Heloise. *The Slaveholding Indians*. 3 vols. Cleveland, 1915–19.
Allsop, Fred W. *Albert Pike, A Biography*. Little Rock, 1928.
Anderson, Ephraim M. *Memoirs: Historical and Personal, Including Campaigns of the First Missouri Confederate Brigade*. St. Louis, 1868.
Andreas, A. T. (comp.). *History of the State of Kansas*. Chicago, 1883.
Barnes, C. R. (ed.). *Switzler's Illustrated History of Missouri from 1541 to 1877*. St. Louis, 1877.
Basler, Roy P. (ed.). *The Collected Works of Abraham Lincoln*. 8 vols. New Brunswick, N.J., 1953.
The Battle of Lexington Fought in and around the city of Lexington, Missouri on September 18th, 19th, and 20th, 1861. Lexington, Missouri, 1903.
Bevier, R. S. *History of the First and Second Missouri Confederate Brigades, 1861–1865*. St. Louis, 1879.
Boggs, William R. *Military Reminiscences*. Durham, N.C., 1913.
Britton, Wiley. *The Civil War on the Border*. 2 vols. New York, 1899.
———. *The Union Indian Brigade in the Civil War*. Kansas City, Mo., 1922.
Brown, Walter L. "Albert Pike, 1809–1891." Unpublished Ph. D. dissertation, University of Texas, 1955.
Cabell, William L. *Report of Gen. W. L. Cabell's Brigade in Price's Raid in Missouri and Kansas in 1864*. Dallas, 1900.
Castel, Albert. *A Frontier State at War: Kansas, 1861–1865*. Ithaca, 1958.
———. *William Clarke Quantrill: His Life and Times*. New York, 1962.
Connelley, W. E. (ed.). *Doniphan's Expedition and the Conquest of New Mexico and California*. Topeka, 1907.
Crawford, Samuel J. *Kansas in the Sixties*. Chicago, 1911.
Crozier, Emmett. *Yankee Reporters, 1861–1865*. New York, 1956.
Davis, Jefferson. *The Rise and Fall of the Confederate Government*. 2 vols. New York, 1881.
Drumm, Stella M. (ed.). *Down the Santa Fe Trail and into Mexico: The Diary of Susan Shelby Magoffin, 1846–1847*. New Haven, 1920.
Edwards, John N. *Noted Guerrillas, or the Warfare of the Border*. St. Louis, 1877.
———. *Shelby and his Men: or, The War in the West*. Cincinnati, 1867.
———. "Shelby's Expedition to Mexico," in Mary V. Edwards (comp.).

John N. Edwards: Biography, Memoirs, Reminiscences, and Recollections. Kansas City, 1889.

Eliot, Ellsworth. *West Point in the Confederacy.* New York, 1941.

Freeman, D. S. *Lee's Lieutenants.* 3 vols. New York, 1942–45.

Grant, U. S. *Personal Memoirs of U. S. Grant.* 2 vols. New York, 1885.

Greeley, Horace. *The American Conflict.* 2 vols. Hartford, 1864–67.

Hartje, Robert G. *Van Dorn: The Life and Times of a Confederate General.* Nashville, 1967.

Harwell, Richard B. (ed.). *Kate: The Journal of a Confederate Nurse.* Baton Rouge, 1959.

Hinton, Richard Josiah. *Rebel Invasion of Missouri and Kansas and the Campaign of the Army of the Border Against General Sterling Price in October and November, 1864.* Chicago and Leavenworth, 1865.

Horn, Stanley F. *The Army of Tennessee.* Indianapolis and New York, 1941.

Jenkins, Paul B. *The Battle of Westport.* Kansas City, 1906.

Johnson, Robert U., and C. C. Buel (eds.). *Battles and Leaders of the Civil War.* 4 vols. New York, 1884–87.

Johnston, William Preston. *The Life of Gen. Albert Sidney Johnston.* New York, 1880.

Klement, Frank M. *The Copperheads in the Middle West. Chicago,* 1960.

Lamers, William M. *The Edge of Glory: A Biography of General William S. Rosecrans.* New York, 1961.

Logan, John A. *The Great Conspiracy: Its Origin and History.* New York, 1886.

McElroy, John S. *The Struggle for Missouri.* Washington, D.C., 1909.

Miller, E. Van Dorn (ed.). *A Soldier's Honor: With Reminiscences of Major General Earl Van Dorn.* New York, 1902.

Miller, Francis T. (ed.). *Photographic History of the Civil War.* 10 vols. New York, 1911.

Missouri Valley Historical Society. *The Battle of Westport October 21–22–23, 1864.* n.p., n.d.

Monaghan, Jay. *Civil War on the Western Border, 1854–1865.* Boston, 1955.

Monnett, Howard N. *Action Before Westport, 1864.* Kansas City, 1964.

Morrow, Norman Potter. "Price's Missouri Expedition, 1964." Unpublished Master's dissertation, University of Texas, 1949.

Nevins, Allan. *Frémont: Pathmarker of the West.* New York, 1939.

———. *Ordeal of the Union.* 2 vols. New York, 1947.

———. *The War for the Union.* 2 vols. New York, 1959–60.

Nicolay, John G., and John Hay. *Abraham Lincoln: A History*. 10 vols. New York, 1890.

O'Flaherty, Daniel. *General Jo Shelby: Undefeated Rebel*. Chapel Hill, 1954.

Parks, Joseph Howard. *General Edmund Kirby Smith, C.S.A.* Baton Rouge, 1954.

Parrish, William E. *Turbulent Partnership: Missouri and the Union, 1861–1865*. Columbia, Mo., 1963.

Peterson, Cyrus A., and Joseph M. Hanson, *Pilot Knob, The Thermopylae of the West*. New York, 1914.

Pollard, Edward R. *Lee and his Lieutenants*. New York, 1867.

———. *The Lost Cause*. New York, 1866.

———. *Southern History of the War*. 2 vols. New York, 1866.

Quaife, Milo M. (ed.). *Absalom Grimes: Confederate Mail Runner*. New Haven, 1926.

Rea, Ralph R. *Sterling Price, The Lee of the West*. Little Rock, 1959.

Rolle, Andrew F. *The Lost Cause: The Confederate Exodus to Mexico*. Norman, Okla., 1965.

Ropes, John C. *The Story of the Civil War*. New York, 1898.

Rose, Victor M. *The Life and Services of Gen. Ben McCulloch*. Philadelphia, 1888.

———. *Ross's Texas Brigade*. Louisville, 1881.

Rowland, Dunbar (ed.). *Jefferson Davis, Constitutionalist: His Letters, Papers, and Speeches*. 10 vols. Jackson, Miss., 1923.

Scharf, John T. *History of St. Louis City and County from the Earliest Period to the Present Day*. 2 vols. Philadelphia, 1883.

Schofield, John M. *Forty-Six Years in the Army*. New York, 1897.

Simmons, Lucy. "The Life of Sterling Price." M.A. thesis, University of Chicago, 1922.

Smith, Edward Conrad. *The Borderland in the Civil War*. New York, 1927.

Smith, Justin H. *The War With Mexico*. 2 vols. New York, 1919.

Snead, Thomas L. *The Fight for Missouri*. New York, 1886.

Snow, William Park. *Southern Generals, Who They Are, and What They Have Done*. New York, 1865.

Stickles, Arndt M. *Simon Bolivar Buckner, Borderland Knight*. Chapel Hill, 1940.

Strode, Hudson. *Jefferson Davis, Confederate President*. New York, 1959.

Violette, Eugene M. *History of Missouri*. Boston, 1918.

The War of the Rebellion: A Compilation of the Official Records of the Union and Confederate Armies. 73 vols., 128 parts. Washington, 1880–1901.

Watson, William. *Life in the Confederate Army.* New York, 1888.
Webb, William L. *Battles and Biographies of Missourians.* Kansas City, 1900.
Williams, Kenneth P. *Lincoln Finds A General.* 5 vols. New York, 1949–59.
Yearns, Wilfred Buck. *The Confederate Congress.* Athens, 1960.

IV. ARTICLES

Bearss, Edwin C. "The Battle of Helena," *Arkansas Historical Quarterly,* XX (Autumn, 1961), 258–93.
———. "The First Day at Pea Ridge, March 7, 1862," *Arkansas Historical Quarterly,* XVII (Summer, 1958), 132–54.
———. "From Rolla to Fayetteville With General Curtis," *Arkansas Historical Quarterly,* XIX (Autumn, 1960), 225–59.
Blunt, James G. "General Blunt's Account of His Civil War Experiences," *Kansas Historical Quarterly,* I (May, 1932), 211–65.
Britton, Wiley. "Resumé of Military Operations in Missouri and Arkansas, 1864–65," *Battles and Leaders of the Civil War,* IV, 364–77.
Brown, Walter L. "Pea Ridge: Gettysburg of the West," *Arkansas Historical Quarterly,* XV (Spring, 1956), 3–16.
Brownlee, Richard S. "The Battle of Pilot Knob, Iron County, Missouri, September 27, 1864," *Missouri Historical Review,* LVIV (October, 1964), 1–30.
Calkins, Homer L. (ed.). "Elkhorn to Vicksburg: James H. Fauntelroy's Diary for the Year 1862," *Civil War History,* II (January, 1956), 7–43.
Cowen, Ruth Caroline. "Reorganization of Federal Arkansas, 1862–1865," *Arkansas Historical Quarterly,* XVIII (Summer, 1959), 32–57.
Covington, James W. "The Camp Jackson Affair: 1861," *Missouri Historical Review,* LV (April, 1961), 197–212.
Darr, John C. "Price's Raid into Missouri," *Confederate Veteran,* XI (August, 1903), 359–62.
Fagan, T. A. "The Battle of Lexington," St. Louis *Globe Democrat,* September 19, 1897.
"The Federal Occupation of Camden As Set Forth in the Diary of a Union Officer," *Arkansas Historical Quarterly,* IX (Autumn, 1950), 214–19.
Frémont, John C. "In Command in Missouri," *Battles and Leaders of the Civil War,* I, 278–88.
Geise, William R. "Missouri's Confederate Capital in Marshall, Texas," *Missouri Historical Review,* LVIII (October, 1963), 37–54.

Grover, George S. "Civil War in Missouri," *Missouri Historical Review*, VIII (October, 1913), 1–28.

———. "The Price Campaign of 1864," *Missouri Historical Review*, VI (July, 1912), 167–81.

———. "The Shelby Raid, 1863," *Missouri Historical Review*, VI (April, 1912), 107–26.

Hamilton, C. S. "The Battle of Iuka," *Battles and Leaders of the Civil War*, II, 734–6.

Harmon, George D. "Confederate Migration to Mexico," *Hispanic American Historical Review*, XVII (November, 1937), 458–87.

Hartje, Robert G. "A Confederate Dilemma Across the Mississippi," *Arkansas Historical Quarterly*, XVII (Summer, 1958), 119–31.

"Hockaday, Isaac to his mother, Mrs. Emily Mills Hockaday," *Missouri Historical Review*, LVI (October, 1961), 56–57.

Huff, Leo E. "The Last Duel in Arkansas: The Marmaduke-Walker Duel," *Arkansas Historical Quarterly*, XXII (Spring, 1964), 36–49.

———. "The Union Expedition Against Little Rock, August–September, 1863," *Arkansas Historical Quarterly*, XXII (Fall, 1963), 223–37.

Kirkpatrick, Arthur Roy. "The Admission of Missouri to the Confederacy," *Missouri Historical Review*, LV (July, 1961), 366–86.

———. "Missouri in the Early Months of the Civil War," *Missouri Historical Review*, LV (April, 1961), 235–66.

———. "Missouri on the Eve of the Civil War," *Missouri Historical Review*, LV (January, 1961), 99–108.

———. "Missouri's Delegation in the Confederate Congress," *Civil War History*, V (March, 1959), 188–98.

Langsdorf, Edgar. "Price's Raid and the Battle of Mine Creek," *Kansas Historical Quarterly*, XXX (Autumn, 1964), 281–306.

Luttrell, Henry C. "Diary of the Price Raid," St. Louis *Missouri Republican*, March 6, 13, 16, 1886.

Lyon, William H. "Claiborne Fox Jackson and the Secession Crisis in Missouri," *Missouri Historical Review*, LVIII (July, 1964), 422–41.

McCausland, Susan A. Arnold. "The Battle of Lexington as Seen by a Woman," *Missouri Historical Review*, VI (April, 1912), 127–35.

Maury, Dabney H. "Recollections of Campaign against Grant in North Mississippi in 1862–63," *Southern Historical Society Papers*, XIII (January–December, 1885), 285–311.

———. "Recollections of the Elkhorn Campaign," *Southern Historical Society Papers*, II (January–December, 1876), 180–92.

Moore, John C. "Missouri," in Clement A. Evans (ed.). *Confederate Military History*. 12 vols. Atlanta, 1899.

Mudd, James A. "What I Saw at Wilson's Creek," *Missouri Historical Review*, VII (January, 1913), 87–113.

Mulligan, James A. "The Siege of Lexington, Missouri," *Battles and Leaders of the Civil War*, I, 307–13.

Newberry, Farrar. "Harris Flanagin," *Arkansas Historical Quarterly*, XVII (Spring, 1958), 3–21.

"Paper by Capt. McNamara," St. Louis *Missouri Republican*, December 5, 1885.

Pearce, N. Bartlett. "Arkansas Troops in the Battle of Wilson's Creek," *Battles and Leaders of the Civil War*, I, 298–303.

Perkins, J. R. "Jefferson Davis and Gen. Sterling Price," *Confederate Veteran*, XIX (October, 1911), 473–77.

Richards, Ira Don. "The Battle of Poison Spring," *Arkansas Historical Quarterly*, XVIII (Winter, 1959), 1–12.

Rister, Carl C. "Carlota, a Confederate Colony in Mexico," *Journal of Southern History*, XI (February, 1945), 33–50.

Robertson, Frank. "The Price Raid," Houston *Daily Telegraph*, December 3, 1864.

Rosecrans, William S. "The Battle of Corinth," *Battles and Leaders of the Civil War*, II, 743–56.

Scroggs, Jack B., and Donald E. Reynolds, "Arkansas and the Vicksburg Campaign," *Civil War History*, IV (December, 1959), 390–401.

Sigel, Franz. "The Flanking Column at Wilson's Creek," *Battles and Leaders of the Civil War*, I, 304–306.

———. "The Pea Ridge Campaign," *Battles and Leaders of the Civil War*, I, 314–34.

Smith, Harold F. "The 1861 Struggle for Lexington, Missouri," *Civil War History*, VII (June, 1961), 155–66.

Snead, Thomas L. "The Conquest of Arkansas," *Battles and Leaders of the Civil War*, III, 441–61.

———. "The First Year of the War in Missouri," *Battles and Leaders of the Civil War*, I, 262–77.

———. "With Price East of the Mississippi," *Battles and Leaders of the Civil War*, II, 717–34.

Snyder, J. F. "The Capture of Lexington," *Missouri Historical Review*, VII (October, 1912), 1–9.

Wherry, William M. "Wilson's Creek and the Death of Lyon," *Battles and Leaders of the Civil War*, I, 289–99.

Zorn, Roman J. (ed.). "Campaign in Southern Arkansas: A Memoir by C. T. Anderson," *Arkansas Historical Quarterly*, VIII (Autumn, 1949), 240–44.

INDEX

Adams, Wirt, 102, 120
Allen, Henry Watkins, 268, 273–74
Anderson, S. S., 271
Anderson, William ("Bloody Bill"), 61, 226
Anthony, Dan, 60
Armstrong, Frank C., 93, 96–97, 99, 100, 103, 106, 114, 121
Atchison, David R., 32

Banks, Nathaniel P., 173, 176, 183–85, 187, 196–97, 285
Baxter, George L., 95
Baxter Springs Massacre, 163–64
Bayou Fourche: engagement at, 158
Beauregard, P. G. T., 84–87, 108
Bell, John, 7
Benjamin, Judah P., 66, 136–37, 169, 192
Bent, Charles, 5
Benteen, Frederick W., 240–41, 248 *n*
Benton, Thomas Hart, 4, 6, 168
Bevier, Robert, 38 *n*
Big Blue, battle of, 230–32
Blair, Frank P., Jr., 5, 7, 9, 12–13, 20–22, 24, 277
Blunt, James G., 163, 229, 232, 235, 238–39, 245–46
Boggs, William R., 178 *n*
Boonville, battle of, 26
Bowen, John S., 116, 118–19, 123, 131
Bragg, Braxton, 67, 86–87, 89–98, 106, 125–26, 198, 206, 282
Breckinridge, John C., 7, 94–95
Broadhead, James O., 11
Brown, B. Gratz, 8, 265
Brown, John Henry, 63–64
Brush Creek. *See* Westport, battle of
Buckner, Simon B., 167, 197, 201, 268, 270–71
Buell, Don Carlos, 93–94, 96–97

Bull, John P., 222–23
Burbidge, John W., 249
Byram's Ford. *See* Big Blue, battle of, and Westport, battle of

Cabell, E. C., 22, 30–32, 57, 66, 169
Cabell, William L., 117, 121, 205, 215, 218, 220, 231, 234–35, 239, 241, 247, 249, 257, 259–60, 262
Camden expedition, 173–83
Camp Jackson Massacre, 12–14, 16, 19
Carthage, Mo.: skirmish at, 27
Chestnut, John, 199
Chilton, Josiah, 203 *n*
Churchill, Thomas J., 173, 176, 181–85, 196, 204
Clark, John B., 25–26, 35, 90–91, 169–70, 188, 265
Clark, John B., Jr., 205, 215, 218, 220, 227, 231, 240 *n*, 244, 247, 249–50
Clemens, Samuel, 51
Cleveland, Marshall, 60
Collins, Richard, 205, 233, 247
Conrow, Aaron H., 22
Cooke, William M., 90
Corinth, battle of, 108–19
Cowskin Prairie: Price's camp at, 27–30, 33
Crawford, Samuel J., 243 *n*
Cumming, Kate, 84–85
Curtis, Samuel R., 65, 68, 70–82, 228–32, 238, 245–48

Darr, John, 220 *n*
Davidson, John W., 154–57, 159 *n*
Davies, Thomas A., 111–12, 116
Davis, Jefferson, 12–13, 18, 20, 30–31, 38 *n*, 58, 64, 66–67, 87–92, 98–100, 126, 130–37, 141, 152 *n*, 161, 163, 166–69, 187–94, 196, 198–99, 202, 257, 259–60, 266, 278, 282–83